TATAR EMPIRE

TATAR EMPIRE

Kazan's Muslims and the Making of Imperial Russia

Danielle Ross

INDIANA UNIVERSITY PRESS

This book is a publication of

Indiana University Press
Office of Scholarly Publishing
Herman B Wells Library 350
1320 East 10th Street
Bloomington, Indiana 47405 USA

iupress.indiana.edu

 The paper used in this publication meets the minimum requirements of the American National Standard for Information Sciences—Permanence of Paper for Printed Library Materials, ANSI Z39.48-1992.

Manufactured in the United States of America

Cataloging information is available from the Library of Congress.
ISBN 978-0-253-04570-6 (hdbk.)
ISBN 978-0-253-04571-3 (pbk.)

1 2 3 4 5 25 24 23 22 21 20

CONTENTS

Acknowledgments vii

Introduction: The Empire That Tatars Built 1

1 The Age of the Settler ʿUlamāʾ 21

2 The Art of Accruing Scholarly Prestige 51

3 Colonial Trade and Religious Revival 70

4 A Shaykhly Rural Gentry 96

5 Knowledge, History Writing, and Becoming Colonial 114

6 Muslim Cultural Reform and Kazan Tatar Cultural Imperialism 140

7 Fundamentalism, Nationalism, and Social Conflict 170

8 At War with the Tatar Kingdom 210

9 An Empire without Russians 229

Conclusion 242

Glossary 247

Bibliography 249

Index 267

ACKNOWLEDGMENTS

THIS BOOK WOULD NOT HAVE BEEN POSSIBLE WITHOUT the support of many along the way. First, I am eternally grateful to David McDonald, who took me in at the beginning of my MA-PhD program at the University of Wisconsin-Madison and became my mentor and guardian angel. His deep knowledge of Russian history never ceased to amaze me and set for me the standard of what a historian should be. I must also express my gratitude to Francine Hirsch, who was both an impeccable guide through the field of Soviet history and a source of emotional support throughout my time in graduate school, and to Michael Chamberlain, who pushed me to think in new ways about social conflict in Islamic history.

I would like to extend my gratitude to Utah State University, Nazarbayev University, University of Wisconsin-Madison, and IREX. This book would not have been possible without their financial and institutional support.

The research that went into this book would not have been possible without considerable assistance on the ground in Russia. Many thanks to Daniya Zagidullina and Gawhar Khasanova at the Russian Academy of Sciences in Kazan, who have always gone above and beyond to help me secure invitations and travel documents. I also extend thanks to Ildus Zagidullin at the Institute of History for his extensive knowledge of Tatar history and unfailing hospitality. Many thanks to the staff of the Institute of Language, Literature, and Art and especially to Ilham Gumerov, Marsel Akhmatjanov, Alsu Khasavnekh, and Nurida Nasibullina, who welcomed me with many cups of tea and took time away from their own research to assist me with mine. Thank you as well to the staff of the Kazan Federal University's Lobachevskii Library, who directed me to sources I would never have thought of consulting. Gratitude is also due to Airat Zagidullin, who assisted me with my work in the Rare Book Collection at the Tatarstan National Library, and to Fluera Daminova and Ramziya Abzallina, who helped me locate materials in the Tatarstan National Museum collections. Nor should I neglect the Ufa Scientific Center of the Russian Academy of Sciences. Words cannot express my gratitude to Ramil Bulgakov, who lent me his encyclopedic knowledge, his good humor, and his camera when

I showed up unannounced at his office door. Thank you as well to Igor Kuchumov and Ildar Gabdrafikov, who welcomed me to Ufa and helped me navigate the city. I am also grateful to the late Gul'farida Abubakirova, founder of the museum at Suleimaniya Mosque in Orenburg, who so generously guided me through the mosque's books and manuscripts collection.

Many thanks to my colleagues from NU, especially Alima Bissenova, Beatrice Penati, Zbigniew Wojnowski, Alexander Morrison, Samuel Hirst, Gabriel McGuire, Meiramgul Kussainova, Stephen Wheatcroft, and Michael Kelly, for their feedback and friendship. Thank you likewise to Susan Cogan, Lawrence Culver, Karen Senaga, Eliza Rosenberg, Kyle Bulthius, Ahmet Izmirlioglu, James Sanders, and Christopher Conte for their support and their insight since I arrived to USU. Finally, thank you to Paolo Sartori, who has never hesitated to challenge me but has also emboldened me to take my research in new directions and has made me a stronger scholar as a result.

Special acknowledgement must go to Stephen Batalden, who recruited me into Arizona State University's Critical Languages Institute so many years ago, and to Agnes Kefeli and Gul'jihan Kashaeva, my first Tatar language teachers, who introduced me to Tatar history and culture.

Nothing in this book would have been possible without the support of my mother-in-law, Liliya Bashirova, who welcomed me into her home and family so many years ago, kindly opened her late husband's papers and personal library to me, and became a second mother, confidant, and friend. Finally, special thanks are due to my husband, Iskander, and our daughter, Maryam, who have followed me back and forth across the Atlantic and relived the history of Kazan's theologians, writers, and revolutionaries together with me. This book is for them.

TATAR EMPIRE

INTRODUCTION

The Empire That Tatars Built

The people came from Semipalatinsk
From the Irtysh Valley in China [. . .]
They came from Karkarinsk Oblast',
From the Urals, and from Turgai.
Good fortune rests with [Shaykh] Zaynullāh.

—**Arginbāy,** *Arginbāy Isḥāq Ḥājjī ila Ḥajjge Uska ulınını Troitskī Ishān Zaynullāh Khaḍratka chıgharghān madkhiyaları*

So Arginbāy wrote lovingly of his Sufi master in 1911. That master was Zaynullāh Ishān Rasūlev, a Naqshbandī-Khalīdī *shaykh* from the South Urals who had established a madrasa and Sufi lodge (*khanaqah*) in Troitsk in what is now Cheliabinsk oblast' near the Russia-Kazakhstani border. Arginbāy describes how thousands of Kazakh, Bashkir, and Tatar disciples came to Zaynullāh bringing charitable donations and asking for healings. They gathered to hear of the Muslim victory at the Battle of Badr, of the pre-Islamic time of ignorance (*al-jāhiliyya*), of the miracles of the Prophet Muḥammad, of the rewards of paradise and the punishments of hell.[1] They sought the knowledge (*ma'rifa*) that would enable them to directly experience God's love.[2]

In 1913, another Cheliabinsk Muslim took up a different kind of mission. Socialist Revolutionary Ḥalilullāh Yenikeyev returned from Kazan to Kiev and was detained by the police. Determined not to be tried and exiled, Yenikeyev fled Kiev with a hundred rubles and a letter of introduction from a fellow Muslim revolutionary in his pocket. His flight took him to Moscow, Odessa, and then out of Russia, across Austria, and into Romania. He climbed mountains, slept in barns, and bribed and begged his way past border guards and train conductors. In December, he reached Istanbul. He wrote a desperate letter to his colleagues back in Russia, asking for more money. He admitted that, if their money failed to arrive, he could take the job he had already been offered: cooking pilaf in the cafeteria of one of the city's madrasas. Despite his difficult financial condition, he was not ready to return home because, as he put it, "There is a whole sea of revolutionary work to be done here."[3]

Ideologically, Rasūlev the Sufi shaykh and Yenikeyev the revolutionary could hardly have been further apart. Yet, as members of the Kazan-based Muslim scholarly networks of inner Russia, both readily took on the role of enlightener and savior of their coreligionists, even when those coreligionists lived hundreds or thousands of miles away from Kazan. This impulse toward instructing, leading, and mediating was not acquired through exposure to Marxism, ethno-nationalism, the modern periodical press, trains, telegraphs, or fundamentalist trends in Islamic thought. Rather, it was rooted in the peculiar historical relationship between the Russian government and its first Muslim subjects: the Muslims of Kazan.

From the 1680s to the 1910s, imams, teachers, students, shaykhs, and merchants from the heartland of the conquered Kazan khanate left their native region to settle in new towns, fortresses, trading posts, and villages in the Urals, western Siberia, the Kazakh steppe, and the Russian-Chinese borderlands. In their capacity as interpreters, messengers, mediators, cultural specialists, and businessmen, they served in the vanguard of Russia's colonial expansion. But as they moved east and south, they also brought with them their own intellectual life, literature, religion, and hierarchies, transplanting their culture and their vision of community identity to new territories. Through these activities, Kazan's Muslims became a distinctive colonizing force within the larger Russian expansion. In the earlier phases of that expansion, Russian officials found these Muslims to be useful allies. By the nineteenth and twentieth centuries, as Russian officials' visions of empire changed, and their opinion of Islam worsened, they came to see Kazan's Muslims as rivals for influence among the non-Russians of the empire's south and east, and as an obstacle to the creation of a stable imperial state.

The title of this chapter has two meanings. First, it highlights the fact that the construction of the Russian empire was not just an ethnic Russian project. It was made possible only through the participation of imperial subjects of many ethnicities and confessions, and these subjects felt a degree of ownership over the empire. For them, it was as much "their" empire as the Russians'. Second, the title nods to the way in which the Kazan Tatars and groups like them created spheres of cultural and economic influence within the boundaries of the empire. These spheres became spaces within which non-Russians could develop their own social, intellectual, and spiritual lives. However, they also became spaces in which the hierarchies and inequities of colonial empire were reproduced among and by non-Russian subjects.

Defining the Kazan Tatars and Kazan ʿUlamāʾ

Historians of the Muslims of Russia's Volga-Ural region rely heavily on Tatar-language biographical dictionaries and local histories composed from the 1880s to the 1920s.[4] They use these works to identify prominent figures within the community from the 1600s to the early 1900s as well as to reconstruct the social, cultural, and legal history of the region.[5] In doing so, they have usually presented the figures and events documented in these works as representative of the Volga-Ural Muslim community as a whole or, at least, of the Muslim educated elite.[6]

However, these sources are far from comprehensive in their presentation of the Volga-Ural region's *ʿulamāʾ* (Muslim scholars). Imperial records, eulogies (*marthiyyas*), and Sufi lineages (*silsilas*) reveal prominent people who were excluded from the biographical dictionaries and village histories of the late 1800s and early 1900s. A comparison of these dictionaries and histories with eulogies penned only a few decades earlier also reveals significant rewritings of the biographies of those ʿulamāʾ who made it into early twentieth-century prosopographies. These exclusions and redactions suggest that the twentieth-century dictionaries and histories were not snapshots of the entire regional ʿulamāʾ, much less of all Volga-Ural Muslim society. Rather, they were carefully curated self-representations of a specific close-knit network of scholarly families, their students, and their clients who dominated social and cultural life in Kazan and its neighboring villages. This book examines the activities of that network's members: men and women who trained in the Islamic sciences, interpreted and transmitted Islamic law and doctrine, educated children, led communal prayers, and presided over life rituals from the late 1600s to the early 1900s as they moved from their villages outside of Kazan to locations across the growing empire and tailored their collective identity in response to their changing circumstances.

In Russian sources, members of this network were often called Kazan Tatars (*kazanskie tatary*) for their association with the districts around the city of Kazan, once the center of the Kazan khanate. Russian officials of the seventeenth and eighteenth centuries were often unaware of or uninterested in the relations and internal politics that bound the network's members together. Rather, they viewed Kazan Tatars, representatives of Russia's oldest conquered Muslim population, as reliable intermediaries with the Muslim peoples of Russia's eastern and southeastern frontiers.

By focusing on the Kazan Tatar ʿulamāʾ network commemorated in the biographical dictionaries and village histories, this book sets out three goals. The first is to reconstruct the social hierarchies and internal dynamics of the Muslim communities of the Volga-Ural region. Kazan's Muslims had lost their preconquest institutions and most of their native noble families by the early 1700s, but that did not mean that their society lacked a meaningful and consistent structure. Understanding that structure is critical for situating individuals within the broader community, so that it becomes possible to move beyond a discussion of generic "Muslims," "clergy," or "laypeople" and gain a nuanced view of how a specific Muslim society responded to Russian rule, economic change, and reform.[7]

The second goal is to trace continuities in community leadership across time. Volga-Ural Muslim history, as currently written, is full of ruptures: pre-Catherine II versus post-Catherine II, pre-Spiritual Assembly versus post-Spiritual Assembly, pre-Jadid reform versus post-Jadid reform.[8] This emphasis on discontinuity masks the fact that influential families, student-teacher relationships, and individuals' careers spanned these ruptures and that the composition of the Volga-Ural Muslim community's social elite—the Kazan-based ʿulamāʾ—did not change much from the early 1700s to the early 1900s. Focusing on the activities of familial and scholarly networks over time enables historians to reevaluate the significance of events that have become central to Volga-Ural Muslim / Volga Tatar history and to reconsider the relationship between the well-studied 1880s–1917 and the less-studied earlier decades.

The third goal of this volume is to disentangle the relationships among the multitude of jurists, shaykhs, merchants, industrialists, bureaucrats, teachers, rebels, and revolutionaries who currently populate the pages of Volga-Ural Muslim history. These individuals never represented a random cross-section of their society. Nor, for the most part, were would-be reformers of any era brought together by chance. A specific group of Muslims dominated publishing and history-writing in Kazan, Orenburg, and Ufa. By the early twentieth century, that group included the Jadid modernist reformers as well as many who have been identified as "*qadim*" traditionalists or conservatives.[9] Eschewing Jadid sources is not an effective strategy for creating a more balanced picture of Volga-Ural Muslim society, for when one turns to so-called traditionalist or conservative sources, one is still immersed in preoccupations and power struggles of the same Kazan Tatar network. Writing a history of this network is vital because doing so makes its boundaries clear. Only once those boundaries are visible does it become possible to distinguish and study the Volga-Ural region's other, less-studied networks and social groups.

The Kazan Tatars in the Context of Empire

The rise of the Kazan Tatars was closely intertwined with the history of empire. Jane Burbank and Frederick Cooper emphasize the demographic and institutional diversity contained within empires and the power of imperial governments to imagine and impose orders of their choosing over spaces and populations that an empire claims as its own.[10] In Russian history, this view of the imperial government as organizer of land and peoples, gatherer of information, and creator of discursive frameworks on governance and subject-state relations has become central to how many historians understand Russian expansion and state-building from the 1600s to 1917.[11] In the Volga-Ural region, this approach has inspired studies of how imperial bureaucrats, missionaries, and orientalist scholars imagined and discussed their empire's non-Russian subjects.[12]

At the same time, historians of empire also point out the limit of imperial power. Confrontations with the diverse societies under imperial rule prompted ruling groups to redefine their identities.[13] Imperial subjects did not always fit themselves neatly into the categories that their governments created for them.[14] Governments were sometimes forced to alter their visions of order in response to their subjects' demands or noncompliance.[15] In remote peripheries, the governments—unable to assert political or cultural hegemony—accepted the existence of hybrid societies and "middle grounds" that would allow them or their agents to maintain a presence and profit economically.[16] Finally, the categories, hierarchies, and institutions imposed by imperial governments carried within them the seeds for other forms of political order, including democracy, citizenship, and the modern nation.[17]

The Kazan Tatars complicate the discussion of imperial power by blurring the categories of colonizer and colonized. The network examined in this book benefited from its ability to navigate the institutions, relationships, and hierarchies constructed by the Russian imperial government. At the same time, Kazan Tatars, like Armenians and Georgians in the Caucasus, Indian merchants in Astrakhan and Central Asia, and German nobility in the Baltic region, occupied a liminal space between Russian officials and a non-Russian population.[18] As a result, they simultaneously looked up to Russian imperial authorities and down on peoples over whom they enjoyed certain powers and privileges. Some of these powers and privileges were explicitly conferred on them by imperial decree. Others were acquired by informal agreement or official neglect. Kazan's Tatar 'ulamā' were part of a colonized community, conquered by a Muscovy, absorbed administratively into the Russian state, and subject to its laws and institutions. At the same time, they were colonizers engaged in the establishment of settler communities, the creation of powerful transregional and international commercial firms that enabled them to employ and exploit members of other ethnic groups, and the compilation of orientalist knowledge. Through these activities, they imagined a geographic space that belonged to them. Within that space, they articulated a hierarchy of peoples with themselves at the top.

The Russian government carried on an ambiguous relationship with Kazan's 'ulamā'. In the 1600s and 1700s, officials relied on them as allies in the integration of the Urals and the Kazakh steppe. In the 1800s and early 1900s, Kazan's 'ulamā' continued to bring benefits to the empire insofar as they shouldered a large part of primary education in Muslim communities (often without financial support from the state), carried on profitable trade and industrial activities, and provided specialist knowledge on Islam and oriental languages (Turkic, Arabic, Persian) to Russian officials and scholars. However, they limited Russian imperial ambitions by refusing to linguistically and culturally assimilate to ethnic Russian society and by creating spaces (from madrasa classrooms to entire urban quarters) that were difficult for the Russian authorities to supervise. Their ventures in education reform, Islamic revival, and philanthropy increasingly collided with imperial officials' efforts to implement more "Russian" visions of imperial identity and order.

The history of the Kazan Tatars is, at once, a story of an empire's success in coopting and mobilizing a diverse population and of the unintended consequences of that success. It also suggests the limits of imperial power by showing how initiatives and relationships established to serve an imperial government could slip from its control and take on lives of their own.

The Kazan Tatars and Modernity

Discussions of modernity and modernization have featured prominently in the Western-language historiography of Russia's Muslim communities since the 1960s.[19] There are two major reasons for this. First, Western scholars writing before 1991 had very limited access to archival and library collections and, so, relied heavily on studies produced in the Soviet Union. Models of societal evolution were central to the Soviet-era Marxist-Leninist historical framework. Already in the 1920s, early Soviet-era Tatar historians/literary scholars such as ʿĀlimjān Ibrāhīmov (Galimzhan Ibragimov) and Jamāladdīn Valīdov (Dzhamaletdin Validov) carved a niche for themselves, their colleagues, and their mentors within the emerging Soviet historical narratives as the harbingers of a new, progressive worldview that, in many ways, foreshadowed the emergence of the "modern" Soviet order.[20] From the 1930s to the 1970s, their narrative was refashioned into one of the rise of the Tatar bourgeoisie (sometimes referred to as Jadids [*dzhadidisty*]) and working class and their struggles against tsarism through the periodical press, "modern" literary genres, liberal-democratic political organizations, and revolutionary activities.[21] Implicit in this narrative were the assumptions that "backward" religion gave way before "modern" science and that the Jadids/Tatar bourgeoisie stood at some intermediate point between "traditional" and "modern" society.

The second reason for the prominence of modernity and modernization narratives in pre-1991 studies historiography of Russia's Muslims was that the history of Islam in the Russian empire began to attract the attention of Western historians at a moment (1950s to early 1980s) when many Western historians of Islamic history viewed secularism and Western liberalism as the inevitable evolutionary endpoint for Muslim societies. Studies of Islamic intellectual history published in the 1960s through the 1980s foregrounded modernizing trends, and especially those trends that seemed to move Islamic societies toward more closely resembling Western European ones.[22] Once Soviet narratives that portrayed the Jadids as advocates of reason, science, and equality in place of superstition, religion, and class oppression had been stripped of their overtly prosocialist rhetoric, they harmonized well with Western scholarship on Islamic reform in Iran, the Ottoman empire, and the Arab world.

The resurgence and/or persistence of faith-based political and social discourses in Egypt, Iran, Pakistan, Saudi Arabia, Indonesia, and Turkey in the last decades of the twentieth century has led to reevaluations of the so-called Islamic modernists and inspired historians to examine other movements and trends in Islamic law and theology in 1700s, 1800s, and early 1900s.[23] In the study of Russia's Muslims, this shift has been accompanied by a growing awareness of the extent to which Soviet narratives shaped

Western studies of Russian and Soviet Islam.[24] Historians of Central Asia have taken a range of approaches to de-Sovietizing the history of Central Asian Islam under Russian rule and bringing their field into line with the discussions transpiring in the fields of Middle Eastern, South Asian, and Southeast Asian history relating to Islamic law under colonialism and the emergence of scripturalism and Salafism. These historians have rejected narratives of the coming of "European modernity" to Central Asia in favor of examinations of preconquest culture and politics and/or legal consciousness, discourses, and practices under Russian rule.[25] By contrast, despite efforts by Allen Frank and Michael Kemper to draw attention to other aspects of Muslim cultural and intellectual life in the Volga-Ural region,[26] the Cold War–era narrative of the Jadids as champions of modernity has persisted. The Jadids' modernity is portrayed as encompassing new technologies, especially those that facilitate expedited transport and communications, mass printing, conspicuous consumption, liberal democratic politics, "secularization," and the replacement of faith-based identities with national ones. Its origins are attributed to western Europe and it is purported to have reached the Volga-Ural Muslim community by way of the publication of Ismail Gasprinskii's newspaper, *Terjuman*, in 1883 and the rapid expansion of the Russian Muslim press following the 1905 Revolution; upon its arrival, it was supposedly embraced by the Jadids and opposed by the defenders of "traditional" society.[27]

Devin DeWeese has explored at length the difficulties of modernity as a concept when applied to the study of Russia's Muslims in the late 1800s and early 1900s. He criticizes, among other things, modernity's self-referential nature, the tendency of historians of modernity to emphasize the novelty of one moment of change over others, and the way in which the dichotomy between "tradition" and "modernity" flattens and essentializes the "premodern" past.[28] However, several more problems with how modernity continues to be discussed in Volga-Ural Muslim historiography should be mentioned. First, studies of the Volga-Ural Jadids' reform programs continue to equate Muslims' becoming "modern" with an embrace of late-nineteenth-century European culture.[29] This formulation ignores or devalues forms of change that do not look recognizably European, denies colonized communities of agency in transforming their own societies, and forces all societies into a set of historical narratives established for and emanating from western Europe. Some critics of this approach have pointed to processes of governmental institutionalization, economic development, and cultural transformation in non-European societies from the sixteenth to the nineteenth centuries.[30] Others have emphasized how European-derived cultural modernity was adapted and nativized as it reached other parts of the world.[31] However, in the historiography of the Volga-Ural region, becoming "modern" continues to consist primarily of donning European suits, printing newspapers, and imitating European forms of social and political organization.[32] This approach downplays the local specificities of Volga-Ural Muslim society and reduces the experiences of its members to another rendition of a story that has been told numerous times elsewhere.

A second problem with the discussions of modernity as it is often applied to the Volga-Ural Muslim community is the portrayal of modernity as something that emerged suddenly, that was actively promoted by select parties, and in which participation was elective. This elective vision of modernity contradicts the characterizations offered in studies of modernity as a historical condition, which present modernity as a global and all-encompassing phenomenon.[33] Phenomena characteristic of modernity are the abstraction and universalizing of time and its divorce from space, the engagement of individuals in ongoing processes of self-revision, the shrinking of the distance between the global and the personal, and the undermining of "local, hierarchical bonds."[34] The problem of determining when Volga-Ural Muslims became "modern" becomes clear when one tries to locate these developments within the history of their community. Disputes over whether to privilege astronomical phenomena or clocks and calendars when calculating prayer times and the start and end dates for the Ramadan fast suggest that Kazan's Muslims were already cognizant of the concept of universalized time by the beginning of the nineteenth century.[35] An examination of calls from ʿulamāʾ to common Muslims to improve their knowledge of Islam and the lifelong participation of Muslim men and women in Sufi study circles and communal readings of didactic texts places the process of self-improvement/self-revision associated with modernity as far back as the 1700s.[36] The growing proximity of the global and the local was certainly present by the early 1800s, as products from as far abroad as China and western Europe began to reshape Muslim consumption habits. However, one could, with equal justification, find the globalizing aspects of modernity in the long eighteenth century, when Muslim military servitors, interpreters, and conscripts were sent to wars with Sweden, Turkey, Khiva, and France.[37] Indeed, for the Kazan Tatars, who lived in settlements scattered from Finland to China and who, from at least the late 1600s, undertook trade and pilgrimage journeys to Central Asia, South Asia, Anatolia, and the Arabian peninsula, local and personal affairs were closely intertwined with global ones long before the 1880s.[38] Finally, if one insists that the breaking down of local hierarchies and kinship networks is an indicator of modernity, then Volga-Ural Muslim society still had not reached modernity in 1917.

In short, framing the history of the Volga-Ural Muslim community as a story of Muslims becoming modern simultaneously flattens a complex history and revives colonial narratives of European "progress" versus Asiatic "backwardness."[39] Rather than attempting to ascertain when Kazan Tatars stopped being "traditional" and became "modern," this volume reconstructs the Kazan Tatar ʿulamāʾ's mobility and successive reinventions of community identity in response to a continually changing set of political and economic circumstances from the 1600s to the early 1900s. When addressing the Kazan Muslim discourses of the late 1800s and early 1900s, this volume approaches "modernity" as a rhetorical device employed by various parties to bolster their claims to authority over Muslims in Kazan and beyond.[40] By positioning themselves as champions of modernity, Kazan Tatar reformers posited that they were the most qualified to lead Russia's Muslims. In this way, the concept of "modernity" became a new weapon in preexisting struggles over social authority within Russia's Muslim communities.

The Kazan Tatars and Secularization

Finally, when addressing the discourse on modernity within Volga-Ural Muslim historiography, one must also address its fellow traveler, secularism. In studies of the Volga-Ural region, "secularization" encompasses a list of purported developments in the late nineteenth and early twentieth centuries: (1) the displacement of the "Islamic" sciences by mathematics, natural sciences, and social sciences;[41] (2) the development of a "desacralized" understanding of Islamic doctrine, law, and history;[42] (3) Muslim scholars' loss of authority to "lay" Muslims;[43] (4) the displacement of Muslim religious identity by national identity;[44] and (5) the transformation of Islam from a system of beliefs and practices permeating all aspects of community life to a matter of inward belief and personal conscience.[45]

The prominence of these developments in Volga-Ural Muslim historiography is primarily a survival from the Soviet-era histories that shaped the field before the 1990s. These histories were based on a reading of pre-Soviet sources that excluded the works of certain writers entirely and drew from a narrow selection of the works of others. When the full corpus of late nineteenth- and early-twentieth-century writers is taken into consideration, the secular trajectory of Volga-Ural Muslim educational and legal culture becomes much less clear. As late as 1917, Kazan Tatar legists and political activists continued to turn to the Islamic legal tradition as a source for building an ethical system of community relations and institutions.[46] Qur'ān and hadith studies, Islamic jurisprudence, theology, and Arabic language remained central to Kazan Tatar madrasa curricula.[47] Kazan Tatar nationalist writers of the early 1900s not only assumed that members of the Tatar nation were necessarily Muslim but also portrayed Islam as the foundation of their nation's future.[48] While it is possible to locate individual cases of common Muslims challenging legal opinions offered by Muslim legal scholars, there is no evidence of a community-wide rejection of the authority of the madrasa educated. On the contrary, madrasa enrollments and the number of licensed imams increased steadily in the years before the 1917 revolution.[49] Sufi shaykhs and sites associated with them continued to draw numerous Muslims even after 1917.[50] When Kazan Tatar attempted to form a government in 1917–1918, Islamic legal specialists assumed leading roles.[51] All of this suggests that at the time of the Russian empire's collapse, Kazan Tatars still had not embraced either the clear separation of "church" and state or the compartmentalization of religious beliefs commonly associated with a secularized society.

When examining the practice of Islam in the Kazan Tatar community, this volume joins a growing body of studies of the evolution of religion in the nineteenth and twentieth centuries that emphasizes how rising literacy rates, popular education, and mass production of sacred texts contributed to new expressions of faith among the general population as well as the educated elite.[52] It also explores how Islamic jurists and theologians responded to nineteenth-century positivism and empiricism and integrated these into their writings on law and doctrine in ways that suggested systematization and popularization rather than desacralization.[53] By taking these two approaches and applying them across the nineteenth century, this volume positions Islam at the heart of pre-Soviet Kazan Tatar culture and as something evolving and expanding rather than retreating. It views the eventual removal of Islam from public life as an outcome of Soviet policy on religion rather than as a trend in the pre-Soviet era. If not for the suppression of Islam in the 1920s and 1930s, the course of Islam in the twentieth-century Volga-Ural region might have been quite different.

The Organization of the Book

This book explores the intersection between the Kazan Tatar 'ulamā''s participation in the Russian expansion and their emergence as leaders of a distinct ethno-confessional community. It focuses on (1) how the 'ulamā' emerged as a coherent regional elite as a result of the Russian expansion; (2) how their strategies for acquiring and exercising influence over their coreligionists in the Urals, the steppe, and Central Asia evolved from the seventeenth to the early twentieth century; and (3) how their engagement in settler migration, long-distance trade, orientalist compilation of data, education reform, and liberal democratic politics fueled conflicts within their ranks and among those over whom they sought to exercise authority.

The first chapter reconstructs the expansion of a key Kazan Tatar 'ulamā' network from Kazan into the Urals and western Siberia from the late 1600s to the late 1700s. Through an examination of the 'ulamā''s roles in illegal settlement, rebellion, and dissent in the South Urals, this chapter demonstrates that there was not a single Muslim community in central Russia during the eighteenth century, but rather numerous competing factions.

Chapter 2 turns to the conflicts surrounding the Orenburg Muslim Spiritual Assembly (OMSA) in the early 1800s. These conflicts illustrate how patronage and public confrontation limited the imperial government's ability to use the OMSA as an effective administrative instrument.

Chapter 3 shifts the focus to wider Muslim society from 1800 to 1850. Russia's growing commodities trade with Europe, South Asia, and China introduced new goods and new tastes. Mass printing and cheaper paper facilitated the growth of education and old and new expressions of popular religiosity. Changes in consumption, public behavior, and literacy levels created concern among the 'ulamā', who lamented their lack of control over the twin forces of mass consumption and unbridled religious revival.

Chapter 4 reconstructs the institutional base and activities of the Machkaran network, a group of 'ulamā' families who wielded authority over some of the most prominent mosques and madrasas of the mid-1800s and shaped Muslim intellectual and social life in Kazan and Orenburg. These families constituted the 'ulamā' elite of Kazan and continued to predominate even as their resources and rhetoric changed during the last five decades of imperial rule.

Chapter 5 uses the careers of Machkaran network scholars Shihābaddīn al-Marjānī and Ḥusayn Fayḍkhānov to explore the participation of Kazan's 'ulamā' in orientalist projects and the effects of this participation on Muslim discourses on faith and community history writing within their network.

Chapter 6 focuses on Muslim education reform in the Urals, the Kazakh steppe, Central Asia, and the Russian-Chinese borderlands from the 1880s to the 1910s as both a continuation and transmutation of the Kazan Tatar 'ulamā''s earlier colonizing activities in the South Urals and the steppe. The promotion of education reform and the establishment of large commercial firms replaced settler migration as the primary modes by which the 'ulamā' and their merchant allies exercised their authority outside of the Kazan heartland.

Chapter 7 focuses on the ascendency of literalist theology and fundamentalist jurisprudential reform in the Kazan Tatar heartland in the early 1900s and their impact on the scholarly networks that formed the backbone of Kazan Tatar society. It traces how young scholars on the margins of the Machkaran network turned to reformed jurisprudence, literalist theology, and, finally, nationalism to claim leadership within the Volga-Ural Muslim community and its diaspora.

Chapter 8 uses the Izh-Būbī investigation and trial of 1911–1912 to explore how conflicting Russian and Kazan Tatar projects of cultural imperialism strained the relationship between Russian officials and their former Kazan Tatar allies.

Chapter 9 views Kazan Tatar political and nation-building ambitions after the February Revolution as directly proceeding from their experience as intermediaries on the Russian frontier and self-appointed heralds of an Islamic modernity.

From their eastward migrations in the 1700s to their formation of revolution-era political organizations, the Kazan Tatar 'ulamā' existed in a state of constant transformation. Imperial expansion continually reshaped the geographical space within which they moved. Expanding trade filled their homes with an ever-changing array of food, drink, clothes, and personal items. Vibrant Islamic and Russian intellectual worlds flooded them with new ideas about faith, citizenship, cosmology, and individuality. However, amid all this change, a group of families, students, and teachers held their own. Their places of residence, their wardrobe, and their collective narratives of their past changed, but their claim to leadership over the Volga-Ural Muslim community and over any other Muslim community Russian expansion drew into their orbit did not. This is their story.

Notes

1. Arginbāy, *Argınbay Iskhāq Ḥajjī ila Ḥajjge Uska ulınını Troitskī Ishān Zaynullāh Khaḍratka chıgharghān madkhiyaları* (Kazan: n.p., 1911), 2–3.

2. "Taṣawwuf kitābī," Kazanskii (Povolzh'skii) Federal'nyi Universitet - Otdel Rukopisei i Redkikh Knig (hereafter K[P]FU-ORRK) No. 205T, 2–3.

3. Tsentralnyi Gosudarstvennyi Istoricheskii Arkhiv—Respublika Bashkortostan (hereafter TsGIA-RB), f. 187, op. 1, del. 504, l. 16–17

4. The most widely used of these prosopographic sources are Rizā' addīn bin Fakhraddīn's *Asār* (Orenburg: Karīmov, Ḥusaynov wa sharkāsī, 1901–1908) (republished with the inclusion of the previously unpublished third and fourth volumes as Rizaeddin Fäkhreddin, *Asar*, ed. Raif Märdanov and Ramil Mingnullin [Kazan: Rukhiyat, 2006]; Rizaeddin Fäkhreddin, *Asar: ikenche tom*, ed. Ilshat Gyimadiev, Ramil Mingnullin and Sirinä Bahavieva [Kazan: Rukhiyat, 2009]; Rizaeddin Fäkhreddin, *Asar: Öchenche häm dürtenche tom*, ed. Liliya Baibulatova et al. [Kazan: Rukhiyat, 2010]) and Shihābaddīn al-Marjānī, *Qism al-Awwāl min Mustafād al-Akhbār fī aḥwāl Qazān wa Bulghār* (Kazan: Tipo-Litografiia Imperatorskago Universiteta, 1897); Shihābaddīn al-Marjānī, *Qism ath-Thānī min Mustafād al-Akhbār fī aḥwāl Qazān wa Bulghār* (Kazan: Tipo-Litografiia Imperatorskago Universiteta, 1900). Others include the sixth volume of Shihābaddīn al-Marjānī's *Wafayāt al-Aslāf* (K[P]FU-ORRK No. 615AR) and M. M. ar-Rāmzī, *Talfīq al-Akhbār wa Talqīḥ al-Athār fī Waqā'i' Qazān wa Bulghār wa Mulūk at-Tatār* (Orenburg: Karīmov, Ḥusaynov wa sharkāsī, n.d.). The village histories include Gabdulla Bubyi, "Bubyi mädräsäseneng kyska tarikhy," *Bertugan Bubyilar häm Izh-Bubyi mädräsäse* (Kazan: Rukhiyat, 1999); Muḥammad Shākir Tūqāyev, *Tārīkh-i Istarlībāsh* (Kazan: n.p., 1899); "Muḥammad Najīb at-Tūntārī, *Tūntūr āwılı*," Natsionalnaya Biblioteka Respublika Tatarstan-Otdel Rukopisei i Redkikh Knig (hereafter NBRT-ORRK) No. 828T; and "Mökhämmätnäjip khäzrät yazmasy," *Gasyr awazy/ Ekho vekhov* 1–2 (2003).

5. See, for example, Michael Kemper, *Sufis und Gelehrte in Tatarien und Baschkirien, 1789–1889: Der islamische Diskurs unter russischer Herrschaft* (Berlin: Schwarz, 1998); Danil' D. Azamatov, "Russian Administration and Islam in Bashkiria (18th–19th centuries)," in *Muslim Culture in Russia and Central Asia from the 18th to the Early 20th Centuries*, vol. 1., ed. Anke von Kügelgen et al. (Berlin: Klaus Schwarz Verlag, 1996), 91–112; Danil' D. Azamatov, "The Muftis of the Orenburg Spiritual Assembly in the 18th and 19th Centuries: The Struggle for Power in Russia's Muslim Institution," in *Muslim Culture in Russia and Central Asia from the 18th to the Early 20th Centuries*, vol. 2, ed. Anke von Kügelgen et al. (Berlin: Klaus Schwarz Verlag, 1998), 355–86; Allen J. Frank, *Bukhara and the Muslims of Russia: Sufism, Education, and the Paradox of Islamic Prestige* (Leiden: Brill, 2012); Nathan Spannaus, "Formalism, Puritanicalism, Traditionalism: Approaches to Islamic Legal Reasoning in the 19th-Century Russian Empire," *The Muslim World* 104 (2014): 354–78; Nathan Spannaus, "The Decline of the Akhund and the Transformation of Islamic Law under

the Russian Empire," *Islamic Law and Society* 20, no. 3 (2013): 202–41; Robert D. Crews, *For Prophet and Tsar: Islam and Empire in Russia and Central Asia* (Cambridge, MA: Harvard University Press, 2009).

6. Allen Frank, through his work with biographical dictionaries and local histories from the steppe periphery, is one of the few historians to break free of the narratives and boundaries imposed by Fakhreddīn and Marjānī to examine networks beyond the one at the core of *Athār* and *Mustafād al-Akhbār*. See Allen J. Frank, *Muslim Religious Institutions in Russia: Islamic World of Novouzenek District and the Kazakh Inner Horde, 1780–1910* (Boston: Brill, 2001); Allen J. Frank, "Islam and Ethnic Relations in the Kazakh Inner Horde: Muslim Cossacks, Tatar Merchants, and Kazakh Nomads in a Turkic Manuscript, 1870–1910," in *Muslim Culture in Russia and Central Asia from the 18th to the Early 20th Centuries*, vol. 2, ed. Anke Kügelgen et al. (Berlin: Klaus Schwarz, 1996), 211–42; Allen J. Frank, "Tatarskikh mulli sredi kazakhov i kirgizov v XVIII–XIX vekakh," in *Kul'tura, isskustvo tatarskogo naroda: istoki, traditsii, vzaimosviazi*, ed. M. Z. Zakiev et al. (Kazan, 1993), 124–31; Allen J. Frank and Mirkasyim A. Usmanov, eds., *An Islamic Biographical Dictionary of the Eastern Kazakh Steppe, 1770–1912, Qurbān ʿAlī Khālidī* (Leiden: Brill, 2005).

7. The tendency to treat "Tatars," "Muslims," "laypeople," and "clergy" as meaningful categories of analysis rather than situating individuals within the social landscape of their specific Muslim communities is especially prevalent in studies of Islamic and imperial legal institutions (Crews, *For Prophet and Tsar*; Spannaus, "Decline of the Akhund"; Stefan B. Kirmse, "Law and Empire in Late Tsarist Russia: Muslim Tatars Go to Court," *Slavic Review* 72, no. 4 [2013]: 778–801). This approach homogenizes cultural practices among communities spread over thousands of miles and atomizes a society characterized by close and intricate social relations.

8. In the historiography of Islam in the Volga-Ural region, Catherine II's reign (1762–1796) continues to demarcate a purported shift from an imperial policy of persecuting Islam to one of tolerating Islam. For recent examples of this, see Mustafa Tuna, *Imperial Russia's Muslims: Islam, Empire, and European Modernity, 1788–1914* (Cambridge: Cambridge University Press, 2015); Charles Steinwedel, *Threads of Empire: Loyalty and Tsarist Authority in Bashkiria, 1552–1917* (Bloomington: Indiana University Press, 2016). Likewise, the most recent studies of Muslim cultural reformism/Jadidism in the late nineteenth- and early twentieth-century Volga-Ural region continue to treat the intellectual culture and political activism of the last four decades of imperial rule as a significant divergence from culture and practices among the Muslim elite in the first half of the nineteenth century and earlier. Frank's and Kemper's work on pre-1880s regional histories and Islamic scholarly writings provide significant insight into Volga-Ural Muslim culture, intellectual life, and world views in the early and mid-1800s (Kemper, *Sufis und Gelehrte*; Allen J. Frank, *Islamic Historiography and 'Bulghar' Identity among the Tatars and Bashkirs of Russia* [Leiden: Brill, 1998]). However, recent works on reform in the late 1800s and early 1900s have done little to position the movements, texts, and individuals they examine in relation to earlier Muslim writers and texts. (See, for example, Tuna, *Imperial Russia's Muslims*; James H. Meyer, *Turks across Empires: Making Muslim Identity in the Russian Ottoman Borderlands* [Oxford: Oxford University Press, 2014]).

9. On post-1991 interpretations of the Jadids' opponents, see Stéphane A. Dudoignon, "Qadîmiya as a Historiographical Category: The Question of the Communal Unity as Seen by 'Reformists' and 'Traditionalists' among the Muslims of Russia and Central Asia in the Early

Twentieth Century," in *Reform Movements and Revolutions in Turkistan: Studies in Honour of Osman Khoja*, ed. Timur Kocaoğlu (Haarlem, Netherlands: Sota, 2001), 159–77; Rozaliya Garipova, "The Protectors of Religion and Community: Traditionalist Muslim Scholars of the Volga-Ural Region at the Beginning of the Twentieth Century," *Journal of Economic and Social History of the Orient* 59 (2016): 126–65.

10. Jane Burbank and Frederick Cooper, *Empires in World History: Power and Politics of Difference* (Princeton, NJ: Princeton University Press, 2010); Anna Laura Stoler and Frederick Cooper, "Between Metropole and Colony: Rethinking a Research Agenda," *Tensions of Empire: Colonial Cultures in a Bourgeois World*, ed. Frederick Cooper and Ann Laura Stoler (Berkeley: University of California Press, 1997), 1–56.

11. Michael Khodarkovsky, *Russia's Steppe Frontier: The Making of a Colonial Empire, 1500–1800* (Bloomington: Indiana University Press, 2004); Willard Sunderland, *Taming the Wild Field: Colonization and Empire on the Russian Steppe* (Ithaca, NY: Cornell University Press, 2004); Steinwedel, *Threads of Empire*; John Le Donne, *The Russian Empire and the World, 1700–1917: The Geopolitics of Expansion and Containment* (Oxford: Oxford University Press, 1996).

12. Crews, *For Prophet and Tsar*; Robert P. Geraci, *Window on the East: National and Imperial Identities in Late Tsarist Russia* (Ithaca, NY: Cornell University Press, 2001); Paul W. Werth, *At the Margins of Orthodoxy: Mission, Governance, and Confessional Politics in Russia's Volga-Kama Region, 1827–1905* (Ithaca, NY: Cornell University Press, 2001); Elena I. Campbell, *The Muslim Question and Russian Imperial Governance* (Bloomington: Indiana University Press, 2015).

13. Peter van der Veer, *Imperial Encounters: Religion and Modernity in India and Britain* (Princeton, NJ: Princeton University Press, 2001); David Schimmelpennick van der Oye, *Russian Orientalism: Asia in the Russian Mind from Peter the Great to the Emigration* (New Haven, CT: Yale University Press, 2010); Vera Tolz, *Russia's Own Orient: The Politics of Identity and Oriental Studies in the Late Imperial and Early Soviet Periods* (Oxford: Oxford University Press, 2011).

14. Frederick Cooper and Ann Laura Stoler, eds., *Tensions of Empire: Colonial Cultures in a Bourgeois World* (Berkeley: University of California Press, 1997); Ann Laura Stoler and Willy Brandt, eds., *Carnal Knowledge and Imperial Power: Race and the Intimate in Colonial Rule* (Berkeley: University of California Press, 2002).

15. Lauren Benton and Richard J. Ross, eds., *Legal Pluralism and Empires, 1500–1850* (New York: New York University Press, 2013); James E. Sanders, *Contentious Republicans: Popular Politics, Race, and Class in Nineteenth-Century Colombia* (Durham, NC: Duke University Press, 2004).

16. Richard White, *The Middle Ground: Indians Empires, and Republics in the Great Lakes Region, 1650–1815* (Cambridge: Cambridge University Press, 2010); Pekka Hämäläinen, *The Comanche Empire* (New Haven, CT: Yale University Press, 2008); Nehemia Levetzion and John O. Voll, eds., *Eighteenth-Century Renewal and Reform in Islam* (Syracuse, NY: Syracuse University Press, 1987); Kwangmin Kim, *Borderland Capitalism: Turkestan Prodce, Qing Silver, and the Birth of an Eastern Market* (Stanford, CA: Stanford University Press, 2016).

17. Frederick Cooper, *Citizenship between Empire and Nation: Remaking France and French Africa, 1945–1960* (Princeton, NJ: Princeton University Press, 2014); Partha Chatterjee, *The Nation and Its Fragments: Colonial and Post-Colonial Histories* (Princeton, NJ: Princeton University Press, 1993).

18. Ronald Grigor Suny, *Looking Toward Ararat: Armenia in Modern History* (Bloomington: Indiana University Press, 1993); Firouzeh Mostashari, *On the Religious Frontier: Tsarist Russia and Islam in the Caucasus* (London: I. B. Tauris, 2006), 41–44; Austin Jersild, *Orientalism and Empire: North Caucasus Mountain Peoples and the Georgian Frontier, 1845–1917* (Montreal: McGill-Queens Press, 2002); Scott Cameron Levi, *The Indian Diaspora in Central Asia and Its Trade, 1550–1900* (Leiden: Brill, 2002).

19. Serge A. Zenkovsky, *Pan-Turkism and Islam in Russia* (Cambridge, MA: Harvard University Press, 1967); Azade-Ayşe Rorlich, *The Volga Tatars: A Profile in National Resilience* (Stanford, CA: Hoover Institute, 1986); Geoffrey Wheeler, *The Modern History of Soviet Central Asia*, (London: Praeger, 1964); Hélène Carrère d'Encausse, *Islam and the Russian Empire: Reform and Revolution in Central Asia* (Berkeley: University of California Press, 1988); Edward Allworth, *The Modern Uzbeks: From the Fourteenth Century to the Present: A Cultural History* (Stanford, CA: Hoover Institute, 1990); A. Bennigsen and Chantal Lemercier-Quelquejay, *Les mouvements nationaux chez les musulmans de Rusie: Le "sultangalievisme" au Tatarstan* (Paris: Mouton, 1960); Alexandre Bennigsen and Chantal Lemercier-Quelquejay, *Islam in the Soviet Union* (London: n.p., 1967); Alexandre Bennigsen and Chantal Lemercier-Quelquejay, *La presse et le movement nationaux chez les musulmans de Russie avant 1920* (Paris: Mouton, 1964); Edward Lazzerini, "Ismail Bey Gasprinskii and Muslim Modernism in Russia, 1878–1914" (PhD diss., University of Washington, 1973).

20. Dzhamaliutdin Validov, *Ocherki istorii obrazovannosti i literatury Tatar* (Kazan: Izdatel'stvo "Iman," 1998); Galimjan Ibrahimov, "Tatarlar arasynda revoliutsiia khäräkätläre," *Galimjan Ibrahimov: Äsärlär sigez tomda* (9 vols.), ed. S. Kh. Alishev (Kazan: Tatarstan kitap näshriyaty, 1984), 7:242–435.

21. A. Arsharuni and Kh. Gabidullin, *Ocherki Panislamizma i Panturkizma v Rossii* (Moscow: Izdatel'stvo Bezbozhnik, 1931); R. I. Nafigov, *Formirovanie i razvitie peredovoi tatarskoi obshchestvenno-politicheskoi mysli* (Kazan: Tatarskoe knizhnoe izdatel'stvo, 1964); M. Kh. Gainullin, *Tatarskaia literatura i publitsistika nachala XX veka* (Kazan: Tatarskoe knizhnoe izdatel'stvo, 1966); M. Kh. Gainullin, *Tatarskaia literatura XIX veka* (Kazan: Tatarskoe knizhnoe izdatel'stvo,1975); M. S. Mähdiev, *Ijtimagi häm estetik fikerneng tatar ädäbiyatı üseshenä yogyntysy* (Kazan: Kazan universitety näshriyaty, 1977).

22. Albert Hourani, *Arabic Thought in the Liberal Age, 1798–1939* (Cambridge: Cambridge University Press, 1983); Şerif Mardin, *The Genesis of Young Ottoman Thought* (Syracuse, NY: Syracuse University Press, 2000); Nikki R. Keddie, *Sayyid Jamāl ad-Din "al-Afghānī": A Political Biography* (Berkeley: University of California Press, 1972); Hamid Algar, *Mīrzā Malkum Khān: A Study in the History of Iranian Modernism* (Berkeley: University of California Press, 1973).

23. Muhammad Qasim Zaman, *Islamic Thought in a Radical Age: Religious Authority and Internal Criticism* (Cambridge: Cambridge University Press, 2012); Muhammad Qasim Zaman, *The Ulama in Contemporary Islam: Custodians of Change* (Princeton, NJ: Princeton University Press, 2010); Michael Laffan, *The Makings of Indonesian Islam: Orientalism and the Narration of a Sufi Past* (Princeton, NJ: Princeton University Press, 2011); Henri Lauzière, *The Making of Salafism: Islamic Reform in the Twentieth Century* (New York: Columbia University Press, 2016); *Global Salafism: Islam's New Religious Movement*, ed. Roel Meijer (New York: Columbia University Press, 2009); Barbara Daly Metcalf, *Islamic Revival in British India: Deoband, 1860–1900* (Princeton, NJ: Princeton University Press, 2014); Francis

Robinson, *The 'Ulama of Farangi Mahall and Islamic Culture in South Asia* (London: C. Hurst, 2001).

24. Adeeb Khalid, *The Politics of Muslim Cultural Reform: Jadidism in Central Asia* (Berkeley: University of California Press, 1998), 1–9; Frank, *Islamic Historiography*, 1–11; Nathan Spannaus, "The Ur-Text of Jadidism: Abū Naṣr Qūrsāwī's *Irshād* and the Historiography of Muslim Modernism in Russia," *Journal of the Economic and Social History of the Orient* 59 (2016): 93–125.

25. Paolo Sartori, *Visions of Justice: Sharia and Culture in Russian Central Asia* (Leiden: Brill, 2017); Paolo Sartori, "Ijtihād in Bukhara: Central Asian Jadidism and Local Genealogies of Cultural Change," *Journal of the Economic and Social History of the Orient* 59 (2016): 193–236; James Robert Pickett, "The Persianate Sphere during the Age of Empires: Islamic Scholars and Networks of Exchange in Central Asia, 1747–1917" (PhD diss., Princeton University, 2015); B. M. Babadzhanov, *Kokandskoe khanstvo: Vlast', politika, religiia* (Tokyo/Tashkent: NIHU Program Islamic Area Studies Center at the University of Tokyo/Institut vostokovedeniia Akademii nauk Respubliki Uzbekistan, 2010).

26. Frank, *Islamic historiography*; Frank, *Bukhara and the Muslims of Russia*; Kemper, *Sufis und Gelehrte*.

27. Meyer, *Turks across Empires*; Tuna, *Imperial Russia's Muslims*; Mustafa Tuna, "Madrasa Reform as a Secularizing Process: A View from the Russian Empire," *Comparative Studies in Society and History* 53, no. 3 (2011): 540–70; Norihiro Naganawa, "Maktab or School? Introduction of Universal Primary Education among the Volga-Ural Muslims" in *Empire, Islam and Politics in Central Eurasia*, ed. Kimitaka Matsuzato (Sapporo, Japan: Slavic Research Center, 2007), 65–97; Norihiro Naganawa, "Molding the Muslim Community through the Tsarist Administration: Mahalla under the Jurisdiction of Orenburg Muhammadan Spiritual Assembly after 1905," *Acta Slavica Iaponica* 23 (2006) 101–23; Ahmet Kanlıdere, *Reform within Islam: The Tajdid and Jadid Movement among the Kazan Tatars (1809–1917): Conciliation or Conflict?* (Istanbul: Eren, 1997); Christian Noack, *Muslimscher Nationalismus im Russischen Reich: Nationsbildung und Nationalbewegung bei Tataren und Bashkiren, 1861–1917* (Stuttgart, Germany: Franz Steiner Verlag, 2000).

28. Devin DeWeese, "It Was a Dark and Stagnant Night ('til the Jadids Brought the Lights): Clichés, Biases, and False Dichotomies in the Intellectual History of Central Asia," *Journal of the Economic and Social History of the Orient* 59 (2016): 59–68.

29. For a recent example of this tendency, see Tuna, *Imperial Russia's Muslims*.

30. James E. Sanders, *The Vanguard of the Atlantic World: Creating Modernity, Nation, and Democracy in Nineteenth-Century Latin America* (Durham, NC: Duke University Press, 2014); Andre Gunder Frank, *ReOrient: Global Economy in the Asian Age* (Berkeley: University of California Press, 1998); Andre Gunder Frank, *The 19th Century: Global Economy in the Continuing Asian Age*, ed. Robert A. Denemark (London: Routledge, 2015); Kenneth Pomeranz, *The Great Divergence: China, Europe, and the Making of the Modern World Economy* (Princeton. NJ: Princeton University Press, 2009); Scott C. Levi, *The Rise and Fall of Khoqand, 1709–1876: Central Asia in a Global Age* (Pittsburgh, PA: University of Pittsburgh Press, 2017); Sanjay Subrahmanyam, *Penumbral Visions: Making Polities in Early Modern South Asia* (Ann Arbor: University of Michigan Press, 2001).

31. Dipesh Chakrabarty, *Provincializing Europe: Postcolonial Thought and Historical Difference* (Princeton, NJ: Princeton University Press, 2000); Dilip Parameshwar Gaonkar, ed., *Alternative Modernities* (Durham, NC: Duke University Press, 2001); *Multiple Modernities*, ed. Shmuel N. Eisenstadt (London: Routledge, 2017).

32. Tuna, *Imperial Russia's Muslims*; Meyer, *Turks across Empires*.

33. Anthony Giddens, *Modernity and Self-Identity: Self and Society in the Late Modern Age* (Stanford, CA: Stanford University Press, 1991), 22.

34. Ibid., 1–34; Marshall Berman, *All That Is Solid Melts into Air: The Experience of Modernity* (New York: Penguin, 1982), 6–16; Peter van der Veer, "The Global History of 'Modernity'," *Journal of the Economic and Social History of the Orient* 41, no. 3 (1998): 285.

35. Michael Kemper, "Imperial Russia as Dar al-Islam?: Nineteenth-Century Debates on Ijtihad and Taqlid among the Volga Tatars," *Islamic Law and Society* 6 (2015): 95–124.

36. Surviving vernacular-language sources written in the 1700s about Quran memorization, basic Islamic obligations, and Islamic history suggest the existence of an audience of Volga-Ural Muslim readers in this period who were not madrasa educated but sought Islamic knowledge for self-improvement and/or for participating a broader enactment of Islamic norms and values within their communities. The Turki-language didactic stories composed by Urgench-born scholar Ishniyaz bin Shirniyaz (1725–1790) ("Ädib Ishniyaz bine Shirniyaz Khäräzmi," *XVIII yöz Tatar ädäbiyaty: Proza*, ed. M. Äkhmätzhanov [Kazan: G. Ibrahimov isemendäge Tel, ädäbiyat häm sängat' instituty, 2012], 359–76) is a known example of these kinds of texts, but many others exist in fragmentary form in manuscript collections in Kazan and have yet to be properly identified and studied in detail.

37. "XVIII gasyr Tatar sugyshchysynyng yulyazmasy," *Säyakhätnamälär*, ed. Raif Märdanov (Kazan: "Milli kitap," 2011), 5–13; "Liubizar," *Tatar khalyk ijaty: Tarikhi häm lirik jyrlar*, ed. I. N. Nadirov (Kazan: Tatarskoe knizhnoe izdatel'stvo, 1988), 44; "Parizh köe," *Onytyrga mömkin tügel: Tatarstan Respublikasynyng fol'klor muzıkasy däülät amsamble repertuarynnan*, ed. A. F. Fayzrakhmanov (Kazan: n.p., 2013), 89.

38. "Ismägyil' Aga Säyakhätnamäsy," *XVIII yöz Tatar ädäbiyaty: Proza*, 313–41; "Mökhämmädämin Säyakhätnamäsy," *XVIII yöz Tatar ädäbiyaty: Proza*, 342–58.

39. On the difficulty of mapping European narratives of tradition and modernity onto Islamic history and cultural production, see Hamid Dabashi, *The World of Persian Literary Humanism*, (Cambridge, MA: Harvard University Press, 2012), 301–28.

40. Frederick Cooper, *Colonialism in Question: Theories, Knowledge, History* (Berkeley: University of California, 2005), 116.

41. Tuna, "Madrasa Reform," 540–70.

42. Agnès Nilüfer Kefeli, *Becoming Muslim in Imperial Russia: Conversion, Apostasy, and Literacy* (Ithaca, NY: Cornell University Press, 2014), 213–54; Adeeb Khalid, "What Jadidism Was and What It Wasn't: The Historiographical Adventures of a Term," *Central Eurasian Studies Review* 5, no. 2 (2006): 5.

43. Crews, *For Prophet and Tsar.*

44. Rorlich, *The Volga Tatars;* Aidar Khabutdinov, *Ot obshchinay k natii* (Kazan: Tatarskoe knizhnoe izdatel'stvo, 2008).

45. Kefeli, *Becoming Muslim*, 218, 230–31.

46. Mūsā Bīgīev, *Zakāt* (Petrograd: Tipografiia Mukhammadalima Maksudova, 1916).

47. Gabdulla Bubyi, "Bubyi mädräsäseneng kyska tarikhy," *Bertugan Bubyilar*, 33, 35, 36, 39, 46–7, 50–1, 55–7; *Madrasa-i Muḥammadiyya Programmasī, 1913 m./1331 h.* (Kazan: Elektro-tipografiia Milliat, 1913), 8, 24–25; *Ufada berenche masjid jāmiʿ khuḍūrındaghī madrasa-i ʿUthmaniyyaning mufaṣṣal programmasī* (Ufa: Elek-tip. 'Tūrmish', 1917), 4; "Madrasa-i Shamsiyya niẓāmnamāsī," K(P)FU-ORRK, No. 1240 T, 30b-4; Madina Rakhimkulova, *Medrese "Khusainiia" v Orenburge* (Orenburg: n.p., 1997), 18–20, 22.

48. Fatikh Ämirkhan, "Fätkhulla Khäzrät," *Fatikh Ämirkhan: Äsärlär dürt tomda* (4 vols.) (Kazan: Tatarskoe Knizhnoe Izdatel'stvo, 1984), 2:7–118.

49. Il'dus Zagidullin, *Islamskie instituty v Rossiiskoi imperii: Mecheti v evropeiskoi chasti Rossii i Sibiri* (Kazan: Tatarskoe Knizhnoe Izdatel'stvo, 2007), 143.

50. Galimjan Barudi, *Qyzylyar säfäre* (Kazan: "Iman," 2004), 59.

51. *'Ulamā' ittifaghī: berenche nadwasī* (Kazan: Tipo-litografiia T. D. "Br. Karimovy,"1917).

52. Nathan O. Hatch, *The Democratization of American Christianity* (New Haven, CT: Yale University Press, 1991); Paul E. Johnson, *A Shopkeeper's Millennium: Society and Revivals in Rochester, New York, 1815–1837* (New York: Hill and Wang, 2004); Nehemia Levetzion and John O. Voll, eds., *Eighteenth-Century Renewal and Reform in Islam* (Syracuse, NY: Syracuse University Press, 1987).

53. David Smith, *Hinduism and Modernity* (Oxford: Blackwell Publishing, 2003); B. M. Pietsch, *Dispensational Modernism* (Oxford: Oxford University Press, 2015).

1

THE AGE OF THE SETTLER ʿULAMĀʾ

IN 1680, MUSLIMS IN KAZAN OBSERVED THAT A bright new star had appeared in the sky. It remained there for forty days.[1] This was the Great Comet of 1680, also called Kirch's Comet or Newton's Comet, one of the great astronomical events of the seventeenth century. However, Kazan's Muslims interpreted it as a sign that great unrest was about to break out among the Russian "nonbelievers" and that many Muslims would abandon their faith.[2]

The late 1600s have been characterized either as a moment at which relations between the Russian government and its Muslim subjects worsened or as part of a longer period of anti-Muslim policy stretching from the 1552 conquest of Kazan to the 1762 ascension of Catherine the Great.[3] Policies enacted by the Russian state and growing unrest in the Urals and western Siberia indeed created a precarious situation for some of Kazan's Muslims. However, they also created opportunities and social upheaval from which others benefitted. The history of how the Kazan's Muslims crafted a new identity for themselves began not with the 1552 conquest, but with a series of seventeenth-century crises and the response to them by a small group of Kazan Tatar ʿulamāʾ.

A New Time of Troubles (1649–1682)

The Muslims of Kazan *prikaz*—a sprawling administrative unit lying east of Moscow and encompassing the conquered khanate of Kazan, the Urals, and the lower Volga basin—had been through difficult times before. During the 1552 conquest, the city of Kazan and its inhabitants suffered the same destruction and brutality that Ivan the Terrible meted out to most of the lands he subdued. Instead of relief, Ivan's death was followed by a devastating famine in 1601 and the Time of Troubles, a period of pretenders, civil war, and foreign invasion that lasted from 1605 until 1613.[4]

Alexei Mikhailovich's ascension to the Muscovite throne in 1645 heralded a distinct change in Russia's policy toward its Muslims. The Sobornoe Ulozhenie, the new Russian legal code issued in 1649, included a clause forbidding Muslims from converting Russians to Islam "by force or trickery." Any Muslim caught doing so was to be burned at the stake.[5] In 1651, Alexei Mikhailovich forbade the Qasim khanate, a small Muslim buffer state established by Muscovy in 1452 and the only Muslim ruling dynasty then within Russian borders, from communicating with Muslims beyond the borders of Russia, including the diplomats and couriers from Iran, Bukhara, Urgench, and the Nogay horde who passed through the khanate on their way to and from Moscow along the Oka River.[6]

By the 1660s, the eastern edge of Kazan Muslims' world grew increasingly perilous. In February 1662, Irka Mullā, a Kazan Muslim working as a diplomat from Moscow to the Kalmyk leader Abylai Tashi, was robbed by Arlsan-bek and his Bashkir followers outside Ufa. He complained to the tsar and requested that they be punished.[7] By October, a group of Bashkirs joined forces with Abylai and attacked settlements around Ufa and Menzelinsk. Alexei Mikhailovich called on officials from Kazan and Perm to raise an army of newly baptized subjects, Muslim Tatars, *mirzas* (noblemen), and Chuvashes to halt and disperse the "traitors" before they could cross the Kama River and threaten Kazan.[8]

In 1670, Stepan Razin's uprising brought yet more violence to Kazan province. Razin made an appeal to the Muslim spiritual leaders and nobles of Kazan.[9] Some Kazan Muslims supported him, while others did not.[10] One *mirza*, Prince Safar Tenishev, described in a 1671 petition how his wife and children had fled into the woods with the family's livestock to escape Razin's followers. They had the misfortune to stumble across a village where they were taken hostage, beaten, and robbed by the local peasants.[11]

The early 1680s dealt several more blows to Russia's Kazan Muslim subjects. In 1680, a brutal famine struck the Middle Volga region, killing thousands.[12] In the same year, Alexei Mikhailovich returned to newly baptized Tatar nobles of the Romanov district the lands that had previously been confiscated from them and exempted them from state service for three years as a reward for their conversion to Christianity.[13] In 1681, his son, Tsar Fedor, decreed that Muslim nobles who refused to convert to Christianity would have their lands confiscated. In short order, the remaining non-Christian nobles of Romanov and Yaroslav complied.[14] In the same year, the mother of the last Shibanid khan of Qasim died. Her son, the last khan, had passed away two years before.[15] Instead of being assigned a new dynasty, the Qasim khanate was dissolved and its territory absorbed into the Kazan *prikaz*.[16] Qasim had been created by the Muscovites as a buffer state between Muscovy and the Kazan khanate.[17] Nonetheless, after the Russian conquest of Kazan, Qasim, with its Turkic Muslim royal court, had served as a last bastion of Muslim-Chinggisid rule for Muslims in the conquered khanates, preserving the historical link to the Golden Horde and allowing Kazan's Muslim aristocracy and ʿulamāʾ to imagine they still dwelt in a Muslim land even as they lived under the rule of an Orthodox Christian tsar and served in his armies.[18]

In 1682, another bout of violence began. A man named Sayyid Jaʿfar appeared among the Bashkirs and began to call them to convert to Islam and live by the rules of the faith. Later histories would dub him a saint (*awliya, karamat*) or a miracle worker.[19] In some sources, he is identified as a khan of the Bashkirs, and in others, as a person who strove to make himself a khan.[20] In either case, some Bashkir leaders had no wish to see him become (or remain) a khan. They went over to the Russians and took up arms against him and his supporters.[21] The resulting conflict lasted until 1683, and according to Kazan Muslim sources, "many people perished."[22]

Imagining Russia as the Abode of Islam: Yūnus bin Iwānāy and His Sons (mid-1600s–1720s)

Muslims were not the only ones to suffer in the second half of the seventeenth century. Alexei Mikhailovich's reign was the era of the Nikonian Reforms and the Great Schism of the Russian Orthodox Church. However, for Muslims living in the Volga Basin and on Russia's eastern frontier, the combination of anti-Muslim legislation against the nobility and the constant civil unrest may have made the situation of Islam in the former Kazan khanate seem dire. It certainly appeared so to Kazan Tatars living two hundred years later. Ḥusayn Amirkhanov, in his 1883 *Tawārīkh-i Bulghāriyya*, characterized the reign of Alexei Mikhailovich as a time when Muslim scholars were killed and Muslim books were burned.[23]

In fact, the situation was much more complex. Russian decrees against Islam most impacted Kazan's Muslim aristocrats, who gradually receded from local Muslim political and social life.[24] At the same time, however, Kazan's ʿulamāʾ took on more prominent roles in regional politics. Irka Mullā, Alexei Mikhailovich's emissary to the Kalmyks, was one example of this. Another was Ishbūlāt Mullā, who, together with Roman Limkov, led a combined Russian-Tatar army out of Kazan to drive rebels out of the surrounding countryside during the 1704–1708 Bashkir Revolt.[25] Religion was only one of many factors that united and divided people in late seventeenth-century Russia's conflict-ridden east.

One Muslim religious scholar who navigated the complicated terrain of the late 1600s was Yūnus son of Iwānāy son of Usay. Yūnus styled himself as descended from a long line of holy men and scholars, some of whom may have come from Syria.[26] His father served as imam of Kache village near the city of Kazan until his death in 1689.[27] Yūnus was born in 1639. He married the daughter of Yanisarı bin Ḥāfiz, imam of Ūri village near Kazan.[28] This marriage secured Yūnus's and his descendants' position as imams of Ūri for several generations.

Yūnus traveled extensively, going to Bukhara, where his learning and intelligence supposedly gained him the title of "Famous Mullā Yūnus" (*Shahīr Mella Yūnus*), and making the pilgrimage to Mecca twice. On one of his journeys south in the early 1700s, he reportedly made the acquaintance of one of the sons of Abu'l-khayr Khan of the Kazakh Junior Horde.[29] At home, he busied himself with Islamic scholarship and with making basic Islamic learning accessible to his students. He composed an Arabic-language commentary detailing the basic duties (*farāʾiḍ*) of Muslims.[30]

In the late 1600s or early 1700s, another Kazan Muslim scholar, ʿAbdalkarīm ash-Shirdānī, wrote to Yūnus. He inquired as to whether Kazan, Astrakhan, and Qasim, which had fallen under the rule of the infidels (the Russians) belonged to the Abode of Islam or the Abode of War. Could Muslims still trade in these cities? Could they continue to live in these regions, or were they, as faithful Muslims, obliged to relocate to lands still under Muslim rule?[31]

Yūnus responded with a *tarjiḥ*, a treatise laying out the various Islamic legal precedents related to ash-Shirdānī's question. He started with Abū Ḥanīfa, the titular founder of the Ḥanafī legal school (*madhhab*), with which most Islamic jurists of Kazan identified. He noted that Abū Ḥanīfa designated three conditions for declaring a territory the Abode of War. First, such a territory was under the rule of idolaters. Second, there was no Muslim land adjacent to it. Third, life there had become so hazardous that neither Muslims nor dependent People of the Book (*dhimmī*) could safely remain there. For a territory to truly become the Abode of War, a place Muslims had a religious obligation to emigrate from, it had to meet all three of these conditions. He also noted that it had been established by consensus of Muslim scholars (*ijmāʿ*) that the presence of nonbelievers in the Abode of Islam did not automatically render it the Abode of War. Likewise, lands that had previously belonged to the Abode of Islam but had fallen under the rule of nonbelievers did not become the Abode of War if Muslims remained there and were able to practice their religion and if that territory was still adjacent to/in contact with some other part of the Abode of Islam.[32]

Yūnus cited the opinions of illustrious scholars of the past rather than formulating a new ruling in response to ash-Shirdānī's question. He did so because, in his mind, the question had already been addressed clearly and sufficiently by earlier jurists and required no further elaboration. However, in the context of Kazan in the late 1600s, Yūnus's compilation and reiteration of these legal opinions was, in fact, a declaration of sorts. It offered an Islamic legal justification for Kazan's Muslims to remain where they were despite the measures that the Russian government had taken against the Muslim nobility and the periodic rebellions in the Volga basin and the Urals. It also implicitly defined the conquered Muslim territories in Russia as primarily Muslim spaces despite the changes in administration. At the same time, it left the door open for those Muslims who had set their minds on leaving Russia to go to other lands.

Yūnus himself chose not to emigrate and continued to live in Ūri. His son, Safar, also chose to stay in Ūri, and Yūnus's grandson, Muḥsin, studied under another scholar from Ūri and later became the imam of Ūri, a position he held until his death in 1790. Another of Yūnus's sons, Maqṣūd, also remained in Russia, but his career took a very different turn from that of his brother and nephew. In 1722, following in the footsteps of Yūnus, Maqṣūd journeyed to Bukhara together with his son, Raḥmatullāh. The main purpose of their trip appears to have been trade, as they traveled with a significant number of pack animals. (Maqṣūd subsequently complained to Russian officials that the "impudent Kazakhs" had robbed them of their camels and horses along the road.)[33] During his trips between Bukhara and Russia from 1723 to 1725, Maqṣūd took on an additional profession. In 1718, Peter I sent Florio Beneveni to deliver a charter to the Bukharan emir. Beneveni remained in Central Asia as a Russian diplomat and intelligence gatherer, and Maqṣūd became his courier, receiving his dispatches in Bukhara and delivering them to Ufa.[34] From 1725 to 1726, Maqṣūd also appears to have served briefly as a Russian emissary to Abu'l-khayr Khan of the Kazakh Junior Horde, perhaps building on his father's relationship with the Kazakh khan.[35] The connection of Maqṣūd bin Yūnus's family with the Russian advance into the steppe did not end in the 1720s. By the late 1700s, Maqṣūd's descendants had moved east to settle around the village of Kirdas in the South Urals.[36]

Yūnus and his family exemplified a new kind of Kazan Muslim subject that had emerged by the late 1600s. These subjects were Muslim scholars and merchants rather than the landed aristocrats and servitors who defended the eastern frontier in the sixteenth and early seventeenth centuries. However, these newcomers took on many of the roles that had been previously filled by the aristocracy. They carried messages, organized new settlements, and mediated between the Russian state and the various Muslim populations it encountered. They did so while imagining themselves as acting within a geographic space that was spiritually Muslim despite being administratively Russian and Christian. For them, the spread of Russian rule and Islamic faith were not mutually exclusive nor contradictory projects. If Muslims were free to practice their religion and lead prosperous lives, "infidel" Russian rule was not necessarily a bad thing. When it brought order, security, and wealth, so that Kazan 'ulamā' could build mosques and madrasas, make money, and spread knowledge of their faith, it could even be thought of as a good thing.

In assessing how safe Russia really was for Islam, Kazan Muslim jurists like Yūnus focused on real-life consequences rather than government decrees. What the tsar or the Orthodox Church said about Islam was less important than how Muslims were treated. In this way, 'ulamā' who entered state service or settled on the frontier excelled at turning a blind eye to periodic flare-ups of anti-Muslim sentiments and continued to pursue longer-term projects of conversion, community building, social climbing, and profit seeking.

When working together in the late 1600s and early 1700s, Kazan 'ulamā' and Russian officials gained benefits that they would not have enjoyed individually. Russian officials gained eyes and ears in places that would have been closed to non-Muslims. 'Ulamā' gained the protection and legitimacy of being connected to the Russian government. For example, Maqṣūd bin Yūnus, upon being waylaid by the Karakalpaks in 1723, introduced himself as an emissary of the Russian tsar. Not only was he able to secure his own safety during his stay among them, but he was also able to obtain the release of two other emissaries who had been previously taken captive.[37] After traveling with the Karakalpaks, he reported back to the College of

Foreign Affairs on the war among the leaders of Samarkand, Bukhara, and Khiva and the latest conflicts between the Kazakhs and the Zungars over the city of Turkistan.[38]

Allies in Maintaining Order: The Bashkir Uprising of 1735–1740

From the 1680s to the 1760s, officials in Russia's eastern borderlands and Kazan's ʿulamāʾ developed a codependent relationship. No official decree from the Russian state initiated this relationship, nor was there a single moment at which these two groups agreed to work together. Rather, their relationship grew out of myriad small interactions between individuals. Both parties in these interactions pursued their own interests but found that cooperation was the easiest way to achieve their respective goals. Deals were struck without either party foreseeing the long-term ramifications of their cooperation.

By the 1730s, both Russian officials and Kazan ʿulamāʾ set their eyes on the steppe on the empire's southeastern frontier. The idea of creating a more permanent Russian outpost at the northern end of the north-south trade route that ran from Russia to the cities of Central Asia was one that both the imperial government and Kazan's Muslims stood to profit from.

In the seventeenth and early eighteenth centuries, the South Urals had been a loosely governed hinterland. The 1735 announcement of plans to construct the fortress city of Orenburg and extend the existing fortified lines to the east and south initiated the transformation of the region into an imperial province.[39] State Councilor Ivaṇ Kirilov envisioned the transformation of the South Urals as including a resettlement of Russian peasants eastward to move the region toward an agrarian economy resembling that of the western parts of the empire. However, when he surveyed the region in 1735, he complained that "between the Siberian settlements and Ufa, no small expanse, a distance of about seven hundred versts, there is not a single Russian inhabitant."[40] Moreover, he was shocked by a seeming lack of imperial law and order in the region. He characterized Taininsk *volost* as "separated from Ufa and, because of all the Bashkirs, a very nest of runaway soldiers and peasants," including "Tatars, Cheremises, Votiaks, Mordvins and Chuvashes," and much of the land on the road to the Or River as "lying empty."[41] Already in 1735, before construction of Orenburg fortress had begun, Kirilov drew up a plan for how to reorganize the

South Urals. Non-Russian fugitives and squatters who turned themselves in would be sent back to Kazan province, where they would be settled as peasant farmers and required to the pay the poll tax. Those who resisted deportation would be enlisted in the imperial navy or sent to hard labor in Rogorvik in the Baltic region.[42]

Kirilov lamented the disorderly nature of society in the South Urals and repeatedly highlighted the pervasiveness of non-Russians in the region. However, he did not see all non-Russians as agents of disorder. His plans for the construction of Orenburg and the pacification of the surrounding region hinged on the cooperation of the region's small population of "service people": irregular military forces such as the ethnically mixed Cossacks and the Turkic-speaking Mishars, the Bashkir *tarkhans* (who had been granted lower tribute and other privileges in return for past service to the Russian state), and "service" Tatars from Kazan, who had been permitted to resettle east in earlier decades. As the Orenburg project got underway, Kirilov and other officials called on these communities to provide military and logistical support to the arriving expedition.

Two of the communities called on were Almat and Nadir villages. Founded in the first two decades of the eighteenth century, these two villages were part of a network of Muslim settlements that had emerged along the Sviaga River. Most of the residents of these villages were Muslims from Kazan and its surrounding villages. In 1735, Nadir village was under the leadership of Mullā Nadir son of Urazmet (Urāz Muḥammad), a descendant of an old *mirza* family from west of Kazan. In addition to the land on which Nadir village was situated, Mullā Nadir's family claimed that they had been awarded the land along the Sviaga, Kichui, Sheshma, and Sok rivers and "the lands and forests on a territory the size of Khiva" in return for their loyal service to Muscovy during the conquest of Kazan and/or the conquest of the Urals.[43] However, by Nadir's time, the family's members appeared to have abandoned their function as landowners, and Nadir's status among his fellow Muslims came from his learning rather than from his being a landed aristocrat.

In the early 1700s, Nadir sold part of his family's land to Sarmakay and Kadermat (Qadīr Muḥammad), two brothers originally from a village near Menzelinsk. On this land, the brothers founded the village of Kakre Elga around 1709.[44] While Kadermat's son remained in Kakre Elga and his grandson eventually became the imam of that village, Sarmakay's son

Almat (al-Muḥammad) left and began a new settlement in the same region, which, by 1735, had become the village of Almat. Mullā Almat bore the distinction of being one of the first community leaders in his region to pay a tribute in furs (*yasak*) to the Russian state.[45]

Aside from being Muslims and imams, Nadir Urazmetev and Almat bin Sarmakay represented the kind of settlers that Kirilov imagined as part of his project to tame the South Urals. They and their families had demonstrated their loyalty to the Russian state through service and taxpaying. They held authority over peasant communities, and they had already proven their ability to lead those peasants on expeditions to establish new settlements and bring "empty" land under cultivation.

But the land in the South Urals was not empty. As Kazan Tatars moved east, they came into conflict with the nomadic Bashkirs on whose territory they attempted to settle. As Russian subjects, the Bashkirs expected the Russian government to enforce their land rights. However, Russian officials did not prove especially effective in keeping settlers off the Bashkirs' lands. As one Bashkir complained in 1734:

> Kadyr and Klych [Qadīr and Qılıch] and their companions, having settled with their households, have set up their residences on our hereditary land on the Sarysakal River and have taken it by force and have committed great offenses against us Bashkirs. And, in the past years, we have written petitions to the Ufa clerical office concerning those incoming Tatars and concerning those offenses, for which the Tatars Kadyr and Klych and their friends were sent back to their previous place of residence in the village of Sartyk in Kazan *uezd*. And when the census was taken, those Tatars ran away [from Kazan uezd], and again settled on that same hereditary land of ours and [now] live there in tents.[46]

For the native population of the South Urals, the conflict that unfolded in the 1730s proceeded directly from this illegal settlement of migrants from Kazan. As the Orenburg expedition began, Kirilov sent word to Cossack, Mishar, Bashkir, and Tatar villages to provide military forces and labor for the construction of the new fortified line.[47] In modern historical studies of the 1735 uprising, this call for labor combined with the prospect of a new fortress on Bashkir land drove some Bashkirs to take up arms.[48] However, a locally written Turkic-language history of the 1735 uprising suggests a different origin. In that account, a group of Chuvash settlers from Kazan stole horses from the Bashkir leader, Akay. Upon apprehending the thieves, Akay and his followers proceeded to beat them to death. However, one offender escaped and made his way to Ufa, where he alerted Russian forces to Akay's savage treatment of the settlers. The Russians responded by launching a punitive campaign against the Bashkirs.[49]

Whatever the immediate causes of the 1735 uprising, the arrival of Kirilov's forces in the South Urals tore apart the fragile equilibrium between natives and settlers. Bashkir supporters of Akay rode to the settler villages of Nadir and Almat and gave their residents two choices: join the armed opposition to the Orenburg project or be killed.[50] In response, Nadir Urazmetev of Nadir village wrote a panicked letter to Colonel I. N. Tatishchev explaining that the Bashkirs had announced their intention to kill him and his people. He begged Tatishchev to assist them by evacuating their families and livestock to the fortified Russian settlement of Sheshma.[51]

The 1735 Bashkir Uprising put the lives of Kazan Tatar settlers like Nadir Urazmetev and Almat bin Sarmakay at risk, but it also confronted them with an ideological challenge. As the uprising's leaders rallied the inhabitants of the Urals and western Siberia against the construction of Orenburg, they presented their cause in terms of their faith. As the Bashkir leader Akay agitated against the Russians, he reportedly reminded Muslim villagers that "our laws come from the Qur'ān."[52] In addition, he and other Bashkir leaders presented the Muslim inhabitants of their region with a world divided into two camps: "us" (Muslim rebels) and "the Russians."[53] Any Muslim who failed to support the uprising became, by default, a Russian (*rusak*) and a potential target for violence.[54] As rebel leaders tried to cast their revolt in confessional terms, in Kazan, the governor Musin-Pushkin surveyed the city's garrison and reported in dismay that "there are very few soldiers here and the majority of them are Muslims and other non-Christians."[55]

Akay and other rebel leaders tried to use confessional identity to entice or frighten Muslim settlers from Kazan into joining the uprising, but their aggressive tactics yielded the opposite result. Muslim service people and settlers living along the Sviaga River and around towns such as Ufa and Menzelinsk had followed the Russian advance east and had been willing to offer service and tax or tribute in return for land and security. The founding of more Russian fortresses in the Urals would open further opportunities for state-sanctioned migration and settlement. By contrast, Bashkir control of the region offered them no benefit. This lack of motivation for settlers to join the rebellion was epitomized in Bashkir leaders' most common argument for why settlers should join the revolt: they would be killed if they did not. Kazan Tatar settlers needed protection of their persons and property from rebel violence. Russian officials attempting to put down the uprising needed soldiers, scribes, and intelligence gatherers.

As the disorder in the South Urals continued, service people and ʿulamāʾ from the Mishar and Kazan Tatar villages became the eyes and ears of the Russian forces. Nadir Urazmetev and the people under his authority joined the Russian campaigns against the Bashkir rebels.[56] They organized themselves into bands to capture Bashkirs and sell them to the Russians.[57] Maqsūd bin Yūnus, who had worked as an emissary and courier to Central Asia a decade before, gave reports on the movements of the rebel Bashkir forces.[58] Saʿīd Aitov-Khalevin (Gadal-Khayali) a peasant-turned-merchant from Saba village in Kazan province, joined the Russian side, working as a translator of letters from Tatar into Russian.[59] He was also worked as a courier between A. I. Rumiantsev and the Bashkir rebel leaders.[60]

The Kazan Tatar settlers' cooperation with Kirilov's forces brought devastating consequences for the Bashkirs. In spring 1736, a large group of Bashkirs who wanted no further part in the uprising gathered on the banks of the Knali River and fled into the forest to where the Knali branched from its source, the Sazly-Elgan River. Kazan settlers—Tatars, Chermises, and others—fled together with them. Unknown to the Bashkirs, some of these were, in fact, spying on behalf of Kirilov's forces. They sneaked away and reported the Bashkirs' location to the Russians. During the night, the Russians and their settler allies surrounded the Bashkir camp with cannons. At dawn, they bombarded the camp: "The poor Bashkirs, not understanding where the shots came from, ran in all directions; many women and children threw themselves in the river. The wounded also perished in the river. During the battle, a bridge of corpses formed over the Sazly-Elgan River. They killed the elderly like dogs, with rocks and sticks. They chopped up the infants with their sabers. They sliced open the women's stomachs. The young people they simply killed."[61]

By 1740, the Bashkir Uprising had ended. Roughly one-third of the Bashkir population had died in battle, of starvation, or of exposure.[62] According to one local historical account, "so many people had perished that they threw the bodies away as if they were animals. On the Menzele River, they broke through the ice and, for every person they saved, they threw thirty-nine into the water. The river became blocked with corpses. Such horrible things were done that it is impossible to describe them in any human tongue."[63]

In 1736, as part of their recommendation for how to govern the region around Ufa and end Bashkir resistance, Kirilov and Rumiantsev proposed that the number of *akhunds* (senior Islamic scholars) in each of the four Bashkir administrative divisions (*doroga*) be reduced to one (for a total of four across the entire Bashkir population). Each akhund would be required to take an oath of loyalty to the Russian state upon assuming his post.[64] This new policy arose in direct response to the Bashkir rebels' appeal to Islam to mobilize other Muslims in the region and to the prominent role taken by Bashkir ʿulamāʾ in the revolt. By regulating the appointment of akhunds, Russian officials sought to utilize the authority they believed Muslim scholars wielded within the Muslim communities of the South Urals to promote imperial policies and oversee those communities. The new policy also provided officials with a means of formalizing existing relationships and rewarding services rendered by the Kazan ʿulamāʾ to the Russian state.

Those who profited most from this new state-imposed religious hierarchy were the Kazan Tatar settlers who had supported Kirilov and his successors during the uprising. One of these settlers was Mullā Manṣūr bin ʿAbdarraḥman (Abdrakhmanov). He studied at a madrasa in Simet village, northeast of Kazan. In the late 1600s or early 1700s, he traveled to Bukhara to continue his education and had supposedly brought back new books and new methods of Islamic scholarship. After a dispute with his old teacher in Simet, he opened his own madrasa in Burındıq village southwest of Kazan.[65] In 1738, he was appointed akhund of newly built Orenburg. In this role, in addition to spiritual and Islamic legal duties, he monitored events among the Bashkirs as well as Kazakh khan Abu'l-khayr's efforts to increase his influence in the South Urals and reported all he learned to his superiors, Vasilii Tatishchev and Alexei Ivanovich Tevkelev.[66] His relationships with these two officials continued well beyond the end of the Bashkir Uprising.

Consolidating Gains and Creating a Kazan Tatar South Urals (1740–1755)

By turning to Kazan ʿulamāʾ, Russian officials such as Kirilov, Tatishchev, and Rumiantsev gained the allies they needed to extend Russian rule into the South Urals. But in doing so, they also began to empower specific networks within Kazan Tatar society and to facilitate the extension of those networks from their homeland into the territory around newly built Orenburg.

The madrasa in Simet village in which akhund Manṣūr Abdrakhmanov had studied belonged to an imam and jurist named Murtaḍa bin Qutlıghısh as-Simetī. Like his student Manṣūr, he had traveled to Bukhara in the late 1600s, either to study or while on *hajj*. The trip became a years-long journey that took him through most of the major towns of Central Asia, Iran, Iraq, the Levant, and Anatolia, in addition to Mecca and Madina. In the process, he visited not only the holy sites of Mecca but also the graves of the figures of the early Islamic community and shrines of dozens of Sufi saints.[67]

By the time of Murtaḍa's death, sometime after 1724, he had acquired numerous students and disciples. One of these was Manṣūr Abdrakhmanov, the akhund of Orenburg. Another was Manṣūr's brother, Ḥusayn Abdrakhmanov. After studying with Murtaḍa, Ḥusayn migrated east and established a madrasa in the village of Istarlībāsh in Ufa province in the 1720s.[68] Though he did not boast the same connections with Russian officials that his brother had cultivated, Ḥusayn's relocation was made feasible by the growing Russian presence in the South Urals. And while Manṣūr's employment solidified his family's relationship with the regional officials, Ḥusayn's madrasa-building extended his late teacher's network eastward by providing a new center for attracting and training students and disciples.

Manṣūr and Ḥusayn Abdrakhmanov were not the only students of Murtaḍa as-Simetī to benefit from relationships forged during the Bashkir Uprising. In 1745, former translator-turned-merchant Saʿīd Aitov-Khalevin received permission from Orenburg governor-general I. I. Nepliuev to establish a settlement outside of Orenburg. When he set out in 1749, he took with him ʿAbdassalām bin Urāz Muḥammad Urayev, imam and madrasa director of Tāshkichū village in Kazan province and another of Murtaḍa's students.[69] Leading two hundred families of merchants and peasants east from the villages around the town of Arsk, Aitov and Urayev founded the Muslim trading community of Seitov Solboda or Qarghalı several miles from Orenburg. Seitov quickly became not only an important outpost for Muslim merchants trading in Orenburg, but also, like Istarlībāsh, an important center for Muslim learning and legal culture in the South Urals.[70] Once settled in Seitov, Urayev became the first imam of the new settlement. He subsequently married his daughter to Maʿsūd bin Afaq, another student of Murtaḍa, who had migrated to the Ufa region from Yanga Sala village northeast of Kazan. Once he arrived, he founded a new village outside of Ufa.[71] Two other students of Murtaḍa as-Simetī, Rafīq bin Tayyib al-Qūrṣāwī and ʿAbdassalām bin Ḥasan al-Qarile, founded their own madrasas in closer proximity to Kazan. They trained scholars who found work in villages in the regions around Kazan, Ufa, and Orenburg and in the previously established villages along the Sviaga River.[72]

In short, the two decades after the 1735 Bashkir Uprising saw the movement of multiple disciples of a single Muslim teacher across the space between Kazan and Orenburg. As Muslim scholars, leaders of peasant groups resettling east, merchants, and village elders (*starshinas*), they juggled multiple tasks. Living in a region where imperial authority was still not thoroughly established, they took charge of personal and community defense. While traveling in Belujistan on their way from Seitov to Mecca in the early 1750s, Mullā Ismāʿīl bin Bikmuḥammad and his companions were stopped in one of the towns and told that they would have to surrender their weapons or risk being attacked by the Afghans. Ismāʿīl responded by promising that "if the Afghans come, we'll fight them." He refused to hand over his sword.[73]

As advocates for the welfare of common Muslims, the Kazan Tatar ʿulamāʾ mediated between their communities and the Russian government. They also cooperated with Russian officials to guarantee their people's prosperity (through the negotiation of settlement and trade terms) and their safety (through service against rebel forces in the borderlands).

Advocating for the Wrong Muslims: The Case of Batırshah Aliyev (1755)

After the uprisings of 1735–1740, important changes swept through the Muslim South Urals. One was a change in nomenclature. *Abız,* a term once used in the region to refer to men of learning, gradually disappeared. It was replaced by mullā, imam, *mudarris*, and akhund, terms that, while not altogether alien to the South Urals, had been in wider use among the Muslims of Kazan province. New villages established by migrants from Kazan appeared on the landscape and with them new madrasas opened. This created new educational opportunities for would-be South Urals scholars, but it also transplanted ʿulamāʾ and Muslim culture from Kazan into what would eventually become Orenburg and Ufa provinces. Rather than empowering the Urals' indigenous ʿulamāʾ, the opening of new madrasas (run by Muslim scholars who enjoyed the favor of local imperial officials) heralded the assimilation of the indigenous Muslim leadership to the culture of the settler ʿulamāʾ from Kazan.

Kirilov's establishment of the system of four akhunds for the supervision of religious practice and political views among the Bashkirs hastened this process of assimilation. This transformation of the post of akhund did much more than simply reduce the number of claimants to the title and create a formal relationship between Russian officialdom and Muslim scholars in the South Urals. It created state-recognized Muslim spiritual leaders in the region. Able to rely on the support of imperial officials, these four akhunds wielded a level of power that no nonstate Muslim scholar could match. Not all ʿulamāʾ were equal competitors for these four positions. When selecting candidates, imperial officials sought advice from "experts" whom they already trusted. By the 1750s, those trusted advisors and specialists were the Kazan Tatar imams and jurists who had aided the Russians during the Bashkir Uprising or otherwise demonstrated their loyalty. These ʿulamāʾ played a role in appointing and approving akhunds of the Bashkirs. Not surprisingly, they favored their own students, acquaintances, and kin.

The complex and often unequal relationship between the settler ʿulamāʾ from Kazan and the indigenous ʿulamāʾ of the South Urals and western Siberia can be seen in the career of Batırshah Aliyev, the instigator of the 1755 uprising. Aliyev received his first education in Gainin volost' in the Siberian doroga.[74] Once he determined to pursue a career as a religious scholar, he traveled to Taisugan village in Bugulma uezd, Kazan province, where he studied with akhund ʿAbdarraḥman bin Tuy Muḥammad, a scholar who through his sons and grandsons was connected to Murtaḍa as-Simetī's students and founded a scholarly network influential in Bulguma, Menzelink, and Seitov.[75] In addition, Aliyev became a student of ʿAbdassalām Urayev either while the latter was still in Tāshkichū village or after he relocated to Seitov.[76] By attaching himself to these scholars and madrasas, the Siberian-born Aliyev gained entry into the dominant Kazan ʿulamāʾ networks. After completing his education, Aliyev returned to his native Siberian doroga, where, like many other ʿulamāʾ educated in the Kazan Tatar networks, he founded a madrasa and began teaching the boys and young men of his region.[77]

In 1754, the Muslims of the Siberian doroga, frustrated with the poverty and corruption in the South Urals and western Siberia, put Aliyev forward as a replacement for the doroga's incumbent akhund. Fearful of Aliyev's influence, the doroga's *starshina*, Yanısh Abdullin, sent a charter to Orenburg proposing the elevation of a different Siberian imam to the akhundship. After examining this imam and finding his knowledge of theology and Islamic law inadequate, the other akhunds gathered the notable scholars of Orenburg and settled on Aliyev as the most fitting candidate.[78] The choice was far from coincidental. Among those involved in the selection were Aliyev's former teacher ʿAbdassalām Urayev, now akhund of Seitov.

By the 1750s, indigenous South Urals ʿulamāʾ, whether akhunds or simple imams, found themselves in an untenable situation. Confronted by rising taxes, restrictions on hunting and fishing rights, illegal settlers, and corrupt local officials, South Urals inhabitants demanded that their ʿulamāʾ protect their interests. As Aliyev recalled, on the eve of the 1755 uprising:

> After I had been in that village for ten days, the Bashkirs of Saldzhugutskaia *volost'* invited us Meshcheriaks to visit. We, the Meshchariaks, about 60 or 70 riders, went to Saldzhugutskaya. Bashkirs had gathered from many villages—mullas and simple people. They prepared a circle and served *kumis*. When they were drunk, they began to speak at length: "They have forbidden us from using the salt we used to collect and hunting the animals we used to hunt. The faithless Russians have ruined many of our brother Muslims in this volost' by sending them to be baptized. Likewise, there is no mercy from the administrators or the general. Under this *tsarina*, the poverty and torment have become intolerable."[79]

Aliyev and other ʿulamāʾ in South Urals Bashkir and Mishar villages felt obliged to resolve the problems faced by their communities. However, in protesting these wrongs, they faced opposition not only from Russian officials but also from their own coreligionists from Kazan, who had benefited from the very policies that undermined the old order in the South Urals.

Aliyev used his journey to Orenburg (to receive his akhund documents) as an opportunity to draw the attention of the town's ʿulamāʾ to the grievances of the Bashkir population. According to Aliyev, those ʿulamāʾ voiced sympathy for the cause, commenting on "how much disorder has broken out among the people because of that fool general!"[80] The Kazan Tatar ʿulamāʾ of Orenburg noted that they had instructed the recruits sent out from Seitov to maintain order among the Bashkirs, and told them than that "if the Bashkirs prove stronger and are victorious, go over to their side. If they prove weak, try to help them save themselves and not get killed."[81]

In the end, the support of the Orenburg and Seitov ʿulamāʾ for a Bashkir-Mishar revolt went no further than words. Urayev and Ibrāhīm bin Muḥammad Tulak had built their careers on maintaining a mutually beneficial relationship with the imperial administration. Ibrāhīm had been invited to become akhund of Orenburg in 1743 by Alexei Tevkelev.

His family maintained a close relationship with the Tevkelev family, with Ibrāhīm's son composing the lengthy inscription on the grave marker of Tevkelev's wife in 1752.[82] Urayev had arrived in the Orenburg region as a member of the party of migrants given permission by Orenburg governor Nepliuev to settle. Their careers and fates were intertwined with the very Russian administrators that Aliyev wished to see removed. When asked to choose between Aliyev's struggle for justice for indigenous Muslims in the South Urals and supporting the empire, Ibrāhīm chose the latter, penning, at Nepliuev's request, a fatwā that decried Aliyev as being anti-Muslim and called on "true Muslims" to support Russian rule.[83] With many Muslims opposing the revolt or refusing to participate in it, Russian officials quickly suppressed Aliyev's movement.

The Last Gasp of a Doomed Elite: The Bashkir and Mishar ʿUlamāʾ of Pugachev's Revolt (1773–1774)

In the years after Batırshah's Revolt, Russian administrative influence increased rapidly in the South Urals, and the pressure on the region's Bashkirs and Mishars increased with it. Bashkir, Mishar, and Cossack servitors faced more restrictions on their hunting, fishing, and salt-gathering rights. As irregular military forces, they also found themselves subject to greater regulation by the imperial government, including the transfer of Bashkirs and Mishars from the South Urals to Malorossia, the Baltic provinces, the Siberian line, and Tobolsk.[84] In 1770, a new rumor circulated in the Bashkir settlements that Bashkir fighters would be sent south to establish outposts deeper in the Kazakh steppe.[85]

While the autonomy of Ural Bashkir and Mishar communities continued to diminish, the flow of Kazan Tatar settlers into the South Urals increased. In what became Orenburg uezd, the Tatar population rose from zero in 1719, to 9,200 in 1747, to nearly 15,000 by 1782.[86] Some of these settlers petitioned Russian officials, explaining that their land around Kazan was no longer adequate to support them and asking for permission to resettle around Orenburg. In some cases, they claimed that they had already agreed to purchase or rent land from Bashkirs in the region and were prepared to relocate as soon as they received official permission.[87] However, once they arrived in the South Urals, these settlers clashed with their Bashkir neighbors, refusing to pay rent they had promised or resorting to various schemes, including underestimating the amount of land they occupied, in order to pay less rent than they actually owed.[88] Another tactic that settlers used to gain ownership of Bashkir grazing lands was to claim that Russian law declared that participants in previous uprisings had forfeited their rights to their land. In some cases, settlers claimed that children and grandchildren of Bashkir "rebels" were also subject to this law.[89] There was in fact no such law, but in the time that it took for Bashkirs to petition imperial officials and report such abuses, the settlers had already established themselves on Bashkir land. Once settlers had succeeded in setting up a new village, officials rarely forced them to move.[90] In such cases, the best that Bashkirs could hope for was that the settlers would be ordered to pay compensation for the seized land.[91]

By the 1770s, Kazan Tatar settlers and indigenous Bashkirs and Mishars, though coreligionists, stood on different sides of the Russian expansion and held conflicting interests in the region. These conflicts were mapped onto the Pugachev Revolt in 1773 and dictated which Muslims supported Emil'ian Pugachev (a Cossack who claimed to be Emperor Peter III, the late husband of Catherine the Great, and rallied the discontented military servitors of the Volga Basin and the Urals to overthrow the empress) and which sided with St. Petersburg.

ʿAbdullāh bin Muslīm's father had founded the village of Muslim near Cheliabinsk in the early 1700s. Following in his father's footsteps, ʿAbdullāh dedicated much of his life establishing Akhun village between Troitsk and Uralsk. He traveled as an emissary from Russia to Bukhara. He also made recommendations on the appointment of imams. His services to the state were rewarded with money and medals. During the uprising, he rallied the Muslims of his district to support the Russian government against Pugachev.[92] Qaraqay bin ʿUthmān, who had married his daughter to a migrant imam from Kazan province, took up arms against Pugachev's forces.[93] Mawlīd bin Mustafa, imam of Qaltay village outside Ufa and a kinsman of a prominent member of Murtaḍa as-Simetī's scholarly network, took a less violent strategy of resistance. He remained in his village after the other residents had fled and bore witness as Pugachev's followers burned it to the ground.[94]

Passive or active resistance to Pugachev's movement by Kazan Tatar settler ʿulamāʾ was matched by strong support for Pugachev among the ʿulamāʾ of the Mishar and Bashkir villages and Muslim Cossack regiments. More than forty ʿulamāʾ are mentioned by name in the documents of Pugachev's War College.[95] While Kazan Tatar ʿulamāʾ who had settled in the South Urals tended to come from peasant or merchant communities, many pro-Pugachev scholars lived among irregular military servitors

(Cossacks or Mishars) and possessed military or administrative experience in addition to their Islamic education. This experience allowed them to rise to positions of importance in Pugachev's army. Such warrior-scholars included Abdey Abdulov, the colonel in command of the Osin-Sarapul' forces; Adigut Timachev, ataman/colonel of Ufa uezd; Adil Bigashev, ataman in Krasnoufimskii, Birskii, and Kungur uezds; Bakhtiyar Kankaev, colonel/brigadier in Kungur, Ufa, and Kazan uezds; Kanzafar Usayev, colonel/brigadier in Zakamye and Prikamye regions; Kinzia Arslanov, colonel of the Nogay doroga and a member of Pugachev's secret council; and Ishmen Itkulov, colonel in Kungur and Krasnoufimskii.

The activities of the Pugachev ʿulamāʾ reflected the role of the Muslim scholar as it had developed over the course of the eighteenth-century Russian expansion. High-ranking Pugachev ʿulamāʾ not only led troops into battle but also mobilized troops, presided over legal proceedings, and coordinated agricultural production and logistics. These community leadership activities paralleled the earlier roles of the Kazan Tatar settler ʿulamāʾ in coordinating the founding of new villages and using their knowledge of Islamic law to resolve legal disputes. Similarly, Pugachev ʿulamāʾ's service as messengers and secretaries (*pisar'*) resembled the scholar-diplomats and messengers to Central Asia employed by Russian officials in the seventeenth and eighteenth centuries.

By mid-1774, as Russian forces gained ground against Pugachev's supporters, those pro-Pugachev ʿulamāʾ who could fled into the Kazakh steppe. Those who could not were captured by imperial forces. As organizers and agitators in a rebel army, they faced harsh punishments, including torture, maiming, and execution. Mullā Abūbakr Tilyachev, a Pugachev secretary, was sentenced to have his hand "by which he wrote to the people" cut off. He was then decapitated.[96] Others were sentenced to hard labor and exiled to the Baltic region. By contrast, the Kazan Tatar settler ʿulamāʾ around Orenburg and Ufa profited from Catherine II's policies of tolerance toward Islam and the use of monotheism as a medium for spreading civil order and enlightenment.

The Kazakh Crisis and the Creation of the Spiritual Assembly (1781–1788)

In the wake of Pugachev's Revolt, Catherine II enacted policies to improve administrative control of regions where the uprising had been most intense. Under the 1775 land reform, boundaries of the empire were redrawn, and the sprawling Kazan and Orenburg provinces were divided into a number of smaller units, each of which received its own administrative staff.[97] In 1782, an urban police code was implemented and subsequently extended to create a land police in the countryside to handle tax collection and internal security.[98] However, like the creation of the akhund system in the Urals, the formalization of imperial administration of Islam across the empire was driven primarily by the needs of the empire on the southeastern frontier.

In 1731, Kazakh khan Abu'l-khayr, who had been at war with the Zungars since the 1720s, reached out to Empress Anna Ioanovna to seek Russian protection against the Zungars and the Kalmyks. At a meeting between with Alexei Tevkelev, Abu'l-khayr promised to submit to the Russian monarch. This submission was problematic from the start. When the Kazakhs accompanying Abu'l-khayr found out about his promise, they nearly killed Tevkelev.[99] Whether Abu'l-khayr submitted on behalf of himself, the Junior Horde Kazakhs accompanying him, or all Kazakhs was never clear, nor were Kazakh leaders and Russian officials of one mind on precisely what submission entailed. Russian rulers and officials, wishing to exert control over the Kazakh steppe and its trade routes, tended to interpret the submission as amounting to the transformation of Kazakhs into Russian subjects in perpetuity.[100] Abu'l-khayr and Kazakh leaders after him used recognition of their status by the Russian and Qing empires to gain favorable short-term arrangements with these two sedentary states and to bolster their authority among their own people.[101] These differing interpretations of submission were an ongoing source of conflict as Russia attempted to extend its influence into the steppe.

In 1781, Kazakh khan Ablai died. In the 1750s, Orenburg governor I. I. Nepliuev had tried to cultivate a relationship with Ablai, going so far as to secure his release after he was taken captive by the Zungars.[102] Later, as Ablai rose to prominence as a supporter of Middle Horde khan Almambet, Russian officials sought his aid in countering Chinese incursions and influence in the eastern steppe and Siberia. At the same time, Ablai himself carried on diplomatic relations with both Russia and China and was claimed as a subject by both states. With the death of Almambet in 1771, Ablai became khan of the Middle Horde. In 1777, he received an official communication from the Russian government that Catherine II was prepared to acknowledge his authority over all three of the Kazakh Hordes. However, in 1778, Catherine II recognized him only as khan of the Middle Horde. In response, Ablai refused to take an oath of loyalty to Russia and so had remained a powerful but unpredictable element in Russia's steppe borderland.[103]

After Ablai's death, a fierce competition for leadership began among the Kazakh aristocracy. Ablai left behind thirty sons, whom he had used during his lifetime to maintain his rule over his various subjects and allies, and a variety of other Kazakh nobles who hoped to lead the conglomerate of clans and tribes he had brought together. The descendants of Abu'l-khayr, the Russian-appointed leaders of the Junior Horde, also sought to claim leadership of the Middle Horde. In addition to raiding their Bashkir, Kalmyk, and Cossack neighbors, Kazakh leaders turned to raiding one another. What began as an internal Kazakh power struggle had direct ramifications for the Russian empire. Fragmentation and warfare in the steppe interfered with the north-south trade between Russia and Central Asia and India. Raids and armed conflicts harmed Russian subjects and property on the frontier. With Ablai's death, there was no single authoritative leader with whom Russian diplomats could negotiate.

In 1785, Catherine appointed Baron Osip Igel'strom as governor-general of Ufa and Siberia. This Baltic German nobleman had spent a significant part of his career working to integrate Russia's non-Orthodox communities into the empire. In the 1770s, he served on the staff placed in charge of newly annexed Poland.[104] In 1783, Catherine placed him at the head of the military administration in charge of the annexation and reorganization of the Crimean khanate.[105] Catherine now tasked him with resolving the Kazakh problem, a problem that she characterized as "attacks and banditry perpetrated by her Kazakh subjects against other of her subjects."[106] What Catherine described was the destabilization of steppe political life precipitated by the death of Ablai four years before. In the Junior Horde, Erali and Nurali, the sons of Abul'khayr, called for Russian recognition of their status as the khans of both the Junior and Middle Hordes. Wali, son of Ablai, sought Russia's recognition of him as khan of the Middle Horde, where he competed with sultans Khodaimendei and Kaip. Another figure, Sırım Datov, began an uprising against the aristocratic contenders for power in the Middle Horde in 1783.[107] What was for Catherine a struggle to bring "her subjects" back under control was for the Kazakh sultans a civil war for the rule of an independent political entity. Catherine was not entirely unaware of this difference, as she charged Igel'strom in a subsequent correspondence to "rein in the autonomous tendencies of the Kazakh horde."[108]

The strategy Catherine recommended to Igel'strom was one of diplomacy rather than show of force: "We need for you to go immediately to the province over which you were appointed, to look over all that have been appointed to that location, to become acquainted with all the leadership of the horde, and to convince them of everything that was already assigned to your predecessor."[109] To this end, two days later, she recommended to Igel'strom akhund Mukhamedzhan Khusainov of the Seitov settlement: "With his abilities, you can use him in matters in that region, and for conveying communications [to the Kazakhs] as you find it convenient."[110] In return for his services to Igel'strom, Catherine proposed to pay Khusainov an annual salary of 150 rubles.[111]

The choice of Khusainov as Igel'strom's assistant was not coincidental. Khusainov's uncle was none other than Mansūr Abdrakhmanov, the legal scholar who had worked with Tatishchev and Tevkelev during the 1730s Bashkir Uprisings and had later been appointed Orenburg akhund. Khusainov was educated at the madrasa that his father, Ḥusayn Abdrakhmanov, had founded in Istarlībāsh village.[112] Like his uncle, Khusainov traveled to Bukhara to study. He also went to Kabul, where he became a student and follower of Fayḍkhān bin Khiḍrkhān, a Naqshbandi-Mujaddidi shaykh.[113] Khusainov was born and raised within the Kazan Tatar ʿulamāʾ network. His family had migrated into the South Urals following the fortress lines and had worked side by side with imperial officials in solidifying Russian control in the region.

Igel'strom gained quick results on his arrival in the southeastern borderlands. By July, he managed to capture several of the sultans responsible for the previous attacks. However, matters took a turn for the worse less than a month later, when a Russian division was attacked by a group of Kazakhs, and some of its members were taken captive. The raid threw Catherine's relationship with Nurali Khan, khan of the Junior Horde and a Russian subject, into doubt. She ordered Igel'strom to put all plans for Nurali (including the appointment of his son as khan of the Turkmens) on hold and to warn Nurali in the strongest terms that the perpetrators of the raid were bandits and that it was within Nurali's power to punish them. The Russian prisoners were to be returned immediately, and no exchange of captured Kazakhs for Russian prisoners would be considered. No further petitions would be accepted from Nurali until he complied with these demands. If Nurali tried to deny responsibility for the raid, Catherine instructed Igel'strom to remind him that he was khan of the horde and therefore responsible for the actions of all its members.[114]

The 1785 raid and what Catherine interpreted as the unwillingness of Nurali and other Kazakh leaders to cooperate with Russian officials in keeping their subjects under control eroded her faith in the usefulness of the Kazakh aristocracy as allies in the establishment of Russian imperial rule in the steppe. By September 1785, she began to articulate an alternate form of imperial governance. This new plan emerged from Igel'strom's descriptions of Muslim prayer in the mosques of Troitsk and the Orenburg line fortresses. Up until the 1780s, these mosques had existed primarily to meet the needs of the fortresses' Muslim inhabitants, but Catherine now proposed to expand this network of Muslim religious institutions to provide services to the neighboring Kazakh populations and to visiting Central Asian merchants.[115]

The principle underlying Catherine's new vision was not making pagan or half-Muslim Kazakhs into better Muslims. Rather, the policy was one of inclusion and cultural influence. By becoming a patron and protector of Islam, the Russian government would earn the appreciation and goodwill of the common Kazakh herdsmen and marginalize the troublesome Kazakh aristocrats. In 1785, she instructed Igel'strom to choose reliable people from among the Kazan Tatars to be sent to work as imams among the Kazakh clans.[116] Less than a year later, Catherine commissioned the printing of a Qurʾān from Johann Karl Shnor's publishing house in St. Petersburg. By distributing free Qurʾāns to the Kazakhs, Russian officials could present the empire as a protector of Muslims and Islam.[117] Igel'strom continued to use Khusainov to negotiate with Kazakh leaders. In November 1786, Khusainov was granted a higher salary and the title of "first akhund."[118] In 1787, Catherine again increased his annual salary, this time to one thousand rubles.[119]

In the meantime, Catherine instructed Igel'strom to proceed with the establishment of schools adjacent to the mosques in the Russian fortresses and border towns, where Kazan Tatar imams could use soon-to-be-printed books in the local languages to teach Kazakh children and instill in them loyalty to the Russian empire.[120] As the raids in the steppe continued, Catherine also charged the imams working among the Bashkirs to admonish them not to steal livestock from the Kazakhs.[121]

A final formalization of the relationship between the imperial government and the Kazan Tatar ʿulamāʾ came in 1788 with the creation of the Orenburg Muslim Spiritual Assembly (OMSA) and the creation of the post of Orenburg mufti as the highest Muslim religious authority in Russia. Though Igel'strom may have drawn inspiration from Ottoman and Crimean Muslim juridical hierarchies as well as from the Russian Orthodox Church, the resulting institution was derived from the evolution of Kazan's Muslim scholarly networks over the previous century.[122] Some elements of the new institution were closely tied to Igel'strom and Khusainov's relationship. During his negotiations with the Kazakhs, Khusainov suggested to Igel'strom that if Russia were to grant him the title of mufti, the Muslim Kazakhs would see him as possessing greater authority than a simple akhund.[123] At the same time, the creation of the OMSA, composed of the mufti and several *qāḍīs*, or judges, built on the earlier administrative relationships of Kirilov's establishment of the akhunds as sworn servants of the Russian state and guardians of civil order. Through the assembly, the system set up within the South Urals was expanded to take in all Muslim regions of the empire, except Crimea.

Simultaneously, the OMSA extended Catherine's expansion and standardization of officials and institutions into the Kazan and South Urals Muslim community. The OMSA was granted exclusive right to bestow religious titles and confirm posts in mosques and *maktabs*.[124] Imams were made subject to the rulings of the assembly, which was in turn placed under the authority of the governor-general of Ufa. All documents produced by the assembly were to be composed in the Russian language and translated into Tatar.[125] Before assuming a post as an imam, a candidate was required to travel to Ufa and take an exam before the assembly, after which he would be granted a license to work in the village where he had been elected. The authority of the licensed 'ulamā' was limited to management of Islamic orthodoxy, education, and marriage and divorce.[126] Arbitration of crimes and the dispensing of corporal and capital punishment were delegated to the imperial state.[127]

In addition, whether Catherine meant it or not, the founding of the OMSA integrated the Kazan Tatar 'ulamā' into the imperial administrative structure. Khusainov, a Kazan Tatar Muslim scholar, occupied the newly established post of mufti. A council of Muslims in Kazan put forward the candidates for the qāḍī-ships. The jurisdictional boundaries of the OMSA officially recognized the territory that the Kazan Tatars had colonized in the South Urals, western Siberia, and the northern steppe as culturally contiguous with their native region around Kazan. Within this jurisdiction, they boasted multiple centers of cultural activity and influence, one of the most significant of which was Orenburg and the adjacent Seitov settlement. What had been a Kazan scholarly network had become a Volga-Ural network.

Notes

1. "Dastān-i Tārīkh (1740s)," K(P)FU-ORRK, No. 4199 T, 2; N. F. Katanov and I. M. Pokrovskii, "Otryvok iz odnoi tatarskoi letopisi o Kazani i Kazanskom khantsve," *Izvestiia obshchestva arkheologii, istorii, i etnografii pri Kazanskom Universitete* 21, no. 4 (1905): 308, 312, 316, 322; *Das Buch der Dschingis-Legende*, trans. and ed. Mária Ivanics and Mirkasym Usmanov (Szeged: Department of Altaic Studies, 2002), 92.

2. Katanov and Pokrovskii, "Otryvok iz odnoi tatarskoi letopisi," 308, 312, 316, 322; *Das Buch der Dschingis-Legende*, 92.

3. Matthew P. Romaniello, *The Elusive Empire: Kazan and the Creation of Russia, 1552–1671* (Madison: The University of Wisconsin Press, 2012), 193; Azade-Ayşe Rorlich, *The Volga Tatars: A Profile in National Resilience* (Stanford, CA: Hoover Institute, 1986), 37–48.

4. "Dāstān-i Tarīkh (1740s)," K(P)FU-ORRK, No. 4199 T, 2, 2ob.

5. *Sobornoe Ulozhenie Alexeia Mikhailovicha 1649 goda* (St. Petersburg: Sinodal'naia Tipografiia, 1907), 186.

6. *Polnoe Sobranie Zakonov Rossiskoi Imperii* [hereafter PSZ] (St. Petersburg, 1830), 1:254–55.

7. RGADA, f. 126, op. 1, 1662 g., d. No. 2, l. 10–13.

8. PSZ, 1:569–71; "Nakaz kazanskikh voevod kn. G. S. Kurakina i M. P. Volynskogo sotennomu golove D. A. Aristovu o nabliudenii za deistviaimi vzbuntovavshikhsia ufimskikh bashkirtsov, chtoby oni ne pereshli cherez Kamu na kazanskuiu storonu, 22, noiabria 1663 g.," *Istoriia Tatarii v Materialakh i dokumetakh* (Moscow: Institut istorii [Akademiia nauk SSSR], 1937), 376.

9. "Pis'mo Razina k kazanskim tataram, 1670 g," *Istoriia Tatarii v Materialakh i dokumetakh*, 378.

10. "Otpiska tsivil'skogo voevody T. Bestuzheva v Prikaz Kazanskogo dvortsa o posylke pod'ezdichikov k razintsam i poluchenii ot nikh 'vorovskoi pamiati', 28 oktiabr 1670 g.," *Istoriia Tatarii v Materialakh i dokumetakh*, 380.

11. "Chelobitnaia Temnikova murzy Safara Mameteva syna kniazia Temnikova o rasprose i pytke krestian, izbivshikh ego zhenu i detei i ograbivshikh ikh, 1671 g.," *Istoriia Tatarii v Materialakh i dokumetakh*, 383.

12. "Dastān-i Tārīkh (1740s)," K(P)FU-ORRK, No. 4199T, 2.

13. PSZ, 2:267.

14. PSZ, 2:313, 315.

15. According to Amirkhanov, the Shibanid line in Russia ended with the death of Kuchum Khan of Siberia (Ḥusayn Amirkhanov, *Tāwārīkh-i Bulghāriyya* [Kazan: Vyatcheslav, 1883], 28). However, Tsar Mikhail Fedorovich granted Kuchum's grandson, Arslan, the khanate in 1614 (V. V. Vel'iaminov-Zernov, *Izsledovanie o Kasimovskikh tsariakh i tsarevichakh* [St. Petersburg: Tipografiia imperatorskoi akademii nauk, 1866], 3:1–2).

16. "Kasimov," *Tatarskaia entsiklopediia*, ed. M. Kh. Khasanov (Kazan: Institut Tatarskoi Entsiklopedii, 2006) 3:257; Vel'iaminov-Zernov, *Izsledovanie o Kasimovskikh tsariakh*, 3:461.

17. Janet Martin, "Muscovite Frontier Policy: The Case of the Khanate of Kasimov," *Russian History* 19, nos. 1–4 (1992): 169–79.

18. To give a sense of the role of Qasim in the cultural life of Muscovy's Muslims in the late sixteenth and seventeenth centuries, the *Chronicle of Qadır 'Ali Bek* ("Sbornik Letopisei" Kadyr-Ali-Beka), the earliest known Turkic-language history to be written after the Russian conquest of the Kazan, Astrakhan, and Siberian khanates, was composed at the royal court in Qasim in 1602 (M. A. Usmanov, *Tatarskie istoricheskie istochniki XVII–XVIII vv.* [Kazan: Izdatel'stvo Kazanskogo Universiteta, 1972], 33–96). On Muslims in Russian military service in the sixteenth and seventeenth centuries, see Martin, "Muscovite Frontier Policy," and Matthew P. Romaniello, *Elusive Empire*.

19. Katanov and Pokrovskii, "Otryvok iz odnoi tatarskoi letopisi," 312, 317, 322. Rychkov mentions this conflict in his *Topografiia Orenburgskoi gubernii*, but gives the wrong date (1676 instead of 1680) (P. I. Rychkov, "Topografiia Orenburgskoi gubernii, chast pervaia," *Zhizn' i deiatel'nost' P. I. Rychkova* [Orenburg: OOO "Izdatel'stvo Orenburgskaia Kniga," 2011], 4:70; *Das Buch der Chingis-Legende*, 93).

20. Katanov and Pokrovskii, "Otryvok iz odnoi tatarskoi letopisi," 312, 317, 322.

21. Ibid., 312, 317, 323.

22. "Dastān-i Tārīkh (1740s)," K(P)FU-ORRK, No. 4199T, 20b.

23. Amirkhanov, *Tawārīkh-i Bulghāriyya*, 3.

24. Allen J. Frank, *Islamic Historiography and "Bulghar" Identity among the Tatars and Bashkirs of Russia* (Leiden: Brill, 1998), 197.

25. Katanov and Pokrovskii, "Otryvok iz odnoi tatarskoi letopisi," 312, 317.

26. Rizaeddin Fäkhreddin, *Asar*, ed. Raif Märdanov and Ramil Mingnullin (Kazan: Rukhiyat, 2006), 34.

27. Ibid.

28. Ibid.

29. Ibid., 33.

30. Shihābaddīn al-Marjānī, *Qism ath-Thānī min Kitāb Mustafād al-Akhbār* (Kazan: Tipo-Litografiia Imperatorskago Universiteta, 1900), 188; "Yunys Oruvi, Shärḥ 'Färaiz al-Sijävendi'," K(P)FU-ORRK, No. 29 gotv.

31. "Shirdānī," K(P)FU-ORRK, No. 399, p. 168a. This document was discussed previously in Alfrid K. Bustanov, "The Bughlar Region as a 'Land of Ignorance': Anti-Colonial Discourse in Khvārazmian Connectivity," *Journal of Persianate Studies* 9 (2006): 183–204.

32. Ibid.

33. *Torgovlia i diplomatiia: Dokumenty o rossiisko-sredneaziatskikh otnosheniiakh, 1723–1725 gg.*, ed. I. M. Vasil'ev (Ufa: Gilem, 2012), 25.

34. Ibid., 3–5.

35. Ibid., 7.

36. Ibid., 11–14.

37. "No. 3, 1724 g. okolo 7 noiabria (rabi-al-awwalia 1 dnia)—Donoshenie Maksiuta Iunusov v kollegiiu inostrannykh del o ego vtoroi poezdke v sredne-aziatskii region," *Torgovlia i diplomatiia*, 70.

38. Ibid., 72–74.

39. Charles Steinwedel, *Threads of Empire: Loyalty and Tsarist Authority in Bashkiria, 1552–1917* (Bloomington: Indiana University Press, 2016), 42–77.

40. "1735 g aprelia ne pozdnee 11—Zapiska I. K. Kirillova ob uchrezhdenii landmilitsii i o polozhenii sluzhilykh liudei v gorodakh ufimskogo uezda," *Materialy po istorii*

Bashkortostana, Tom VI: Orenburgskaia ekspeditsiia i bashkirskie vosstaniia 30-kh godov XVIII v. ed. N. F. Demidova (Ufa: "Kitap," 2002), 26.

41. Ibid., 6:26; "1735 g. aprelia ne ranee 20—Senatskaia vypiska o vysylke s bashkirskikh zemel' na prezhnie mesta zhitel'stva skhodtsev iz drugikh uezdov," *Materialy po istorii Bashkortostana, Tom VI*, 27.

42. Ibid., 27.

43. Fäkhreddin, *Asar*, 49.

44. Ibid., 48.

45. Ibid., 48.

46. A. I. Dobrosmyslov, *Materialy po istorii Rossii: Sbornik ukazov i drugikh dokumentov, kasaiushchikhsia upravleniia i ustroistva Orenburgsako kraia, 1734* (2 vols.) (Orenburg: Tipolitografiia F. B. Sachkova, 1900), 1:216.

47. "1735 g. iunia 9—Donoshenie sotnika Kazanskoi dorogi, Nadyrovoi volosti Nadyra Urazmetova v kantseliariiu Sheshminskogo landmilitskogo polka," *Materialy po istorii Bashkortostana, Tom VI*, 30.

48. Alton Donnelly, *The Russian Conquest of Bashkiria, 1552–1740: A Case Study in Imperialism* (New Haven: Yale University Press, 1968).

49. "O vosstanie bashkir pod rukovodtsvom Akaia syn Kusiuma," *Istoriia Tatarii v Materialakh i dokumetakh*, 402.

50. "1735 g. iunia ranee 24—Pis'mo tatarskogo mully Nadyrovoi volosti Almetia polkovniku I. N. Tatishchevu o s'ezdakh i namereniakh vosstavshikh i ob opasnosti ot nikh dlia naseleniia Nadyrovoi volosti," *Materialy po istorii Bashkortostana, Tom VI*, 32.

51. "1735 g. ranee iunia 22—Pis'mo sotnika Nadyra Urazmeteva polkovniku Sheshminskogo landmilitskogo polka I. N. Tatishchevu," *Materialy po istorii Bashkortostana, Tom VI*, 31–32.

52. "1735 g. iulia 4—Donoshenie kazanskogo gubernatora P. N. Musin-Pushkina v Voennuiu kollegiiu o s'ezdakh bashkir Nogaiskoi dorogi," *Materialy po istorii Bashkortostana, Tom VI*, 34.

53. Ibid., 6:34.

54. "1735 g. ranee iunia 22—Pis'mo sotnika Nadyra Urazmeteva polkovniku Sheshminskogo landmilitskogo polka I. N. Tatishchevu," *Materialy po istorii Bashkortostana, Tom VI*, 32.

55. "1735 g. iulia 4—Donoshenie kazanskogo gubernatora P. N. Musin-Pushkina v Voennuiu kollegiiu o s'ezdakh bashkir Nogaiskoi dorogi," *Materialy po istorii Bashkortostana, Tom VI*, 34.

56. "1735 g. ne ranee avgusta 13—Ekstrakt, sostavlenyi v Senate po donosheniiam iz Kazanskoi gubernii o silakh i namereniiakh vosstavshikh, sviazi s nimi tatar Kazanskogo uezda i ob oborone pogranichnykh krepostei," *Materialy po istorii Bashkortostana, Tom VI*, 48.

57. "O vosstanie bashkir pod rukovodtsvom Akaia syn Kusiuma," 404.

58. "1735 g. ne pozdnee avgusta 7—Ekstrakt, sostavlenyi v Kabinete o napadenii bashkir na roty Vologodskogo dragnunskogo polka, o tatarskoi zaseke okolo Menzelinska i o sviazi tatar Kazanskogo uezda s vosstavshimi bashkirami," *Materialy po istorii Bashkortostana, Tom VI*, 45.

59. "1735 g. sentiabria ne pozdnee 21—Pis'mo bashkir Rysia Psiakova s tovarishchami grafu P. N. Musin-Pushkinu s prosboi prislat' ukaz s tatarskim perevodom, i skaza privezshikh ego bashkir o posylke perevodchika dlia pryneseniia imi povinnoi," *Materialy po istorii Bashkortostana, Tom VI*, 64.

60. "1735 g. sentiabria 28—Skazka podpraposhchika G. Ovinova i tatarina Kazanskogo uezda Seita Aitova Khalevina o sbore v der. Kileevoi Biliarskii volosti bashkir dlia slushaniia universala A. I. Rumiansteva," *Materialy po istorii Bashkortostana, Tom VI*, 76.

61. "O vosstanie bashkir pod rukovodtsvom Akaia syn Kusiuma," 403.

62. Donnelly, *Russian Conquest*, 138.

63. "O vosstanie bashkir pod rukovodtsvom Akaia syn Kusiuma," 405.

64. "1736 g. maia 28—Opredelenie A. I. Rumiantsova i I. K. Kirillova ob upravlenii naseleniem Ufimskogo uezda i o merakh po predotvrashcheniiu bashkirskikh volnenii," *Materialy po istorii Bashkortostana, Tom VI*, 173.

65. Fäkhreddin, *Asar*, 36, 39.

66. "1738 g. fevralia 1—Pis'mo akhuna Mansura Abdrakhmanova V. N. Tatishchevu o prebyvanii Abulkhair-khana u bashkir Nogaiskoi dorogi," *Materialy po istorii Bashkortostana, Tom VI*, 536; "1738 g. aprelia 14—Pis'mo akhuna Mansura Abdrakhmanova A. I. Tevkelevu ob obstoiatel'stvakh aresta Kusiapa Saltangulova," *Materialy po istorii Bashkortostana, Tom VI*, 557. On the career of V. N. Tatishchev, see Vladimir Senenov and Vera Semenova, *Gubernatory Orenburgskogo Kraia* (Orenburg: Orenburgskoe knizhnoe izdatel'stvo imeni G. P. Donkovtseva, 2014). On the career of Alexei Ivanovich/ Qutlu'Muḥammad Tevkelev, see Steinwedel, *Threads of Empire*, 14–15, 45–47, and Michael Khodarkovsky, *Russia's Steppe Frontier: The Making of a Colonial Empire, 1500–1800* (Bloomington: Indiana University Press, 2004), 32–33.

67. Fäkhreddin, *Asar*, 35, 38–39.

68. Ibid., 48.

69. Ibid., 38, 42, 51.

70. Ibid., 42; Mami Hamamoto, "Tatarskaia Kargala in Russia's Eastern Policies," *Asiatic Russia: Imperial Power in Regional and International Contexts*, ed. Tomohiko Uyama (New York: Routledge, 2012): 32–52.

71. Fäkhreddin, *Asar*, 42, 51.

72. Ibid., 1:38, 40, 45–47, 79, 84, 87.

73. Ismägyil' bin Bikmökhämmäd, "Ismägyil' aga Seyäkhätnamäsy," *XVIII yöz tatar ädäbiyaty: Proza*, 314.

74. A. P. Chuloshnikov, *Vosstanie 1755 g. v Bashkirii* (Moscow: Nauka, 1940), 64; *Pis'mo Batyrshi Imperatritse Elizavete Petrovne*, ed. G. B. Khusainov (Ufa: UNTsRAN,1993), 71.

75. Chuloshnikov, 64; Fäkhreddin, *Asar*, 44, 46–47, 52, 59, 60, 80, 86.

76. *Pis'mo Batyrshi*, 71; Fäkhreddin, *Asar*, 42.

77. *Pis'mo Batyrshi*, 71.

78. Ibid., 90.

79. Ibid., 77.

80. Ibid., 97.

81. Ibid.

82. Fäkhreddin, *Asar*, 41–42.

83. I. I. Nepliuev, *Zapiski Ivana Ivanavicha Neplieueva (1693–1773)* (St. Petersburg: A. S. Suvorin, 1893), 50–51.

84. *Materialy po istorii Bashkortostana, Tom VI*, 491–541; William Tooke, *View of the Russian Empire*, vol. 2 (New York: Arno Press, 1970), 248.

85. I. M. Gvozdikova, *Bashkortostan nakanune i v gody krest'ianskoi voiny, pod predvoditel'stvom E. I. Pugacheva* (Ufa: "Kitap," 1999), 241.

86. Iu. S. Zobov, "Nachal'nyi etap formirovaniia tatarskogo naseleniia Orenburzh'ia (40–50-e gg. XVIII v.)," *Tatary v Orenburgskoi krae*, ed. I. M. Gabdulgafarova (Orenburg: Dimur, 1991), 9.

87. *Materialy po istorii Bashkortostana, Tom VI*, 15–56.

88. Ibid., 27, 53.

89. Ibid., 41–43, 51. Kirilov's policy had in fact been that Mishars, Teptiars, and other squatters residing on the land belonging to Bashkir rebels prior to 1735 would receive title to that land if they supported the state against the rebels.

90. Ibid., 51–55.

91. Ibid., 50.

92. Fäkhreddin, *Asar*, 52–53.

93. Ibid., 62–63.

94. Ibid., 87.

95. For more information on the backgrounds and fates of these men, see: *Dokumenty stavki E. I. Pugacheva, povstancheskikh i uchrezhdenii*, ed. P. V. Ovchinikov (Moscow: Nauka, 1975); I. M. Gvozdikova, *Bashkortostan nakanunei v gody krest'ianskoi voiny*; *Pugachvshchina, tom pervyi: iz arkhiva Pugacheva*, ed. S. G. Golubtsov (Moscow: Gos. Izdat, 1926); *Vozzvaniia i perepiska vozhakov Pugachevskogo dvizheniia v Povolzh'e i Priural'e*. ed. Mirkasīm Usmanov (Kazan: Izdatel'stvo Kazanskogo Universiteta, 1988).

96. *Vozzvaniia i perepiska vozhakov Pugachevskogo dvizheniia*, 394.

97. Claus Scharf, "Noble Landholding and Local Administration in the Guberniia Reform of Catherine II: Arguments from the Middle Volga." *Reflections on Russia in the Eighteenth Century*, ed. Joachim Klein et al. (Köln: Bohlau Verlag, 2001), 121–24.

98. Ibid., 124–25.

99. Donnelly, *Russian Conquest*, 56–58.

100. Khodarkovsky, *Russia's Steppe Frontier*, 53.

101. For a detailed analysis of the Kazakhs' relations with Russia and China in the 1700s, see Noda Jin, *The Kazakh Khanates Between the Russian and Qing Empires: Central Eurasian International Relations during the Eighteenth and Nineteenth Centuries* (Leiden: Brill, 2016).

102. *Istoriia Kazakhstana s drevneishikh vremen do nashikh dnei* (5 vols.) (Almaty: Atamura, 1997), 3:171.

103. Ibid., 3:255.

104. "Arkhiv Grafa Igel'stroma," *Russkii arkhiv* 4 (1886): 345–47.

105. Alan W. Fisher, *The Russian Annexation of Crimea, 1772–1783* (Cambridge: Cambridge University Press, 1970), 140–41.

106. "Arkhiv Grafa Igel'stroma," 346.

107. *Istoriia Kazakhstana s drevneishikh vremen do nashikh dnei*, 3:223–27, 230–34.

108. "Arkhiv Grafa Igel'stroma," 347.

109. Ibid., 346.

110. Ibid., 346.

111. Ibid., 347.

112. Muḥammadshākir Tūqāyev, *Tārīkh-i Istarlībāsh* (Kazan: n.p., 1899), 4–5.

113. Fäkhreddin, *Asar*, 99; Hamid Algar, "Shaykh Zaynullah Rasulev: The Last Great Naqshbandi Shaykh of the Volga-Ural Region," *Muslims in Central Asia: Expressions of Identity and Change*, ed. Jo-Ann Gross (Durham: University of North Carolina Press, 1992), 113–14.

114. "Arkhiv Grafa Igel'stroma," 347–48.
115. Ibid., 348.
116. Ibid., 349.
117. A. G. Karimullin, *U istokov tatarskoi knigi: ot nachala vozniknovenniia do 60-kh godov XIX veka* (Kazan: Tatarskoe knizhnoe izdatel'stvo, 1992), 95–98; E. A. Rezvan, "Koran v Rossii," *Islam na evropeiskom vostoke: Entsiklopedicheskii slovar'*, ed. R. A. Nabiev (Kazan: Izdatel'stvo "Magarif", 2004), 169.
118. Ibid.
119. "Arkhiv Grafa Igel'stroma," 357.
120. Ibid., 358.
121. Ibid., 366.
122. On the influence of Ottoman empire on Russian rulers' understanding of Islam, see Robert D. Crews, *For Prophet and Tsar: Islam and Empire in Russia and Central Asia* (Cambridge, MA: Harvard University Press, 2009), 34–49.
123. Danil' Azamatov, "Russian Administration and Islam in Bashkiria (18th–19th centuries)," *Muslim Culture in Russia and Central Asia from the 18th to the Early 20th Centuries*, vol. 1, ed. Anke von Kugelgen et al. (Berlin: Klaus Schwarz Verlag, 1996), 102.
124. *Materialy po istorii Bashkirskoi ASSR* (5 vols.) (Moscow: Izd-vo Akademii Nauk SSSR, 1960), 5:564.
125. Ibid., 564.
126. Ibid., 564–66.
127. Ibid., 566.

2

THE ART OF ACCRUING SCHOLARLY PRESTIGE

In his memoirs, Gabdessalam Gabdrakhimov, mufti of Orenburg from 1825 to 1840, related a dream he had in 1792 while he was still a madrasa student. In this dream, he saw a white elephant with a tent on its back. He climbed onto this elephant and, holding a sword of damasked steel in his hand, gave the elephant a signal to "go to such-and-such a city in such-and-such a state." Traveling in this way, he reached a cave. The inside of the cave was like a palace, and on a throne sat the hero Sayfalmulūk and the fairy princess Badīʿaljamāl, the main characters of Majlīsī's epic poem *The Song of Sayfalmulūk*.[1] Forty or fifty warriors stood about conversing in the hall, each of them bearing a unique weapon. Gabdrakhimov prepared himself for combat, and the warriors asked him, "Will you attack us or shall we attack you first?" Gabdrakhimov told them to step forward one at a time and attack him. After several of them had engaged with him but failed to strike him, he told them to stand back and that he would try to attack them. He cut down many of them with his sword before commanding the rest to stand aside. Then he bowed before Sayfalmulūk and Badīʿaljamāl.[2]

Gabdrakhimov's dream neatly encapsulates the nature of Kazan Tatar ʿulamāʾ culture in the early 1800s. The righteous, knowledgeable jurist girded himself for battle and engaged in single combat with his rivals before the Muslim community and its leaders. In return for displaying his prowess and vanquishing his foes, the jurist was rewarded with public recognition. Such recognition in turn brought material rewards: new disciples, powerful patrons, postings in important towns, and money for the construction and maintenance of mosques and madrasas. Early nineteenth-century Kazan Tatar jurists fought one another with words rather than with swords. Their arsenals consisted of legal and theological commentaries, Aristotelian logic, astronomy, and geometry rather than the bows, blades, and firearms that their fathers and grandfathers had used to defend the frontier settlements in the 1700s. This culture of public intellectual sparring was not unique to the Volga-Ural region.[3] However, it gained a new dimension with the involvement of Russian officials.

Studies of the Orenburg Muslim Spiritual Assembly have emphasized its role in transforming the religious-legal culture of the Muslims of the Volga-Ural region. Crews argues that the OMSA gave the Russian state a means to enforce "clerical discipline and doctrinal uniformity" among its Muslims.[4] Frank credits the OMSA with creating a stable environment within which Muslims could found religious institutions and carry on a robust intellectual life, and codifying, if not creating, a new sense of Muslim community in the Volga-Ural region.[5] Spannaus characterizes the OMSA as a colonial-style intervention into the indigenous Muslim legal culture of the Volga-Ural region. This intervention led to a splintering of the consensus that had existed among Muslim legal scholars before the OMSA's founding and ultimately contributed to a decline in the authority of other Muslim spiritual personnel, particularly the akhunds.[6]

All the above historians emphasize the power of the OMSA, or rather, the Russian state that had established it, to shape Islamic legal culture and Muslim social hierarchies. However, the image of a powerful Russian state in the early nineteenth-century South Urals is contradicted in studies of Russian provincial administration and infrastructure during the same period. The Russian monarchs' ability to enforce their will on their subjects had improved since the early 1700s, but poor roads, vast distances, a difficult climate, and self-interested provincial elites continued to hamper the center's efforts to impose its authority.[7] Recent historical literature on life in Russia's provinces during the nineteenth century have offered a more positive interpretation of such provincial agency by arguing that local identities, loyalties, and initiatives gave coherence to Russian provincial life and drove social and economic development outside of St. Petersburg.[8] However, whether one chooses to view Russia's provinces as stubbornly resistant to the change imposed by the imperial center or as sites of vibrant local development, one factor remains consistent: at no point were the provinces blank slates on which the imperial government could write an order of its choosing. In one way or another, policymakers in St. Petersburg were forced to come to grips with real conditions in the empire's peripheries.

In its first decades, OMSA did not represent a break in either Islamic legal life or the interactions between Kazan Tatar 'ulamā' and Russian officials. In fact, it could not, because from the moment of its founding, the OMSA was deeply rooted in the local, multiconfessional politics of the Orenburg borderlands. Beneath its institutional existence, interpersonal relationships and personal ambitions still determined many of its policies. Even the procedure for selecting the mufti had not been fully articulated. This was because the office of mufti, like the assembly, came about as an extension of interpersonal relationships rather than as a carefully planned institution: Mukhamedzhan Khusainov, in his own view, had earned the office of mufti through his years of service to Igel'strom. He saw the foundation of the OMSA as the beginning of negotiations rather than the end; with further loyal service, he anticipated that he could win still more privileges and prerogatives from the imperial government, the ultimate patron.

However, Khusainov was not the only Kazan scholar to compete for the patronage of the Russian state. Many Kazan ʿulamāʾ built their reputations with the Muslim peasants, merchants, townsmen, and nobles and then reached out to high-ranking Russian officials or were sought out by them for the influence they wielded within the Muslim communities. The accumulation of official titles, prestigious postings, and pensions was not the initial source of ʿulamāʾ power, but a signifier of it. In the early 1800s, interpersonal relationships trumped institutions in Russian-Muslim relations. Rules could be bent to accommodate the demands of a favored Muslim jurist.

By picking favorites and bestowing titles, Russian officials became increasingly involved in a game that they did not fully understand. To return to Gabdrakhimov's dream, Russian officials became Sayfalmulūk and Badīʿaljamāl on their thrones: spectators, arbitrators, and granters of benevolence in the Kazan ʿulamāʾ's contests for reputation and authority. Without understanding the intricacies of Kazan Tatar politics, officials could not anticipate the results of favoring one Muslim over another. This meant that their efforts at enacting policies relating to Islam and Muslims usually had consequences that they had not foreseen. Inter-ʿulamāʾ conflicts had their winners and losers. Complaints of loss of authority and accusations of corruption and incompetence were not signs of a change in Russian Islam or Kazan ʿulamāʾ culture brought on by the OMSA. They were part of ʿulamāʾ conflicts, the frustrated responses of those who found themselves outmaneuvered by their rivals or who failed to receive the rewards they hoped for. Batırshah Aliyev and the Pugachev ʿulamāʾ had found themselves in similar situations before the OMSA came into existence.

Among the Kazan Tatar ʿulamāʾ of the early 1800s, Mukhamedzhan Khusainov competed fiercely for the power that Russian officials and institutions could provide access to. He was not necessarily the poor scholar that later Muslim historians would assert. However, he was highly ambitious and quite willing to lie, cheat, and steal to gain power over his fellow ʿulamāʾ and over Muslim cultural life. His machinations ranged from defrauding his own wife to trying to have himself appointed as a Muslim equivalent of the metropolitan of Moscow. Khusainov was a useful ally to frontier administrators because he would support any policy that would bring him advantage. However, his schemes created conflicts within the Muslim community and inconvenience for his Russian allies. Khusainov embodied the tension in the early years of the OMSA between Russian officials' desire to institutionalize Islam and their tendency to rely on interpersonal relationships. His career also brings to light how authority was negotiated within early nineteenth-century Kazan Tatar communities and between those communities and the state.

The Asiatic Press Scandal (1801–1802)

One of the early struggles over centralization of Muslim culture and religious authority occurred in 1802, shortly after the relocation of the Asiatic Press to Kazan. Established in St. Petersburg in the 1780s, the press's equipment was transferred to Kazan's First Gymnasium by imperial order in 1800, where it was meant to fill the demands made by the Muslims of Kazan and Orenburg provinces for Arabic-script books.[9] A warrant officer named Abu'l-Ghazi Burashev was instrumental in petitioning the government for the right to open a Muslim press in Kazan and for the transport of the printing equipment, which he paid for out of his own pocket. Once the equipment reached Kazan, he also shouldered the expense of paying the salaries of the press's staff; covering the costs of paper, ink, and binding; and paying a tax of five rubles for every one thousand pages he printed. In return, he received official permission to print Qurʾāns, prayer books, and similar material. The printing equipment reached Kazan in 1800, but before any printing could take place, Burashev, Kazan's governor, and the Imperial Senate had to come to a formal agreement on the terms under which the press would be used. The negotiations took nearly two years.[10] By 1801, despite still not having a formal contract, Burashev began to take on printing jobs. The first edition of the *Haft-i Yak* (a seventh-part of the Qurʾān) to come to press in Russia appeared in 1801. A Tatar-language primer was released in the same year, followed by the Sufi works *Thabāt al-ʿAjizīn* and *Fawz an-Najāt* in 1802.[11]

In 1801, Mufti Khusainov began to take an interest in the new press. The OMSA was charged with circulating an advertisement seeking a Muslim censor for the press. Three candidates responded: Ibrāhīm Khalfin, a teacher of Tatar language at Kazan's First Gymnasium; Sabit Sadıqov, a village imam from Saba uezd in Kazan province; and Muḥammad Abdrazakov, an imam from Kazan. Khusainov appointed Abdrazakov to act as censor for future printings of the Qurʾān and claimed for himself the right to act as censor on all other publications. In September of 1801, Abdrazakov was appointed as an official censor and awarded an annual salary of fifty rubles. However, it then came to light that he was in fact appointed to act as a representative for Khusainov, who made all the censorial decisions.[12]

This situation was not satisfactory to Russian officials in Kazan, and a conflict ensued. In April 1802, Khusainov appealed directly to Emperor Pavel I. He related how the governor of Kazan province had sent him copies of recently printed Arabic-script books for his approval and lamented that no one involved in the censorship procedures in Kazan possessed sufficient knowledge of Arabic, Persian, Turkish, and Tatar to properly inspect books in those languages. He pointed out that, despite the censorship system in place, dubious texts had already made it to press. He noted as an example the recently printed *Thabāt al-ʿAjizīn*, citing a passage in which readers were told to wait for a right-believing Muslim ruler. Khusainov argued that to an educated, loyal Muslim, it was clear that when the author used the term "Muslim," he really meant only "right-believing" and that the Russian emperor, with his devotion to Orthodox Christianity, filled the role of a "right-believer" perfectly as far as loyal Russian Muslims were concerned. However, "devious," anti-Russian Muslims might use ambiguous phrases like this one to mislead believers and engender hostility against the imperial government. To monitor the production of Muslim books and to cultivate literature that would inculcate Muslim loyalty to the Russian state, Khusainov volunteered to inspect every Arabic-script book printed.[13]

In that same year, a minor scandal broke out over the printing of *Fawz an-Najāt* when it was discovered that the text that went to press contained three more pages than the text that had been sent to Khusainov for inspection. Abdrazakov was fired as censor, and Burashev was relieved of his duties as manager of the press. In late 1802 and early 1803, Burashev petitioned the

Ministry of Internal Affairs to reinstate him as operator of the press under the conditions that Abdrazakov be fired, that manuscripts would no longer be sent to Khusainov for approval, and that gymnasium teacher Khalfin would be placed in charge of censorship. Burashev received no answer to his petition. However, by December of 1802, the post of state censor was unofficially transferred to Khalfin. The appointment soon became official, and Khalfin remained censor until the 1820s. Khusainov was excluded from the censorship process.[14]

Khusainov had lost the battle for control of the Asiatic Press, but his 1802 petition to Pavel contained tropes that he used repeatedly during his tenure as mufti, including the danger posed by "crooked" or manipulative Muslim scholars and holy men and the role of the mufti and the OMSA in encouraging Muslim loyalty to the empire. These tropes echoed those in Catherine II's letters to Igel'strom in the mid-1780s, which portrayed Kazan Tatars as cultivators of loyalty and obedience among the Kazakhs. Good imams could be instruments of imperial rule and imperial expansion. Bad imams could foment rebellion and undermine imperial rule. While Khusainov may not have invented this discourse, his deployment of it as mufti legitimized it in Russian officials' eyes. For Khusainov, this rhetoric became a weapon to be deployed to increase his own influence over Muslim legal and cultural life in Russia and to crush those who challenged him.

The Shaykh Ḥabībullāh Affair (1804)

By 1804, Khusainov was embroiled in another conflict, this time with the powerful Naqshbandi shaykh Ḥabībullāh Khusainov (of no relation to the mufti). Ḥabībullāh bin al-Ḥusayn (Ḥusaynov) was the son of the Ḥusayn bin ʿAbdalkarīm, who had served as the imam of several villages near Kazan, among them the village of Ūri, where he died in 1791.[15] Ḥabībullāh (b. 1762) studied in Bukhara and then in Kabul under Shaykh Fayḍkhān bin Khiḍrkhān, from whom he received permission to gather disciples of his own.[16] He returned to Ūri Village in 1787 and was invited to become the first imam of a new stone mosque built by a local merchant, Nazir Bāy. There he began to teach and gather disciples until he fell into conflict with Nazir and other wealthy men of the village, who fired him.[17] His former patrons replaced him with his younger brother, Fatḥullāh (b. 1767), who received a license from the OMSA in 1799, formalizing his status as imam of the Stone Mosque of Ūri.[18] When Ḥabībullāh protested this new order, Nazir Bāy reportedly told him that "I built the mosque for me and my children, not for Mullā Ḥabībullāh." To retain his place in Ūri, Ḥabībullāh claimed that the village needed another mosque. With the help of his disciples, he set out to build a new one close to the existing one.[19]

This situation was not atypical in the eighteenth-century Volga-Ural region. Until 1788, the Russian empire possessed no mechanism for regulating either the construction and repair of mosques or the appointment and dismissal of imams. Imams were left to their own devices to obtain posts, negotiate sponsorship, and build support networks. By mobilizing his supporters to build a new mosque, Ḥabībullāh demonstrated to his brother and his former patrons his influence and authority as a Muslim scholar and Sufi shaykh. He set out to prove that he was a powerful spiritual leader with a devoted following who had best not be crossed.

As the conflict between Fatḥullāh and Ḥabībullāh escalated, it began to disrupt community life. The brothers designated different times for prayers and fasts.[20] Ḥabībullāh's position as a shaykh made him particularly formidable. He had established a Sufi meetinghouse in the Ūri village and attracted a large following, especially among the Mishars, who often traveled to "holy Ūri."[21] On at least one occasion, Ḥabībullāh mobilized these disciples to accost his opponents and beat them with sticks.[22]

As the highest-ranking Muslim jurist in Russia, Mufti Khusainov was a potential mediator for the conflict between Ḥabībullāh and Fatḥullāh. But Khusainov also had a more personal stake in the brothers' dispute. Ḥabībullāh was highly influential among the Muslims of Saratov and Nizhnii Novgorod. As nineteenth-century historian Ḥusayn Amirkhanov described the matter:

> It was a known fact: if a Bashkir or a Mishar wanted to become an imam, the first thing they asked him was, "Did you kiss the hand of Ḥabībullāh Ishān? Did you recite the *tanbīḥ*?" And no matter how good a scholar [the candidate] was, if he answered no, they [the qāḍīs of the OMSA] would not accept him for examination. And no matter how ignorant he was, if he said, "yes, I kissed his hand and recited the tanbīḥ," they would take him on as an imam. And if a person suddenly showed up and said he was going to see Ḥabībullāh Ishān or had just returned from seeing him, men gave him their last article of clothing and women got out their best tablecloths and linens. They would kiss his [the traveler's] hands and feet and treat him better than someone returning from *hajj*.[23]

Mufti Khusainov sought to monopolize authority over Muslim scholarly life. Ḥabībullāh, with the strong influence he exerted over part of the Muslim population, presented the mufti with a potential rival. On April 1,

1804, Khusainov wrote a lengthy report to Orenburg's military governor on behalf of the OMSA. He claimed that other 'ulamā' had informed him that Shaykh Ḥabībullāh was spreading his influence among the Muslim villages of Saratov district. He accused Ḥabībullāh of sending out his disciples, including other imams, to rally support for him and of creating his own organization, which he supposedly called the "Secretariat of the Court." The facility for this new organization was rumored to contain an expensive chair that only Ḥabībullāh was permitted to sit in. He had even acquired a Russian Christian mistress. But most disturbingly, Khusainov informed the governor, Ḥabībullāh was opposed to Russian rule and encouraged the common people to follow him rather than the Russian government. Khusainov requested that an investigation be made of the Muslims living under the authority of the OMSA to determine what was going on.[24]

At first the imperial government seemed willing to uphold Mufti Khusainov's authority. In answer to his complaint that Ḥabībullāh had gone to St. Petersburg without permission, Khusainov received a letter from Prince Lopukhin within a few weeks assuring him that the matter had been investigated and that by order of the emperor, Ḥabībullāh had been sent home to his village.[25] However, in August, matters took a different turn. In answer to a request from the Ministry of Internal Affairs to find out whether there was any sort of Muslim Spiritual Assembly in Saratov province, the provincial governor replied there was not, but forwarded a request from the Muslims of Saratov that one be created for them to enforce "Muslim law" in their region. The governor of Saratov argued that the OMSA was too distant to handle the affairs of the fifteen thousand Tatars of Saratov. He reported that the Tatars had proposed a new Saratov assembly headed by its own mufti. They had already chosen Kazan province imam and madrasa director Ḥabībullāh Khusainov of Ūri village to fill the post.[26]

The Saratov assembly never came into being. But the case illustrated two points about imperial policy toward Islam in the early 1800s. First, it demonstrates the fundamental lack of consensus among imperial officials and Kazan Tatars as to the purpose of the OMSA. Its founders (Catherine II and Baron Igel'strom) envisioned it as fulfilling two goals: serving as a diplomatic tool for increasing the Russian government's cultural influence among the Kazakhs and vetting the imams who would be employed in that project. The Saratov report proposed an entirely different function for the assembly: the administration of Islamic law among Russia's Muslim subjects. The Saratov proposal suggests that this latter interpretation of the assembly's purpose was not confined to the Muslim communities; it was shared by imperial officials as well. For those who believed that the assembly had been founded primarily to serve Russia's Muslim population in and around Kazan, its location in the South Urals made no sense. As the historian Shihābaddīn al-Marjānī later put it, "After three years [. . .] they moved it [the assembly] to that black hole that is the town of Ufa. But it was clear to everyone that the most convenient location for the organization would have been Kazan."[27] What both Marjānī and those who supported the creation of an assembly closer to the Kazan heartland failed to see was that the Orenburg Assembly had not been designed for Kazan's Muslims. There was no need for the imperial government to court the loyalty of that population because it was thoroughly under imperial control and relatively well integrated into the Russian state. Moving the OMSA deeper into the heartland of the empire would have negated its purpose as a tool of foreign relations and imperial expansion. Creating multiple assemblies would have created multiple Muslim authorities with which the Kazakhs and Muslim diplomats from Central Asia would have had to engage. That multiplicity would have diminished the effectiveness of the assembly as a tool for disseminating an image of Russia as friendly to Islam. The problem of multiple state-approved authorities on Islam had been apparent as far back as Batırshah's Revolt, when one state-appointed akhund told Muslims to revolt against the empire while a second called such behavior un-Islamic. While the Orenburg mufti served as the face of Russian Islam to the Kazakhs and Central Asia, there could be only one.

Secondly, the Habībullāh affair revealed the degree to which institutionalization was still a work in progress where Russia's Muslim communities were concerned. Outside St. Petersburg, politics were still very much about personal relationships. Rather than acting in unison, individual governors tended to speak for constituencies inside of their provinces and to promote local favorites. This had already occurred in the case of the Asiatic Press, when the governor of Kazan had favored the local teacher Khalfin (who was well connected in Kazan bureaucratic and intellectual circles) over Khusainov and his agents. Similarly, if the Orenburg governor succeeded in obtaining a special assembly for his Muslims, there was no reason why the Saratov governor could not get the same for *his* Muslims. Muslim aristocrats and merchants served as patrons to prominent ʿulamāʾ, and they petitioned and pressured provincial officials to reward those ʿulamāʾ with new mosques, pensions, and authority. In this context, provincial officials and Muslim elites did not necessarily view the OMSA as an instrument for centralizing Muslim legal and religious affairs, but as the first of a new kind of prize in the ongoing competition among the 'ulamā' to establish their reputations and disseminate their legal and theological views.

This vision stood in stark contrast to Mufti Khusainov's understanding of the OMSA. Khusainov had achieved what no Muslim jurist in Russia had achieved before: the Russian government had designated a single Muslim scholar as superior to all others, and Khusainov had obtained that status. He now sought to invest his post with true authority and fought rabidly against anyone whom he perceived as a rival. Habībullāh was popular among the Muslims of Saratov, Kazan, and Nizhnii Novgorod provinces, had the support of at least one highly placed Russian official, and was therefore a threat. Khusainov set out on a campaign to destroy him by casting him as an imminent threat to the Russian state. Not content to accuse him of preaching "against Russian law," he characterized him as an example of the sort of spiritual leader—"false prophets, shaykhs, and ishāns"—who stirred up the "Asiatic population" and caused revolts.[28] This was a cliché characterization of popular Muslim mystical leaders that dated back at least to the Mullā Mūrād Affair in 1767–1772 and would be used again numerous times over the course of the nineteenth century.[29] In Habībullāh's case, the accusation seems to have had no basis in fact. Granted, few of Habībullāh's writings have survived, but one that has is the *Treatise of Reverend Habībullāh of Ūri*. Written in Turki, the text enumerates the obligations of Muslims, giving especial attention to the ritual ablutions and daily prayer. It is a handbook that would have been copied and read by Habībullāh's students and disciples as a basic guide to Muslim rituals and morality. Not only does the text say nothing against the Russian government but also it never mentions government or politics at all.[30]

Khusainov's efforts to cast Habībullāh as an anti-Russian rabble-rouser did not win over imperial administrators. Not only was Habībullāh put up as a potential candidate for mufti by the Saratov governor in 1804, but he also received support from the governor of Nizhnii Novgorod when the merchants there petitioned to have him appointed to serve as an imam to the Muslims who attended Nizhnii Novgorod's annual trade fair, one of the largest commercial events in the empire.[31] When all else failed, Mufti Khusainov became so frustrated that he wrote an order to have Habībullāh's mosque in Ūri burned down. However, he stopped short of putting that order into effect.[32]

The Orenburg Asiatic Mosque Scandal (1805)

As Mufti Khusainov fought to put down the real and imagined threats to his authority posed by Habībullāh al-Ūriwī, he became embroiled in yet another conflict in Orenburg. Gabdessalam Gabdrakhimov was a young imam on the make. Gabdrakhimov was born in 1774 into an ʿulamāʾ family in the village of Abdrakhman on the Sviaga River. The village had been named after his paternal grandfather, who had founded it in the late seventeenth or early eighteenth century. He was trained by prominent teachers in Seitov and Orenburg.[33] In 1797, at the age of twenty-three, he was chosen by the Muslim notables of Orenburg to teach their children. He frequented the homes of Orenburg's prominent Kazakh residents, including those of the Junior Horde sultans and their families, and quickly won their trust.[34]

Gabdrakhimov's public battle with Mufti Khusainov began in the late 1790s. In 1797, Emperor Pavel relocated the OMSA from Ufa to Orenburg. Shortly after Khusainov arrived in Orenburg, he began to attend Gabdrakhimov's classes. After he had done so on several occasions, the people in Gabdrakhimov's congregation asked whether the mufti would issue their new teacher a license. Khusainov refused, making various excuses, and the matter was left unresolved.[35]

Sometime later, Khusainov left for the town of Yaik to negotiate a marriage with the daughter of Junior Horde Kazakh noble Yishem son of Nurali Khan. While he was absent from Orenburg, Gabdrakhimov's supporters wrote a petition to the governor. The governor's office sent Gabdrakhimov to the OMSA to take the licensing exam, but with the mufti absent, the assembly's qāḍīs were afraid to administer the exam. When Khusainov returned and heard about the matter, he was enraged. He promised that if the qāḍīs would not administer the exam, then he would do so himself and that Gabdrakhimov would fail in any case. In Khusainov's opinion, Gabdrakhimov was not fit to serve as village mullā, much less as an imam and madrasa director in Orenburg.[36]

Khusainov soon found a way to rid himself of Gabdrakhimov. The First Teptiar Regiment wrote to the assembly to request a new imam to replace their old one, who was too ill to fulfill his duties. Khusainov wrote to the imperial administration, explaining that the Teptiar Regiment required a new imam and that he would be glad to appoint someone himself. He informed the governor that he had the perfect candidate on hand, a young Teptiar named Gabdrakhimov, who had passed the licensing exam, but for whom there was no work in Orenburg. He explained that with a mufti and the assembly's qāḍīs, Orenburg possessed adequate personnel to fulfill local Muslims' spiritual needs. Gabdrakhimov could be sent immediately to the regiment.[37]

The order for Gabdrakhimov's transfer came straight from the military governor of Orenburg. When Gabdrakhimov received it, he appealed to his Kazakh patron, Princess Taikara, and her husband, Colonel Nūr Muḥammad Abdeljamilov. Princess Taikara in turn wrote to the military governor, complaining that their imam had been reassigned. She requested that the people of Orenburg be allowed to keep "their dear mullah." Her letter began a discussion among Russian officials that ended with Gabdrakhimov being reassigned to Orenburg. An order was sent to the assembly explaining that he was being reinstated at the request of Princess Taikara and was to be issued a license. The order reminded Khusainov that, according to the terms under which the OMSA had been established in 1788, its prerogative was to examine candidates and determine whether they were fit for service, not to choose which candidates would go to which posts. The right of nominating candidates rested with the individual congregation (*maḥalla*).[38] Khusainov was not yet willing to give up the fight to remove Gabdrakhimov from Orenburg. When the Muslims of the Teptiar Regiment sent their own candidate, Khusainov reported to the governor that he was unfit for the job and again proposed to transfer Gabdrakhimov. The Russian administration informed him that this solution was unacceptable; if the first candidate was unfit, then the Teptiar Regiment should send another.[39]

Khusainov's failure was twofold. On the one hand, he had failed to co-opt the imperial bureaucracy to remove his potential competitor. On the other, he had failed in his bid for the imperial state to grant him the power to appoint or dismiss individual imams at will. However, his conflict with Gabdrakhimov was far from over.

In 1802, the Bukharan ambassador, 'Eid Muḥammad, left St. Petersburg and set out on the return trip to Bukhara, stopping along the way at Nizhnii Novgorod and then at Orenburg. He arrived in Orenburg on the twenty-ninth day of Ramadan and reported that Muslims from that town, including his travel companions, were still fasting in observance of the holy month, though by his count, the fast should already have come to an end. Apparently, in Orenburg, Khusainov himself was not holding the fast. He explained to the ambassador that those who were fasting had begun late and were still fasting, so as not to cut the traditional fast period short. The

Bukharan ambassador responded by calling Orenburg a "faithless town" and told Khusainov that by his own count, they should hold the 'Eid al-Fitr celebration (which marked the end of Ramadan) at dawn the next day. Gabdrakhimov and two qāḍīs from the OMSA who were present accepted the ambassador's opinion and sent word to the 'ulamā' in neighboring Seitov to prepare for the 'Eid. In Orenburg, Gabdrakhimov and the town's Muslim elites celebrated the 'Eid with the Bukharan diplomats.[40]

Mufti Khusainov refused to participate in the celebration. Instead, he informed the provincial governor that Gabdrakhimov had held the 'Eid a day early in defiance of Khusainov's authority. Khusainov recommended that Gabdrakhimov be dismissed from his post. The provincial administration called on Gabdrakhimov to answer for what he had done. There are two versions of what followed. By Gabdrakhimov's own account, he wrote a response, explaining that he had acted on the opinion of the Bukharan ambassador and that two of the OMSA's three qāḍīs and several prominent 'ulamā' of Seitov had agreed with the decision. In addition to arguing for the unanimity of the decision, he pointed out that the choice was upheld by the Russian calendar, according to which the moon was in the phase signaling the end of Ramadan. Gabdrakhimov was found innocent of any wrongdoing.[41] However, the records from the district court stated that Gabdrakhimov, when accused of defying the mufti, claimed that he had made his decision to break the fast based on the consensus (*ijmā'*) of Orenburg's Muslims, the 'ulamā' of Seitov, and two qāḍīs of the OMSA. The court found him not guilty because it was determined that he was not a congregational imam but was only licensed to teach children and preside over burial rites. Therefore, he was not qualified to formulate a legal opinion on something as important as when to end Ramadan.[42] In either case, he was absolved of all wrongdoing.

Khusainov continued to try to turn the imperial bureaucracy against Gabdrakhimov. Gabdrakhimov was summoned to stand before the OMSA in 1803. He was found guilty of defying the assembly, and his imam's license was revoked.[43] However, Khan Ayshuaq of the Junior Horde intervened on his behalf and requested that Gabdrakhimov be returned to his post, pointing out that he considered Gabdrakhimov to be part of his retinue.[44] Gabdrakhimov's close relationship with the Junior Horde nobility made it nearly impossible for Khusainov to remove him from office.

The building of the Asiatic Mosque in Orenburg became another moment of conflict between Khusainov and Gabdrakhimov. According to

Gabdrakhimov, the idea of building a mosque in Orenburg to serve Kazakh aristocrats and the visiting Central Asian merchants was first raised by his patron, Princess Taikara and other Muslims of Orenburg, but with the death of Catherine II and then Pavel I, the petition had been stalled or lost. While attending the coronation of Pirʿali Sultan, the newly elected khan of the Turkmens of Mangyshlak, Gabdrakhimov took advantage of the moment to advise the khan that he might use his newly bestowed authority to act as an advocate for the mosque project. His appeals apparently moved Pirʿali, who proclaimed quite loudly that he would "sacrifice himself body and soul" for such a worthy cause. The petition was drafted and sent, made its way to Emperor Alexander I, and was approved. Military Governor Bakhmet'ev informed Orenburg's Muslims that the project could go forward if the Muslim community sent architectural plans to him for approval and if the proposed building was not excessively large.[45] Working through established administrative channels, Bakhmet'ev turned the matter over to Mufti Khusainov. Khusainov, aware of Gabdrakhimov's role in the project, did what he could to thwart it. He pointed out to Bakhmet'ev that Orenburg's Muslims already had a mosque in the town's Trading Yard (*Menovyi Dvor*) and did not need another. The new mosque would serve only merchants from Bukhara, Khiva, Urgench, Tashkent, and Khoqand and visiting sultans from the Kazakh steppe. As such, a small building capable of holding no more than fifty people would suffice. It would not be necessary to include even one minaret on the structure.[46]

In this instance, Gabdrakhimov did not need to defend his position. Bakhmet'ev himself intervened on behalf of the imperial government. He informed Khusainov that a small, minaret-less structure would reflect poorly on the power and prestige of the Russian state. What would khans and sultans from the steppe and the emissaries from the Central Asian khanates think when they came to negotiate with Russia and were directed to such a modest building to pray? Reportedly, he tore up the mufti's plan in front of him and ordered him to come up with a more fitting proposal. A new, more impressive architectural plan was sent to Bakhmet'ev and approved. Over eight thousand rubles were provided from the state treasury to cover the cost of construction and for beautifying the surrounding grounds. The mosque was completed in 1804.[47]

Mufti Khusainov determined that Gabdrakhimov would not become imam of the new mosque. He submitted reports and complaints to various Russian officials in which he listed all Gabdrakhimov's previous misdeeds and noted his lack of qualifications for the position. He highlighted Gabdrakhimov's defiance of the OMSA and forged a connection between Gabdrakhimov and another "defiant" Muslim scholar: Shaykh Ḥabībullāh al-Ūriwī. He warned that Gabdrakhimov liked to "act of his own accord" and that if he was permitted to remain an imam in Orenburg, he would cause the same kinds of problems with popular unrest and noncompliance with the OMSA that Ḥabībullāh had.[48] Once again, Khusainov used tropes of dangerous, rebellious, anti-Russian Muslims to mobilize imperial officials against his rival. However, he met with little success.

As the construction of the mosque began, Khusainov wrote to Major General Lebedev that he had heard that a new mosque was being constructed in Orenburg at the government's expense. He asked who would determine the proper positioning of the mosque. He pointed out that if the mosque was not oriented precisely according to the *qibla* (the direction in which Mecca is located), the government's money would be wasted. Lebedev inquired in Orenburg as to whether this issue had been addressed and was told that Gabdrakhimov and the architect had made certain that the mosque would be oriented toward Mecca.

Shortly after the new mosque was completed, Prince Grigori Volkonskii, Orenburg's military governor, left for Uralsk to put down unrest among the soldiers of the Bashkir and Teptiar regiments, who had recently been informed that they would have to shave off their beards to conform to the new military dress code. Taking advantage of Volkonskii's absence, Khusainov arrived in Orenburg and demanded to be let into the new mosque. Upon entering, he immediately claimed that the wall that should have had been oriented with the *qibla* faced thirty-four degrees too far to the east. Volkonskii returned two months later and tried to settle the difference between the two ʿulamāʾ, but when the mosque was officially opened, Khusainov stood among the ʿulamāʾ from Seitov, the nobles of the Junior Horde Kazakhs, and representatives from Bukhara, and restated his accusation against Gabdrakhimov that the mosque had been oriented incorrectly. He laid a prayer rug in the prayer niche, but instead of laying it straight, he angled it toward the west to indicate where, in his calculation, Mecca was located. He forbade anyone from moving it. The congregation quickly descended into argument, with many coming to the defense of Gabdrakhimov.

At a later prayer, one of Khusainov's supporters noticed that the prayer rug had been moved so that its angle corresponded to that of the prayer niche. He demanded to know, on behalf of the mufti, who had dared to move the prayer rug. The guilty party, an interpreter named ʿUbaydullāh, came forward and acknowledged that he had done it, because the rug had looked crooked to him. He confessed that he had no idea that the mufti had laid it out that way. Gabdrakhimov instructed the mufti's informant to tell Khusainov that the mosque was facing in the right direction.

The next day, people gathered at the mosque to perform their morning prayers. Upon completing their prayers, they stood up and moved to leave, but when they reached the door, they were prevented from exiting by two of Khusainov's men. Those men informed the people that the mufti had told them not to let anyone out of the mosque and that they were to cease recognizing Gabdrakhimov as their imam. From now on, their new imam would be Muzaffar Mujir. In answer to this announcement, Mirsalim Bikchurin, a high-ranking imperial official, told the mufti's men that if Khusainov wished to give such an order, then he at least needed to issue it in written form. This demand bought time for Bikchurin to gather the Muslim nobles, merchants, and military officers of Orenburg. It was Volkonskii's saint's day and the provincial prosecutor had come to Orenburg from Ufa. Gabdrakhimov's supporters went to Volkonskii's saint's day celebration to address their complaint against the mufti directly to him. On receiving the complaint, Volkonskii expressed shock at the fact that Khusainov was still in Orenburg, as he was supposed to have returned to Ufa. Angered by the disruption of his saint's day banquet, he ordered his adjunct to bring Khusainov to him at once, but was stopped by another nobleman, who told Volkonskii to send a message to the "little mufti" (*muftiyushka*) instead: "Why are you offending our beloved mullā [Gabdrakhimov]? By tomorrow, you'd better be gone from here." Khusainov fled Orenburg before dawn and made his way back to Ufa.[49]

In August 1805, Gabdrakhimov was appointed to serve as imam-mudarris and akhund of the newly built Asiatic Mosque. He was awarded an annual salary of 150 rubles from the imperial government while he held this post. The recommendation was put forward by Volkonskii and was supported by Ayshuaq Khan of the Kazakh Junior Horde.[50]

Conclusion

In 1804, several ʿulamāʾ petitioned Volkonskii about Khusainov's investigation and harassment of Ḥabībullāh al-Ūriwī and his disciple, Shaban. They complained that "the mufti was behaving improperly."[51] This complaint captures the essence of the hostility between Khusainov and many of his colleagues. Conflicts among rival scholars could be vicious and very public. In fact, they needed to be public, because a victory was valuable only if the wider community knew about it. However, as evident from Gabdrakhimov's dream, these conflicts were governed by rules and accepted conventions. Shaykh Ḥabībullāh and Gabdrakhimov fought by the rules. Khusainov's gravest sin was not that he accepted a salary from the Russian government or worked actively with Russian officials, but that by trying to use his office as mufti to single-handedly dominate Muslim scholarly life, he had broken the rules of engagement. When other influential ʿulamāʾ determined that Khusainov had overstepped his bounds, they reacted by ignoring him or mobilizing their allies and supporters to undermine him.

Khusainov might have enjoyed more success in imposing his will over the ʿulamāʾ of Kazan and Orenburg if imperial officials had consistently supported him. However, in the early 1800s, officials themselves struggled to decide how involved the imperial government needed to become in the administration of Islam. The failure of Khusainov's attempt to gain control of Arabic-script publishing and the posting of imams suggests that officials were not in favor of a highly centralized administrative organ tasked with handling all matters relating to Islam. At the same time, the rejection of the proposal to open additional spiritual assemblies in the Volga basin and the South Urals suggests that at least some officials did not want to see the development of a more decentralized organization. The question of whether the OMSA was an organ for foreign relations or designed for the administration of Russia's domestic Muslim communities also recurred through the first decade of the nineteenth century.

The OMSA continued to evolve during the nineteenth century, but its early years revealed a problem that would continue to plague the administration of Islam in the Volga-Ural region to the end of the imperial period. Officials were torn between the impulse to administer Islam and reluctance to construct an administrative organ that was too comprehensive, systematic, and potentially powerful. They settled for something in between: an OMSA with no regional branches and such a small full-time staff that it functioned only through reliance on the broader scholarly networks and the division of other responsibilities (i.e., civil suits, education, Muslim publishing) among the various ministries and provincial administrations. This left plenty of space for Islamic culture to develop outside the imperial government's direct control.

Notes

1. Mäjlisi, *Sayfelmölek*, ed. Farit Yakhin (Kazan: Tatarstan kitap näshriyaty, 2007).

2. Gabdessäläm Gabderäkhimov, "Khäter däftäre," *Gabdessäläm Möfti: Khäter däftäre, tärjemäi Gabdessäläm Möfti, Säfärnamäi shahzadä Alexander*, ed. Masgud Gaynetdin (Kazan: Iman, 2002), 28–29.

3. Michael Chamberlain, *Knowledge and Social Practice in Medieval Damascus, 1190–1350* (Cambridge: Cambridge University Press, 1994).

4. Robert D. Crews, *For Prophet and Tsar: Islam and Empire in Russia and Central Asia* (Cambridge, MA: Harvard University Press, 2009), 91.

5. Allen J. Frank, *Islamic Historiography and 'Bulghar' Identity among the Tatars and Bashkirs of Russia* (Leiden: Brill, 1998), 34–39, 197–98.

6. Nathan Spannaus, "The Decline of the Akhund and the Transformation of Islamic Law under the Russian Empire," *Islamic Law and Society* 20, no. 3 (2013): 202–41.

7. Robert E. Jones, *Provincial Development in Russia: Catherine II and Jacob Sievers* (New Brunswick, NJ: Rutgers University Press, 1984); Dmitri Ivanovich Rostislavov, *Provincial Russian in the Age of Enlightenment: The Memoir of a Priest's Son*, trans. Alexander M. Martin (De Kalb: Northern Illinois University Press, 2002).

8. Catherine Evtuhov, *Portrait of a Russian Province* (Pittsburgh: University of Pittsburgh Press, 2011); Mary W. Cavender, *Nests of the Gentry: Family, Estate, and Local Loyalties in Provincial Russia* (Newark: University of Delaware Press, 2007).

9. A. G. Karimullin, *U istokov tatarskoi knigi: ot nachala vozniknovenniia do 60-kh godov XIX veka* (Kazan: Tatarskoe knizhnoe izdatel'stvo, 1992), 106.

10. Ibid., 108.

11. Ibid., 110–11; "Protokol tsenzurnago komiteta pri Kazanskom Universitete uchrezhdennago 1822 goda," K(P)FU-ORRK, No. 4174, 1–2; "Po otnoshenniiu bibliotekira universiteta s prepovozhdenii raznyikh knig' dlia khraneniia," K(P)FU-ORRK, No. 4175 no. 1, 1.

12. Karimullin, *U istokov tatarskoi knigi*, 112–13.

13. GAOO, f. 6, op. 2, del. 763/2 l. 1–20b.

14. Karimullin, *U istokov tatarskoi knigi*, 113–15; "Khalfin, I. M," *Bibliograficheskii slovar' otechestvennykh tiurkologov: dooktiabrskii period*, ed. A. N. Konanov (Moscow: Glavnays redaktsiia vostochnoi literatury, 1974), 281.

15. Rizaeddin Fäkhreddin, *Asar*, ed. Raif Märdanov and Ramil Minggnullin (Kazan: Rukhiyat, 2006), 49.

16. Ibid.

17. Shihābaddīn al-Marjānī, *Qism ath-Thānī min Kitāb Mustafād al-Akhbār fī aḥwāl Qazān wa Bulghār* (Kazan: Tipo-Litografiia Imperatorskago Universiteta, 1900), 190–91.

18. Rizaeddin Fäkhreddin, *Asar: Ikenche tom ikenche tom*, ed. Ilshat Gyimadiev, Ramil Miggnullin, and Sirinä Bahavieva (Kazan: Rukhiyat, 2009), 2–6.

19. Shihābaddīn al-Marjānī, *Qism ath-Thānī min Kitāb Mustafād al-Akhbār*, 191.

20. Michael Kemper, *Sufis und Gelehrte in Tatarien und Baschkirien, 1789–1889: Der islamische Diskurs unter russischer Herrschaft* (Berlin: Schwarz, 1998), 100.

21. Shihābaddīn al-Marjānī, *Qism ath-Thānī min Kitāb Mustafād al-Akhbār*, 191; Fäkhreddin, *Asar*, 86.

22. Shihābaddīn al-Marjānī, *Qism ath-Thānī min Kitāb Mustafād al-Akhbār*, 191; Kemper, *Sufis und Gelehrte*, 100.
23. Ḥusayn Amirkhanov, *Tawārīkh-i Bulğāriyya* (Kazan: Vyatcheslav, 1883), 42–43.
24. GAOO, f. 6., op. 2, del. 654/1, l. 1–2ob
25. Fäkhreddin, *Asar*, 103.
26. GAOO, f. 6, op. 2, del. 654/1, l. 3–5ob.
27. Shihābaddīn al-Marjānī, *Qism ath-Thānī min Kitāb Mustafād al-Akhbār*, 187.
28. GAOO, f. 6, op. 2, d. 654/1, l. 2.
29. I. M. Gvozdikova, *Bashkortostan nakanune i v gody krest'ianskoi voiny pod predvoditel'stvom E. I. Pugacheva* (Ufa: "Kitap," 1999), 238–44. See also the 1821 case of M. Kurmanov preaching among the Kirgiz-kaisaks (*Kazakhsko-russkie otnosheniia v XVIII-XIX vekakh [1771–1867 gody]: Sbornik dokumentov i materialov* [Alma-Ata: Nauka, 1964], 197–200) and the justification for exiling Shaykh Zainulla Rasulev from the South Urals in the 1860s (UNTsRAN, f. 22, op. 1, del. 1, l. 83–85).
30. "Risāla-i Dāmallā Ḥabībullāh al-Ūrıwī," IIaLI, f. 39, no. 3442, l. 35ob-42ob.
31. Fäkhreddin, *Asar*, 103.
32. Ibid., 85.
33. Ibid., 154–55; al-Marjānī, *Qism ath-Thānī min Kitāb Mustafād al-Akhbār*, 298; Masgud Gainetdin, "Möfti-Reformator," *Gabdessäläm Möfti: Khäter däftäre*, 3.
34. Gabdessalam Gabderäkhimov, "Khäter daftare," *Gabdessäläm Möfti: Khäter däftäre*, 29–30.
35. Ibid.
36. Ibid.
37. Ibid., 30–31.
38. Ibid., 31–32.
39. Ibid., 32–33.
40. Ibid., 34–35.
41. Ibid., 35–36.
42. GAOO, f. 6, op. 2, del. 1090, l. 22–22ob.
43. Ibid., 1.
44. Ibid., 7.
45. GAOO, f. 6, op. 2, del. 763/31., l. 2.
46. Gabderäkhimov, "Khäter däftäre," *Gabdessäläm Möfti: Khäter däftäre*, 23–24.
47. Ibid., 25.
48. GAOO, f. 6, op. 2, del. 1090, l. 1 ob, 22.
49. Gabderäkhimov, "Khäter däftäre," *Gabdessäläm Möfti: Khäter däftäre*, 40–42.
50. Ibid., 42
51. GAOO, f. 6, op. 2., del. 942, l. 1.

3

COLONIAL TRADE AND RELIGIOUS REVIVAL

IN MARCH 1857, SEMIPALATINSK CUSTOMS OFFICIALS ARRESTED MERCHANT Nazim Murtazin and confiscated his goods. They had found undeclared tea concealed under his other cargo.[1] Nazim was one of hundreds of Russian, Tatar, Kazakh, and Tashkendi merchants to try his hand at what had become a major business in Russia in the first half of the nineteenth century: the smuggling of tea from China.

During the first half of the nineteenth century, Russia expanded rapidly. In the east, the Qing defeat of the Zungars and the subsequent extermination of most of the Zungar population of the Ili Valley in 1758 led to the resettlement of the Chinese side of the border with Muslim populations (Taranchi, Dungan, Hui) and opened the way for more active trade between Russia and China.[2] Russia and China had designated the towns of Kiakhta and Tsouroukhaitou centers for Russian trade in 1728.[3] However, the demographic transformation of the borderland led to an increase in trade across the territory previously occupied by the Zungar khanate. Three towns on the Russian-Chinese border particularly profited from this new trade: the Chinese towns of Kulja and Chawchak and the Russian outpost Semipalatinsk. In 1851, in recognition of the steady increase in commerce between these towns, Russia and China concluded a treaty that formally sanctioned this trade and established rules for governing it.[4] As the trade with China grew, so did Semipalatinsk. Kazan Tatar merchants and settlers, people like Nazim Murtazin, headed east looking for cultivatable land and business opportunities.

While trade expanded on Russia's eastern frontier, on its western borders, British, French, Dutch, and German manufacturers looked abroad for new consumers. In the early 1800s, the flow of European manufactured goods into Russia reached such levels that Pavel I and Alexander I issued decrees banning the importation of mirrors, crystal, silk, paper, linen, and fine china from Europe.[5] The primary goal of these declarations was to provide protection to the nascent Russian manufacturing sector. Both from the east and the west, early nineteenth-century Russia witnessed not only a rise in trade but also a fundamental transformation in commerce. Eighteenth-century long-distance traders had specialized in luxury goods (precious gems, spices, India-made silk and cotton textiles) intended for a small market of wealthy consumers.[6] Even tea and paper were imported primarily for consumption by government officials and a small class of wealthy nobles and merchants. However, by the late 1700s, trade culture began to shift in response to the rise of a continent-wide economy of mass consumption.

The aspect of Russian Muslims' participation in transcontinental trade that is most often emphasized in historical studies of the Volga-Ural region is the accumulation of merchant wealth. Muslim merchants took money earned in commerce and put it toward the construction of mosques and madrasas, the maintenance of madrasa students, and the sponsorship of legal scholars and shaykhs. New wealth reshaped life in Russian Muslim communities from the 1780s to the 1860s. An account from an ʿEid al-Adhā celebration in Semipalatinsk in the 1860s describes how the wealth merchants dressed in cloth of gold and set up carpets and vast tables of food in front of their homes to feed passersby.[7] Other prosperous residents sponsored horse races beyond the outskirts of the town and rode through the streets mounted on saddles covered with silver.[8] Ostentatious displays of wealth were as much a part of the new prosperity as were charity and mosque sponsorship.

Besides generating wealth, Kazan Tatar participation in long-distance trade and the flourishing of a continent-wide commodities trade through the first half of the nineteenth century brought new goods to Muslim communities. Tea, once a luxury good, became a staple of Kazan Tatar households by the 1830s. Kazan Tatar thirst for tea created a new demand for a range of accoutrements connected with tea consumption: teacups, teapots, teaspoons, saucers, serving dishes, and finally the samovar.[9] Sugar also gained a foothold in Kazan Tatar homes, both as an additive to tea and an ingredient in a new range of sweets served with tea.[10]

Both the east-west and north-south trade introduced Kazan Tatars to new cultures and inspired new tastes. At Muslim tables in Semipalatinsk, Kazakh, Tatar, Tashkendi, and Taranchi food and drink met and mixed: *qazı* (cured horse meat), dried fruit, walnuts, pistachios, meat pies, rice, kumis, and tea.[11] Shaykhs and wealthy Muslims in Russian provincial towns donned colorfully dyed cotton robes from Central Asia, India, and Iran; lined their eyes with kohl; and treated their guests and disciples to opium-based substances such as *majun* and *nospay*.[12] Russia's merchants also traded opium to the Chinese for tea, at least until 1840, when the Russian government condemned the practice.[13] By the mid-1800s, British calicos and chintzes were made into turbans for Tashkendi merchants and shirts for Kazakh aristocrats.[14] From Britain, France, and central Europe came factory-made textiles, leather goods, china, and a variety of small household and personal items. The accordion, which arrived in the Volga Basin from factories in central Europe and western Russian by the mid-1800s, transformed Kazan Tatar music, and together with the samovar became a fixture at social gatherings.

Improving transportation technology facilitated more rapid movement of goods and people across the Russian empire. The first steamboats appeared on the Volga River in 1820. In 1844, a new larger model was introduced.[15] This shift in transportation technology led to Kazan's integration into the expanding system of waterway commerce that linked many of the cities of the western half of the empire.[16] Development of modern transportation in the eastern and southern parts of the empire proceeded more slowly. Muslim traders in the early 1800s packed thousands or occasionally tens of thousands of rubles worth of merchandise onto camels, mules, and wagons. They traversed steppes, deserts, and mountains on journeys that took weeks or months and could prove hazardous. They made protection arrangements with Kazakh leaders, worked in concert with Turkic-speaking merchants from China and Central Asia, and dodged Russian and Qing border guards and customs agents.[17] The potential for high profits made the risks worthwhile.

This new culture of foreign goods and conspicuous consumption was not without its critics. Shihābaddīn al-Marjānī characterized Ibrahīm bin Khūjāsh's tenure as imam of Kazan's First Congregational Mosque at the end of the eighteenth century as bringing harmful innovation and perversion to the city's Muslims. One of these innovations was permitting men and women to sit together at feasts and holiday gatherings. Other "innovations" were also closely intertwined with the new commodities trade. For example, some of Kazan's wealthy merchants and horse traders returned from Moscow with new white hats. These hats became the new fashion in the Kazan Tatar quarter. They were soon joined by a new, Russian-inspired version of the *jilan* (a long coat worn by urban Muslim men) and *ichigi* (high-heeled leather boots with colorful appliqué). Once wealthy Muslims began to sport these new garments, less affluent members of society imitated them, ordering their own, less costly versions of these clothing items. Workshops sprang up in Kazan to satisfy the new sartorial demands.[18]

Poet and jurist ʿAbdarraḥīm bin ʿUthmān Ūtiz-Īmānī al-Bulghārī emerged as a particularly vocal commentator on early nineteenth-century consumption.[19] He was born in Ūtiz-Īmān village in Kazan province in 1754. His father had died a few months earlier and his mother had returned to her native village to stay with her relatives. She died a few years later. At an early age, Ūtiz-Īmānī was handed over to the director of the village's madrasa, where he performed chores to pay for his room, board, and education.[20] At some point, likely in the 1770s, he moved to Seitov and began to study with Walīd Ishan.[21] Living in Seitov in the 1770s and the 1780s, Ūtiz-Īmānī was surrounded by the rapid growth, lavish displays of wealth, and fierce scholarly competition that characterized the Kazan Tatar trade settlements of the late 1700s and early 1800s. If he wrote anything during this period, it has not survived, but life in Seitov played a role in shaping the views he later expressed concerning wealth, consumption, and spiritual authority.

In 1788, Ūtiz-Īmānī took his two wives and his children and left for Bukhara. Some historians have linked his departure to a conflict with future mufti Mukhamedzhan Khusainov in 1785, but there is no direct reference to such a conflict in Ūtiz-Īmānī's own writings.[22] Over the next decades, Ūtiz-Īmānī and his family traveled to Bukhara, Samarkand, and Kabul. During this time, he read the writings of South Asian Muslim scholars Aḥmad Sirhindī and Shah Walīullāh. Ūtiz-Īmānī kept a personal copy of the *Maktubāt al-Imām al-Rabbānī*, a compilation of Sirhindī's letters to his disciples and fellow shaykhs.[23] When Ūtiz-Īmānī returned to Russia, he assumed the identity of the son of a Bashkir from Sterlitamak district in the South Urals and settled there.[24] He was likely aided in this subterfuge by Jaʿfar ibn ʿAbdi, a shaykh who had fallen afoul of Mufti Khusainov and lived in that region.[25] Ūtiz-Īmānī's identity change led one of his biographers, Riḍāʾaddīn bin Fakhraddīn, to quip that "he came into the world as Mishar [Tatar] and left it as a pure Bashkir."[26]

During his sojourn and after his return, Ūtiz-Īmānī wrote numerous poems and treatises touching on Islamic morality, wealth, consumption, and relations between Muslims and non-Muslims. Sirhindī, writing in the

Mughal empire in the late 1500s and early 1600s, had decried Muslims' toleration of Hindus and their incorporation of Hindu practices into Islam. He urged separation of Muslims from non-Muslims and complete rejection of non-Muslims and their beliefs.[27] Ūtiz-Īmānī took Sirhindī's views on nonbelievers and transplanted them to Russian soil. He denounced the intermixing of Muslims with Russian Christians at all levels.[28] Addressing regional economic activities, he critiqued leather production and consumption in Volga Basin, invoked rules about ḥalāl (permitted) consumption relating to the slaughter of animals and the use of animal products in manufacture. He focused on the use of excrement and gelatins in the production of leather, noting that both in Russia and abroad, tanners and leather manufacturers used substances derived from impure animals as well as derivatives of potentially ḥalāl animals that had been rendered ḥarām (forbidden) by the method of slaughter or by the treatment of the remains and derivatives during the manufacturing process. He admonished Muslims not to purchase leather manufactured by Christians and pagans, who did not know or adhere to Muslim rules of cleanliness.[29]

Ūtiz-Īmānī also attacked the what he saw as the superficial, corrupt, materialistic behavior of his coreligionists. When characterizing the behavior of the Sufi shaykhs of inner Russia, he noted that "their goal is to take their disciples' money / to visit their houses and drink sweet tea. They wear colorful clothing of good quality / so that they can sleep with pleasant women."[30] His criticism of luxury and excessive indulgence extended to the increasingly popular consumption of tea. He listed twenty-five reasons why Muslims should not drink tea, alleging that tea had ignited an arms race in hospitality, with Muslim households devoting more and more of their income to purchasing expensive silver or gold-plated tea services, extravagant table settings, and exotic treats.[31] If Muslims indeed possessed such disposable income, it would have been better spent on charity. He also addressed the moral dimension of tea culture, noting that Kazan Tatars tended to drink the beverage to excess and that tea-drinking became an excuse to sit about for hours chatting and doing nothing. Tea corroded morality, self-restraint, and work ethic.[32]

Ūtiz-Īmānī's criticism also extended to the madrasa culture of Bukhara, a popular destination for young men from the Volga basin. Once in Bukhara, these young men, naïve but flush with cash, became easy marks for dishonest locals and were left destitute before the end of their first year of study.[33] Wealthy students were parted from their money, and handsome students were seduced into their teachers' beds.[34] Ūtiz-Īmānī's portrait of

Bukhara clashed with the popular perception of Bukhara in the nineteenth century Volga-Ural region as well as with the image that the Bukharan elite tried to present of their city as an august center of learning.[35]

By the standards of early nineteenth-century Kazan Tatar society, Ūtiz-Īmānī's views on nonbelievers and wealth were unusual in their severity. Marjānī, in his biography of Ūtiz-Īmānī, credits him with claiming that Muslims should not perform Friday prayers in Russia because Russia was a land of nonbelief. He also attributed to Ūtiz-Īmānī claims that a cow's milk was impure (and therefore unfit for Muslim consumption) for forty days after calving and that the frames of Russia's mosque windows resembled crosses, and that, therefore, these mosques should be considered churches.[36] These and other anecdotes that Marjānī relates should not be taken at face value. Rather, they reflect conflicting views over how to respond to the new wealth, goods, and habits that were becoming part of Volga-Ural Muslim society in the first half of the nineteenth century. Moreover, like Gabdrakhimov's and Mufti Khusainov's very public arguments over when to end the Ramadan fast and which way to orient the mosque, Ūtiz-Īmānī's denigration of Kazan's ʿulamāʾ and his uncompromising rejection of all contact with non-Muslims were part of the broader culture of reputation-building through public dispute. Ūtiz-Īmānī's extreme opinions distinguished him from other Kazan Tatar scholars of his day and allowed him to claim more a profound knowledge of Islamic law and, therefore, moral superiority. Ūtiz-Īmānī never held the offices of mufti or qāḍī, but his poetry and other writings circulated among nineteenth-century ʿulamāʾ and their students.

A Society of Readers

No single commodity wrought such far-reaching changes on nineteenth-century Kazan Tatar society as paper. Paper was not produced locally in the Volga-Ural region in the 1600s and 1700s. In fact, paper was not widely produced anywhere in Russia for most of the eighteenth century. Despite efforts by Peter the Great to foster a Russian papermaking industry, by the reign of Empress Elizabeth (1741–1762), it was estimated that Russia produced less than half the paper its subjects and officials consumed. Both the imperial bureaucracy and the Russian consumer relied on paper imported from the better-developed papermaking industries in the Netherlands, France, and elsewhere in western and central Europe. Muslims living along the trade route from Orenburg to the Central Asian khanates and India might, arguably, have enjoyed access to Indian and Persian paper. However, by the 1700s, Indian and Persian papermakers had not undergone the same level of mechanization as their European counterparts. Using water power harnessed by mills, European papermakers produced paper of higher quality in larger quantities. For Kazan Tatar ʿulamāʾ, often working at or near Russian administrative centers and fortresses, European paper was cheaper and more plentiful than Persian or Indian paper. From the mid-1700s, Russian rulers took stronger measures to promote the growth of domestic paper production, including issuing orders that all official business had to be recorded on Russian paper. This effort began to yield results by the end of the century. The number of Russian papermakers increased. At the same time, European papermaking continued to expand to meet rising demand.[37]

For Russia's consumers, the overall result of these changes was that by the end of the 1700s, the price of paper began to fall, and the supply began to rise. Domestically produced paper became more common in Russia, and European paper made its way into the empire from Britain, France, and central Europe. Like tea, paper went from being a luxury good to a commodity present in the daily life of common Muslims. A peasant or rural ʿulamāʾ family living in Kazan province in the mid-1700s may have owned one or two manuscript books. By the mid-1800s, even rural imams could afford to collect small personal libraries, and peasants increasingly became owners of prayer books, abridged Qurʾāns, poetic works, and collections of folk songs.

This new abundance of paper and manuscript books initiated a transformation in the system of cultural transmission in the Kazan Tatar community. As paper prices fell, madrasa students could afford to make their own copies of the Qurʾān, hadiths, and various law books. They could also copy down the poetry, fatwās, and treatises produced by their teachers. The copying of texts also became an aid for memorization. Not everyone copied their own books. Wealthier scholars could afford to pay others to copy texts for them. By the 1830s, at least one "calligraphy factory" or scriptorium was opened in Kazan for the coordinated production of manuscript books.[38] By the early decades of the nineteenth century, manuscripts could be presented as gifts, bought and sold, and custom ordered.

The introduction of printing in the 1780s also shaped this new culture. When compared with the post-1905 publishing world, the list of Arabic, Turkic, and Persian titles that came to print between 1786 and the 1860 was quite short. However, those works were printed in the thousands or tens of thousands of copies.[39] This output exerted visible influence over a society that was in the process of making the transition from oral to written culture. Over the first half of the nineteenth century, published texts gradually took the place of their handwritten equivalents. With Muslims able to purchase mass-printed Qur'āns, prayer books, and Sufi texts, professional and amateur copyists devoted their time to reproducing texts that were not available in published form.[40]

From 1800 to 1860, written texts became firmly embedded in the religious and cultural life of Kazan Tatar communities. 'Ulamā' accumulated dozens or hundreds of law manuals, hadith collections, histories of Islam, and guides to astronomy and medicine. Madrasa students copied down the lessons and opinions of their teachers. Sufi disciples recorded the teachings of their shaykhs. New maktabs and madrasas opened to provide education to Muslims at all levels of society. Already in the 1810s, literacy had gone from being an arcane, elite skill to a fundamental part of cultural capital. As an article in the newspaper *Kazanskii Vestnik* noted in 1816,

> to all who visit, it seems, without a doubt, strange to find in the Kazan Tatars a people that is more educated than many others, including Europeans. A Tatar who does not know how to read and write is looked down upon by his countrymen, and, as a citizen, receives no respect from others. Because of that, every father tries to enroll his children as early as possible in a school where they will learn, at very least, to read, write, and know the fundamentals of their faith. To facilitate this, there is a school located at every mosque, which is under the supervision of the akhund. The mosque's mullā is the teacher, and once a day he is occupied with teaching all these subjects.[41]

There were certain limitations to this new reading craze. Almost all the popular works in circulation could be broadly labeled as "religious" literature. Faith played a major role in inspiring Kazan Tatars to learn to read or make their children learn. Being literate allowed a Muslim to engage individually and privately with the written texts of prayers and Sufi poems. Written texts, from printed Qur'āns to personal prayer books and blessings inscribed on scraps of paper, also became a regular part of communal rituals.[42] Manuscript books, paper, and ink gained a foothold in the maktab and the madrasa, where the educational process became structured around learning to recognize words and phrases on the page.[43] The teaching of morality/ethics (*akhlāq*) and basic Islamic requirements and obligations (*farā'iḍ*) was likewise bound to paper, with dozens of handbooks and didactic poems being produced in hundreds or thousands of copies and circulated in manuscript form. Reading and writing were also employed with increasing frequency in the transmission of knowledge concerning folk medicine, dream interpretation, protective charms, magic, and curative rituals, information that had previously been transmitted in oral form.

What the early nineteenth-century boom in literacy did not bring was wide exposure to Russian literature, the European writings, or other knowledge from outside the Muslim world. Government restrictions on Arabic-script printing limited the kinds of texts that were published for Muslim consumption.

The Education Boom

Since the 1720s, new madrasas had been appearing across the Volga Basin and the Urals.[44] However, rising literacy and the perception that literacy was a marker of piety and respectability accelerated the growth of Muslim educational institutions. More Muslims sought education for their children. The ʿulamāʾ responded to this new demand by expanding existing maktabs and madrasas and opening new ones. Between 1833 and 1856, 920 new mosques were built, raising the total number of mosques in inner Russia from 3,133 to 4,053.[45] The costs of construction and maintenance were often covered by wealthy merchants who had made their fortunes along the empire's many trade routes.[46] Many of these mosques had maktabs attached to them. The rising number of mosques created more posts for the ʿulamāʾ, and between 1833 and 1868, the number of licensed Muslim religious personnel across inner Russia increased from 3,907 to 6,553.[47]

In a society that linked literacy to piety and prestige, becoming an imam, a mudarris, or even a muezzin was a form of social mobility. In theory, the path to a scholarly career was open to any sufficiently intelligent and motivated young man regardless of his origins. In fact, ʿulamāʾ networks continued to function as they had in the eighteenth century. Being born into a respected ʿulamāʾ family and forging connections with authoritative teachers and shaykhs greatly improved one's chances of gaining a coveted post in a provincial town or wealthy village.

As the number of men with Islamic scholarly training continued to grow, the education they pursued grew broader and deeper. The most respected jurists read and wrote fluently in Arabic, Persian, and Turki. They needed to know Arabic well enough to competently debate points of syntax and morphology in the Qurʾān and hadiths and to compose legal, theological, and philosophical works. Knowledge of Persian language granted access to the great works of medieval Sufi literature (Rumi, ʿAttar, Jamiʿ), which were much in vogue in the mid-1800s, judging by the number of manuscript copies of such works from that era preserved in Kazan's manuscript collections. Persian also served as the gateway to the educational institutions of Bukhara, Khiva, Samarkand, Kabul, and India. By the mid-1800s, any young man who hoped to win a prestigious post pursued education in one or more of these locations. This was not simply a matter of the educational institutions in these societies being perceived as superior to those of inner Russia, but also a question of establishing or reinforcing one's ties with the heads of the major, transnational Sufi and scholarly networks.

In a fiercely competitive employment market, public and written debate remained a vital skill for any would-be scholar. Early and mid-nineteenth-century madrasa instructors devoted a significant part of their curriculum to art of dispute. Students read multiple books on logic (*mantiq*) and syllogisms, including *Isāghūjī*, *Shamsiyya*, *Sullam al-ʿUlūm*, and their commentaries. They also received training in Islamic philosophy (*ḥikmat*). The centrality of dispute to Muslim intellectual and social life shaped the teaching of Arabic language at the madrasa, with instruction being weighted toward linguistic analysis rather than conversational skills.[48]

Not everyone was satisfied with this curriculum. Ūtiz-Īmānī denounced the "meaningless philosophical sciences," equating them with ignorance and nonbelief. He claimed that madrasa teachers, by promoting philosophy and logic and teaching these subjects, had ruined Muslim education. Ūtiz-Īmānī urged young students to reject philosophy and to turn instead to the writings and legal decisions of Abū Ḥanīfa and ʿAli al-Qārī. It was there, in the legal rulings of competent scholars well acquainted with the hadiths, that students would learn what Islamic law really was.[49] Ūtiz-Īmānī's admonishments against studying philosophy were copied into primers for young pupils by the 1830s.[50] Nonetheless, logic and philosophy were still central to the training offered at many madrasas in the 1870s, more than thirty years after Ūtiz-Īmānī's death.

Literacy in the first half of the nineteenth century was not limited to men. Women also took part in the new world of reading and writing. The education of girls and young women transpired in private circles, often conducted by the wife of a local imam in her own home. ʿUlamāʾ families educated their own daughters, training them Arabic, Persian, Qurʾān, and hadith.[51] By the 1850s, female literacy among Muslims in Kazan province was estimated to be as high as 70 percent in the prosperous villages.[52]

Literacy became increasingly central to women's practice of Islam over the course of the nineteenth century. It influenced the way that women engaged with Sufi texts such as *The Tale of Joseph*, becoming a medium for constructing their personal spiritual beliefs and articulating those beliefs to others.[53] As with men's religious culture, written texts became important in women's culture for transmitting knowledge and as physical objects to be used during private and communal rituals.

Literacy and Islamic Revival

Literacy transformed how Muslims interacted with their faith and indeed how their ʿulamāʾ and coreligionists expected them to interact with it. By the early 1800s, Muslim children received a significant portion of their education from manuscript books. If they learned to write, they could copy down some of these texts for reference and rereading. Shaykhs and their followers produced texts containing moral instructions and admonitions. Didactic poems and stories, basic theological texts, and tales of the Prophet Muḥammad, his followers, and numerous other prophets and saints all provided literate Muslims with guidance on what to believe, how to practice one's faith, and in general how to be a better Muslim.

The *Risāla-i Ḥabībullāh al-Ūriwī*, attributed to early nineteenth-century Shaykh Ḥabībullāh bin al-Ḥusayn provides an example of the didactic material circulating among common Muslims in the first decades of the nineteenth century. The *Risāla* is divided into sections containing lists of instructions relating to designated topics. The *Risāla* opened with a section listing the basic obligations incumbent on all Muslims. Further sections elaborated on how and when to perform prayer and the nature of God and the prophet, before turning to a discussion of personal comportment. Many of the *Risāla*'s points addressed interpersonal interactions and relationships. Readers were warned not to rob or kill fellow Muslims. Wives were admonished to obey their husbands.[54]

Written in simple Turki, the *Risāla* was designed to teach Islamic morality to an audience with limited reading skills. It set out specific, defined tasks for readers to undertake, from performing their five daily prayers to calling out or shunning those who did not adhere to Islamic moral standards. *Badavām*, a didactic poem popular for most of the nineteenth century, did the same, warning Muslims to avoid interacting with non-Muslims and to refrain from marrying non-Muslim women. *Badavām* described the end of times, an era in which the basic tenets of Islamic morality would no longer be practiced: ʿulamāʾ would drink alcohol and dress in the manner of nonbelievers, women would commit adultery, and people would cease to observe the five pillars of Islam.[55]

With manuscript and printed books becoming more readily available, the ʿulamāʾ encouraged the people in their congregations not only to become more literate but also to improve their understanding of Islamic law. In "ʿAbdarraḥīm Bulghārī's Poem about the *Laws of Qāḍīzāde*," Ūtiz-Īmānī instructed readers:

> Wherever you may find this book,
> Take it up, and it will soon bring you respect.
> Take it and copy it,
> Or purchase it and make it your own.
> Give lessons from it to your sons,
> and your daughters and your wives.[56]

Miracle stories and apocalyptic literature, already popular in oral form, were printed and consumed in writing by nineteenth-century readers. *The Severed Head*, a poem widely read in the 1800s, relates the story of a Muslim man who is attacked by a demon who takes his wife and leaves behind only the man's severed head. However, because the man is a faithful Muslim, his weeping and laments are heard by Prophet Muḥammad and his companions, and ʿAlī ibn Abi Ṭālib, the son-in-law of the Prophet, sets out to vanquish the demon and restores the man's body and family.

Majlīsī's *The Song of Sayfalmulūk*, another poem that circulated widely in printed form in the Volga-Ural region in the 1800s, reflects the Sufi dimension of nineteenth-century popular Islam. Its titular character is smitten by a fairy princess whose likeness he sees woven into a robe. Though others warn him that such beauty is beyond his grasp, he sets out on a journey to seek her, weathering shipwrecks, savages, demons, dragons, and floods. On several occasions, he should have perished along with his travel companions, but because of his moral purity and his devotion to finding a woman he has never met, but whose beauty he believes in with unshakable faith (a metaphor for the Muslim believer's striving to experience divine love), God rescues him again and again.[57]

Badavām, *The Severed Head*, *The Song of Sayfalmulūk*, and poems like them highlighted the direct role of God in the world and in the lives of individual believers. God intervened to punish sinners and to reward the faithful. At the same time, these works also emphasized the role of individual Muslims in earning their way to salvation by adhering to specific rules, fulfilling mandatory rituals, exhibiting firmness in their belief in God, and making moral choices. Responsibility for the salvation of the whole community rested with each of its members.

The mandate to enforce Islamic morals in the household and the community led more Muslims to engaging directly with didactic and Sufi texts, and, in some cases, with the Qur'ān and the hadiths. However, it also led to scenes like the one that Karl Fuks witnessed in Kazan in the 1830s or 1840s, when the town's Muslims caught sight of one of their coreligionists exiting a pub (*kabak*) during Ramadan. They chased the man down the street trying to beat him until he sought shelter in another pub and remained there until sunset.[58]

The Kazan Tatar 'Ulamā' in the First Half of the Nineteenth Century

For the Kazan Tatar 'ulamā', the first half of the nineteenth century was a period of profound transformation. As the Russian expansion continued south and east, the South Urals region was no longer the frontier territory that it had been in the eighteenth century. Kazan Tatars continued to relocate to Orenburg and its environs, but the era of Bashkir uprisings and Kazakh raids was largely over by the early 1800s. The Nepliuev Military School was founded in 1825 to train military officers and interpreters, the kinds of employment that had earlier been filled by Kazan Muslim scholars and jurists.[59] With the professionalization of frontier diplomatic staff and the development of a full provincial bureaucracy in Orenburg and Ufa provinces, the 'ulamā' transitioned to a civilian life.

At the same time, Kazan Tatar merchant activity at home and in the borderlands and connections with the Kazakh nobles' families brought more wealth into Muslim communities than had been available in the 1700s. Part of that wealth was transferred to shaykhs and religious scholars in the form of zakāt payments and *sadaqa* donations that were used for the construction and maintenance of mosques and madrasas, the support of religious scholars and students, and the provision of basic social services to destitute and disabled community members.[60]

Finally, mass print and cheaper paper made books more obtainable than ever before. 'Ulamā' accumulated more books from their native region and abroad. They wrote legal treatises, poetry, philosophical works, Sufi *silsilas*, and local histories. Given the expense of printing and the imperial government's limitations on which books could go to press, they relied primarily on their students and followers to copy their writings and circulate them.

From the late 1700s to the mid-1800s, the Kazan Tatar ʿulamāʾ transformed from rough-and-tumble frontier preachers and part-time imperial agents into an urbane learned elite. They held social gatherings and holiday feasts, accepted and bestowed charity, dressed in properly impressive clothing, drank tea with cream and sugar, and carried on polite (and sometimes not-so-polite) debates about points of Islamic law and theology. They had come a long way from the days of Batrıshah Aliyev, who ended his life during a failed prison break at Schisselburg Fortress in 1757, killing four guards with an axe before being killed himself.[61]

The eighteenth-century expansion into the South Urals had fundamentally changed the ʿulamāʾ's sense of geography. The histories of the early 1700s focused on events around the cities of Kazan and Bulghar. However, by the early 1800s, a new set of "Bulghar" histories presented the South Urals as an integral part of the history of Islam in the Volga-Ural region. One of the most widely circulated of these was the *Tawārīkh-i Bulghāriyya*, attributed to Ḥusmaddīn bin Sharafaddīn al-Bulghārī. According to the text, Ḥusmaddīn is said to have composed the *Tawārīkh-i Bulghāriyya* in the mid-1500s, but evidence within the text and the absence of any extant manuscripts from before the 1820s points to a composition date in the early nineteenth century.[62] Within the context of early nineteenth-century Kazan Tatar society, the *Tawārīkh-i Bulghāriyya* reconciled conflicting positions in the early nineteenth-century debate over the divine attributes.[63] However, as Frank argues, its foremost purpose was the articulation of a cohesive regional Islamic identity rooted in local historical tradition and sacred geography. For Frank, the *Tawārīkh-i Bulghāriyya* represented a reaction to the growing power that the Volga-Ural ʿulamāʾ came to enjoy during the 1700s as the Muslim landed aristocracy, under increasing pressure from the imperial government to convert to Christianity, lost authority.[64] Frank views this process of identity creation as more or less egalitarian, insofar as it involved writers from different ethnic groups and locales within the Volga-Ural region. For example, in his discussion of South Ural scholar Tājaddīn Yālchīgūl-ulı, he argues that Tājaddīn, through his Bulgarist history, *Tārīkh-nāme-i Bulghār*, was able to "'Bulgharize' his Bashkir identity and 'Bashkirize' his Bulghar identity."[65]

At first glance, the prominent place of the Urals in Ḥusmaddīn's *Tawārīkh-i Bulghāriyya*, which places the Urals first in his list of the different regions of the world, would seem to support this thesis: "A discussion of our own clime, the seventh clime or the seventh part of the Earth or the seventh clime, or a discussion of the seven [climes], the Urals: [This clime] extends from the Indian [Hindustan] Ocean to the Persian or Astrakhan Sea and to the Sea of China . . . It is the best of the seven climes in terms of its native usefulness and beauty. There are in it many rivers, springs, and forests. The taste of its waters is incredible and access to them is easy."[66]

This same foregrounding of the South Urals is evident in the *Tawārīkh-i Bulghāriyya*'s account of the conversion of the Volga-Ural region's people to Islam. The city of Bulghar along the Volga River features as the location at which Islam is first brought to the region, but in its enumeration of the first Muslims, the *Tawārīkh-i Bulghāriyya* lists Bashkir converts immediately after the first converts of Bulghar.[67] Only then does it list the converts from other parts of Kazan, Ufa, Orenburg, and Saratov provinces.

However, there is another, less benign way to read the prominent positioning of the South Urals in these histories. By focusing on the Islamization of Bulghar as the foundational moment for a community of Muslims that stretched from Kazan to western Siberia, these histories transformed a recently constructed geographic space into one that was both ancient and unified. According to these histories, not only had the South Urals been Muslim for nearly a millennium, but its journey to Islam began at the same place and time that Kazan's did; all Islam from Kazan to Tobolsk sprang from a single source, and there was no serious conflict or dissent among regions or peoples within that Islamic space. Thus, any movement of Muslims from Kazan to the South Urals occurred across a homogenously Muslim space rather than being an invasion of one group by another. The Bulghar historical narrative, in addition to legitimizing the authority of the ʿulamāʾ, erased the violence of the eighteenth-century migrations and uprisings from the historical record. So, too, the Russian state, and its role in facilitating the construction of Muslim settlements and institutions, was likewise erased. The absence of the Russian state from the *Tawārīkh-i Bulghāriyya* is particularly striking when compared with the prominent role ascribed to the "infidel" Russian state in the Muslim annals of the eighteenth century.

While the Kazan Tatar ʿulamāʾ imagined a unified and relatively peaceful regional past, they confronted a much more complicated present. The growing availability of books and paper opened before them a range of legal, doctrinal, philosophical, and poetic literature that their seventeenth- and eighteenth-century predecessors could only have dreamed of. Rising levels of literacy provided them with more students and disciples to teach and mentor. But this flood of new information and new readers came with its own perils. Less educated Muslims, eager to learn more about their faith, able to read in their vernacular Turki, and armed with a smattering of Arabic, delved into mystical texts, histories, Sufi handbooks, Hanafī law books, and the Qur'ān. In their search for salvation, they attached themselves to various teachers and spiritual guides.

Ūtiz-Īmānī criticized both these tendencies. He lamented the lack of good vernacular instructional books on Islam, pointing out that this lacuna forced local Muslims to turn to Arabic-language texts to answer questions about their faith.[68]

> The number of copyists has increased dramatically,
> Their work is filled with errors and inaccuracies,
> People who do not know right from left,
> People who cannot tell fat from thin,
> Made these copies.
> These books fall into the hands of the ignorant.
> They don't know how to use them,
> They stray from the straight path and become lost.[69]

Without adequate knowledge of Arabic language and Islamic doctrine, Muslims could not differentiate between good and bad books. Even when they read reliable works, they invariably misunderstood what they read.[70]

Ūtiz-Īmānī also addressed the problems of finding a qualified Sufi shaykh. He started his treatise by describing religious charlatans, who exploited the faith of ignorant Muslims, but either taught them nothing, or worse, encouraged beliefs and rituals that had no basis in Islam.[71] Unlike some of the reformers of the late 1800s, Ūtiz-Īmānī had no objection to Sufism. Indeed, he saw it as an integral part of intellectual and spiritual life. However, he encouraged his coreligionists to seek out Sufi masters who came from established lineages and demonstrated sound knowledge of Islamic law and doctrine.

The proliferation of written and printed texts also led to conflicts among the 'ulamā' themselves over juridical training, legal methodology, and specific points of ritual and doctrine. They debated over the aspects of God and how to schedule daily prayers during Russia's long winter nights and summer days.[72] Such disputes sometimes resulted in the creation of factions and fierce rivalries within the ʿulamāʾ.[73]

Abū'n-Nāṣr al-Qūrṣāwī's *Kitāb al-Irshāḍ lil-ʿIbād* (*The Book of Putting People on the True Path*) was a treatise on Islamic legal reasoning. In it, Qūrṣāwī addressed what he saw as a pressing problem of his time: the incorrect exercise of legal reasoning by people who were not qualified to engage in such activities.[74] Cold War-era historians presented Qūrṣāwī as a champion of *ijtihād*, the process by which an Islamic jurist formulates an original opinion in response to a legal question.[75] However, as Kemper and Spannaus have noted, Qūrṣāwī's presentation of legal reasoning in Qūrṣāwī's book did not promote the widespread use application of ijtihād.[76] Qūrṣāwī places numerous limits on when ijtihād should be undertaken and by whom. Only those men possessing strong reasoning skills, knowledge of the Qurʾān and the hadiths (including their lines of transmission and all their meanings, and the meanings of each individual word within them), and the consensus (*ijmāʿ*) of the Islamic scholarly community on the relevant issues, were qualified to formulate original legal opinions.[77] Qūrṣāwī declared that ijtihād could never be applied to questions relating to theology (*ʿaqīda*) and the foundation of the faith (*uṣūl*).[78] Nor was ijtihād to be undertaken when an answer to the question posed already existed in the Qurʾān and the hadiths or when there was already a consensus among Islamic jurists as to what the answer should be. A decision reached through ijtihād was never to contradict what had already been established in the Qurʾān and hadiths or by ijmāʿ.[79] Qūrṣāwī acknowledged that it was possible for jurists' consensus to vary from one region to another or for a scholar to not have access to a relevant hadith, but one should make every effort to gather all the relevant information, including taking counsel with other jurists.[80] Qūrṣāwī also distinguished between a decision achieved by ijtihād (a long, sincere consideration of the sources of Islamic law) and "personal opinion," the result of whim rather than sincere meditation and divine guidance. He characterized the undertaking of ijtihād as a holy act worthy of divine reward even if the jurist ultimately came to the wrong decision.[81] By contrast, to offer one's opinion without regard for the sources of the law was a grave sin.[82]

Qūrṣāwī wrote that it was the duty of everyone to undertake ijtihād "to his own ability."[83] But in the previous pages, he had already set limits on what kinds of questions ijtihād could be applied to, and he further limited the practice of ijtihād by delineating the different levels of legal reasoning: absolute ijtihād, ijtihād within a legal school (madhhab), and so on. His stance was that those capable of formulating original legal decisions should do so (in the appropriate situations), while those not capable should follow the rulings given by the founding scholars of their legal school, as long as those rulings did not contradict anything in the Qur'ān and the hadiths.[84] Qūrṣāwī did not consider such following (taqlīd) to be a sign of ignorance or stagnation, but rather the responsible behavior of someone who recognized the limits of his or her legal knowledge.[85]

Qūrṣāwī's views on ijtihād were not revolutionary for his time. They closely resemble discussions on legal reasoning in the Arab world and South Asia in the 1700s and early 1800s.[86] Some of Qūrṣāwī's remarks, such as his discussion of what the title of mufti really meant, might be read as a reaction against the creation of the OMSA.[87] However, like the works of Ūtiz-Īmānī, *al-Irshād lil-'Ibād* should also be read in the context of early nineteenth-century Kazan Tatar society, in which the proliferation of books and written communications held the potential to create far-flung, highly varied discussions about points of Islamic law and doctrine. Both Qūrṣāwī and Ūtiz-Īmānī emphasized the primacy of the Qur'ān and the hadiths, the authority of the legal schools, and the complexities of performing ijtihād to create a stable, predictable structure for resolving Islamic legal questions and countering harmful innovations (*bid'a*) in Islamic law and theology.[88] Meticulousness in ijtihād and appropriate application of taqlīd were meant to prevent the spread of legal views that contradicted the revealed texts and to encourage doctrinal consistency in a chaotic era. Adherence to correct and proven precedent was preferable to undisciplined reinterpretation.

Parting Ways with the Russian State

Between the 1770s and the 1860s, the Volga-Ural Muslim community experienced a cultural and religious renaissance. Literacy rates among Muslims surpassed those in Russian Christian communities. All Muslims were encouraged to learn about their religion, participate in its rituals, and enforce its moral norms. At the same time, Sufi shaykhs drew large numbers of followers with cures, blessings, and promises of knowledge of how to reach paradise after death.

However, Russian officials took a different view of this new face of Volga-Ural Islam. Starting in the 1760s, Russian records reported mass gatherings of Muslims in the South Urals and the Kazakh steppe. In the late 1760s, Mullā Mūrād attracted hundreds, if not thousands of followers, whom he reportedly told to gather at the ruins of Bulghar and await the end of the world.[89] Shaykh Ḥabībullāh gathered thousands of disciples in Kazan and Saratov provinces between the 1790s and the 1810s. In the early 1820s, Maral Kurmanov, a Kazakh who claimed to be a Bukharan saint, attracted numerous Tatar, Bashkir, and Kazakh followers as he moved through the steppe in the region of Turgai supposedly working miracles.[90]

As the Islamic revival proceeded, Muslim expressions of piety took on other forms. ʿAbdalkarām ash-Shirdānī's question of whether the Volga Basin and the Urals were the Abode of Islam or the Abode of War reemerged. Literacy was a key component in reigniting this debate. Works such as Allāhyār Sūfī's *Thabāt al-ʿAjizīn*, a popular compilation of Sufi poetry was attributed to an author whose family had supposedly left the Volga region for Bukhara.[91] Ūtiz-Īmānī's poem "ʿAwāʾrif al-Zamān" related his experience of traveling through other parts of the Muslim world and then returning to Russia, only to realize that Russian Muslims were so ignorant and corrupted as to be infidels.[92] These kinds of stories contributed to a narrative of leaving "infidel" Russia to seek shelter in a truly Muslim society. Some Muslims left Russia to reside permanently in Bukhara or Khiva.[93]

As Volga-Ural Muslims engaged in new and, often, very public expressions of their faith in the first half of the nineteenth century, Russian official attitudes toward Islam were changing. In 1817, conflicts between the Russian state and Muslim populations in the recently acquired North Caucasus spiraled into a series of wars that lasted until 1864. Russian military officers attributed stiff Muslim resistance to organization by Sufi networks, a phenomenon which they dubbed "muridism" (*muridizm*).[94] Muridism was tied to another concept: fanaticism (*fanatizm*), fervent, irrational devotion to one's faith. Fanaticism, as it emerged in nineteenth century Russian official discourse, was used as a shorthand for exhibiting a propensity for violence and rejecting Russian imperial rule. It was also associated frequently, if not solely, with Islam. In the late 1700s, Russian officials had used Mufti Khusainov to negotiate with the release of Russian prisoners from the Karbardians.[95] But as Russia became embroiled in the Caucasian wars, Islam and resistance to Russian authority became closely linked in the minds of imperial officials. In the course of the 1800s, officials ceased to view Islam as a tool for spreading Russian influence and instead discussed it as an alien faith and a threat to be contained.[96]

By the mid-1800s, the imperial government no longer needed the Kazan Tatar ʿulamāʾ to work as couriers, intelligence gatherers, and cultural specialists in the southeastern borderlands. In 1789, the Bashkir and Mishar fighters of the South Urals were organized into the Bashkir-Mishar Host.[97] In 1824, Mikhail Speranskii's "Statute on the Siberian Kazakhs" (*Ustav o Sibirskikh Kirgizakh*) laid the groundwork for a different kind of imperial rule in the Kazakh steppe. It used Enlightenment-era language to describe how the Russian state would bring peace and prosperity to the Kazakh nomads, but reached out directly to Kazakh elites rather than working through Tatar intermediaries.[98] The Statute was the first of many law codes and administrative structures to be implemented in the Kazakh steppe from the 1820s to 1917.[99] Kazakh nobles and promising commoners were gradually socialized into the new Russian-built administrative hierarchies through rituals of submission, contact with imperial officials, receipt of state decorations and pensions, and by mid-century, education in the Orenburg and Omsk cadet corps, where they studied side by side with Cossack, Bashkir, and Russian youths. In half a century, the Russian government created a cadre of native Kazakh and Bashkir military officers and bureaucrats.[100] The members of this cadre commanded both Russian and their native languages. They understood both their own culture and that of the imperial bureaucracy.

In the early 1860s, one of these native bureaucrats, Chokan Valikhanov, delivered a devastating assessment of the Kazan Tatars' involvement in the Kazakh steppe:

> Islam cannot help the Russians or any other Christian government. One cannot rely on the devotion of the mercenary Tatar clergy . . . In the old days, when Islam was not as strong on the banks of the Volga as it is today, the Tatars served Russia on the battlefield and in matters of the land. Tsar Shaykh Ali commanded Russian troops during the Livonian War and Pyotr Kazanskii was a *zemskii tsar* during the *oprichnina*. As a result of the spread of ultra-Islamic tendencies, the participation of the Tatars in the government affairs of the Russian state has noticeably decreased. In a word, since the time of the unification of Kazan and Astrakhan to the Tsardom of Russia, that is, for the last 300 years and more, the Tatars have rendered scarcely any notable service to their fatherland.
>
> There is no doubt that the reason for the alienation of the Tatars from the Russians and the reason for this lamentable phenomenon was Islamic Puritanism. There can be no other reason.[101]

By the 1860s, the Russian government took measures to reduce the influence of "fanatic" Kazan Tatars in the steppe. In 1864, Kazan Tatars were forbidden from serving as licensed imams in the steppe. Such positions were to be given to native Kazakh 'ulamā', who were supposedly less infected by "Islamic puritanism" than the Kazan Tatar 'ulamā'.[102] In 1865, the Kazakh steppe was removed from the jurisdiction of the OMSA.

Ironically, the emergence of Kazan Tatar "fanaticism" was a not a product of resistance to Russian rule. On the contrary, Islamic revival in the Volga-Ural region was a result of the imperial government's success in using Kazan Tatars to settle the eastern provinces and to pursue Asiatic trade. In effect, Russian frontier policy created the Kazan Tatar or "Bulghar" community, with its networks of 'ulamā' and its tendency to spread and culturally assimilate the non-Russian peoples it encountered. By the mid-1800s, it had taken on a life of its own, and Russian officials were now uncertain as to how to deal with it.

Notes

1. TsGIARK, f. 478, op. 2., del. 193, l. 121.
2. "N. A. Abramov, "Gorod Semipalatinsk (1868)," Natsional'naya Biblioteka Respubliki Kazakhstan-Fond Redkikh Knig (hereafter NBRK-FTK), No. 58, 4–5; Peter C. Perdue, *China Marches West: The Qing Conquest of Central Eurasia* (Cambridge, MA: Harvard University Press, 2005), 285; James A. Millward, *Eurasian Crossroads: A History of Xinjiang* (New York: Columbia University Press, 2007), 95.
3. Anne L. Fitzpatrick, *The Great Russian Fair: Nizhnii Novgorod, 1840–90* (New York: Palgrave Macmillam, 2016), 47.
4. N. Abramof, "Semipalatinsk," *Journal of the Royal Geographic Society of London* 32 (1861): 556.
5. TsGIARK, f. 478, op. 2. del. 15, l. 62, 65, 68, 75.
6. For a glimpse of the state of Russia's trade with Asia at the time of the founding of Orenburg in the 1730s, see "Razskaz indiiskago kuptsa Baraeva o dorogakh v Indiiu i tovarakh, kororye vyvoziatsia ottuda v Rossiiu i iz Rossii v Indiiu, zapissanyi v orenburgskoi ekspeditsii," A. I. Dobrosmyslov, *Materialy po istorii Rossii: Sbornik ukazov i drugikh dokumentov, kasaiushchikhsia upravleniia i ustroistva Orenburgsako kraia, 1734, Tom 1* (Orenburg: Tipo-litografiia F. B. Sachkova, 1900), 49.
7. "N. A. Abramov, Gorod Semipalatinsk (1868)," NBRK-FRK, No. 58, 44–44ob.
8. Ibid.
9. Karl Fuks, "Kazanskie tatary v statisticheskom i etnograficheskom otnosheniiakh," *Karl Fuks, o Kazani, Kazanskom krae: Trudy, dokumenty, vosponinaniia, issledovaniia* (Kazan: Izdatel'stvo "Zhyen," 2005), 149–50.
10. Ibid., 148, 150–51; Gabdrakhim Utyz-Imiani al-Bulghari, "Zamm shrub al-shai/ Poritsanie chaepitiia (dvatsat' sem' negativnykh posledstivii chaepitiia)," *Gabdrakhim Utyz-Imiani al-Bulghari*, trans. and ed. Ramilia Adygamova (Kazan: Tatarskoe Knizhnoe Izdatel'stvo, 2007), 251.

11. N. A. Abramov, "Gorod Semipalatinsk (1868)," NBRK-FRK, No. 58, 44ob-45.

12. Ibid., 44ob; Mäjit Gafuri, "Tärjemäi Khälem," *Mäjit Gafuri: Äsärlär*, vol. 4 (Kazan: Tatarstan kitap näshriyatı, 1981), 431–32. (Ghafūrī's account describes a meeting in the 1890s, but ethnographic accounts such as Abramov's suggest that these practices had reached the steppe trading towns no later than the 1860s.)

13. TsGIARK, f. 478, op. 2, del. 154, l. 1.

14. "Sobranie dokumentov otnosiashchikhsia do aziatskoi torgolvli. Vypiski iz arkhiva generala S. A. Khruleva," NBRK-FRK, no. 450, 7; N. A. Abramov, "Gorod Semipalatinsk (1868)," NBRK-FRK, no. 58, 40.

15. *Istoriia Tatarskoi ASSR*, (2 vols), ed. N. I. Vorob'ev et al. (Kazan: Institut iazyka, literatury i istorii [Akademiia Nauk SSSR], 1955), 1:246.

16. Ibid., 246–47.

17. "Sobranie dokumentov otnosiashchikhsia do aziatskoi torgolvli. Vypiski iz arkhiva generala S. A. Khruleva," NBRK-FRK, No. 450, 21–22; N. Abramof, "Semipalatinsk," 3.

18. Shihābaddīn al-Marjānī, *Qism al-Thānī min Kitāb Mustafād al-Akhbār fī aḥwāl Qazān wa Bulghār* (Kazan: Tipo-Litografiia Imperatorskago Universiteta, 1900), 227–28.

19. Michael Kemper has noted that Gabderraḥim was likely not called by the nisba "Ūtiz-Īmānī" during his lifetime. However, to call him either "Gabderraḥim" or "al-Bulghārī" here would be to risk confusing him with other nineteenth-century scholars. In this book, for the sake of clarity, he will be referred to as Ūtiz-Īmānī.

20. Ramil Adygamov, "Osnovnye etapy biografii Gabdrakhima Utyz-Imiani," *Gabdrakhim Utyz-Imiani al-Bulgari*, 26; Michael Kemper, *Sufis und Gelehrte in Tatarien und Baschkirien, 1789–1889: Der islamische Diskurs unter russischer Herrschaft* (Berlin: Schwarz, 1998), 175.

21. Adygamov, "Osnovnye etapy biografii Gabdrakhima Utyz-Imiani," 27; Kemper, *Sufis und Gelehrte*, 175.

22. Kemper, *Sufis und Gelehrte*, 176.

23. Rizaeddin Fäkhreddin, *Asar*, ed. Raif Märdanov and Ramil Minggnullin (Kazan: Rukhiyat, 2006), 141.

24. Ibid.

25. Ibid., 97; Kemper, *Sufis und Gelehrte*, 176.

26. Fäkhreddin, *Asar*, 141.

27. Yohanan Friedman, *Shaikh Ahmad Sirhindi: An Outline of His Thought and a Study of His Image in the Eyes of Posterity* (New Delhi: Oxford University Press, 1971); John Obert Voll, *Islam: Continuity and Change in the Modern World* (Syracuse, NY: Syracuse University Press, 1994), 39; *Dhalik faḍl Allāh yuʿtihi man yashāʿ wa Allāh ḍū al-faḍl al-ʿaẓīm* (Istanbul: Evner Baytan Kitabevi, n.d.), 1:77–78, 238–40.

28. Kemper, *Sufis und Gelehrte*, 196–99.

29. Gabdrakhim Utyz-Imiani al-Bulghari, "Risāla-i dibāğa/Traktat o vydelke kozh," *Gabdrakhim Utyz-Imiani al-Bulghari*, 79–89.

30. Gabdrakhim Utyz-Imiani al-Bulghari, "ʿAwārif al-zamān," *Gabdrakhim Utyz-Imiani al-Bulghari*, 81.

31. Gabdrakhim Utyz-Imiani al-Bulghari, "Zamm shurb al-shāi/Poritsanie chaepitiia," *Gabdrakhim Utyz-Imiani al-Bulghari*, 250

32. Ibid., 252.

33. Gabderäkhim Utyz-Imäni äl-Bolgari, "Tuḥfat al-ğurabā' wa laṭā'if al-'āzā'," *Gabderäkhim Utyz-Imäni äl-Bolgari: Shigyrlär, poemalar*, ed. Änvär Shäripov (Kazan: Tatarstan kitap näshriyaty, 1986), 58–59.

34. Ibid., 59–68.

35. Allen J. Frank, *Bukhara and the Muslims of Russia: Sufism, Education, and the Paradox of Islamic* Prestige (Leiden: Brill, 2012); James Robert Pickett, "The Persianate Sphere during the Age of Empires: Islamic Scholars and Networks of Exchange in Central Asia, 1747–1917" (PhD diss., Princeton University, 2015), 107–75.

36. Shihābaddīn al-Marjānī, *Qism ath-Thānī min Kitāb Mustafād al-Akhbār*, 240.

37. Olga Mashkina, "The Pulp and Paper Industry Evolution in Russia: A Road of Many Transitions," *The Evolution of Global Paper Industry, 1800–2050*, ed. Juha-Antti Lamberg, Jari Ojala, Mirva Peltoniemi, and Timo Särkkä (London: Springer, 2012), 288; Dard Hunter, *Papermaking: The History and Technique of an Ancient Craft* (London: A. A. Knopf, 1947).

38. Shihābaddīn al-Marjānī, *Qism ath-Thānī min Kitāb Mustafād al-Akhbār*, 103.

39. A. G. Karimullin, *U istokov tatarskoi knigi: ot nachala vozniknovenniia do 60-kh godov XIX veka* (Kazan: Tatarskoe knizhnoe izdatel'stvo, 1992), 110–16.

40. The impact of mass printing in the first half of the nineteenth century is evident in the IIaLI and K(P)FU Arabic-script manuscript collections, where the reduction in the production of popular Sufi works often corresponds to the date at which they were first printed by Kazan's Asiatic Press.

41. "Tatarskie uchilishcha," *Istoriia Kazani v dokumentakh i materialakh XIX vek: Obrazovanie: vysshee, srednee, nachal'noe 4* (Kazan: Tatarskoe knizhnoe izdatel'stvo, 2012), 519.

42. The reading and/or copying down of Muslim sacred texts was a key part of rituals of healing and blessing in the Volga Basin. G. Gmelin, traveling through the region in the mid-1700s, describes how Tatar *abızes* would read aloud from the Qur'ān over the sick to heal them. (K. V. Kharlampovich, "Izvestiia G. Gmelina o Kazani i o kazanskikh inorodtsakh," *Izvestiia Obshchestva arkheologii, istorii i etnografii pri Imperatorskom Kazanskom universitete* XIX, v.1-6. 1903, 269). Copying down Qur'ānic citations or bits of mystical poetry is part of many of the rituals described in early and mid-nineteenth-century books of "medicine" and charms. Majit Gafuri, in his memoirs, recounts a childhood memory of communal reading of *The Book of the End Times* in the late 1800s (Mäjit Gafuri, "Tärjemäi khälem," *Mäjit Gafuri*, 4:356–57). In the 1800s, many of these rituals were carried out by common Muslims rather than scholars. This only became possible once a significant number of men and women attained an adequate level of literacy.

43. This is the much-maligned "old method" (*uṣūl-i qadīm*). A description of it can be found in Adeeb Khalid, *The Politics of Muslim Cultural Reform: Jadidism in Central Asia* (Berkeley: University of California Press, 1998), 22–25. Despite late nineteenth-century critiques of it, this system was the one in use during the rapid rise in literacy in the first half of the 1800s.

44. Allen J. Frank, *Islamic Historiography and 'Bulghar' Identity among the Tatars and Bashkirs of Russia* (Leiden: Brill, 1998), 26.

45. Il'dus Zagidullin, *Islamskie instituty v Rossiiskoi imperii: Mecheti v evropeiskoi chasti Rossii i Sibiri* (Kazan: Tatarskoe Knizhnoe Izdatel'stvo, 2007), 143.

46. Fuks, "Kazanskie tatary v statisticheskom i etnograficheskom otnosheniiakh," *Karl Fuks, o Kazani, Kazanskom krae*, 149.

47. Zagidullin, *Islamskie instituty v Rossiiskoi imperii*, 143.

48. See the discussion of *Sharḥ Mullā Jamī'*, a work of Arabic grammar commonly taught in madrasas in Russia and in many other parts of the Muslim world (Ebrahim Moosa, *What Is a Madrasa?* [Chapel Hill: University of North Carolina Press, 2015], 117–18).

49. "ʿAbdarraḥīm Ūtiz-Imānī al-Bulghārī, 'Manẓūm,'" K(P)FU-ORRK, No. 1265, 41.

50. Ibid.

51. A. Kh. Mäkhmütova, "Mökhlisa Bubī," in *Millät Anaları: Tarikhi-dokumental' häm biografik jyentyk*, ed. A. Kh. Mäkhmütova (Kazan: Jyen, 2012); Liliia Gabdrafikova, *Tatarskoe burzhuaznoe obshchestvo* (Kazan: Tatarskoe Knizhnoe Izdatel'stvo, 2015), 209–10; Al'ta Makhmutova, *Pora i nam zazhech' zariu svobody!: Dzhadidizm i zhenskoe dvizhenie* (Kazan: Tatarskoe Knizhnoe Izdatel'stvo, 2006); T. A. Biktimirova, *Stupendi obrazovaniia do Sorbonny* (Kazan: Tatarskoe Knizhnoe Izdatel'stvo, 2011); Ismägyil Rämiev and Räis Dautov, *Ädäbi Süzlek* (Kazan: Tatar kitap näshriyaty, 2001), 272–73.

52. Khösäen Fäezkhanov, "Islāḥ-i Madāris," in *Khösäen Fäezkhanov: Tarikhi-dokumental' jyentyk*, ed. Raif Märdanov (Kazan: "Jyen," 2006), 39.

53. Agnès Kefeli, "The Tale of Joseph and Zulaykha on the Volga Frontier: The Struggle for Gender, Religious, and National Identity in Imperial and Postrevolutionary Russia," *Slavic Review* 70, no. 2 (2011): 373–98.

54. "Risāla-i Dāmallā Ḥabībullāh al-Ūriwī," IIaLI, f. 39, no. 36–37.

55. *Badavām* (Kazan: Tipografiia B. L. Dmobrovskago, 1907), 4–5, 9.

56. Gabderäkhim Utyz-Imäni äl-Bolghari, "Naẓm-i ʿAbdarraḥīm Bulghārī fī Ḥaqq-i Qaḍīzāde," *Gabderäkhim Utyz-Imäni äl-Bolghari: Shigyrlär, poemalar*, 37.

57. Mäjlisi, *Säyfelmölek*, ed. Farit Yakhin (Kazan: Tatarstan kitap näshriyaty, 2007).

58. Fuks, "Kazanskie tatary v statisticheskom i etnograficheskom otnosheniiakh," *Karl Fuks, o Kazani, Kazanskom krae*, 148.

59. This institution became the Nepliuev Cadet Corps in 1844.

60. Danielle Ross, "Muslim Charity under Russian Rule: Waqf, Sadaqa, and Zakat in Imperial Russia," *Islamic Law and Society* 24 (2017): 77–111.

61. V. N. Vitevskii, *I. I. Nepliuev: vernyi sluga svoego otechestva, osnovatel' Orenburga i ustroitel' Orenburgskago kraia* (Kazan: Tipografiia V. M. Kliuchnikova, 1891), 191–92.

62. Frank, *Islamic Historiography*, 53–58.

63. Ibid., 58; Kemper, *Sufis und Gelherte*, 58.

64. Frank, *Islamic Historiography*, 197–8.

65. Ibid., 198.

66. "Tawārīkh-i Bulghārī Husmaddīn al-Bulghārī," St. Peterburgskii otdel Instituta Vostokovedeniia Rossiiskoi Akademii Nauk, B 749, 150b.

67. Ibid., 20.

68. Gabdrakhim Utyz-Imiani al-Bulgari, "Risalā-i muhimma" / "Traktat o vazhnom," *Gabdrakhim Utyz-Imiani al-Bulgari*, 254.

69. Gabderäkhim Utyz-Imäni äl-Bolgari, "ʿAwāʾrif az-Zamān," *Gabderäkhim Utyz-Imäni äl-Bolgari: Shigyrlär, poemalar*, 85.

70. Gabdrakhim Utyz-Imiani al-Bulgari, "Risāla-i muhimma" / "Traktat o vazhnom," *Gabdrakhim Utyz-Imiani al-Bulgari*, 254.

71. Gabdrakhim Utyz-Imiani al-Bulgari, "as-Sayf as-Ṣārim" / "Ostryi mech," *Gabdrakhim Utyz-Imiani al-Bulgari*, 184–85.

72. Michael Kemper, "Imperial Russia as Dar al-Islam?: Nineteenth-Century Debates on Ijtihad and Taqlid among the Volga Tatars," *Islamic Law and Society* 6 (2015): 95–124.

73. For example, in his biography of Qūrṣāwī, Fäkhreddin notes how the major scholars of Qūrṣāwī's time responded to his views on the divine attributes and his treatment in Bukhara. (Fäkhreddin, *Asar*, 69, 74–75).

74. Abū Nāsr ʿAbd al-Nasīr al-Qūrsāwī, *Kitāb al-Irshād lil-ʿIbād* (Kazan: Lito-tipografiia I. N. Kharitonova, 1903), 2.

75. Azade-Ayşe Rorlich, *The Volga Tatars: A Profile in National Resilience* (Stanford, CA: Hoover Institute, 1986), 49–50.

76. Kemper, "Imperial Russia as Dar al-Islam?"; Nathan Spannaus, "The Ur-Text of Jadidism and the Historiography of Muslim Modernism in Russia," *Journal of the Economic and Social History of the Orient* 59 (2016).

77. Abū Nāsr ʿAbd al-Nasīr al-Qūrsāwī, *Kitāb al-Irshād lil-ʿIbād*, 24.

78. Ibid., 27.

79. Ibid., 26.

80. Ibid., 4, 25–26.

81. Ibid., 27–28.

82. Ibid., 28.

83. Ibid., 29.

84. Ibid., 32.

85. Ibid., 21, 29, 30.

86. Voll, *Islam: Continuity and Change*, 24–83; Bernard Haykel, *Revival and Reform in Islam: The Legacy of Muhammad al-Shawkani* (Cambridge: Cambridge University Press, 2003).

87. al-Qūrṣāwī, *Kitāb al-Irshād lil-ʿIbād*, 30.

88. Ibid., 35–45; Gabdrakhim Utyz-Imiani al-Bulgari, "Jawāhir al-bayān," *Gabdrakhim Utyz-Imiani al-Bulgari*, 16–63; Gabderäkhim Utyz-Imäni äl-Bolgari, "ʿAwāʾrif az-Zamān," *Gabderäkhim Utyz-Imäni äl-Bolgari: Shigyrlär, poemalar*, 93–95.

89. I. M. Gvozdikova, *Bashkortostan nakanune v gody krest'ianskoi voiny pod predvoditel'stvom E. I. Pugacheva* (Ufa: "Kitap," 1999), 238–43.

90. "1821 g. iiunia 9—Zapis' pokazanii starshiny Biuidaly-Uvakovskoi volosti Kurkumbaia ob agitatsii sektanta M. Kurmanova sredi kazakhskogo naseleniia," *Kazakhsko-Russkie otnosheniia v XVIII-XIX vekakh (1771–1867 gody): Sbornik dokumentov i materialov* (Alma-Ata: Nauka, 1964), 197–98; "1821 g. sentiabia 12.—Donesenie Oremburgskoi pogranichnoi komissii orenburgskomu voennomu gubernatoru o merakh presecheniia agitatsii M. Kurmanova sredi kazakhov," *Kazakhsko-Russkie otnosheniia v XVIII–XIX vekakh*, 198–200.

91. Tājaddīn Yalchigul, *Risāla-i ʿAzīza* (Kazan: Elektro-tipografiia "Umid," 1912), 6.

92. Gabderäkhim Utyz-Imäni äl-Bolgari, "ʿAwāʾrif az-Zamān," *Gabderäkhim Utyz-Imäni äl-Bolgari: Shigyrlär, poemalar*, 78–80.

93. Alfrid Bustanov, "The Bulghar Region as a 'Land of Ignorance': Anti-Colonial Discourse in Khārazmiam Conectivity," *Journal of Persianate Studies* 9 (2006): 183–204.

94. Anna Zelkina, *In Quest for God and Freedom: The Sufi Response to the Russian Advance in the North Caucasus* (London: Hurst and Company, 2000). Recent scholarship had challenged the idea that anti-Russian resistance in the North Caucasus was led by Sufi masters or organized around the Sufi networks. See Alexander Knysh, "Sufism as an Explanatory Paradigm: The Issue of the Motivations of Sufi Resistance Movements in Western and Russian Scholarship," *Die Welt des Islams* 42, no. 2 (2002): 139–73; Michael

Kemper, "The North Caucasian Khalidiyya and 'Muridism': Historiographical Problems," *Journal of the History of Sufism* 5 (2006): 111–26.

95. Fäkhreddin, *Asar*, 99.

96. Daniel R. Brower, "Islam and Ethnicity: Russian Colonial Policy in Turkestan," in *Russia's Orient: Imperial Borderlands and People, 1700–1917*, ed. Daniel R. Brower and Edward J. Lazzerini (Bloomington: Indiana University Press, 1997), 115–37.

97. Charles Steinwedel, *Threads of Empire: Loyalty and Tsarist Authority in Bashkiria, 1552–1917* (Bloomington: Indiana University Press, 2016), 86.

98. "1824 g. ianvaria 7.—Proklamatsiia general-gubernatora Zapadnoi Sibiri, adresovannaia kazakhskomu naseleniiu, biiam, sultanam v sviazi s vvedeniia Ustava o sibirskikh kirgizakh," *Kazakhsko-Russkie otnosheniia v XVIII–XIX vekakh*, 207–9.

99. Virginia Martin, *Law and Custom in the Steppe: The Kazakhs of the Middle Horde and Russian Colonialism in the Nineteenth Century* (London: Routledge, 2001).

100. G. S. Sultangalieva, "Vvedenie," *Kazakhskie chinovniki na sluzhbe Rossiiskoi imperii: Sbornik dokumentov i materialov* (Almaty: Qazaq universitetı, 2014), 3–5.

101. Chokan Valikhanov, "O Musul'manstve v stepi," in *Smert' Kukotai Khana* (Semei: Mezhdunarodnyi klub Abaia, 2001), 114–15.

102. Gabderashit Ibrahimov, *Tärjemä-i Ḥälem* (Kazan: "Iman", 2001), 56.

4

A SHAYKHLY RURAL GENTRY

On October 6, 1859, Tājaddīn bin Bāshir wrote to ʿAbdullāh al-Chirtūshī, the director of Machkara Madrasa near the town of Malmyzh. He wished his teacher health, good fortune, and a long, prosperous life. He briefly mentioned his arrival in Kazan and delivered news from a mutual acquaintance.[1]

At first glance, there is nothing extraordinary about Tājaddīn's letter. In it, he provides little concrete information about his journey. Indeed, most of his letter is taken up with formulaic greetings and blessings. However, the letter offers a window into Tājaddīn's social world. For example, nowhere in the letter does he mention ʿAbdullāh al-Chirtūshī by name. Rather, he addresses the letter to "the teacher of Machkara village" (*Machkara dāmallāsı*) and refers to him as "reverend" (*ḥaḍrat*) throughout the body of the letter. Although Tājaddīn reports on his trip to Kazan, his account of himself and his affairs takes up less space in the letter than his well-wishing to ʿAbdullāh al-Chirtūshī. Tājaddīn's letter is a sort of epistolary obeisance in which he reaffirms his subordination to his teacher and the bonds of patronage that tied them together.

The economic and cultural boom that swept through Volga-Ural Muslim communities in the first half of the nineteenth century raised to prominence a new rural elite. Two kinds of Muslims came together to form this new elite: merchants who had made their wealth in Russia's increasingly globalized trade and Naqshbandi Sufi shaykhs. The merchants brought money to this relationship. The shaykhs brought the social prestige and moral authority they gained through their command of arcane knowledge and in many cases the popular belief that they possessed divinely derived powers, such as the ability to heal illness with a touch, an incantation, or a breath.

By the mid-1800s, relationships between teachers and student and between shaykhs and disciples, which are often only hinted at in the eighteenth century, emerge into full view in surviving sources. Merchants and peasants became followers of specific shaykhs, often based on some combination of community geography, family ties, and the belief in the shaykh's power. They attended meetings, holiday gatherings, and public lectures held by that shaykh. When they had enough money or goods to do so, they made charitable donations to him. When they suffered from poor health or ill fortune, they came to him seeking medical treatment, blessings, and financial assistance. Madrasa-educated men enjoyed an even more intense relationship with their chosen teachers. A future imam might spend ten years or more of his childhood and early adulthood living at the shaykh's madrasa, where he learned the shaykh's dhikr, Sufi teachings, and views on Islamic law and philosophy. Favored students might aspire to marry one of the shaykh's daughters and become permanent members of his extended family.

This chapter lays out the topography of the Machkaran network, a group of scholarly families and their merchant patrons who exercised growing authority over social and intellectual life in and around Kazan from the mid-1800s to the 1910s. The term "Machkaran" denotes the fact that many of the network's older members received their education with Muḥammad Raḥīm bin Yūsuf or ʿAbdullāh al-Chirtūshī at the Machkara village madrasa near the town of Malmyzh in Viatka province. Although they left Machkara to assume posts in other towns and villages, they, their students, and their descendants remained in contact with one another through social gatherings, education, and marriage. The Machkarans were not the only ʿulamāʾ network active in the Volga-Ural region, but they were so successful in generating and transmitting information about themselves, especially in mass-printed form, that at first glance they appear to represent the whole of the Volga-Ural ʿulamāʾ. In fact, they were but one of multiple networks in the region, albeit an extremely influential one. The amount of information they left behind makes possible the reconstruction of their activities and relationships in more detail than is currently possible for neighboring networks. This chapter will present the network as it existed from its origins in the late 1700s to the 1870s. The subsequent chapters will follow its evolution from the mid-1800s to 1917.

The Ūtamishevs

Machkara village (RUS: Maskara) is located thirty-three kilometers south of the town of Malmyzh (now the center of Malmyzh District, Kirov Oblast in the Republic of Tatarstan). Its rise to prominence as a center of Muslim scholarly activity began with an alliance between a merchant family and two Muslim scholars. In 1759, ʿAbdalḥamīd bin Ūtagan became madrasa director of Machkara. He found support from one of the village's wealthy merchants, ʿAbdassalām bin Ūtamish, and his son, ʿAbdullāh, who became a student of ʿAbdalḥamīd upon his arrival.[2] ʿAbdalḥamīd served as madrasa director until 1768, when the wealthy men of Machkara, among them ʿAbdassalām and ʿAbdullāh, invited Muḥammad Raḥīm bin Yūsuf of Ashıt village to replace him.[3]

In 1771, Muḥammad Raḥīm set out with his brother-in-law, Ibrahīm bin Khūjāsh, for Dagestan. They remained for ten years and studied with ʿAlī ash-Shirvānī. From there, they went to Sivas and Diyarbakir in eastern Anatolia before returning to Russia via Astrakhan in 1781.[4] During their absence, ʿAbdullāh bin ʿAbdassalām, by then a First Guild merchant, arranged for his old teacher, ʿAbdalḥamīd, to return to Machkara to oversee the village's madrasa.[5] Muḥammad Raḥīm, upon his return in 1781, resumed control of Machkara, becoming imam and madrasa director, and was eventually promoted to the office of akhund.[6]

Muḥammad Raḥīm's return to Machkara in the 1780s marked the beginning of the village's rise as a scholarly and social center. It also marked the rise to prominence of the Ūtamishevs, the Machkaran merchant family of ʿAbdassalām and his son, ʿAbdullāh, first in the Malmyzh area and then across Kazan and Viatka provinces.[7] ʿAbdullāh provided the money for the construction of a stone mosque in Machkara, which was completed in 1791.[8] Muḥammad Raḥīm, now madrasa director in Machkara, allied himself with ʿAbdullāh by marriage, wedding ʿAbdullāh's sister, Maḥbūba, and then, after her death, another of ʿAbdullāh's sisters, Ḥabība.[9]

ʿAbdullāh, now a brother-in-law to Muḥammad Raḥīm, established further connections with the Kazan ʿulamāʾ by marrying Marḥāba bint Ibrāhīm, the sister of Muḥammad Raḥīm's student, Abū'n-Nāṣr al-Qūrṣāwī, whose views on the divine attributes led to his exile from Bukhara and divided Volga-Ural Muslim scholars.[10] In the midst of this conflict, Mūsā Ūtamishev, ʿAbdullāh and Marḥāba's son, defended his uncle.[11] In the early 1800s, he and Mūsā bin Ismaʿīl Āpānāev wrote to Ibrahīm bin Khūjāsh, then imam of Kazan's First Stone Mosque. They described how Mūsā Apanaev had attended a banquet with his son-in-law, and an argument had erupted over Abū'n-Nāṣr's views. He cautioned Ibrahīm that if the latter openly supported the accusations that were already being circulated in private behind Abū'n-Nāṣr's back, he was likely to start a public conflict.[12] In writing this letter, Mūsā Ūtamishev intervened not only as Abū'n-Nāṣr's kinsman but also as a wealthy, powerful patron stepping forward to shelter a client.

Another of Mūsā Ūtamishev's uncles and Abū'n-Nāṣr's elder brother, ʿAbdalkhalīq al-Qūrṣāwī (d. 1843), returned from *hajj* in 1812 and became a shaykh and the madrasa director of Qūrṣā village.[13] He developed a reputation as a specialist in both Sufism and the hadiths, assembled a hadith collection based on his study of the existing collections, and drew students from across Kazan province.[14] He married his daughter to another Machkara Madrasa student, Ḥasan bin Ḥamīd. After ʿAbdalkhalīq's death, Ḥasan succeeded him as the shaykh and madrasa director of Qūrṣā.[15]

The Ūtamishevs' influence also reached into Kazan. In 1802, ʿAbdullāh bin ʿAbdassalām paid for the replacement of the wooden mosque in Kazan's Sixth Maḥalla with a stone one and brought Abū'n-Nāṣr al-Qūrṣāwī to calculate the orientation of the building to make certain it would face toward Mecca.[16]

Mūsā's son, Ismāʿīl Ūtamishev (1803–1888), continued to extend the influence and authority of the Ūtamishev family. He first studied in Machkara with Muḥammad Raḥīm's student and successor, ʿAbdullāh al-Chirtūshī (1774–1859).[17] In the late 1830s or early 1840s, Ismāʿīl traveled to Bukhara, at which time Kazan historian and theologian Shihābaddīn al-Marjānī met with him to request permission to copy the version of Abū'n-Nāṣr al-Qūrṣāwī's *Sharḥ al-ʿAqāʾid Nafīsa al-Jadīda*.[18] Ismāʿīl returned to Russia and was chosen to become the director of Qıshqār village madrasa in 1846.[19] Under his management, Qıshqār Madrasa became one of the most prominent Volga-Ural madrasas of the mid-1800s.

The Āpānāevs

The Āpānāevs, like the Ūtamishevs, began their rise to social prominence as a merchant family. They claimed to be descended from leather workers who served the Russian tsars of the seventeenth century and founded the village of Yanbulat in Laish uezd of Kazan province. Some members of the family resettled to the Tatar Quarter in Kazan in the 1700s and shifted their interests from leatherwork to trade. By the 1760s, one member of the family, Ismāʿīl bin Āpānāy, achieved the status of First Guild merchant. He made his fortune importing silk and other expensive textiles from China and Iran. Ismāʿīl's son, Yūsuf Āpānāev, opened the largest soap factory in Kazan in the late 1700s. His other son, Mūsā Āpānāev, owned Kazan's largest tannery.

By the late 1700s and the early 1800s, the Āpānāevs wielded significant power within Kazan's Old Tatar Quarter. Mūsā Āpānāev was the patron to the Second Maḥalla and its stone mosque, one of the oldest mosques in the city.[20] In the first decade of the nineteenth century, he financed the construction of a new mosque in the Eighth Mahalla in the New Tatar Quarter in memory of his deceased daughter. Like ʿAbdullāh Ūtamishev, he called on Abū'n-Nāṣr al-Qūrṣāwī to establish the proper orientation for the mosque.[21] Both Yūsuf and Mūsā regularly made donations to help the poor, especially during Ramadan and ʿEid al-Aḍḥā'.[22] Yūsuf and Mūsā's children continued their fathers' businesses and expanded them so that, by the mid-1800s, there were multiple Āpānāev merchants and factory owners who held First or Second Guild status and/or served on Kazan's city duma and other civic organizations.[23] Like the Ūtamishevs, the Āpānāevs also began to send their sons to the madrasas for education. Mūsā's sons Munāsib and Muzaffar served as the imams of Ashıtbāshı village and Yanga Tāzlār village, and Kazan's First Stone Mosque.[24] Another of his sons, Mustafa, succeeded Ibrāhīm bin Khūjāsh, Muḥammad Raḥīm bin Yūsuf's brother-in-law, as imam of Kazan's First Stone Mosque.

The Āpānāevs left their mark across the landscape of Kazan province. In 1839, ʿUbaydullāh bin Mūsā Āpānāev and his brother ʿAbdalkarīm built a new mosque in Qūrṣā village for Shaykh ʿAbdalkhalīq al-Qūrṣāwī.[25] They added to it in the 1860s while ʿAbdalkhalīq's son-in-law, Ḥasan bin Ḥamīd, was the imam and shaykh of Qūrṣā.[26] By the 1870s, in addition to the two mosques they sponsored in Kazan, they were also patrons of Muḥammad Dhākir aṣ-Ṣāṣnāwī's mosque and madrasa in Chistopol. By the end of the nineteenth century, various Āpānāevs owned fourteen buildings in the Old Tatar Quarter alone. In 1890, ʿAbdullāh Āpānāev (1862–1919), Yūsuf Āpānāev's great-grandson, was appointed imam-*khatip* of Kazan's Haymarket Mosque.[27] Other members of the family continued to act as patrons of Āpānāev Mosque on the shore of Kazan's Kaban Lake in the Old Tatar Quarter as well as its associated madrasa, which was variously called Āpānāev Madrasa, Qāsimiyya Madrasa, and Lakeside (*Külbuye*) Madrasa.[28]

The Āpānāevs' and the Ūtamishevs' spheres of influence overlapped, and the two families sometimes worked together. During the controversy over Abū'n-Nāṣr al-Qūrṣāwī's views on the divine attributes, the Āpānāevs and Ūtamishevs closed ranks to defend Abū'n-Nāṣr, who was an Ūtamishev in-law and an Āpānāev client. In the second half of the nineteenth century, the Āpānāevs and Ūtamishevs tried to forge a union through the marriage of Muḥammad Walī Āpānāev (1825–1885) and Naʿīma Ūtamisheva. However, the couple divorced in 1870.[29] The Āpānāevs also seem to have had ties to Malmyzh District, the native district of the Ūtamishevs and the location of Machkara village. For example, although ʿAbdullāh Āpānāev's father was a merchant in Kazan, his mother left Kazan for Ṣāṣnā village in Malmyzh district, where she gave birth to her son.[30]

The Tūqāyevs of Istarlībāsh Village

Muḥammad Raḥīm bin Yūsuf and his Ūtamishev allies spread their influence beyond Malmyzh district through the training of future imams, madrasa directors, and Naqshbandi shaykhs. In 1801, Niʿmatullāh bin Bīktimir Tūqāyev (1772–1844), the son of a well-to-do merchant from Istarlībāsh village, went to study in Bukhara. Along the way, he traveled to Machkara village, where he studied with Muḥammad Raḥīm bin Yūsuf.[31] In 1813, he obtained the directorship of Istarlībāsh Madrasa in the South Urals.[32] Under Niʿmatullāh's direction, Istarlībāsh Madrasa emerged as a major center for Islamic education, literature, and Sufism. Niʿmatullāh attracted enough new students that it was necessary to build a larger mosque and madrasa to accommodate them.[33] Visitors to Niʿmatullāh's madrasa included the Kazakh aristocrats Jahāngīr Khan and Shirghāzī Khan. Jahāngīr possessed kinship ties to the Istarlībāsh through his wife, Faṭīma, daughter of Mufti Mukhamedzhan Khusainov, whose family had built the madrasa's first building in the 1720s and served as madrasa directors there in the eighteenth century. Jahāngīr and Faṭīma's sons studied under Niʿmatullāh until the 1830s.[34]

Niʿmatullāh was remembered not only as a popular shaykh but also as purifier of local Islamic practice. He vehemently opposed *jiyens*, the celebration of Nowruz, and the commemorative gatherings that were traditionally held on the third, seven, and fortieth days after a Muslim's death. He encouraged his followers toward more orthodox expressions of religious zeal.[35] He is said to have spent a great deal of money commissioning copies of manuscript books and to have copied many books himself.[36]

After Niʿmatullāh's death in 1844, Istarlībāsh Madrasa passed to his eldest son, Muḥammad Ḥarīth (1810–1870), who also became the new shaykh of Istarlībāsh.[37] He attracted numerous students and disciples from

Kazan, Menzelinsk, Orenburg, and the Kazakh steppe and became known for his lectures on hadith and *tafsīr*, which lasted from two to three hours.[38] By the 1850s, the Istarlībāsh congregation had again outgrown its mosque, and a new, enlarged mosque, which could hold up to four hundred people, was constructed in 1858.[39]

The Tūqāyev family aligned itself with Muslim education reform during the second half of the nineteenth century, and in 1870, Muḥammad Ḥarīth was among the first of Russia's madrasa directors to introduce Russian-language courses into his school's curriculum.[40] He also took part in philanthropic work, sending three thousand *puds* of food to famine victims in 1866–1868, for which Alexander II awarded him the status of tarkhan in 1869. He opened a poorhouse and an orphanage in Istarlībāsh.[41] In addition, he maintained a wide range of friendships and alliances with other ʿulamāʾ, hosting Orenburg muftis Gabdulvakhid Suleymanov (1768–1862) and Salimgarey Tevkelev (1805–1885) as well as numerous jurists and imams, many of whom made annual visits to Istarlībāsh.[42]

The Shaykhs of Tūntār Village

ʿAlī bin Sayfullāh at-Tūntārī (1780–1874) was another of Muḥammad Raḥīm bin Yūsuf's students and trained at Machkara Madrasa beside ʿAbdullāh al-Chirtūshī.[43] He subsequently traveled to Bukhara to continue his studies, then to Afghanistan, and finally to India.[44] He returned to Russia in 1831 and became madrasa director in his father's village of Tūntār. He provided education and spiritual guidance to the villagers alongside his rather formidable wife, Gīzzatannisaʾ bint ʿAbdalghafūr, who on one occasion sold the family's silver to pay for repairs to Tūntār's madrasa building.[45]

By the middle of the nineteenth century, ʿAlī bin Sayfullāh (or ʿAlī Ishān) had become the most influential Naqshbandī shaykh in Volga-Ural region, attracting thousands of followers.[46] As a teacher, he was renowned for his mastery of the Persian language, his knowledge of hadith and tafsīr, and his skill in debating speculative theology (kalām).[47] In jurisprudence, he earned a reputation among his students and fellow scholars for advocating strict adherence to the rulings of the Hanafī madhhab.[48] In 1869, his madrasa enrolled forty-five male students and thirty-nine female students.[49] He also gave lessons for students of other madrasas.[50]

For the Muslims of the Volga-Ural region, and especially those in Malmyzh District, ʿAlī bin Sayfullāh was a holy man and spiritual guide.

According to his grandson, Muḥammad Najīb Shamseddinov-Tūntārī, ʿAlī became a shaykh not out of the desire for wealth, but to help others. He gave away much of the money that came to him, and at various times made hundreds or thousands of rubles of charitable donations.[51] His kindness and decency extended beyond human beings to animals and especially to horses, which he treated with great respect.[52] His teachings also gained popularity among the baptized non-Russians of the Volga region and contributed to the Kraishen apostacies of the mid-1800s.[53] Among his fellow ʿulamāʾ, he was a respected authority and played a leading role in selecting appointees to prestigious postings in and around Kazan.[54]

After ʿAlī's death in 1874, the directorship of Tūntār Madrasa passed to Shamsaddīn bin Raḥmatullāh (1830–1876), the husband of his only daughter, ʿAfīfa. ʿAlī's widow, Gīzzatannisaʾ, continued to command authority, settling a conflict that erupted between the madrasa students and the villagers while Shamsaddīn was away on *hajj*.[55] Unfortunately, Shamsaddīn never returned to Tūntār. He died in Istanbul.[56] ʿAlī's daughter, ʿAfīfa, remained in the village, teaching the local girls. Her son, Muḥammad Najīb (1862–1930), was too young to be appointed madrasa director in his father's place. As such, the directorship passed to one of Shamsaddīn's students, Ishmuḥammad Dīnmuḥammadov.

From 1876 to 1917, Tūntār retained the reputation it had acquired under ʿAlī at-Tūntārī as a center of learning. Under Dīnmuḥammadov's management, enrollment rates at Tūntār Madrasa rose to one hundred male students and forty female students.[57] However, in the second half of the nineteenth century, Tūntār became an increasingly complex community. Many households turned to clothing production, leatherwork, and shoe manufacture.[58] A growing number of families were also drawn into long-distance trade in Russia's new Central Asian market. The individuals at the center of Tūntār's cultural life—madrasa director Dīnmuḥammadov and the widowed *abıstay* ʿAfīfa bint ʿAlī—were both strong willed and appear to not have gotten along. In 1878, Dīnmuḥammadov wrote to Shihābaddīn al-Marjānī, then imam of the First Stone Mosque in Kazan, to request his aid in obtaining a post in the city. He intimated that ʿAfīfa was attempting to seduce him and that he needed to leave the village to preserve his honor. Marjānī, instead of assisting him, shared this private communication with his students, making the situation public knowledge.[59] This was only a prelude to the conflicts that would sweep through Tūntār village in the late 1800s and early 1900s.

ʿAbdullāh al-Chirtūshī

The Ūtamishevs, Āpānāevs, Tūqāyevs, and Tūntārīs were multigenerational elite families within the Machkara network who linked Muḥammad Raḥīm bin Yūsuf and the ʿulamāʾ of the early 1900s. By contrast, ʿAbdullāh al-Chirtūshī, Muḥammad Raḥīm's student, created a network primarily based on teacher-student relationships.

ʿAbdullāh al-Chirtūshī began his career as a student of Muḥammad Raḥīm bin Yūsuf at Machkara Madrasa. He befriended fellow student ʿAlī at-Tūntārī, who intervened on his behalf to help him receive a teaching appointment at Machkara Madrasa.[60] ʿAbdullāh married Muḥammad Raḥīm's daughter, Rābiʿa, and, after Muḥammad Raḥīm's death in 1818, was appointed director of Machkara madrasa.[61] The friendship between ʿAbdullāh and ʿAlī at-Tūntārī continued until ʿAbdullāh's death, when ʿAlī came forward to pay ʿAbdullāh's debts.[62]

Under ʿAbdullāh al-Chirtūshī's leadership, Machkara remained an important center for building scholarly networks. ʿAbdullāh al-Chirtūshī trained Muḥammad Karīm bin Muḥammad Raḥīm al-Qazānī and Shah-i Aḥmad bin Abū Yazīd, who were appointed imams of Kazan's Second and Eighth mosques, increasing the influence of the Machkara network in Kazan.[63] He also trained Niʿmatullāh bin Munāsib, who went to become the madrasa director of Izh-Būbī village in Viatka province, a position that would pass to Niʿmatullāh's son, ʿAbdalʿallām in 1845, and then to Niʿmatullāh's grandson, ʿAbdullāh Būbī, in 1901.[64] However, in the context of the second half of the nineteenth century, ʿAbdullāh al-Chirtūshī's most important student was Muḥammad Dhākir bin ʿAbdalwahhāb aṣ-Ṣāṣnāwī, shaykh and director of a large madrasa in the town of Chistopol.[65]

Reconstructing a Rural Elite Network

When taken together, ʿAbdullāh al-Chirtūshī, the Ūtamishevs, the Āpānāevs, the Tūntārīs, and the Tūqāyevs constituted stable nodes in a regional social network. This network included Kazan's Second, Sixth, and Eighth mahallas, Chistopol, Malmyzh, and the villages of Machkara, Tūntār, Qūrṣā, Qıshqār, Istarlībāsh, Tāshkichū, Izh-Būbī, and Ṣāṣnā.

As they built their network, the Machkarans did two things very well. First, they worked through local politics, influential merchants, and gatherings of the regional ʿulamāʾ to have their students appointed to important posts in and around Kazan. Second, they excelled at self-promotion. Their madrasas gained reputations as great centers of learning in the Volga-Ural region and attracted students from as far away as Siberia and the Kazakh steppe. From the 1860s onward, they produced a body of odes, silsilas, and eulogies praising their living and departed colleagues. Eulogies listed relatives, students, teachers, and colleagues, emphasizing the ties among those within the network and binding them to the network's exalted history.

In their quest for social authority, the Machkarans thoroughly supported Bulghar historical narratives and expanded on them to make space for their own ancestors in them. Ḥusayn Amirkhanov's *Tawārīkh-i Bulghāriyya*, published in 1883, presented a narrative that wove together the story of the Islamic conversion at Bulghar with the history of the ʿulamāʾ and Sufi shaykhs of the late 1700s and 1800s. The scholars of the Machkara network and its branches were not the only ones to appear in Amirkhanov's history, but they occupied a significant amount of space. Amirkhanov dedicated a full page to the madrasa directors of Machkara village, about a page and half to the Tūqāyevs of Istarlībāsh, more than three pages to Abū'n-Nāsr, ʿAbdalkhalīq al-Qūrṣāwī, and ʿAbdalkhalīq's son-in-law, Ḥasan.[66]

The Machkarans and Their Madrasas

Madrasas were central to the maintenance and expansion of the Machkaran ʿulamāʾ's authority. Madrasas served as the sites at which teachers and students met and formed lifelong relationships. Through these relationships, new members (newcomers as well as sons of the network) were socialized into the culture of the network and learned its history and its internal politics. The madrasa was the setting in which future network members mastered the skills they would require to present themselves to the broader Muslim community as authoritative in the fields of Islamic law, doctrine, ritual, and philosophy.

Although the Machkarans were bound together by their relationships to specific teachers, they did not adopt a single template for education. All madrasas, and not just those within the Machkara network, began with the teaching of Arabic morphology and syntax, without which the student could not proceed through the rest of the curriculum. These books were themselves written in Arabic or Persian, so the student learned to read in the language as he learned the rules of the language. Arabic grammar books were not meant to be read in solitude, but in the presence of an instructor (most likely a senior student or teaching assistant), who could guide the new student through the text.

Having mastered the Arabic grammar books, the student could proceed to the books of admonition (*wa'ẓ*), such as *'Ayn al-'Ilm*, and the basic jurisprudential manuals, such as *Mukhtaṣar al-Wiqāya* and *Mukhtaṣar al-Qudūrī*, and to foundations of jurisprudence (*uṣūl al-fiqh*). Through these books, again with the mediation of an instructor, the student learned the Hanafī legal school's accepted rulings on various questions of ritual, family law, economic law, and sumptuary law. He also learned the proofs (*dalil*) for these rulings. This information would be of the most practical use to a madrasa graduate in his professional life, because much of his time as an imam would be consumed answering basic legal questions and resolving disputes for the people of his maḥalla. In this capacity, his main task, from a juridical perspective, would be to identify the most acceptable solution within the Hanafī madhhab to a legal problem and not to formulate a new answer based on original legal reasoning (ijtihād).[67]

The student was also trained in the books of Aristotelian logic (*manṭiq*), such as *Isāghūjī* and *Sullam al-'Ulūm*, and in speculative theology (kalām). Skills in these fields, together with advanced knowledge of Arabic grammar and a thorough understanding of Hanafī jurisprudence, helped a student to build a reputation as a great scholar. With them, he could wrestle with difficult questions of jurisprudence and theology and prove his mettle in public dispute (*munāẓara*).

Machkara Madrasa, managed by Muḥammad Raḥīm and then 'Abdullāh al-Chirtūshī, reached the peak of its influence and popularity in the mid-1800s. A notebook compiled by students at Machkara Madrasa in the 1850s offers a glimpse of the curriculum for that period. The notebook, composed entirely in Arabic and Persian, includes multiple tracts on how to distribute inheritance. The tracts include charts and equations to be used in various scenarios for dividing property among heirs.[68] These tables, formulas, and calculations provide valuable insight into how mathematics was taught in the mid-nineteenth-century madrasa—that is, as part of inheritance law, which was in turn part of the students' education in jurisprudence. Mathematical training included basic arithmetic (addition, subtraction, multiplication, and division) and the application of the theoretical models of property division established in Islamic law (often expressed in terms of fractions and proportions) to concrete sums of money. The ability to calculate sums and work with money, though taught in the context of inheritance division, was readily transferable to other occupations that demanded arithmetic and bookkeeping skills.

Tūntār Madrasa's reputation rose to new heights under the directorship of ʿAlī at-Tūntārī. His years of study and travel in Central Asia and India had helped him perfect his Persian-language skills. Persian language figured prominently in the curriculum of his madrasa. Students copied down Persian-language poems to help them memorize the basic obligations incumbent on Muslims and major points of Muslim theology.[69] This strong focus on Persian language granted the students access to Persian literature on law and theology and prepared them for their future studies in Bukhara.

In addition to Persian, ʿAlī at-Tūntārī used vernacular-language texts to teach basic doctrine and theology. One such text, copied down by Tūntār Madrasa students in the 1850s or 1860s and entitled "The Meaning of Faith," instructed students in the meaning of the profession of faith (*shahāda*) using a combination of linguistic analysis and didactic stories.[70] The same notebook includes other texts in the Turki vernacular, among them a text entitled "Dogmatics in Verse" (*ʿAqīda Manẓuma*) and a brief Qurʾānic commentary (tasfīr).[71] The presence of such vernacular texts suggests that the use of Turki as a language of reading and instruction in the madrasas predated the education reforms of the 1880s. ʿAlī at-Tūntārī was also known for his knowledge of theology and jurisprudence.[72]

By the time ʿAlī at-Tūntārī's son-in-law, Shamsaddīn bin Raḥmatullāh, began to teach at Tūntār Madrasa in the 1860s and 1870s, instruction was offered in arithmetic, algebra, and astronomy.[73] Shamsaddīn's son, Muḥammad Najīb Shamseddinov, recalled his father as a lover of astronomy, who would take his children and students outside in the evening to teach them the names and positions of the stars.[74] Shamsaddīn was also deeply interested in medicine. He kept a large personal library of medical books, including a Latin-Russian dictionary of medical terms, and was known to order medications from as far away as Istanbul.[75] He was also a reader of newspapers, subscribing to *Turkestan Wilayate Gazetası*.[76]

Qıshqār Madrasa, under the directorship of Ismāʿīl Ūtamishev from 1846 to 1888, was among the most highly regarded of the Machkara-affiliated madrasas in the second half of the nineteenth century. Ismāʿīl adopted the Machkaran curriculum but also added books that were not taught at Machkara. Students traveled from Siberia and the Kazakh steppe to study with him.[77] The Machkarans themselves touted the madrasa's reputation, listing it alongside Cairo, Damascus, and Istanbul, and "Dāmallā Ismāʿīl" was much loved by his students.[78]

Early twentieth-century jurist and Ismāʿīl's niece's husband, ʿĀlimjān Bārūdī, later criticized Ismāʿīl for his tendency to accept the rulings given in the classic Hanafī law books without evaluating the methods by which they were reached. Muḥammad Najīb Shamseddinov also remarked on Ismāʿīl's firm adherence to the Hanafī madhhab.[79] However, this was standard approach to Islamic jurisprudence in the Volga-Ural region and Central Asia in the mid-1800s. Bārūdī also criticized Ismāʿīl for not traveling more extensively in the Islamic world (i.e., further than Bukhara) to put himself in touch with the latest trends in Islamic jurisprudence, but this remark reveals more about Bārūdī's generation of scholars than about Ismāʿīl's competence.[80] By the standards of the mid-1800s, Ismāʿīl's Bukharan education would have been considered state of the art.

In general, Ismāʿīl Ūtamishev does not fare well in the biographical dictionaries of the early 1900s. Riḍāʾaddīn bin Fakhraddīn accused him of sophistry, recalling how he justified collecting interest on the money he placed in Russian banks by arguing that Russia was the Abode of War, and therefore Islamic laws forbidding the collection of interest did not apply.[81] However, another way of viewing this remark is to point out that Ismāʿīl, a prominent Muslim scholar of the mid-1800s, interacted freely with Russian economic institutions, making the journey to town several times per year to collect his interest payments and dividends.

One of the reasons that Ismāʿīl attracted such ire from early twentieth-century scholars was that he was a master of all the skills that nineteenth-century scholars most valued. As these skills fell out of favor with scholars of the early 1900s, Ismāʿīl was cast as the embodiment of everything they rejected.

Nowhere is this tendency more obvious than in the field of public dispute. Ismāʿīl was an expert debater, and Qıshqār Madrasa graduates were renowned beyond all others for their oratory skills. They were apparently such impressive rhetoricians and debaters that even their rivals and critics grudgingly acknowledged their level of accomplishment. Jamaladdīn Valīdov, writing in the early Soviet period, recalled an earlier encounter between his madrasa director, ʿAbdullāh Būbī, and a Qıshqār graduate:

> The Qıshqārans, with whom none of the other Tatar madrasas could compete in the field of "rationalism" (*ʿaqlīyat*), were, in general, poor students of Arabic language, but this did not stop them from being good orators and rhetoricians. To this day, I cannot forget how one Qıshqāran "debater" (*munāẓir*) laid out his dissenting views to our madrasa director and the way he knew how to

> carry himself freely in the midst of all that and how we students looked on enviously and, for a long time, could not bring ourselves to interrupt his fluent and sonorous speech.[82]

Validov's awe at the Qıshqāran's skill says much about the level of education instituted by Ismāʿīl Ūtamishev at Qıshqār Madrasa. Educated at reformist Būbī Madrasa, Validov had been conditioned to scorn the style of education offered at mid-nineteenth-century madrasas. His praise suggests that, even in the early 1900s, more than a decade after Ismāʿīl's death, when the culture of learning he had championed was under fire by reformers, Qıshqār's students had lost none of their edge. They continued to devastate their opponents in public disputes. As will be seen in later chapters, one of the only ways that early twentieth-century legal reformers could avoid this sort of rout was to refuse to engage in such competitions. Instead, they attempted to delegitimize them.

Conclusion

Adeeb Khalid, in his study of the Jadids in Russian-ruled Central Asia, turns to Pierre Bourdieu's theory of *habitas* to defend the pre-reform maktabs and madrasas. In this way, he presents the difference between nineteenth-century Central Asian education and Jadid education as one of kind rather than quality. The curricula and teaching methods of Central Asian maktabs and madrasas were well suited to socializing young Muslim men into their communities and transmitting the cultural capital they required to participate in adult society. Central Asian Jadids believed that the habits, values, and knowledge that these educational institutions instilled were a poor fit for Central Asian society as it was developing under Russian rule, and they sought to replace the old culture capital with a new one.[83]

While Khalid's invoking of *habitas* is a useful way of considering education in Central Asia, it risks implying that the value of nineteenth-century Muslim education must be explicated through academic theory because it is otherwise not immediately obvious. Machkaran education certainly harmonizes with Khalid's view on *habitas*; studying at madrasas such as Machkara, Tūntār, or Qıshqār socialized young people into a patronage network and provided the skills they would need to assume a specific role in their community as adults. However, Machkaran education was also provided many of the same applied skills that post-1880s reformers would claim to have introduced into Muslim education. Mathematics was very much part of the nineteenth-century madrasa curriculum, and students still gained enough mastery of it to pursue careers as managers and accountants in nineteenth-century Muslim trading firms. Similarly, madrasa students did not display difficulty writing in their native tongue. They learned to write by reading examples of "good" writing (often Chagatay poetry), memorizing them, imitating them, and eventually composing texts of their own. In terms of Arabic instruction, the Machkaran madrasas did not teach conversational Arabic, but that was not their purpose. They imparted grammar and classical Arabic, which enabled a generation of scholars to analyze juridical and theological problems and to record their conclusions. The best Islamic scholars of the nineteenth-century Volga-Ural region were men of accomplishment not only within their villages but also across their native region and beyond. More than a few found that their madrasa-imparted skills were transferable to other lines of work.

The greatest difference between the treatment of these subjects in the nineteenth-century madrasas and in the reformed madrasas of the post-1880s was that nineteenth-century madrasa directors and students did not view mathematics, astronomy, medicine, literature, history, and geography as disciplines distinct from "Islamic" learning. They were taught not simply beside jurisprudence, theology, and doctrine, but as part of those fields. The opposition of "religious" knowledge to "worldly," "secular," "European," or "universal" knowledge did not exist within the walls of the pre-1880s madrasas. Rather, it was all "science" (*ʿilm*). Acquisition of ʿilm was what separated the scholar (*ʿalīm*) from his less-educated fellow believers.

Another aspect of mid-nineteenth-century Machkaran education that differentiated it from post-1880s education was its classist nature. The pursuit of knowledge was a luxury rather than a right or an obligation. Those with the most opportunity to master ʿilm came from prominent families and possessed powerful patrons. As Riḍāʾaddīn bin Fakhraddīn stated rather bitterly in his biography of Ismāʿīl Ūtamishev, he could not judge Ismāʿīl's debating skills because "poor students" like him were not invited to the gatherings that Ismāʿīl frequented.[84] Not every imam or imam's son had the time and money to indulge his passion for horses, feed hungry peasants, or gaze at the stars. The great ʿulamāʾ of the Machkaran network were in effect a Muslim rural gentry. They claimed that their status was justified by their outstanding accomplishments in the Islamic sciences, but in fact it was their privileged place within their networks that enabled them to pursue advanced training in those sciences in the first place. The Machkaran network would face its own crisis, but that crisis would not come from Russia or Europe. Rather, it would emerge from contradictions inherent in the network itself. The Machkaran network and its educational institutions would eventually become victims of their own success.

Notes

1. "Machkara dāmallāsınā khātı," NBRT-ORRK No. 499T.

2. Shihābaddīn al-Marjāni, *Qism ath-Thānī min Kitāb Mustafād al-Akhbār fī aḥwāl Qazān wa Bulghār* (Kazan: Tipo-Litografiia Imperatorskago Universiteta, 1900), 161.

3. Ibid.

4. Rizaeddin Fäkhreddin, *Asar*, ed. Raif Märdanov and Ramil Mingnullin (Kazan: Rukhiyat, 2006), 83, 109. M. M. ar-Ramzī, *Talfīq al-Akhbār wa Talqīḥ al-Athār fī Waqā'i' Qazān wa Bulghār wa Mulūk al-Tatār* (Orenburg: Karīmov, Ḥusaynov wa sharkāsī, n.d.), 420–21.

5. Shihābaddīn al-Marjāni, *Qism ath-Thānī min Kitāb Mustafād al-Akhbār*, 161.

6. Ibid., 83, 109.

7. Frank notes that the father of the author of *Tawārīkh-i Barangawiyya* studied at Machkara. (Allen J. Frank, *Bukhara and the Muslims of the Russian Empire: Sufism, Education, and the Paradox of Islamic* Prestige [Leiden: Brill, 2012], 18). He also notes that a stone mosque was constructed in Machkara in 1872 at the cost of seven thousand rubles (Allen J. Frank, *Muslim Religious Institutions in Imperial Russia: Islamic World of Novouzenek District and the Kazakh Inner Horde, 1780–1910* [Boston: Brill, 2001], 208). The most complete examination of Machkara and its influence in nineteenth-century Kazan society can be found in A. Khabutdinov, *Instituty rossiiskogo musul'manskogo soobshchestva v Volgo-Uralskom regione* (Moscow: Izdatel'stvo "Mardzhani," 2013).

8. Shihābaddīn al-Marjāni, *Al-Qism ath-Thānī min Kitāb Mustafād al-Akhbār*, 159–60. This mosque stood until 1871, when it was gutted by a fire. It was a rebuilt a year later by 'Abdullāh's grandson, Iṣḥāq.

9. Fäkhreddin, *Asar*, 83.

10. Ibid., 67.

11. Rizaeddin Fäkhreddin, *Asar: Öchenche häm dürtenche tom*, ed. Liliya Baibulatova et al. (Kazan: Rukhiyat, 2010), 144; On Abū'n-Nāṣr al-Qūrṣāwī and the debate over the divine attributes, see Nathan Spannaus, "Islamic Thought and Reformism in the Russian Empire: An Intellectual Biography of Abu Nasr Qursawi (1776–1812)" (PhD diss., McGill University, 2013).

12. Shihābaddīn al-Marjānī, *Qism ath-Thānī min Kitāb Mustafād al-Akhbār*, 38.

13. Ibid., 176–77; Fäkhreddin, *Asar*, 183.

14. Ḥusayn Amirkhanov, *Tawārīkh-i Bulghāriyya* (St. Petersburg: n.p., 1883), 52.

15. Fäkhreddin, *Asar: ikenche tom*, ed. Ilshat Gyimadiev, Ramil Minggnullin, and Sirinä Bahavieva (Kazan: Rukhiyat, 2009), 135–36; Shihābaddīn al-Marjānī, *Qism ath-Thānī min Kitāb Mustafād al-Akhbār*, 177–78.

16. Shihābaddīn al-Marjānī, *Qism ath-Thānī min Kitāb Mustafād al-Akhbār*, 98.

17. Fäkhreddin, *Asar: Ikenche tom*, 79–80.

18. Shahr Sharaf, *Marjānī* (Kazan: Magārif, 1915), 58; Fäkhreddin, *Asar*, 68.
19. Fäkhreddin, *Asar: Öchenche häm dürtenche tom*, 146; M. M. ar-Ramzī, *Talfīq al-Akhbār wa Talqīḥ al-Athār*, 478.
20. Shihābaddīn al-Marjānī, *Qism ath-Thānī min Kitāb Mustafād al-Akhbār*, 61–62.
21. Ibid., 107.
22. L. Deviatykh, "Apanaevy," *Iz istorii Kazanskogo Kupechestva* (Kazan: Titl-Kazan', 2005), 134–36.
23. Ibid., 136–37.
24. Shihābaddīn al-Marjānī, *Qism ath-Thānī min Kitāb Mustafād al-Akhbār*, 39.
25. Ibid., 167.
26. Deviatykh, "Apanaevy," 136–37.
27. Ibid.,137.
28. "Apanaevskaia Mechet'," *Tatarskaia Entsiklopedia*, ed. M. Kh. Khasanov (Kazan: Institut Tatarskoi Entsiklopedii, 2006) 1:164–65; "Kasimiia Madrasa," *Tatarskaia Entsiklopedia*, 3:257.
29. "Wālī Āpānāev belan Naʿima Ūtamishevning aerilshūlarī turinda dokument (1870)," NBRT-ORRK, No. 962T.
30. "Apanaev, Gabdulla Abdukarimovich," *Tatarskaia Entsiklopedia*, 1:164.
31. Muḥammad Shākir Tūqāyev, *Tārīkh-i Istarlībāsh* (Kazan: n.p., 1899), 6.
32. Ibid., 6; Fäkhreddin, *Asar*, 11.
33. Tūqāyev, *Tārīkh-i Istarlībāsh*, 7.
34. Ibid., 5–7.
35. Ibid., 7.
36. Ibid., 8.
37. Ibid., 9.
38. Ibid., 10.
39. Ibid., 10.
40. *Islam na Evropeiskon Vostoke: Entsiklopedicheskii slovar'*, ed. R. A. Nabiev (Kazan: Izdatel'stvo "Magarif", 2004), 323.
41. Ibid., 12–13.
42. Ibid., 10. On ʿAbdalwaḥid bin Sulaymān, see Fäkhreddin, *Asar: Ikenche tom*, 90. On Salimgarey Tevkelev, see Fäkhreddin, *Asar: Öchenche häm dürtenche tom*, 128.
43. Fäkhreddin, *Asar: Öchenche häm dürtenche tom*, 16–42.
44. Ibid., 17–8, 21, 30; "Qasīda Madaḥa Shaykhinā wa Ustādhinā Ustādh al-Kull Ishān ʿAlī Muḥammad at-Tūntārī," Institut iazyka, literatury i iskusstva (hereafter IIALI), f. 39, op. 1, del. 3772, l. 29; Muḥammad Najīb Tūntārī, "Tūntār awilī," NBRT-ORRK No. 828T, 12; Amirkhanov, *Tawārīkh-i Bulghāriyya*, 50.
45. Fäkhreddin, *Asar: Öchenche häm dürtenche tom*, 18–19; Tūntārī, "Tūntār awılı," 14–15.
46. R. Sh. Zaripov, *Gali Ishan, Ishmi Ishan häm Tüntär mädräsäse* (Kazan: n.p., 2002), 6.
47. Ibid., 20; [Aqmulla], *Dāmallā Shihābaddīn Ḥaḍrateneng Marthiyyase*, 11.
48. Tūntārī, "Tūntār awilī," 14.
49. Zaripov, *Gali Ishan*, 11.
50. Tūntārī, "Tūntār awilī,"14.
51. Ibid., 14.
52. Ibid.
53. Agnés Nilüfer Kefeli, *Becoming Muslim in Imperial Russia: Conversion, Apostasy, and Literacy* (Ithaca, NY: Cornell University Press, 2014), 134–35.

54. Sharaf, *Marjānī*, 80–83.
55. Ibid., 18–19.
56. Fäkhreddin, *Asar: Öchenche häm dürtenche tom*, 87–88.
57. Zaripov, *Gali Ishan*, 11.
58. Tūntārī, "Tūntār awilī," 7.
59. Fäkhreddin, *Asar: Öchenche häm dürtenche tom*, 348–49.
60. Ibid., 16–17.
61. Fäkhreddin, *Asar: Ikenche tom*, 79.
62. Ibid., 80.
63. Ibid., 5–6, 105–6; Fäkhreddin, *Asar: Öchenche häm dürtenche tom*, 97–98; *Kitāb Sham' aḍ-Ḍīyā' fī tadkira qaum ahl aḍ-ḍīyā'* (Kazan: Vyacheslav, 1883), 6–7.
64. Fäkhreddin, *Asar: Ikenche tom*, 80; Fäkhreddin, *Asar: Öchenche häm dürtenche tom*, 375; Gabdulla Bubyi, "Bubyi mädräsäseneng kyska tarikhı," *Bertugan Bubyilar häm Izh-Bubyi mädräsäse: tarikhi-dokumental' jyentyk*, ed. Raif Märdanov, Ramil Mingnullin, and Söläyman Räkhimov (Kazan: Rukhiyat, 1999), 16–18.
65. Fäkhreddin, *Asar: Ikenche tom*, 80.
66. Amirkhanov, *Tawārīkh-i Bulghāriyya*, 43, 45–47, 52–54.
67. As in mid-nineteenth-century Central Asia, the madrasa directors of the mid-nineteenth-century Volga-Ural region tended to approach fiqh as "content rather than as a methodology." Students were expected to master the compendia of past legal opinions of the Hanafī madhhab and know when to apply them, and not to formulate their own, original legal decisions (see Paolo Sartori, "Ijtihād in Bukhara: Central Asian Jadidism and Local Genealogies of Cultural Change," *Journal of the Economic and Social History of the Orient* 59 [2016]).
68. "'Abdaljabbār bin Mullā 'Abdalḥakīm ham Bahā'addīn bin Mullā Sirājaddīn, Machkara madrasase daftare, 1854," IIaLI, f. 39, op. 1, del. 5942.
69. "Shah-i Aḥmad bin Batirshah ham Fatḥullāh bin Ḥabībullāh, "Tūntār madrasase daftare," IIaLI, f. 39, op. 1. del. 3772, l. 1–70b.
70. Ibid., 18ob-27.
71. Ibid., 8ob-11ob, 15–15ob.
72. [Aqmullā], *Dāmallā Shihābaddīn Ḥaḍrateneng Marthiyyase*, 11.
73. Ibid., 16.
74. Ibid.
75. Ibid.
76. Ibid.
77. Fäkhreddin, *Asar: Öchenche häm dürtenche tom*, 146.
78. [Aqmullā], *Dāmallā Shihābaddīn Ḥaḍrateneng Marthiyyase*, 8; "Ismā'īl al-Qıshqārī marthiyyase," IIaLI, f. 39, op. 1, del. 2768, l. 269.
79. Tūntārī, "Tūntār awılı," 14.
80. Fäkhreddin, *Asar: Öchenche häm dürtenche tom*, 146.
81. Ibid.
82. Dzhamaliutdin Validov, *Ocherki istorii obrazovannosti i literatury Tatar* (Kazan: Izdatel'stvo "Iman," 1998), 42.
83. Adeeb Khalid, *The Politics of Muslim Cultural Reform: Jadidism in Central Asia* (Berkeley: University of California Press, 1998), 20–21.
84. Fäkhreddin, *Asar: Öchenche häm dürtenche tom*, 147.

5

KNOWLEDGE, HISTORY WRITING, AND BECOMING COLONIAL

THE 1860S MARKED A DECISIVE TURNING POINT IN both the relationship between the Russian state and the Kazan Tatar ʿulamāʾ as well as in the ʿulamāʾ's internal politics. There was no single event that drove this shift. Rather, it was shaped by a convergence of international, imperial, and regional factors. Kazan's Muslims entered the 1850s having experienced half a century of rising literacy, expansion of education institutions, and growing popular engagement with Islam. By the 1860s, they found themselves caught between two new forces: European colonial domination of the Islamic world and Russia's Great Reforms. These two forces led some Russian Muslim scholars to question the viability of Islamic intellectual culture, the role of the ʿulamāʾ, and the very sources of knowledge and truth.

Allen Frank has termed the ʿulamāʾ debates of the late 1800s and early 1900s a "manufactured crisis."[1] Indeed, the roots of the crisis that shook Volga-Ural Muslim society in the 1850s and 1860s were not as obvious as the origins of similar crises among the Kazakhs and the Central Asians. Volga-Ural Muslims experienced neither European conquest in the mid-1800s nor the culmination of a longer process of disempowerment. Rather, their crisis was a psychological one, a moment of realization that the broader Islamic world with which they identified was under siege. Fierce debates broke out among Kazan's ʿulamāʾ over the role of Russian language, the efficiency of nineteenth-century teaching methods, and the relationship between Muslims and Russian-speaking societies. The fabric of Kazan ʿulamāʾ society and its narratives of community identity were rent by these conflicts and were never fully mended. For imperial officials, the motives of the Kazan

Tatars, who shared a faith with more recently conquered Muslim peoples elsewhere in the empire, became increasingly suspect.

A Son of the Machkara Network

Shihābaddīn al-Marjānī was born into a family with deep roots in the powerful networks of Kazan province. His father, Baha'addīn (1786–1856), the son of Subḥān al-Marjānī, was a student of Muhammad Raḥīm bin Yūsuf of Machkara, and traced his lineage back to 'Abdalqudūs, founder of Marjān village in Kazan province.[2] After studying in his native Baraska and then in Ashıt village, Baha'addīn set out for Bukhara in 1812. He studied with prominent teachers and established a relationship with the Bukharan amir. Amir Haydar reportedly provided him with a room at Mella Tursunjan's madrasa and rendered him other forms of assistance. In 1815, when Baha'addīn prepared to return to Russia, Amir Haydar supposedly appealed to him to remain in Bukhara. When Baha'addīn refused, the amir presented him a year's salary as a parting gift.[3]

Upon returning home, Baha'addīn married Bībī Ḥabība, the daughter of 'Abdannaṣīr bin Sayfalmulūk al-Jabalī, his former teacher from Ashıt village. A year later, at the request of a local merchant, Baha'addīn was appointed imam and madrasa director of Yabınchı village. In 1821, he relocated to Tāshkichū village, where Shihābaddīn spent his youth. In 1822, Bībī Ḥabība died giving birth to the family's fourth child. A year after her death, Baha'addīn remarried, this time to his late wife's sister, Bībī Ḥubayda, reestablishing the kinship bond between him and his old teacher, 'Abdannaṣīr.[4]

Shihābaddīn al-Marjānī grew up surrounded by 'ulamā'. He inherited from his paternal grandfather, Subḥān, a love of history. His maternal grandfather, 'Abdannaṣīr, hailed from a family that traced its lineage back to Murtaḍa bin 'Ali al-Bulghārī, an ally and sympathizer of the late seventeenth-century scholar, Murtaḍa as-Simetī. 'Abdannaṣīr was also a disciple of Shaykh Ḥabībullāh al-Ūriwī.[5] Baha'addin and 'Abdannaṣīr were deeply engaged in the political and intellectual conflicts that divided the 'ulamā' in the early 1800s. Amid the controversies surrounding Mufti Khusainov, Baha'addin joined the ranks of those who spoke highly of Khusainov's intelligence and skill as a jurist.[6] 'Abdannaṣīr, a former student of Shaykh Ḥabibullah, held a less favorable view of the first mufti. When conflict emerged over Abū'n-Naṣr al-Qūrṣāwī's view on the divine attributes,

Baha'addin, a supporter of Amir Haydar, sided against Qūrṣāwī and reportedly said on more than one occasion that Amir Haydar should have killed Qūrṣāwī while he had the chance.[7]

At age twenty-one, Shihābaddīn al-Marjānī set out for Bukhara by caravan. He spent ten years in Bukhara and Samarkand, studying in the madrasas, attending gatherings of students and teachers in the evenings, reading new books, and finally working as a junior instructor.[8] In 1849, he returned to Russia.[9] Two months later, he was put forward by merchant Ibrāhīm Yūnusov to serve as the imam of Kazan's First Mosque. Before sending Marjānī to take the licensing exam in Ufa, Yūnusov called a meeting of the prominent 'ulamā' of Kazan province. At the meeting, the scholars asked Marjānī numerous questions to test his knowledge of Islamic law, doctrine, and philosophy, but several men took his side, including 'Alī at-Tūntārī. Marjānī was found fit to serve as imam of Kazan's First Stone Mosque and was sent to the OMSA to take his official exam.[10]

The New Student: Marjānī and Fayḍkhānov

Marjānī's career took a new turn with his relationship with a student. Ḥusayn Fayḍkhānov, born in 1828, came from the Mishar village of Sabachay in Simbirsk province. Unlike Marjānī, he was not well connected within Kazan 'ulamā' circles. He was a peasant's son whose intelligence had caught the attention of his teachers and set him on the road to a career in the 'ulamā'. He traveled to Kazan, where he hoped to gain the education and the social contacts necessary to secure a respectable post. When he began to study with Marjānī in the early 1850s, he was only ten years younger than his teacher.[11]

In the 1850s, Kazan was a thriving cultural center. Its university, then the easternmost of the imperial universities, was located close to Russia's Asiatic borderlands. The city and the surrounding countryside boasted large Turkic-speaking and Muslim populations. As a historical center of Orthodox missionary activity in Russia's east, it was the home of an Orthodox ecclesiastical academy and was the urban center closest to the sites of the *inorodtsy* apostasies of the nineteenth century.[12] It became a center for a small but influential Orthodox clergy and imperial officialdom concerned with the problem of administering populations of Muslims and ethnic non-Russians.[13] Its Asiatic Press, Russia's oldest Arabic-script printing facility, published the Qur'ān and Islamic law books, popular Islamic literature, and Tatar-language grammars.

Kazan was the intellectual center of Russia's colonial project. By the mid-nineteenth century, that project had expanded in focus from territorial acquisition to orientalist concerns with knowing, mapping, and ruling the diverse population of the empire's southern and eastern frontiers. Linguists, ethnographers, and archaeologists affiliated with the city's educational institutions and scholarly societies compiled information on local languages and cultures that was used by the Ecclesiastical Academy's Anti-Islam department to discourage apostasy or by bureaucrats assigned to administer non-Russian provinces.[14] Broad categories such as Muslim, Tatar, and inorodtsy were broken down into ethnic groups defined by their specific dialects, clothing, and day-to-day cultural practices. Kazan produced orientalists who were posted elsewhere in the empire, the most notable example being Nikolai Ostroumov, who went on to play a prominent role in the administration of Russian Turkestan.[15]

Local non-Russians played a significant role in the compilation of orientalist knowledge. Kazan Tatar ʿulamāʾ and their students volunteered their services as interpreters, messengers, and cultural intermediaries, as they had done in the previous century. However, their interactions and experiences were different than they had been in the 1700s. With the growth of Kazan's Russian educational and cultural institutions, Muslims were drawn into the orbit of Russian academic conferences, scholarly societies, and universities.[16] This new world was characterized by fascination with empirical research, positivism, and concepts such as individual consciousness, historical progress, and humankind's mastery over the natural world. Muslim scholars discovered that if they could embrace such ideas, they could be accepted into Russian-language orientalist circles.

Not long after arriving at Marjānī's madrasa, Fayḍkhānov began to attend lectures at Kazan University. His knowledge of Arabic and Persian caught the attention of orientalists A. K. Kazem-bek and I. I. Berezin.[17] In 1854, these two men helped Fayḍkhānov to secure a job as a lecturer of Tatar and Turkish language at Kazan University. A year later, he received a similar job at St. Petersburg University and left Kazan for the imperial capital city. By 1859, he joined the Russian Archaeological Society and in 1863 became a state lecturer.[18]

Fayḍkhānov's entry into the world of Russian orientalism transformed him. In 1854, he had been a madrasa student, seemingly destined to pursue a career in Islamic law. Over the next decade, he exchanged research notes with V. V. Vel'iaminov-Zernov, wrote letters to V. V. Grigor'ev and

D. Khvol'son, and socialized with Moscow archeologist Count A. S. Uvarov.[19] With his move to St. Petersburg, Fayḍkhānov discovered the fields of cataloguing and book acquisition and was soon sending inquiries to libraries, private collections, and archives in Europe and the Ottoman empire, seeking manuscripts and scholarly works to add to the university collection.[20]

Through all this, Fayḍkhānov did not forget his former teacher, Marjānī. He wrote numerous letters to him, expressing excitement over the resources, people, and possibilities he found in St. Petersburg. The two men corresponded regularly, discussing conditions in Kazan as well as the latest theories and discoveries in the fields of Russian ethnography and archeology. Fayḍkhānov regularly forwarded new books and manuscripts to Marjānī and encouraged Marjānī to send him the titles of books he needed, so that Fayḍkhānov could purchase them. In 1856, Fayḍkhānov, traveling through western Europe for the first time, noted: "Oh, the works of these states! In Europe, it doesn't matter where a book was first printed; you'll be able to buy it within two months. Here, the stores have catalogues. Whatever kind of book is published here gets to be known throughout Europe. They print up whole catalogues of the books they keep in their libraries. If you can't find a copy of it, then you can get a friend to copy it for you and mail it to you."[21]

During Fayḍkhānov's trip, other aspects of western European life also made a deep impression on him. He was quick to share his excitement with Marjānī: "In the natural sciences and mathematics, their efforts and mastery are unquestionable, and they advance further every day. If there is a new question in mathematics, it is written about in all the newspapers and it will be the object of every European scholar's attention. Everyone busies himself with proofs and questions at his own level of knowledge. Finally, after the discussions and research of several thousand scholars, the question is answered."[22]

Fayḍkhānov returned to Russia fascinated not only by the kinds of knowledge that Europeans had mastered and accumulated, but also by the technologies that existed for disseminating information and the ways in which those technologies allowed scholars to collaborate. This willingness (and technological ability) to exchange ideas contrasted sharply with the world that he and Marjānī knew, a world in which knowledge was jealously guarded and carefully transmitted from teacher to student and in which reputations were made and broken by public scholarly dispute. Competition, dispute, and petty rivalry were, of course, part of the European scholarly world as well, but Fayḍkhānov, as a visitor, did not linger long enough to notice. His critiques of Muslim intellectual life were based on Europe as he imagined it rather than Europe as it was.

Fayḍkhānov's introduction to the Russian and western European academies took place against the backdrop of what was, for many parts of the Muslim world, the most turbulent part of the nineteenth century. From 1853 to 1856, the Crimean War between Russia and Britain brought new misfortunes to the peninsula's Muslim population. Men, women, and children were imprisoned as potential British agents or were deported to other Russian provinces. Thousands of Muslims fled Crimea for the Ottoman empire.[23] The British brutally suppressed the Indian Rebellion of 1857 and all but cleansed Islam from Delhi, imprisoning or exiling Muslim jurists and students and demolishing the city's madrasas.[24] In Central Asia, the Russians moved slowly but implacably south, seizing Ak-Mechet from the Khoqandis in 1853, establishing a fortress at Vernyi in 1854, and strengthening their hold over the Kazakh steppe.

Muslim governments and educated elites scrambled to hold their ground against colonial expansion. In 1856, Sultan Abdulmecid issued the *Hatt-i Humayun*, redefining citizenship in an effort to generate solidarity among his diverse subjects and halt the rising nationalist sentiments of the empire's Christian minorities. In the 1850s, the Ottoman empire opened its first state-sponsored schools for civil engineers, economists, and political scientists.[25] In Iran, from the late 1840s, Amir Kabir, sought to counteract growing Russian and British influence by enacting a series of military, administrative, and fiscal reforms.[26] In India, while Sayyid Ahmad Khan appealed to the British government to take a more tolerant approach toward its Muslim and Hindu subjects, many 'ulamā' left Delhi for towns further away from the British administration. Some went to Deoband, in northern India, where they founded a new madrasa, in which Islamic learning was combined with aspects of British school organization.[27] Their goal was no longer to win political independence from Britain, but to save what they could of their religion and culture by promoting correct Islamic knowledge.[28]

While the Kazan 'ulamā' were not under the threat of imminent conquest, the spread of European influence through Muslim lands upended their world. Kazan Tatars may not have agreed as to whether their homeland could be considered the Abode of Islam, but they could take heart in the fact that the Abode of Islam existed in Bukhara, Delhi, Istanbul,

Damascus, and Cairo. These Muslim lands not only offered refuges to those Kazan Tatars who believed that it was unethical to live under Christian rule but provided what they imagined as a setting in which true Islamic learning persisted. It was tolerable for Islam to be imperfectly realized in Kazan and Orenburg because proper models of Islamic morality, law, and governance existed somewhere. But as the colonial powers swallowed up one Muslim state after another, the Islamic world grew smaller, and the Kazan Tatar ʿulamāʾ faced the possibility that, one day soon, there might be no more great centers of Islamic learning. Indeed, there might well be no independent Muslim societies at all.

As the Islamic world seemed under siege, the new Russian emperor, Alexander II, responded to his own state's crisis. Over the course of Nicholas I's reign, Russia had gone from being the liberator of Europe from Napoleon to losing the Crimean War. Blaming their empire's defeat on the conservative policies of the late Nicholas, the new emperor and his government set into motion the Great Reforms, a series of decrees designed to make governance more efficient, strengthen the military, and improve infrastructure across Russia. Russia's serfs were emancipated in 1865, and new administrative and judicial institutions were established to enable the government to interact more directly with its subjects. In 1864, the first zemstvos were established in thirty-four of Russia's provinces (including Kazan province) with the goal of engaging provincial elites in local governance. These new organizations turned to building and repairing roads, founding schools, and providing health care and social services to Russian subjects.[29]

By 1857, Fayḍkhānov began to take advantage of the reformist attitude of Alexander II's regime. On the model of the Tanzimat reforms in the Ottoman empire and Rifāʿa Ṭahṭāwī's activities in Egypt, he petitioned Russia's Ministry of Education for permission to open a Tatar-language newspaper, *The Morning Star* (*Chulpan*), in Kazan.[30] His proposal was rejected. Unfazed, Fayḍkhānov launched an attack on Islamic education. He proposed the establishment of a new kind of madrasa, which would adopt many of the organizational components of the Russian gymnasium (formal admission periods, grade levels, a fixed ten-year program). Instruction was to be in vernacular Tatar, and an Islamic legal curriculum was to be augmented by courses in history, geography, arithmetic, and the Russian language.

Fayḍkhānov's goal was not to turn Kazan's madrasas into gymnasia or to replace Islamic legal education with mathematics and civil engineering, but to restructure how jurists were trained and change how they would participate in Muslim society. He attacked the madrasas' emphasis on the art of debate and the monopoly that many teachers and masters claimed over their pupils' education. He argued that these two factors distanced ʿulamāʾ from Muslim society as a whole and created a class of elitists who used their esoteric education and social connections for personal gain while providing nothing of use to the broader Muslim population.[31] Fayḍkhānov's concerns reflected an interest that had grown steadily in mid nineteenth-century Russian official circles in cultivating cadres of educated professionals (doctors, veterinarians, engineers, military officers) to provide services in the empire's provinces. However, they also mirrored anxieties in both the Ottoman empire and India over the quality of Islamic education and its applicability in a colonized world. Fayḍkhānov's response to these anxieties was to call for greater measures of quality control and a formalized structure for education.

Unfortunately for Fayḍkhānov, the two main targets of his reform plan—"useless" public disputation and a clannish scholarly network—formed the backbone of ʿulamāʾ professional and social life. Networks gave structure to what was otherwise a diffuse collection of scholars scattered over hundreds of miles of territory. Teachers and students were bound together by ties of kinship, obedience, and mutual obligation. Public dispute provided the means for individual scholars to distinguish themselves as reliable bearers of Islamic knowledge. Cultivating the patronage of a senior scholar and mastering classical logic and philosophy were vital for any young man who wished to become more than an imam in a remote village. Fayḍkhānov's model turned this entire paradigm of ʿulamāʾ authority on its head. He imagined madrasa-educated men not as members of a privileged class, but as servitors, who like country doctors used their knowledge to improve the lives of common Muslims.

Aspects of Fayḍkhānov's plan found supporters, most notably Marjānī, Salimgarey Tevkelev (who became mufti of the OMSA in 1865) and Muḥammad Ḥarīth Tūqāyev, shaykh of Istarlībāsh Madrasa.[32] The plan also had its opponents, most notably Ismāʿīl Ūtamishev, director of Qıshqār Madrasa and an old friend of Marjānī. Marjānī derided Ūtamishev mercilessly for failing to support Fayḍkhānov, and the breaking of their friendship reflected a broader break among Kazan Tatar madrasa directors.[33] On one side stood those who wanted organizational change in madrasa education, a curriculum tailored to the vocational needs of the village imam, and/or a greater focus on the transmitted sciences (Qur'ān, hadith, jurisprudence) over the instrumental sciences (Arabic grammar, logic, philosophy). On the other side were those scholars who believed that the madrasas functioned satisfactorily as they were, that the instrumental sciences were vital to textual interpretation, and that the madrasas should continue to offer a classical Hanafi legal education.

Conflicts over Fayḍkhānov's school project raged through 1864, reaching such a fever pitch that in October, Fayḍkhānov wrote to Marjānī to apologize for having caused so much trouble.[34] Then, in 1866, Fayḍkhānov took six months leave from St. Petersburg University, ostensibly to conduct research on the Kazakh language. In fact, the trip to the drier environment of the Kazakh steppe was a last effort to treat his tuberculosis, which had advanced rapidly during the previous year.[35]

1866 proved a difficult year for Marjānī. In May, the Russian army dealt Bukhara a stinging defeat. It would be two more years before the emirate was fully defeated and reduced to the status of a Russian protectorate. Colonial expansion went from being a distant rumor to a very real force acting on Marjānī's former teachers, schoolmates, and friends. It affected Marjānī himself in a more indirect but psychologically crushing way. For Marjānī's generation and his father's, Bukhara had served as a sort of anchor, a place to which Kazan's Muslims could turn as a source of true Muslim learning uncorrupted by the rule of nonbelievers. However, neither holiness nor Islamic knowledge proved adequate to protect Bukhara. When faced with the full force of the Russian expansion, the Bukharans fared no better than the Muslims of Kazan had centuries earlier. Then, in autumn of 1866, Fayḍ khānov succumbed to his illness.[36]

These two tragedies, one global and the other deeply personal, fundamentally altered Marjānī's worldview. For him, Russian expansion abroad and reform at home posed very real threats to the transmission of Islamic learning and to the survival of Islam itself. In response to the prospect of the Russian state opening schools for Muslims, he wrote in the late 1860s:

> It is known that the government endeavors to open schools of this type [for non-Russians]. When that happens, there will be nothing we can do. They will be administered such they will be of no use to the Muslim community, and they will not help revitalize the [Muslims'] sciences, preserve their honor, or return their condition to what it was in days past. If the Russian government opens these schools and funds them with money from its treasury or taxes paid by its subjects, more likely than not, the teachers of philosophy will be

> Russians, they will teach in their own language and their students will imitate them in language and dress. Further, though the sciences will be Muslim, they will be taught in a foreign language, like the rest of the administration and the courses. No desire will awaken in the students to read Islamic books and they may begin to perceive that Islam is incompatible with knowledge and science, especially if they hear that from their teachers during lessons and discussions.[37]

By the late 1860s, with the Great Reforms policies underway in Kazan province and growing interest in non-Russian education among Russian educators, missionaries, and officials, non-Muslim intervention into Muslim education seemed inevitable. For Marjānī, the best that Muslims could do was to take the lead in restructuring their own institutions before the Russian ministries became too deeply involved.

The Education Disputes of the 1870s–1880s

In the years following Fayḍkhānov's death, Marjānī undertook a series of new activities. In 1867, the OMSA awarded him the ranks of *mukhtasib* and akhund. He used his new status to gather money and moral support from the wealthy merchants of his parish, purchased a plot of land, and built a new madrasa. When it was complete in fall of 1871, he and his students abandoned his former madrasa, which had been sponsored by Kazan merchant Ibrāhīm Yūnusov, for the newly constructed one. This move enraged Yūnusov, who suddenly found himself with an empty madrasa on his hands and his authority in the community preempted. Yūnusov publicly accused the people of the parish of being "sheep" and informed them that they had no right to exclude him from decisions concerning the community's Islamic institutions.[38] His remarks alienated his neighbors even further; they petitioned the OMSA to transform the mosque and madrasa into a community-managed waqf and to appoint Marjānī as its administrator. Yūnusov appealed to the new inorodtsy school inspector, V. V. Radlov, from the Ministry of Internal Affairs, to thwart Marjānī and his supporters, but in the end he was forced to accept the new order.[39]

As Marjānī fought for greater control of his madrasa, the new minister of education, Dmitri Tolstoy, grappled with his ministry's continuing failure to attract Kazan's Muslim students to government-sponsored schools. This frustration was shared by Radlov, who had recruited ʿulamāʾ to teach the Russian language in 1871, only to have the residents of Kazan's

Tatar quarters and the nearby villages harass them and try to run them out of town.[40] In 1870, a new law was passed requiring that all madrasas offer courses in the Russian language or make provisions for their students to study Russian elsewhere. Two years later, state inspectors were appointed to oversee the maktabs and madrasas.[41] This new state intervention caused heated discussions among madrasa teachers and directors, but very few madrasas complied.[42] Many madrasas could not afford to employ full-time Russian teachers.[43] Also, as popular engagement with Islam had grown during the first half of the nineteenth century, so too had popular concern over maintaining proper Islamic behavior within the community. By the 1870s, many Volga-Ural Muslims viewed Russian language and Russian-style clothing as attributes of an outside, non-Muslim culture. Kazan Muslims acted to keep the Russian *kafir*s and their culture out of the Muslim community.

Those madrasa directors who encouraged Muslims to gain fluency in Russian did not do so for the same reasons that education minister Tolstoy did. In the late 1860s, Muḥammad Ḥarīth Tūqāyev had introduced Russian language instruction into the curriculum of Istarlībāsh Madrasa.[44] Marjānī encouraged his students to sit in at university lectures and defended his own position on Russian-language fluency by arguing: "It is necessary to learn Russian. It is obligatory and necessary that the people of [one nation] living under the rule of another nation know the language of the press and the language in which the laws and regulations of the state [in which they live] are written."[45] However, Marjānī did not favor full cultural assimilation of Kazan's Muslims into Russian society: "It is [also] necessary to preserve your own language, by simply continuing to draw upon your language, poetry and customs, by not speaking Russian among yourselves and by not mixing Russian words [with Tatar]."[46]

In the early 1870s, Radlov proposed that the Ministry of Education should open a Russian-Tatar teachers' school like the ones that had been created in Simferpol and Ufa in 1870.[47] By using the Tatar vernacular as the language of instruction and inviting prominent 'ulamā' to fill some of the teaching positions, the ministry might counteract Kazan Muslims' aversion to Russian education. However, the main purpose of the school remained the same: to introduce would-be 'ulamā' to European knowledge and, in doing so, to forge a permanent relationship between the Muslim community and the Russian state in which the latter became guide and guardian to the former. Tolstoy's approach represented an innovation in the imperial government's attitudes toward Kazan's Muslims. In the eighteenth century, officials may have viewed Kazan's ʿulamāʾ as culturally alien, but those aliens had proven useful as settlers, traders, and mediators between the Russian state and the Muslim peoples on its borders. Under Tolstoy's plan, the ʿulamāʾ would remain mediators conveying Russian knowledge and culture to their communities, but the ultimate purpose of this mediation would be the transformation of Muslim society into something more closely resembling Russian society. Unlike Fayḍkhānov, Tolstoy saw no inherent value in Islamic knowledge, culture, and teaching. These things were valuable only insofar as they could be used to win Muslims' trust and draw them to the Ministry of Education's schools. Tolstoy's approach established the ministry's schools as problematic institutions for Muslim teachers concerned about the future of Islam in Russia. On the one hand, these schools offered access to Russian-language training and academic subjects that most madrasas could not afford to offer. On the other, they posed the threat of Russian encroachment into Muslim educational and cultural life.

In the 1870s, Marjānī received several invitations from Radlov to teach in the new teachers' school to be established in Kazan. Initially, Marjānī rejected these offers and focused on implementing changes within his own madrasa. In the 1870s, he instituted mandatory attendance for all students at his madrasa, issued required reading lists, and ordered books according to level of difficulty. He composed a basic code of student conduct. He also established a council of teachers and senior students charged with administering the madrasa and making decisions about the curriculum and student life.[48] All of these changes were intended to improve students' learning by creating a more rigorous study regime and improved living conditions. The problems Marjānī's reforms addressed—lack of structure and rigor, lack of student discipline, and the dilapidated state of many madrasa buildings—were the same ones that Fayḍkhānov had raised.

Radlov's and Tolstoy's Kazan Russian-Tatar Teachers' School opened in 1876. Despite his initial refusals, Marjānī eventually accepted a post at the school as a teacher of Islamic law.[49] In retrospect, he argued that he had only done so to prevent Radlov from awarding the job to a lesser, "ignorant" scholar, whose teachings would do more harm than good to Islam.[50] Marjānī was joined by Tayyib Yākhin (a former Qıshqār student), Ibrāhīm Tergulov (the scion of an Ufa service family), and Muḥammad ʿAlī Maḥmūdov (a teacher of Tatar language at one of Kazan's gymnasia).[51]

However, as Marjānī taught at the school, he began to have his doubts about the motives behind the Ministry of Education's project. He fell into conflict with the ministry's school inspectors over various topics and finally clashed with Radlov himself. The substance of their argument was the purpose of the school. Marjānī, like Fayḍkhānov, was in favor of Muslim youth pursuing other kinds of education (Russian language, pedagogy, etc.) in addition to the subjects taught in the madrasas. But he was not in favor of educating a new class of scholar-teachers who would lack strong ties to their native ethno-confessional community. As a buffer against cultural assimilation, he insisted that prospective students should be fluent and literate in their native language before they were accepted into the teachers' school.[52] Radlov, by contrast, stood by the priorities of his supervisor, Tolstoy, for whom the primary purpose of the school was to introduce future Muslim elites to the fruits of Russian culture and to forge a new kind of community leader capable of leading Kazan's Muslims into closer assimilation with Russian-speaking society.[53] Radlov did not see literacy in Tatar as necessary for achieving this end, and in 1884 he proposed that students should be admitted regardless of whether they knew how to read in Tatar. Marjānī protested the decision. When Radlov would not be swayed, Marjānī quit his job at the school.[54]

By the early 1880s, Marjānī was not the only Kazan Tatar scholar who sought to augment or restructure Muslim education in Russia. ʿAbdalqayyūm an-Naṣīrī (1825–1902) gained exposure to Russian teaching methods and school organization while teaching Tatar at Kazan's Ecclesiastical Academy. He took these sensibilities with him when he attempted to return to the Muslim community as a teacher of Russian for Muslim children and as a compiler of textbooks, folklore collections, and guidebooks for a popular audience. He found limited success in his teaching endeavor, but his textbooks and compilations on subjects as diverse as Sufism, fairytales, grammar, history, and accounting, gained such popularity that by 1906, they were granted their own section in publishers' catalogs.[55] Naṣīrī's work built on the Arabic and Tatar publishing market that had emerged since the foundation of the Asiatic Press, but he turned from the editing and printing of well-known madrasa textbooks, law books, and poems to the publication of new works that had not previously circulated in manuscript form. In this way, his activities foreshadowed the rise of a new Tatar publishing industry, which focused increasingly on bringing new works into circulation. He was also responsible for penning the first generation of printed textbooks organized in Russian/European pedagogical style but written in Turki-Tatar by a Muslim author for a Muslim audience.[56]

Meanwhile, in St. Petersburg, military akhund ʿAtaʾullah Bayazitov wrestled with the question of how to transmit reliable information about Islamic law, ritual, and doctrine to a popular audience. He identified the Arabic-language textbooks used in the madrasas as one of the main obstacles to this goal. In 1880, he published *The Book of Islam*, a textbook crafted to teach young Muslims the basics of their religion in their own language. He believed that Islamic education in the vernacular not only guaranteed that students would gain a clearer understanding of their religion but would do so more quickly than under the Arabic-heavy education system. This would free time for them to study other subjects or finish their education earlier and enter the workforce.[57]

Marjānī, Fayḍkhānov, Tūqāyev, Naṣīrī, and Bayazitov did not constitute an organized movement for Muslim education reform. They lacked either a collective identity or a unified program of action. Rather, they responded to the apparent decline of the core Islamic lands in the mid-1800s by attempting to maintain or improve the transmission of Islamic knowledge. In these efforts, they drew on education projects from other parts of the Muslim world and discussions with Russian educators. However, they also built on a base of popular literacy and educational institutions that had been growing steadily since the late 1700s. The goal of mid-nineteenth-century education reformers was to harness and direct that growth, using what they now knew about both colonial expansion and Russian imperial reform projects. The changes they made to institutional organization, study materials, and language of instruction raised larger questions about the purpose of Islamic education and the relationship between Muslim schools and the Russian state that would trouble Muslim educators and imperial officials for decades to come.

The Importance of Being Bulghar

As Marjānī introduced innovations into his madrasa, he also threw himself into another project: the revision of the history of the Volga-Ural Muslim community. Like Marjānī and Fayḍkhānov's education reform, Marjānī's history writing was shaped by multiple forces. It was built on a preexisting structure of "Bulghar" historiography that contributed to multiple discourses on Islamic orthodoxy, proper knowledge, and local identity. It attempted to critique all of these.

Like Marjānī's interest in education, his interest in regional history blossomed during his friendship with Fayḍkhānov. While teaching Kazan and St. Petersburg universities, Fayḍkhānov began to follow the results of Russian-led archaeological expeditions in the Volga basin. In the 1860s, he and Marjānī exchanged letters discussing how new archaeological finds confirmed or challenged the theories that they had begun to formulate about the history of their native region.[58]

Marjānī may have studied history previously, but the way that Russian archaeologists and ethnographers studied history was different from anything he had ever done. His biographical dictionary, *Wafayāt al-Aslāf*, was based on two kinds of sources: (1) written records, mostly official histories and previous biographical dictionaries, and (2) oral and living history, including Marjānī's own recollections and information related to him by others. But the Russian scholars at work at sites such as Bulghar turned to the study of material culture, numismatics, and epigraphy to reconstruct parts of history that had not been preserved in chronicles, dictionaries, genealogies, and oral tradition.

At the same time, a revolution was underway in Russian history writing by the mid-1800s: the cataloging of official chronicles and state archival documents and their use in the writing of comprehensive histories of the empire. The first major historical work to result from this effort, N. I. Karamzin's *History of the Russian State*, was published between 1816 and 1826. In 1856, M. S. Solov'ev began to publish *The History of Russia from the Earliest Times*, the final volume of which appeared in 1879. K. N. Bestuzhev-Riumin, who took a post on the history faculty at St. Petersburg University during Fayḍkhānov's time there, published his *Russian History* in 1872. V. O. Kliuchevskii's *A Course in Russian History in Five Parts* (1904) and V. N. Vitevskii's five-volume *I. I. Nepliuev and the Orenburg Frontier from its Founding to 1758* (1897) would only be published after Marjānī's death, but both historians published actively during his lifetime, Kliuchevskii starting in the 1860s and Vitevskii in the 1870s.

Marjānī and Fayḍkhānov may not have agreed with all the conclusions that these historians drew, but both were captivated by their "scientific" approach to reconstructing the past. That approach brought together archaeology, philology, and paleography with a close study of the history and nature of the sources themselves (*istochnikovedenie*). Russian historians presented these methods as neutral, empirical, and objective. Like physics or mathematics, these new historical methods were not the exclusive property of Russians or Orthodox Christians (indeed, Russian historians borrowed freely from their counterparts in western Europe). Rather, for their practitioners, they represented the only correct way to study history. History and its study became universal.

This view of a single, sweeping narrative of human history and a set of universally applicable methods for historical study contrasted with the practice of history as Marjānī had initially learned it from his family and in Bukhara. Muslim history writing in the Volga-Ural region grew out of the Islamic historical tradition. The guiding narrative of that tradition was the rise, spread, and eventual triumph of Islam. Its practitioners concerned themselves primarily, if not exclusively, with Islamic societies and turned mainly to Muslim sources (the Qur'ān, the hadiths, the works of earlier Muslim authors, and oral traditions) to gather information about the past. Russian and European sensibilities about how to write history implicitly challenged Muslim ones. If European-Russian history-writing methods were not only correct but universal, then other methods and approaches were necessarily incorrect.

Fayḍkhānov was the first to break ranks with the nineteenth-century Volga-Ural Muslim historiographical tradition. This was primarily for practical reasons. As he petitioned the Russian government to sponsor his madrasa project, he sought to define in ethnic, confessional, and historical terms the target population. He began with "Russia's Muslim Tatars" who lived along the "Volga and Belaia rivers." As he proceeded, he abandoned the word "Tatars" for "Muslims" and emphasized geographic location of the population as its defining characteristic: "Muslims of Kazan, Saratov and Kasimov."[59]

By the early 1860s, Fayḍkhānov became increasingly invested in the history of the populations for whom he was trying to construct a new education system. In a letter to Marjānī in 1864, he discussed the latest advances Volga regional history and his own writings.[60] In the mid-1860s, Fayḍkhānov began to write *The History of Kazan* (*Qazān tārīkhī*). The work utilized Russian-European methods of history writing and standards of evidence, but it was composed in Tatar-Turki and addressed to a Muslim audience. Fayḍkhānov framed *The History of Kazan* as a polemic work. It was not meant to merely reconstruct history, but to also drive home broader points about the state of Islamic learning in Muslim society and the proper (and improper) methods for carrying out scholarly inquiry. Fayḍkhānov began by attacking any potential sense of superiority that his Muslim readers might have held: "Even if the Kazan khanate was a very well-known state three or four hundred years ago and [even if], in those times, the Tatar people now located in the Russian state were at the center of praiseworthy science and culture, since that time, a curtain of ignorance had descended upon our people concerning its past condition in general and especially the history of the khans who founded that kingdom."[61]

Fayḍkhānov went on to explain to his readers the methods he intended to use to reconstruct the "forgotten" history of Kazan's Muslims and simultaneously to rationalize those Muslims' ignorance of their past. He started by pointing out the lack of reliable chronicle accounts produced by the people of the khanate:

> If we say that we will wait until some correct and reliable text written by scholars from those [past] times should appear, God knows, we will be waiting a long time. It seems to me, that this is because, although after the destruction of Sarai, the so-called Golden throne, the Kazan khanate was founded in one corner of that great empire [the Golden Horde], declared its independence and lasted for a century or two, it lived in fear of attacks from a people that would in the future become known as the Russians and suffered from internal disunity. [Therefore] they could not give their attention to spreading knowledge and the remaining scholars could not put together works like histories. [. . .] Even if there were histories written at that time, because the technology of printing did not exist in those times and such works could not be spread [to other regions]; they perished in the catastrophe and chaos that descended upon Kazan.[62]

Nor, by Fayḍkhānov's judgment, had the khanate fared well in the histories of neighboring Muslim peoples: "Kazan was separated from them [Mawarannahr, Khwarazm, Crimea] by the endless Dasht-i Kipchak steppe, and because of their own unrest, they could not interact with Kazan. You won't find one word about Kazan in the works of [Antiochus] Kantemir (1708–1744) and the histories of his time. So, where [among them] are we supposed to find that person who wrote a special history of Kazan?!"[63]

Nor could Russian primary sources be fully relied on: "In those days, the Russians were an ignorant people. They did not write their information honestly and for the sake of the science of history-writing. They did not check [their information], they did not try to prove anything correct. They wrote down what people heard and what fit with their politics. Therefore, in many places [in their works] conclude that because the Tatars were their enemies, they were hostile people and violators of justice. For this reason, one cannot entirely believe Russian accounts."[64]

Having accused every known written source of unreliability, Fayḍkhānov proposed a different course. If would-be historians of Kazan and its people could not look to a single primary source as an unimpeachable authority on the history of the Kazan khanate, they could still exercise logic and weigh the existing sources, Muslim and non-Muslim, against one another to sift out fact from legend and political bias.[65]

Fayḍkhānov's line of argument fell squarely within the bounds of Russian historical scholarship in the mid-1800s. But for Kazan's Muslim audience, it was scandalous. Fayḍkhānov's method stressed the practical application of logic and personal judgment and the need to consider the culture, education, and motivation of the writer of any historical source, but as he used them, these approaches could be applied to any source, Muslim or "infidel" Russian, which implied that Russian sources of knowledge were no less reliable or worthy of study than Muslim ones. Fayḍkhānov even encouraged Muslims to read Russian texts. Like Fayḍkhānov's madrasa project, his invitation to Muslims to study "infidel" texts and even use them to evaluate Muslim writings blurred the boundary between Kazan's Christian and Muslim communities and raised questions about the relationship between Islam and knowledge. Once non-Islamic sources could be used to confirm the reliability of Islamic ones, Islam ceased to be the totality of knowledge and became merely one of many sources of knowledge.

The History of Kazan remained unpublished at the time of Fayḍkhānov's death. It was passed to Marjānī together with the rest of Fayḍkhānov's unpublished writings. Rather than publishing the text, Marjānī cannibalized it and combined its fragments into the introduction of his own work, *Mustafād al-akhbār fī aḥwāl Qazān wa Bulghār (A Compendium of News on the Affairs in Kazan and Bulghar)*, the first volume of which appeared in 1885. On the surface, this work was a history of the Bulghar khans, the Golden Horde, and the Kazan Khanate. However, Marjānī also used it as a forum to present views on Volga-Ural Muslim community identity, education, and intellectual culture that he had developed in his correspondences with Fayḍkhānov in the 1860s and during his employment in the teachers' school in the 1870s. Like Husmaddīn's *Tawārīkh-i Bulghāriyya*, *Mustafād al-akhbār* was more than a retelling of regional history. In it, Marjānī attacked the entire Bulghar historical tradition and the Islamic knowledge culture of Kazan's ʿulamāʾ. He began with an assault on his readers' understanding of their own identity:

> Because the Russian people themselves use the word Tatar in a distasteful and hateful way and interpret it as demeaning, some among us understand being Tatar as a defect. They reject this name and declare "We are not Tatars, we are Muslims!" [. . .] O you misguided ones, if they did not know any other

> name for you but Muslim, the enemies of your faith and nation would call you "Muslim" with [the same] hatred. You are not Arab or Tajik or Nogay; you are still less Chinese or Russian or French or Prussian or German. If you are not Tatars, then who are you?[66]

The term "Tatar" had long been used in Russian official documents to refer to the Turkic-speaking Muslims of the Volga Basin, the Urals, and Siberia. It was also used to refer to the Turkic-speaking Muslim inhabitants of Crimea and the south Caucasus. In Russian historical writings, it was also applied to the Mongol invaders of Rus' and the rulers of the Golden Horde. It was used by eighteenth- and nineteenth-century Kazan Tatars to identify themselves when they communicated with the imperial state through petitions or the courts. Tatar (*tatarin*) was not, however, a term commonly used in internal community discourses, where Muslim and, among the ʿulamāʾ, Bulghar (*bulghārchā/Bulghārī*) were the preferred forms of self-identification. These two terms (Muslim and Bulghar) emphasized Kazan Muslims' belonging to a larger Islamic community and expressed their spatial and chronological location within it: they were the Muslims who had joined the community of the faithful through the conversion of Volga Bulghar. By contrast, the term "Kazan Tatars" situated them within the political, ethnic, and confessional hierarchies of the Russian empire. A third term, Nogay, situated them within the Chinggisid cultural world, differentiating them from Kazakhs, Bukharans, Khivans, Khoqandis, and other Turkic and Persian speakers who encountered one another on the trade routes and in the towns of what had once been Mongol-ruled Inner Asia.

Marjānī had little patience with these overlapping worlds. He viewed these shifting, situational, contingent identities as a weakness rather than a strength. He pointed out that the powerful peoples of the world—the Russians, the French, the Germans, the Chinese—neither called themselves by multiple names nor allowed others to determine their identity for them.[67] Certainty of one's identity and the ability to choose and craft that identity became marks of a well-educated people in control of their own past and future.

Although Marjānī attacked the use of "Muslim" and "Nogay" as terms of identification, his full ire was reserved for "Bulghar" identity and the entire framework of Islamic knowledge that supported it:

> Science and education and, especially, the science of history and origins have been entirely abandoned [among Kazan's Muslims]. Enthusiasm and concern for one's heritage have disappeared. Foolishness remains. Learning among our

> people has descended to the level of works like *Khwaja Naṣreddīn*, *Būzyeget*, [Ḥusmaddīn] Muslīmī's *Tawārīkh-i Bulghāriyya* and the *Adventures of Seyyid Baṭṭāl Ghāzī*, and [people] mistakenly set up their lives around these worthless utterances. A group of people who call themselves scholars ('ulamā') content themselves with the poor studies and condensed writings of false scholars [. . .] and have no knowledge of the authentic works of the great scholars. Indeed, if we are still waiting for a good, comprehensive, articulate discourse, a faithful and adequate history book on the topic of the land and deeds of our ancestors [to emerge] from the works of the abovementioned scholars, God knows how long we will wait.[68]

These remarks were in no way an accurate characterization of Muslim education in the mid-nineteenth-century Volga-Ural region. In the madrasas, students continued to read the grammars, legal commentaries, and logic manuals of the great scholars of the early and medieval Islamic periods. The poetic works of Rumi, Sa'di, and 'Attar were not only widely read among the educated, but by the mid-1800s were being adapted into Turki for non-Persian-speaking audiences. The major Islamic works on astronomy, though perhaps not taught in every madrasa, had continued to be copied and transmitted even in the most difficult periods of the seventeenth and eighteenth centuries. With increased mobility and falling paper prices, Volga-Ural scholars gained access to a growing range of old and new Islamic scholarship. While literate Muslims probably laughed at the comical antics of Khwaja Naṣreddīn and enjoyed the adventures of Baṭṭāl, there is no evidence that they took these works literally or used them to construct their sense of history and geography.

It was the third work, the Husmaddīn-attributed *Tawārīkh-i Bulghāriyya* that was Marjānī's main target, and his citing of it alongside two works that his Muslim readers would have immediately identified as fantasy was a tactic for undermining its legitimacy. If Khwaja Naṣreddīn was silly and not to be taken seriously, neither was Husmaddīn's history or by extension any of the Bulghar histories, all of which were based on sources as unreliable and fanciful as the Khwaja Naṣreddīn anecdotes.

Marjānī did not reject the idea that his people were descended from the Volga Bulghars or that the Bulghars represented a cultural high-water mark in the history of the Volga Basin that was worthy of emulation: "The people of Bulghar traveled and expanded their commerce. They called the ignorant tribes to the faith of Islam to guide them to the path of truth and lead them away from the delusion of untruth and the path of error."[69] Rather, Marjānī decried the evidentiary basis and the historical methodology on which the nineteenth-century regional scholarly tradition had been built and the people who upheld and profited from that tradition: "Were the catastrophes and chaos (*fitna*) that descended upon our states of Bulghar and Kazan the cause of our ruin? After that, the 'ulamā' remaining in our country became parasites and, in their letters and local books, in their sayings and utterances, the legends heard by our fathers and grandfathers came to be disseminated among our people as fact."[70]

He devoted an entire section of his new history to debunking the Bulghar historiographical tradition and challenging the competence of the prominent nineteenth-century scholars who contributed to it.[71] He then proceeded with his own history, one that brought together the writings of Islamic scholars such as Ibn 'Arabī and Ibn Khaldūn with nineteenth-century Russian historical and archaeological studies. Like Fayḍkhānov, Marjānī refused to give local Islamic sources of knowledge precedence over sources that were nonlocal or produced by non-Muslims. Instead, he emphasized the need to compare information across sources, consider the credibility of the authors, and consider the veracity of the information being given.

In narrative terms, *Mustafād al-Akhbār* took the separate identities—Bulghar, Nogay, Tatar—claimed by and assigned to the Muslims of the Volga-Ural region, historicized them, and connected them. The Bulghar khanate, the Kazan khanate, and finally the Kazan Muslim community inside of Russia were made to occupy specific spaces in a chronological framework, as historical developments and not simultaneously existing spheres. The overarching framework was itself borrowed from Russian historiography. The history of the Volga-Ural region began before the arrival of Islam, and it continued after the Russian conquest of Kazan. *Mustafād al-Akhbār* also bridged the macro and micro histories of Marjānī's region, beginning with the history of khanates and ending with histories of Muslim villages and urban quarters.

While criticizing the existing systems of scholarly discourse and arguing for the value of non-Islamic sources, Marjānī also used *Mustafād al-Akhbār* for a third purpose: to elevate Kazan as a legitimate center of Islamic learning. During the first half of the nineteenth century, Kazan's Muslims came to conceive of their own region as a flawed or lesser reflection of the Muslim-ruled societies of Central Asia. For Marjānī, the Russian conquest of Bukhara made the vision of "holy Bukhara" untenable. In *Mustafād al-Akhbār*, he presented Kazan and the Volga-Ural region as having a long and distinguished history as a center of Islamic culture before the misfortunes of the Russian conquest. He urged his countrymen to reclaim that legacy through the active pursuit of "true" knowledge and the cultivation of Islamic education at home.

Conclusions

In the 1880s, two works of Kazan Muslim regional history appeared in print: Ḥusayn Amirkhanov's *Tawārīkh-i Bulghāriyya* and the first volume of Marjānī's *Mustafād al-Akhbār*. These works shared much in common. Both Amirkhanov and Marjānī strove to provide a narrative of regional history based on reliable sources and free of errors and falsehoods. Both authors identified Bulghar as the cultural and spiritual cradle of their people. Both also viewed Islam as a fundamental part of their people's identity and history. In both histories, conversion to Islam distinguished the Bulghars/Tatars from the other peoples of the Volga Basin and brought them together as a recognizable community. As Amirkhanov and Marjānī wrote their histories, each of them engaged with, borrowed from, and criticized earlier works of regional history.

At the same time Amirkhanov and Marjānī's histories reflected a broader shift occurring in Kazan Muslim intellectual life. Amirkhanov's work was a continuation and elaboration of the Kazan Muslim intellectual culture of the early and mid-1800s. He turned to Muslim-authored sources and tried to expand, refine, and when necessary correct earlier accounts of regional history. This impulse toward compiling, correcting, and refining had been a key factor in Kazan Muslim religious, literary, and legal life since the early 1800s and was directly connected to rising literacy and the increase in the circulation of written texts. Amirkhanov's selection of historical sources is comparable to Ūtiz-Īmānī's statements on Islamic law books and Sufi writings and Qūrsāwī's discussion of legal theory and methodology in that all three writers, confronted with a flood of printed knowledge, sought to filter reliable information from unreliable, and to create a purer, more accurate finished product.

By contrast, Marjānī took the impulse to compile and refine beyond the boundaries of the Volga-Ural Muslim intellectual world. He borrowed freely from non-Islamic sources and privileged them over sources by Muslim authors. He presented his history as a model of how this non-Islamic knowledge could be integrated into the Islamic intellectual tradition to further Muslims' knowledge of history. Marjānī's (and Fayḍkhānov's) views that empirical knowledge could be correct and useful regardless of the society that produced it and that scientific observation would lead to indisputable truths signaled the entry of Kazan Tatar intellectuals into an emerging global knowledge culture. This culture had developed in western Europe in the seventeenth and eighteenth centuries but only gained interest in non-European societies in the nineteenth century, as Britain, France, and Russia won significant military victories in Asia and Africa and extended their influence to societies across these continents. For Marjānī, Russian expansion abroad and Russian archaeology and interference into local education made it necessary to come to terms with Russian intellectual culture. In the first volume of *Mustafād al-Akhbār,* Marjānī sought to bridge the gap between local Islamic knowledge culture and the global culture in which the Russian archaeologists and ethnographers of Kazan took part. Kazan's Muslims had benefited from Russian expansion since the late 1600s and global commodities trade since the late 1700s. From the 1860s to the 1880s, educated Kazan Muslims like Fayḍkhānov and Marjānī became much more aware of the political contours of the globalized, colonized world and where they and their people fit within it. Once they had gained that awareness, the Islamic intellectual world of the nineteenth century no longer seemed adequate to address the challenges that lay before them.

Sadly, Fayḍkhānov and Marjānī had little appreciation for the constructive aspects of the Bulghar historiographical tradition and especially the way it served as a source of cohesion among diverse Muslim groups within the Volga-Ural region and the role it played in legitimizing the authority of their own scholarly-kinship network. In their quest for unassailable, scientific truth, they set into motion destructive forces that would tear their community apart.

Notes

1. Allen J. Frank, "Muslim Cultural Decline in Imperial Russia: A Manufactured Crisis," *Journal of the Economic and Social History of the Orient* 59, nos.1–2 (2016): 166–92.
2. Ibid., 4.
3. Shihābaddīn al-Marjānī, *Qism ath-Thānī min Kitāb Mustafād al-Akhbār fī aḥwāl Qazān wa Bulghār* (Kazan: Tipo-Litografiia Imperatorskago Universiteta, 1900), 314–15.
4. Ibid., 284.
5. Ibid., 281–83; Shahr Sharaf, *Marjānī* (Kazan: Magārif, 1915), 4.
6. Shihābaddīn al-Marjānī, *Qism ath-Thānī min Kitāb Mustafād al-Akhbār,* 213.

7. Ibid., 253; *Ocherki Mardzhani o vostochnykh narodakh*, trans. and ed. A. N. Yuzeev (Kazan: Tatarskoe knizhnoe izdatel'stvo, 2003), 133.

8. Sharaf, *Marjānī*, 33–76.

9. Ibid., 77.

10. Ibid., 80–83.

11. Ismägyil' Rämi and Räis Dautov, *Ädäbi Süzlek* (Kazan: Tatarstan kitap näshriyaty, 2001), 270–71; Flera Safiullina, "Khusein Feizkhanov," in *Khösäen Fäezkhanov: Tarikhi-dokumental' jyentyk*, ed. Raif Märdanov (Kazan: Rukhiyat, 2006), 544–45.

12. Agnès Nilüfer Kefeli, *Becoming Muslim in Imperial Russia: Conversion, Apostasy, and Literacy* (Ithaca, NY: Cornell University Press, 2014).

13. Robert P. Geraci, *Window on the East: National and Imperial Identities in Late Tsarist Russia* (Ithaca, NY: Cornell University Press, 2001); Paul W. Werth, *At the Margins of Orthodoxy: Mission, Governance, and Confessional Politics in Russia's Volga-Kama Region, 1827–1905* (Ithaca, NY: Cornell University Press, 2001).

14. Geraci, *Window on the East*, 54–56.

15. Adeeb Khalid, *The Politics of Muslim Cultural Reform: Jadidism in Central Asia.* (Berkeley: University of California Press, 1998), 87–88.

16. In the 1850s and 1860s, scholarly societies in St. Petersburg such as the Imperial Geographic Society became important loci for reform-minded, "enlightened" bureaucrats in the capital as a result of the insight that these societies' members gained into the problems facing the empire through conducting research and gathering data in the provinces. (Bruce W. Lincoln, *In the Vanguard of Reform: Russia's Bureaucratic World, 1825–1855* [DeKalb: Northern Illinois University Press, 1982], 99–100). A similar argument can be made for the role of scholarly societies in Kazan, particularly where the Muslim elites were concerned.

17. A. N. Konanov, *Biobibliograficheskii slovar' otechesvennykh tiurkologov: dooktiabr'skii period* (Moscow: Nauka, 1989), 232–33.

18. Ibid., 232–33; Rämi and Dautov, *Ädäbi Suzlek*, 271.

19. "Khösäen Fäezkhanovnıng B. A. Dornga yazghan khatı," *Khösäen Fäezkhanov*, 427, "Khösäen Fäezkhanovnıng V. V. Grigor'evka yazghan khatı," *Khösäen Fäezkhanov*, 455, "Zhurnal sobraniia Fakul'teta vostochnykh iazykov za 1867 g., Sobranie ot 10 marta 1867 g. Protokol No. 5," *Khösäen Fäezkhanov*, 495; A. N. Konanov, *Biobibliograficheskii slovar'*, 233.

20. "2 khat," *Khösäen Fäezkhanov*, 319–21; "13 khat," *Khösäen Fäezkhanov*, 348.

21. "2 khat," *Khösäen Fäezkhanov*, 321.

22. Ibid.

23. Sirri Hakan Kirimli, "National Movements and National Identities among the Crimean Tatars (1905–1916)" (PhD diss., University of Wisconsin-Madison, 1990), 13–14.

24. Barbara D. Metcalf, *Islamic Revival in British India: Deoband, 1860–1900* (Princeton, NJ: Princeton University Press, 2014), 84–85.

25. Şerif Mardin, *The Genesis of Young Ottoman Thought* (Syracuse, NY: Syracuse University Press, 2000); M. Sukru Hanioglu, *Young Turks in Opposition* (Oxford: Oxford University Press, 1995), 7–32; Stanford J. Shaw and Ezel Kural Shaw, *History of the Ottoman Empire and Modern Turkey*, vol. 2 (Cambridge: Cambridge University Press, 1977),106–12.

26. Hamid Algar, *Religion and the State in Iran, 1785–1906: The Role of the Ulama in the Qajar Period* (Berkeley: University of California Press, 1969), 122–68.

27. Sayyid Ahmad Khan, "Asbab-e-Baghawat-e-Hind," *Writings and Speeches of Sir Syed Ahmad Khan* (Bombay: Nachiketa Publications Limited, n.d.); Metcalf, *Islamic Revival in British India*, 93.

28. Metcalf, *Islamic Revival in British India*, 85, 87, 100.

29. B. B. Veselovskii, *Istoriia Zemstva za sorok let'* (4 vols.) (St. Petersburg: Izdatel'stvo O. N. Popovoi, 1909–1911); George Fischer, *Russian Liberalism: From Gentry to Intelligentsia* (Cambridge, MA: Harvard University Press, 1958); Derek Offord, *Nineteenth-Century Russia: Opposition to Autocracy* (New York: Longman, 1999); G. M. Hamburg, *Boris Chicherin and Early Russian Liberalism* (Stanford, CA: Stanford University Press, 1992); Larissa Zakharova, "Autocracy and the Reforms of 1861–1867 in Russia: Choosing Paths of Development," and Fedor Petrov, "Crowning the Edifice: The Zemstvo, Self-Government and the Constitutional Movement, 1864–1881," *Russia's Great Reforms, 1855–1881*, ed. Ben Eklof, John Bushnell, and Larissa Zakharova (Bloomington: Indiana University Press, 1994).

30. Khösäen Fäezkhanov, "Risāla," *Khösäen Fäezkhanov*, 70–71; "Dokument 10," *Khösäen Fäezkhanov*, 480–82.

31. Khösäen Fäezkhanov, "Risāla," *Khösäen Fäezkhanov*, 77.

32. "22 Khat," *Khösäen Fäezkhanov*, 376.

33. Shihābaddīn al-Marjānī, *Wafāyāt al-Aslāf* (6 vols) K(P)FU-ORRK, No. 615 AR, 6: 245–47.

34. "24 Khat," *Khösäen Fäezkhanov*, 381–382.

35. "Dokument No. 18," *Khösäen Fäezkhanov*, 487–88.

36. "Dokument No. 22," *Khösäen Fäezkhanov*, 490.

37. Shihābaddīn al-Marjānī, *Wafāyāt al-Aslāf* (6 vols.), K(P)FU-ORRK, no. 615 AR, 6:244ob.

38. Sharaf, *Marjānī*, 98–99.

39. Ibid., 99–100.

40. *Qayyum Nasīrī: Saylanma äsärlär dürt tomda* (4 vols.), ed. Khujiäkhmät Makhmutov (Kazan: Tatarskoe Knizhnoe Izdatel'stvo, 2005), 1:328–32.

41. Sharaf, *Marjānī*, 126.

42. Ibid., 126.

43. Ibid., 127.

44. *Islam na evropeiskom vostoke: Entsiklopedicheskii slovar'*, ed. R. A. Nabiev (Kazan: Izdatel'stvo "Magarif," 2004), 323.

45. Sharaf, *Marjānī*, 126.

46. Ibid., 126–27.

47. Geraci, *Window on the East*, 143.

48. Ibid., 102–5; "Marjānī madrasase niẓānāmasī," K(P)FU-ORRK, 749 AR, 46ob-48ob.

49. Sharaf, *Marjānī*, 129.

50. Ibid., 128.

51. Ibid., 129; Rämi and Dautov, *Ädäbi Süzlek*, 174–75, 250, 324.

52. Sharaf, *Marjānī*, 133–34.

53. *Kazanskaia Tatarskaia Uchitel'skaia shkola, 1876–1917: Sbornik dokumentov i materialov*, ed. L. V. Gorokhova (Kazan: Izdatel'stvo Gasyr, 2005), 23.

54. Sharaf, *Marjānī*, 133.

55. *Baldāt-i Qazānda Sabākh kitāpkhānasīning asma-i kutūbdir* (Kazan: Knigoizdatel'stvo Sabakh, 1906), 26–27.

56. ʿAbdalqayyūm ʿAbdannaṣīr-ulī, *Khisāblıq yaʿnī ʿilm khisāb qaʿīdalar, yaki arifmetika wa ham khisābliq masʾalalare* (Kazan: Universitet tipografiiasī, 1873); ʿAbdalqayyūm ʿAbdannaṣīr-ulī, *Anmuzāj: Lisanimizning ṣarf wa naḥw qaʿīdalare bayanīnda risāldir* (Kazan: Universitet tipografiiasī, 1895); ʿAbdalqayyūm ʿAbdannaṣīr-ulī, *Lahja-i Tatār* (Kazan:

Universitet tipografiiasī, 1896); ʿAbdalqayyūm ʿAbdannaṣīr-ulī, *Zubda min tawārīkh al-Rūs* (Kazan: Universitet tipografiiasī, 1890); ʿAbdalqayyūm ʿAbdannaṣīr-ulī, *Istilaḥāt Jaghrafiyya* (Kazan: Universitet tipografiiasī, 1890).

57. ʿAtāʾullāh Bayazitov, *Islam Kitabī* (Kazan: n.p., 1880).

58. "20 Khat," *Khösäen Fäezkhanov*, 367.

59. Khösäen Fäezkhanov, "Risāla," *Khösäen Fäezkhanov*, 73–76.

60. "23 Khat," *Khösäen Fäezkhanov*, 379.

61. Khösäen Fäezkhanov, "Kazan Tarikhy," *Khösäen Fäezkhanov*, 109.

62. Ibid., 109.

63. Ibid., 110.

64. Ibid.

65. Ibid., 110–11.

66. Shihābaddīn al-Marjānī, *Qism al-Awwāl min Mustafād al-Akhbār fī aḥwāl Qazān wa Bulghār* (Kazan: Tipo-Litografiia Imperatorskago Universiteta, 1897), 4.

67. Ibid.

68. Ibid., 4–5.

69. Ibid., 5.

70. Ibid., 5–6.

71. For a full discussion of Marjānī's critique of the Bulghar histories, see Allen J. Frank, *Islamic Historiography and 'Bulghar' Identity among the Tatars and Bashkirs of Russia* (Leiden: Brill, 1998), 149–57.

6

MUSLIM CULTURAL REFORM AND KAZAN TATAR CULTURAL IMPERIALISM

Introduction

In April 1865, as the Russian conquest of Tashkent was underway, ʿAbdalghanī Ḥusaynov, a small-time trader from Seitov set out from Orenburg into the steppe. His was not the luxurious cargo of the eighteenth-century Russian-Indian trade. He hauled 861 rubles worth of turpentine, wooden cups, needles, tarps, and buckets.[1] His prospective customers were not Bukharan scholars or Khivan courtiers, but common Kazakh herders. Nor was he alone in this venture. Merchant families from Orenburg had been cultivating trade contacts with the Kazakh auls and Russian fortresses as they worked to supply the Russian armies that were heading south on campaign against Central Asia.[2] In return for his humble goods, Ḥusaynov would receive payment in kind, mostly in the form of sheep, cattle, leather, and wool.[3]

These animals and animal products would be fed into a growing network of slaughterhouses and factories that by the late 1800s offered its goods for sale across the empire and in central Europe. To give a sense of the scale of this economy, between 1909 and 1911, over 1.3 million sheep met their end in the slaughterhouses of Seitov, a Muslim suburb of Orenburg with a population of ten thousand. The impact of this inflow of animals did not affect Orenburg alone, but sent ripples across the empire, to the soap factories of Kazan and to the shoemakers and leatherworkers in Muslim villages such as Tūntār. By the 1880s, the potential profits to be made in this economy dwarfed the merchant economy of the late 1700s and early 1800s. The scale and geographic extent of this economy drove Muslim businessmen, managers, and accountants to think about themselves and their community in a new way. As company secretaries sent letters among Malmyzh, Tashkent, and Berlin, Bulghar historical narratives and the mid-nineteenth century madrasa began to seem a bit provincial and perhaps not quite up to the task sustaining an ambitious new generation of merchants and scholars who believed that they boasted much broader horizons than their father had.

Rethinking Jadidism

This chapter explores the roots of the Muslim educational reform in the Volga-Ural region that began in the 1880s and 1890s. This period continues to appear in the historiography of Russia's Muslims as the era of Jadid cultural reform. In the Volga-Ural region, adherents of Jadidism have been portrayed as promoting "modern" culture and technology, secular worldviews, and national identities, which distinguished them from the "traditional" Muslim culture that had come before.[4]

This chapter challenges Jadidism's novelty by placing education reform and early newspaper projects in the context of economic change and social structure in the 1850s–1890s. It examines discussions of educational and cultural reform in the late 1800s as emerging from the social hierarchies, institutions, and debates within the Volga-Ural ʿulamāʾ and, especially, the Machkaran network. These were but the latest phase in a long negotiation of scholarly authority and knowledge transmission that had been underway since the late 1700s. The intellectual figures that will be discussed in this chapter owed their education, careers, and social status to the nineteenth-century Machkaran network and its madrasas, no matter how vocally they critiqued nineteenth-century Muslim society. Machkaran intellectual culture shaped who they were and who they wanted to be.

As these Machkarans left their madrasas in the 1860s–1890s, the rapid expansion of transregional and international firms promised new geographic and financial horizons and indeed a new kind of expansion. Community expansion in the 1700s and early 1800s had been characterized by migration and settlement. In the late 1800s and early 1900s, it became about the movement of massive quantities of goods, the creation of markets, and the spread of cultural influence through mass publishing and education. Claims of "modernity" were a part of this new expansion insofar as they were used to articulate and justify a hierarchical relationship between Kazan Tatars and the Muslim populations they interacted with in the Kazakh steppe and newly conquered Central Asia.

This chapter follows in the footsteps of Adeeb Khalid's and Paolo Sartori's work on Central Asian Jadidism in that it emphasizes the local forces and mentalities behind late nineteenth-century Muslim cultural reform in the Volga-Ural region rather than approaching such reform as an empire-wide movement with a single point of origin.[5] It also builds on recent writings that question the Jadids' uniqueness when compared with earlier Muslim intellectual movements and the usefulness of "coming-of-European-modernity" paradigms for making sense of the Jadids' ideas and goals.[6]

Chistopol Madrasa: Machkarans in Transition

Nothing perhaps is more emblematic of the Jadids than newspapers. Crimean Tatar writer and activist Ismāʾīl Gasprinskii, editor of Russia's first Russian-Turkic bilingual newspaper, *Terjuman* (first published in 1883), is often portrayed as the founder of Jadidism, and it is from his phonetic "new method" for teaching literacy (*uṣūl-e jadīd*), that the term Jadid is derived. The embrace of newspapers as a medium for communication and popular enlightenment has been identified as a central element of the Jadids' program and one that links them to phenomena associated with modernity: mass literacy, a sense of simultaneity of events, and the creation of imagined communities. As such, newspapers offer a good point of entry for examining Jadidism in the Volga-Ural region.

If the history of Turkic-language newspapers in the Volga-Ural region does not belong entirely to the Machkarans, they still owned a large portion of it. Other ʿulamāʾ, including Ḥusayn Fayḍkhānov, had petitioned to open vernacular-language newspapers but had their requests denied.[7] The lack of Tatar-language newspapers published in Russia did not mean that the Machkarans and other educated Muslims did not read newspapers. By the latter half of the nineteenth century, Ottoman newspapers circulated in the Muslim regions of Russia. ʿUlamāʾ who knew Russian, especially men in state service, such as ʿAtaʾullah Bayazitov, military akhund of St. Petersburg, or Muḥammadsalīm Umetbāev, interpreter for the OMSA, could also read Russian newspapers.

The roots of the Muslim periodical press in the Volga-Ural region go back to the madrasa of Muḥammad Dhākir ibn ʿAbdalwahhāb Kamālov aṣ-Ṣaṣnawī al-Chistāwī (1815–1893) in the town of Chistopol, 140 miles southeast of Kazan. A student of ʿAbdullāh al-Chirtūshī of Machkara village and a prominent shaykh, Muḥammad Dhākir was appointed imam of Chistopol to replace the previous imam, Aḥmad bin Khālid al-Manggarī, who left Chistopol to take an appointment in the town of Troitsk on the steppe frontier. As the son-in-law of wealthy Kazan merchant, Ḥasan bin Mūsā Āpānāev (1799–1863), Muḥammad Dhākir enjoyed the largesse of the Āpānāev clan. Ḥasan built him a new mosque, a new madrasa building, and a house.[8] In addition to teaching, Muḥammad Dhākir took part in Russia's tea trade and donated the money he made to charity.[9]

Muḥammad Dhākir was also notable for his unusual family. He had eighteen children by his two wives. Most of these were daughters. This had two important implications. First, it meant that Chistopol Madrasa offered educational services for women, primarily for the numerous Kamālov daughters, but also for girls from prominent local families. Second, Muḥammad Dhākir became a father-in-law to many prominent ʿulamāʾ, among them Muḥammad Najīb Shamsaddīnov and Mūsā Bīgī. Other daughters married into the Amirkhan and Akchurin families.[10]

Muḥammad Dhākir's main educational experience came from Machkara Madrasa. (Unlike many of his contemporaries, he did not study in Bukhara.) According to Riḍāʾaddīn bin Fakhraddīn (1858–1938)—who did not study with Muḥammad Dhākir but visited his madrasa director a few times in the company of his brother-in-law, Ghilmān Karimov, in the late 1860s—Muḥammad Dhākir was unimpressive as a scholar. In his early career, he supposedly reproduced the curriculum and culture of Machkara in Chistopol. Theology figured prominently in that curriculum. He dressed in the fashion of Machkara's students, closely monitored his students' sartorial choices and grooming habits, and supposedly forbid them from reading newspapers.[11]

Tatar nationalist writer and one-time socialist revolutionary ʿAyaḍ Isḥāqī, who studied at Chistopol Madrasa in the early 1890s, offers a more positive account of Muḥammad Dhākir. He estimated that madrasa's multi-building complex housed between six hundred and eight hundred students, most of whom had come from outside of Chistopol.[12] The madrasa's large student population was mostly due to Muḥammad Dhākir's reputation as a Naqshbandi shaykh. At the time of his death, he had earned comparison with ʿAlī at-Tūntārī and Ḥasan bin Ḥamid al-Qūrṣāwī.[13] By this time, elements of the educational reorganization that had been promoted by Fayḍkhānov and Marjānī and later Bayazitov and others, were becoming evident in Chistopol. The madrasa's large population was organized into divisions, the highest-ranking of which was the "junior teacher" (*khalfa*) division. These junior teachers lived in their own quarters, wore different uniforms to distinguish them from the rest of the student body, and had access to the "special" library, where the rare books were stored. The next division in terms of prestige was the "junior teacher candidate" division, who were also housed in their own dormitory. The third and lowest division was populated by the "students" (*ṭāliblar*), the children and teenagers still in their first years of their studies.[14] Like Marjānī's madrasa in the 1870s, life at Chistopol Madrasa in the 1880s and early 1890s was highly regimented. The madrasa had a code of conduct presented to new students, who were expected to learn its rules and routines. Students were awakened for morning prayers. At tea and meal times, they were divided into "teams" of four to seven boys, each of which was assigned to a samovar.[15] The third-division students were charged with sweeping and basic cleaning chores on the madrasa grounds.[16] Even the poor and the sickly students ate relatively well at the madrasa's expense, thanks to a large network of donors.[17]

Muḥammad Dhākir placed most of the responsibilities of teaching the third-division boys in the hands of the first-division students.[18] It was a special occasion when Muḥammad Dhākir gathered all the students together to deliver a lecture or test their knowledge. Decades later, Isḥāqī still recalled with pride how, after he had answered several questions, the shaykh asked his name and complimented him on being as bright as his father, who had also been one of Muḥammad Dhākir's students.[19] In the classroom, in addition to the classical books on Hanafī law, logic, and dogma, Isḥāqī recalled being assigned to read books on the history of al-Andalus and the Ottoman empire. He also recalled how his education there awakened in him a deep love of reading.[20]

The discrepancies between Riḍā'addīn bin Fakhraddīn's account of Chistopol Madrasa in the 1860s and Isḥāqī's account of the school in the 1880s–1890s suggests how Machkaran education patterns changed over two decades. Some of these changes, especially the organizational ones, can only have been instituted by Muḥammad Dhākir himself, and even Riḍā'addīn bin Fakhreddīn, a harsh critic of the shaykh, grudgingly admitted that Muḥammad Dhākir's journey on *hajj* brought him into contact with new books and gave him a new appreciation for scholarship.[21] However, the sheer number of students that he attracted allowed for the formation of a sizeable community of young scholars, who were perhaps more amenable toward new trends in Islamic literature and scholarship than their shaykh was.

Isḥāqī's parents withdrew him from the madrasa after the death of Shaykh Muḥammad Dhākir in 1893 and transferred him to another Āpānāev-sponsored institution, Lakeside Madrasa in Kazan. However, Chistopol Madrasa's community of teachers and students was still thriving in 1895 when Murtaḍa Wahapov, a local merchant and sponsor of the madrasa, enrolled his six-year-old daughter, Faṭīma-i Farīda Wahapova, in 1895. Tutored alongside the Kamalov girls by one of Muhammad Dhākir's kinsmen, Ibrāhīm Kamalov, Faṭīma-i Farīda greatly enjoyed her time at the school, which she credited with teaching her grammar, Arabic literature, mathematics, history, and geography.[22]

The descriptions of Chistopol Madrasa by Isḥāqī and Wahapova suggest a large community of young scholars who were very much in touch with developments in Islamic law and education around the world in the late 1800s. Whether or not Muḥammad Dhākir's aversion to newspapers disappeared by the 1880s, his students certainly read them. Unfortunately, Russian law did not permit them to open one of their own. They made do with what they could get their hands on.

Gasprinskii and His Newspaper in Context

Gasprinskii was an unlikely candidate to lead an intellectual movement among Kazan's 'ulamā'. He was a Crimean Tatar, and despite his marriage into the wealthy Akchurin merchant-industrialist clan from Simbirsk, he was an outsider in relation to powerful familial and scholarly networks that dominated social life in the Volga-Ural region. The son of a minor nobleman, he had received his education in military academies in Sevastopol and Voronezh and then in the Miliutin Cadet Corps in Moscow.[23] He lacked an education in Islamic law and had little direct experience in the madrasa. But by 1883 he had one thing that none of the powerful Machkaran shaykhly and scholarly families did: permission from the imperial government to print a newspaper.

Gasprinskii's early writings on the plight of Russia's Muslims were composed in the Russian language and crafted primarily to appeal to Russian-speaking educated society. Having passed his school days in Moscow in the home of Russian publicist and nationalist Mikhail Katkov and his early career serving as the mayor of Bakchasarai, Gasprinskii had spent his youth socializing with Russian intellectuals and civil servants.[24] His views on the problems confronting Muslims in Russia primarily reflected the situation in the Crimean peninsula, a region that had witnessed multiple waves of emigration of its Muslim inhabitants to the Ottoman empire and weathered the Crimean War.[25] The main purpose of his book *Russian Muslims* (*Russkoe Musul'manstvo*), composed in the Russian language, appears to have been to inform Russian educated society of the condition of the empire's Muslim subjects, especially in Crimea, and to engage them to aid in the regeneration of these Muslim communities (projecting the Crimean case onto the rest of the empire's Muslims) and the eventual integration of those communities into the liberal policies of the Great Reforms era.[26]

Zuhra Akchurina read *Russia's Muslims* and was apparently so moved by it that she married its author. However, there is little evidence that the book won Gasprinskii much support from Russian society, nor that it was widely read by Kazan's Muslims. But Gasprinskii's newspaper, *Terjuman*, written in Tatar-Turki as well as Russian, was a different case. Within a year of its establishment, the newspaper had acquired one thousand subscribers. Of those, three hundred lived in Inner Russia and Siberia. 'Ulamā' and merchants from Kazan likely also numbered among the two hundred subscribers from Turkestan and Central Asia. Of *Terjuman*'s one thousand subscribers, five hundred identified themselves as 'ulamā' and three hundred as merchants.[27]

For the students and graduates of Shaykh Muḥammad Dhākir's Madrasa, *Terjuman* likely slipped in among the other periodicals they read.[28] At four pages long, it would have looked rather slight when set beside the more established Russian, Arab, and Ottoman publications. What would have made it stand out was that it was produced by a Russian Muslim subject and addressed issues of specific interest to them. Moreover, in the 1880s and 1890s, *Terjuman* seemed to appeal to a specific kind of Machkaran scholar. Mosque-building in inner Russia had continued unabated in the second half of the nineteenth century. Much of this growth occurred in the villages rather than in the major cities. As the number of mosques and madrasas increased, so too did the number of young men entering the madrasas to pursue careers as Muslim scholars. Between 1868 and 1908, the number of licensed Muslim spiritual personnel increased from 6,553 to 8,312.[29] With the ranks of the 'ulamā' growing faster than the number of mosques and madrasas and with many of the available posts appearing in rural areas, even affiliation with a powerful shaykh or madrasa did not guarantee a desirable posting. Many madrasa graduates, including those who studied with shaykhs as prominent as Muḥammad Dhākir, returned to their parents' peasant existence, working in the fields to feed their families while performing their duties as imams.[30]

The autobiography of Ghilmān Karīmov captures the frustration experienced by former madrasa students confronted with the realities of their chosen profession. A peasant from Samara province, he had studied with Shaykh Muḥammad Dhākir at Chistopol Madrasa in the 1860s and then at Marjānī's madrasa in Kazan. He received his imam's license by 1870.[31] But once he had settled at his new post, everything fell apart. His mosque burned down, and it took two years for his congregation to raise the funds to rebuild it.[32] He attempted to operate a maktab, but found the peasant children lazy and uninterested in learning.[33] After sixteen years of preaching and teaching in this "small," "poor," "dark" village, Karīmov decided to quit his job.[34]

And then, in the mid-1880s, an issue of *Terjuman* came into his hands.

Karīmov read it. At first, he opposed Gasprinskii's ideas. He wrote a long letter to Gasprinskii explaining that the views expressed in *Terjuman* about Muslim society and Muslim education were wrongheaded. As Gasprinskii's urging, Karīmov traveled to Bakchasarai to debate with Gasprinskii in person. During those debates, he began to make connections between Gasprinskii's arguments about Muslim backwardness and his unhappy career as a rural imam. His disputes with Gasprinskii provided him with a new sense of mission. Rather than viewing himself a failure in his career, Karīmov came to see his misfortune as an opportunity: he stood on the frontline of a campaign to save benighted Muslim societies across the empire.[35]

At first glance, Karīmov's narrative seems to confirm a familiar story of Gasprinskii awakening educated Muslims to the backwardness of Russian Muslim society. However, Karīmov was not a naïve village imam encountering reformist rhetoric and newspapers for the first time. He had come of age at Muḥammad Dhākir's and Marjānī's madrasas surrounded by people engaged in discussions of education reform, Islamic law, and colonial expansion. Moreover, he had studied in the heart of the most influential scholarly network in Kazan before being condemned to a post in the countryside. *Terjuman* did not introduce him to new ideas so much as it confirmed things that he already believed: that Muslims outside of their scholarly network were poor and ignorant, and that he, as a madrasa-educated person and disciple of an important shaykh, was worthy of more prestigious, meaningful work than herding peasants to Friday prayer. In a time when the Russian government refused to let Kazan's Muslims print their own newspaper, Gasprinskii's newspaper provided a forum in which Machkaran scholars, especially those on the fringes of the network, could vent their frustrations. They could imagine these experiences not as isolated incidents, but as manifestations of broader cultural and structural problems in their society.

ʿUlamāʾ throughout the Volga-Ural region used *Terjuman* to complain about uneven distribution of resources and the self-interested behavior of the most privileged provincial scholarly and merchant families. An anonymous contributor writing from Ufa in 1888 lamented that his city, despite being the location of the OMSA, had no madrasas. Ufa citizens blamed their city's lack of madrasas on a lack of funding for Muslim education, but the contributor argued that Ufa had more than enough wealthy Muslim citizens. It was these citizens' disinterest in contributing to the community and their preference for taking up minor posts in the provincial bureaucracy to "steal from and confound [their] illiterate countrymen" that prevented them from funding community education.[36] *Terjuman* contributors from the Volga-Ural region used the newspaper as a forum to collectively imagine an alternate reality in which talent and merit were rewarded over social connections, in which the enlightened wealthy gave freely of their largesse to aid in community development and support the educated, and in which all community members were literate, pious, and socially conscious. It should be noted that ʿulamāʾ like Ghilmān Karīmov, who hailed from middle and lower ranks of the Machkaran network, studiously overlooked their own privilege and social connections as they imagined this alternate reality. Yet it was those very social connections that enabled *Terjuman* to circulate through Kazan ʿulamāʾ society and find new subscribers.

The October Manifesto of 1905 was the beginning of the end of *Terjuman*'s dominance of the Kazan Muslim periodical market. Kāmil Mutiʿī was educated at Uralsk Madrasa by his father, madrasa director Mutiʿullāh Tuḥfatullin, an alumnus of Qıshqār Madrasa and then al-Azhar.[37] Tuḥfatullin was prepared to send Kāmil to Qıshqār, but his wife objected, arguing that "I don't want my son to become some village mullā like you [Tuḥfatullin]."[38] Kāmil was sent to Lakeside Madrasa in Kazan instead, and then to Cairo and Istanbul. By January 1906, Kāmil had returned to Uralsk and opened the monthly journal *The New Century* (*al-ʿAṣr al-Jadīd*).[39] With each issue between forty and sixty pages long, *The New Century* dwarfed *Terjuman*. Its list of contributors heavily featured Machkarans and especially writers from families connected with Muḥammad Dhākir's madrasa: Faṭīma-i Farīda Wahapova, Riḍā'addīn bin Fakhraddīn, 'Ayāḍ Isḥāqī, and Fatīḥ Karīmī (son of Ghilmān Karīmov). *The New Century* also featured poet 'Abdullāh Tūqāyev, a friend of Kāmil Muti'ī and his father's former student.

The New Century closed by early 1907, but its editors and contributors migrated to other publications. Karīmī became the head editor of the Orenburg newspaper, *Waqt* (*Time*), starting in February 1906. Riḍā'addīn bin Fakhraddīn worked as the head editor of *Waqt*'s supplement, the journal *Shūrā*, from 1908 to 1918. In 1906, Isḥāqī opened several newspapers—*Tāng yūldızı*, *Tāng majmū'ası*, and *Tāwısh*—one after the next; the pronounced anti-autocratic tone of these publications guaranteed that they were shut down by the police in short order.[40] Tūqāyev relocated to Kazan by 1908, where he took over editorship of the student-focused journal *al-Iṣlāḥ* and played a major role in the production of the satirical journals *Yāshen* and *Yālt-Yūlt*. These publications quickly eclipsed *Terjuman* in the Volga-Ural region in terms of circulation and cultural impact. The range of these publications—biweekly newspapers, literary journals, satire—also suggests that by 1906 the students of Chistopol Madrasa and other Machkaran network institutions had been exposed to a much wider range of periodicals (Russian, Ottoman, and Arab) than *Terjuman*.

Commerce, Educational Reform, and the New Cultural Imperialism

While some young men who studied in Machkara-network madrasas strove to escape rural posts for the city or turned to publishing, others sought opportunities farther afield. The Russian conquest of Bukhara, Khiva, and Khoqand, as well as the empire's continued involvement in China's western borderlands, created new economic opportunities. As these newly conquered territories were fully integrated into the empire, traders from towns along the northern and eastern fringes of the steppe rushed to take advantage of new markets. An ambitious, lucky businessman might turn a few hundred rubles of capital into hundreds of thousands.

Aḥmad (1837–1906), 'Abdalghanī (1839–1902), and Maḥmūd (1845–1910) were three of six children born to Seitov merchant Muḥammad 'Alī bin Ḥusayn and his two wives. Muḥammad 'Alī inherited significant wealth from his father, but by the late 1850s, the family had fallen on hard times.[41]

When Muḥammad ʿAlī died in 1858, his five sons set out to rebuild his business. Like many other would-be merchants, they started out traveling from village to village selling small items, but soon turned to the steppe, buying up manufactured goods in Orenburg and trading them to the Kazakh herders for wool, hides, and livestock to be sold in the city. It was the Orenburg-Kazakh trade that brought them enough money to purchase an apartment in Orenburg and shortly afterwards an office and a warehouse.[42] They began to bring their wares to the annual trade fair in Nizhnii Novgorod and founded the trading firm Aḥmad Ḥusaynov & Bros. Co. As Central Asia fell under Russian rule in the 1860s, the firm spread its commercial networks south. By 1869, the brothers had stationed themselves strategically in Russia's southeastern borderlands, with ʿAbdalghanī residing in Kazalinsk in the south of the Kazakh steppe and Maḥmūd dividing his time between Turkestan and Orenburg.[43] They brought Russian manufactured goods (kerosene, pitch, steel, pig iron, and buckwheat flour) to the steppe and traded them for wool, felt, cow hides, sheep, and camels to be sold in Orenburg. Between 1873 and 1878, they made more than three hundred thousand rubles.[44] By the 1880s, they had become major players in the livestock and animal byproduct trade along the Syr Darya River, in Semirech'e, and in Turgai oblast'. They built strong connections with the herdsmen of the southern steppe and organized sheep, camel, and cattle drives to bring livestock to market in the absence of a well-developed railway system.[45] In the 1890s, they tried to extend their business to western Europe. In 1894, they shipped sheep to Paris for sale. However, transportation expenses made the venture unprofitable.[46]

As the Ḥusaynov brothers grew wealthy, they undertook philanthropic work to cement their reputation within the Muslim communities in which they worked. In Kazalinsk, ʿAbdalghanī hosted madrasa students traveling to and from Bukhara, paid for the construction of a large stone mosque, and donated money for the construction of a hospital. When famine struck the Syr Darya region in 1880 and grain prices rose, he opened the doors of his warehouses to the poor and sold them grain and flour below market price.[47]

From the 1860s to the 1910s, other Muslim firms such as Yaushev and Sons, G. ʿA. Ḥamidullin, and Muḥammad ʿAlī Yūnusov Co. followed a similar trajectory to that of the Ḥusaynovs, accumulating vast wealth through their economic involvement in the empire's eastern and southeastern territories. Stories of families such as the Yaushevs of Kulja, who had left Kazan penniless in the 1880s and by the early 1900s had become sponsors of Muslim education in western China, were celebrated by the Machkaran ʿulamāʾ to whom they became patrons.[48] These companies and their founders built their fortunes processing livestock and grain produced in the Urals, Siberia, the Kazakh steppe, and Central Asia and shipping it to other parts of the empire and eventually to central and western Europe. These Muslim businessmen owned commercial offices, factories, warehouses, and pastures in locations scattered across the empire, where they employed hundreds of people of various ethnicities as shepherds, butchers, wool washers, tanners, mill workers, packers, teamsters, and shop clerks. Managing these far-flung enterprises and numerous employees required sustained communication and careful recordkeeping. Aḥmad Ḥusaynov, whose writing skills were so poor that he could not even sign his own voting records during his tenure on the Orenburg city duma, was not equipped to handle such management personally. But others were.

Muḥammad Kamāl Muzaffarov was born in Tūntār village in 1855 to the family of a junior officer who had just been demobilized after twenty-three years of service in the Russian army. He received his education at Tūntār Madrasa from ʿAlī at-Tūntārī until 1868, when, at age thirteen, he went to the Nizhnii Novgorod fair. He worked for various merchants until 1876, when he was recruited into the Russian army. He returned from his service three years later and relocated to Orenburg, where he found work with Aḥmad Ḥusaynov & Bros. Co. In 1882, he married Faṭīma Fayḍullina, the daughter of the Fayḍullin merchant family of Orsk, and by 1890 he had returned to his native district, settling in the town of Malmyzh, where he worked as a secretary in Ḥakīmov Trading House, a Malmyzh commercial firm run by a family from Tūntār.[49]

Muzaffarov and his family left behind copious correspondences relating to their business and personal lives. From these letters and papers, it is possible to piece together Muzaffarov's broader kinship and commercial networks. His father-in-law, Mustafa Fayḍullin, was also employed with the Ḥusaynov firm, where he worked as the secretary to Aḥmad Ḥusaynov in Orenburg and Orsk in the 1880s and 1890s.[50] His brother-in-law, Maḥmūdgaray Fayḍullin, worked as a secretary to Maḥmūd Ḥusaynov in Orenburg in the 1890s and early 1900s before eventually opening his own firm, Makhmud-Garay Mustafin Fayzullin and Co., by 1904.[51] Maḥmūdgaray's brother, Sayyidgaray, studied at Tūntār Madrasa at Muzaffarov's advice. He married Faṭīma Dinmuḥammadova, the daughter of

Tūntār Madrasa's director, Ishmuḥammad Dinmuḥammadov, and gained a post as imam of the Second Congregational Mosque of Shoda (Shudinsk) village in Malmyzh *uezd*, where the couple opened a school for Muslim girls.[52]

Tūntār graduates such as Muzaffarov had been trained as Islamic legal experts. However, that training included skills that were transferable to professions outside of the field of Islamic law. First, they could read and write fluently in their native language. Second, the mathematics they had mastered while learning how to divide inheritances and calculate zakāt payments could easily be turned to calculating profits and losses and keeping accounting books and company inventories.

With their millions of rubles in capital, their large staffs, and their expansive institutional networks, the Tatar livestock and grain firms made the ideal investors for cultural and educational projects. As frontier adventurers-turned-nouveau riche, the owners of these firms were eager to trade their financial resources for respectability and social capital. In 1893, Gasprinskii approached ʿAbdalghanī Ḥusaynov at the latter's office in Samarkand. Gasprinskii opened the discussion with the question of primary school education, a topic that happened to be on ʿAbdalghanī's mind because he had school-aged children. By the end of the discussion, Gasprinskii convinced ʿAbdalghanī to return to Orenburg, where he joined the Rāmīev brothers, owners of a mining concern in the Urals, in a quest to transform Muslim education and publishing.

The entry of the Ḥusaynov brothers and firms like theirs into the fields of education and publishing strengthened their ties with the Machkarans. Former Chistopol student Ghilmān Karīmov was appointed akhund of Bugelma district in Kazan province, but in 1899 he surrendered his imam's license and his akundship and relocated to Orenburg at the urging of the Rāmīevs and Ḥusaynovs.[53] His son, Fatīḥ, taught at Ḥusayniyya Madrasa for a short time, then traveled to Moscow, where he studied accounting and researched how to open a press. Ghilmān dabbled in the grain trade until 1900, when Fatīḥ returned and the two of them opened the printing house Ḥusaynov, Karimov, and Co. With financial help from Aḥmad Ḥusaynov, Ghilmān purchased orchards outside the city, which he used to teach local Muslims how to tend fruit trees in the steppe.[54]

Since the early 1700s, Kazan ʿulamāʾ had helped other Kazan ʿulamāʾ build wealth and influence on Russia's frontiers. They established new settlements and madrasas to which they anchored the Sufi and scholarly networks that guided the cultural and socioeconomic life of the Volga-Ural region's Muslim villages and urban quarters. By the 1870s, the Machkaran ʿulamāʾ were expert players at this game and had carved out a significant space for themselves in Kazan and the villages east of the city. But in the 1880s and the 1890s, a set of circumstances emerged that allowed the Machkarans to imagine their community on a completely different scale. Imperial trade in Central Asia sent Machkarans far afield. Accounting, management, editing, and printing offered alternate career paths to Machkarans who could not find a posting in the Volga-Ural mosques or did not especially want one. Newspapers and journals helped patrons and clients connect across the vast expanses of the growing empire. In the 1870s, the Machkarans held significant influence in the politics of the Volga-Ural Muslim communities. By the 1890s, some of them began to imagine themselves guiding a much larger Muslim community, one that included the Muslims of the Kazakh steppe and Central Asia.

Gasprinskii, with his newspaper and his agenda on education reform, fit well into this new Machkaran vision of cultural imperialism. He remained a potent symbol for the Machkarans and their children down to 1917 because his status as a Crimean Tatar made him an outsider and lent a veneer of universality to their various projects. But once these projects got underway, Gasprinskii's control over them was questionable at best. For example, the Ḥusaynovs claimed to promote Gasprinskii's program of study, purchased textbooks from Gasprinskii, and supplied them to their schools.[55] However, as they entered the field of education, they brought with them the strategies they had perfected in the livestock trade. They gave money to build schools and pay teachers' salaries in Kazan, Orenburg, and Ufa provinces, but they also funded schools in Tashkent, Irgiz, Perovskii, Kazalinsk, Turkistan, and Samarkand, where they already possessed warehouses, commercial contacts, and company staff. They did not simply give money to needy teachers and school directors; they insisted that the schools they funded be operated according to the educational model they prescribed. They kept in touch with those they sponsored, discussing residents' reactions to the schools, staffing issues, and resistance from local elites.[56] As the Ḥusaynov brothers had come to dominate the livestock trade between the Syr Darya and Orenburg, they now sought to dominate in Muslim education in Orenburg and beyond. ʿAdbdalghanī wrote to his brother, Aḥmad: "This year, as you noted, we trained 100 teachers. They will teach hundreds of children. There are also the teachers that we have trained previously. [. . .] Where do these teachers come from? Where are they teaching? Write and give me the details."[57] The Ḥusaynovs' goal was not simply to enact Gasprinskii's education program, but to control the production of educated people in Orenburg and its hinterland.

By the end of the 1890s, the Galikeevs of Kazan, the Āpānāevs of Malmyzh, the Yaushevs of Troitsk, and the Saydyukovs of Tiumen had joined the Ḥusaynovs and the Rāmīevs as sponsors of maktabs, madrasas, and public libraries across inner Russia, in the steppe, and in the empire's Chinese and Central Asian frontiers.[58] In inner Russia, a network of newly founded madrasas trained boys and young men in literacy, Islamic law, mathematics, and natural sciences. Many of these madrasas were founded by scholars with ties to the Machkaran network. ʿĀlimjān Bārūdī, founder of Muḥammadiyya Madrasa in Kazan, was married to Māhrūi bint Isḥāq, a daughter of the Ūtamishev clan and the niece of Qıshqār Madrasa director Ismāʿīl Ūtamishev.[59] Ḥusayniyya Madrasa in Orenburg was founded by the Ḥusaynov brothers in 1889 and staffed by members of the same Chistopol- and Malmyzh-connected families that were so well represented in their firms.[60] Izh-Būbī Madrasa, a rural madrasa in Viatka province two hundred kilometers east of Malmyzh, was under the directorship of ʿAbdalʿallām Būbī and then his sons, ʿAbdullāh and ʿUbaydullāh. These were the son and grandsons of the son of Nigmatullah bin Munasib, who studied with ʿAbdullāh al-Chirtūshī in Machkara.[61]

These new schools differed in structure from Tūntār, Qıshqār, and Machkara madrasas. They took the organizational changes enacted earlier at Chistopol and Marjānī madrasas and pushed them further. Designed to produce more educated people at a faster rate, they accepted large numbers of students. Whereas by 1892 Tūntār Madrasa enrolled 140 students, by 1905 Muḥammadiyya Madrasa enrolled 330.[62] The new madrasas enforced stricter gender separation. Whereas Tūntār Madrasa had enrolled girls and boys in the same facility since the 1860s, Muḥammadiyya, Ḥusayniyya, and Izh-Būbī madrasas were exclusively male institutions at which women's education was channeled into separate divisions or schools.[63] Classes were shifted to a lecture format, academic disciplines were divided among instructional hours and grade levels.[64] Such measures were intended to enable the madrasas to produce larger numbers of graduates than most nineteenth-century madrasas could have managed.

These graduates would go on to fill teaching posts and administrative positions across the Urals, the steppe, and Central Asia. For example, at

Izh-Būbī Madrasa, instructors encouraged their students to seek summer work as teachers among the Kazakhs. Some of the madrasa's teachers also undertook such work. Izh-Būbī instructor Quddus 'Abdrakhmānov wrote to his fellow teacher, Ḥarīth Saymanov, prior to the latter's departure to teach among the Kazakhs of Turgai oblast':

> On the one hand, you are very fortunate because for the sake of your faith, your nation, and progress, you have agreed to sacrifice yourself and travel to a far-off country to enlighten our brothers. Was that not always our dearest dream? We and others always have the words "progress" and "learning" on the tip of our tongues. We all talk, but we have very few people among us who really do anything. There are those among us who weep tears of blood for the nation and their names will live forever. I count you in their number. [. . .] Farewell, brother. Be well. Burn for our faith and nation [. . .] Take up the banner of Islam and Allah and set right the failings of the Kazakhs.[65]

Gasprinskii may have pioneered the concept of Russian Muslim identity, but in the hands of the Machkaran 'ulamā', it took on a new purpose: it gave them and their merchant-industrialist brethren a vocabulary for describing their place in the post-1860s political and economic order of the Russian empire. Conceiving of themselves as Russian Muslims enabled them to articulate their relationships with the other Muslim communities of the empire in a way the Bulghar historiography did not. Likewise, Gasprinskii's education reform, combined with earlier experiments in madrasa reorganization and venularization, gave the Machkarans the means to expand their ranks more rapidly and to increase their cultural footprint in newly conquered regions. These goals owed so little to Gasprinskii that he was quickly relegated to a figurehead onto which the Machkarans projected their own ambitions for leadership of Russia's other Muslim communities.

Lakeside Madrasa and Constructing Hierarchies of Muslim Backwardness

While Chistopol Madrasa's sheer size enabled it to host a vibrant community of young scholars, Lakeside Madrasa's greatest asset was its location. The Āpānāev-sponsored madrasa took its name from Kazan's Kaban Lake, beside which it stood, though it was also known successively as Khūjāsh's Madrasa, Bāimurād's Madrasa, 'Abdalkarīm's Madrasa, 'Abdal'allām's Madrasa, and finally Qāsimiyya Madrasa after Muḥammad Qāsim 'Abdal'allām-ulı Saliḥov, its director from 1899 to 1918. It was also known as Āpānāev Madrasa after its main sponsors.[66]

From the 1870s to the 1890s, Lakeside Madrasa's reputation rose under the directorship of Muḥammad Qāsim's father, ʿAbdalʿallām bin Salīḥ, a descendant of seventeenth-century scholar Yūnus bin Iwānāy.[67] By 1875, the madrasa enrolled three hundred students and was perceived as a prestigious school, especially by middling rural ʿulamāʾ families looking to raise their social status.[68] By the 1880s and 1890s, Lakeside boasted the most cosmopolitan environment of any Volga-Ural madrasa. Isḥāqī, who studied there in the 1890s, remarked on the supply of the Ottoman newspapers and novels circulating at Lakeside, which was fed by Kazan's booksellers, who made regular trips to Istanbul to purchase the latest literature in Turkish and Arabic. Ottoman émigré publications from Paris and Cairo also flowed into the school. Lakeside also served as a portal to Russian literary culture. Isḥāqī recalls making his first trips to the Russian theater during his years at Lakeside.[69]

Like Chistopol Madrasa, Lakeside does not fit the definition of a "Jadid" school, as the cultural influences and organizational tendencies that piqued its students' interest in Gasprinskii's ideas were already in motion as Gasprinskii was formulating and publishing his views. Lakeside encompassed many of the tensions of the 1870s–1890s period: (1) the influence of growing industrialist wealth, (2) middling and poor ʿulamāʾ families' desire to raise their status, (3) rapidly expanding Kazan Muslim trade networks and the possibilities they opened in terms of new careers, identities, and worldviews. From the 1880s to the 1890s, Lakeside counted among its alumni writers Muḥammad Ẓāhir Bīgī, ʿAyaḍ Isḥāqī, ʿAbdarrakhmān Ilyāsī, and ʿAliaskar Kamāl, the jurists ʿĀlimjān Bārūdī, Mūsā Bīgīev, and Aḥmad Hādī Maqsūdī, historians Ḥasanʿatā ʿAbashī and Zaki Validi Togan; and writer-publisher and duma deputy Ṣadraddīn Maqṣūdī. This list, when combined with Chistopol graduates listed previously and a handful of men and women from other branches of the Machkaran network, accounts for most of the historical actors commonly termed Jadids in the historiography of the Volga-Ural region.

Although some Lakeside students traveled to Bukhara to continue their studies, the prominence of Turkish, Arabic, and Russian published literature in the madrasa's culture gradually reoriented its students' gaze westward. At the same time, the emergence of transregional trade and manufacturing firms bridging the Volga-Ural region and Central Asia transformed the latter into a periphery that provided raw materials and purchased finished products. Lakeside's proximity to Kazan's orientalist and missionary projects provided a vocabulary through which the Kazan ʿulamāʾ could begin to make sense of their new world.

Lakeside alumnus Muḥammad Ẓāhir Bīgī described a journey he had made to Central Asia in 1893. He enthusiastically recited for his readers the region's history, from the ancient Greeks to Armin Vambery.[70] He called to mind the long and distinguished intellectual traditions of Mawarannahr's cities by invoking the image of philosophers Saʿadaddīn at-Taftāzānī and ʿAlī al-Jurjānī debating in the court of Tamerlane in Samarkand.[71] He delightedly noted that, thanks to the new system of riverboats and trains established by the Russian state, the journey from Rostov-na-Donu to Central Asia had been rendered faster and more convenient than travelers a decade earlier could ever have imagined.[72]

Near the end of Bīgī's journey, he reached Bukhara. In some ways, the ancient city of Islamic learning did not disappoint. Everywhere Bīgī turned, he saw madrasas, charitable endowments, and learned people.[73] But not all in Holy Bukhara was as it should have been. Students who arrived from Kazan to pursue their studies were treated with especial disdain. They were forced to pay exorbitant fees for their lodgings despite the abundant profits generated by Bukhara's endowments. They came with pure and naïve intentions of learning at the feet of great scholars but instead were exploited, abused, and pushed to the margins of Bukharan society.[74] He noted that every Islamic legal school forbid waqf managers from accruing profits from endowment property, yet the Bukharans did so, although they were learned enough to know better.[75] Their oppression of foreigners did not end with the Kazan Tatar madrasa students. He claimed that of one hundred Kazan Tatar teachers employed in Bukhara, eighty lived in poverty.[76] In one of the Muslim world's greatest centers of learning, talent, hard work, and piety counted for nothing. The Bukharan educational sphere operated on profits and connections.

Bīgī then turned his attention to what transpired in the Bukharan madrasa classroom. He noted the progression from Arabic grammar to theology and finally to logic and philosophy. The teachers of Bukhara used the same books as instructors in inner Russia, they picked and chose lessons instead of teaching any single textbook from beginning to end, and they assigned only one book for a given subject. Being instructed in this way, students gained a very limited range of knowledge and required fifteen to eighteen years to master it. Once they had completed this general program, students could proceed to take courses in jurisprudence, astronomy, and other advanced subjects, but individual subjects and, in some cases, individual books, were taught by different teachers, and sometimes by only one teacher in the entire city.[77] History as an academic subject was taught nowhere in the city, and instruction in the Qur'ān and hadith were not emphasized as much as Bīgī thought they should have been.[78] Overall, he admitted that there were many intelligent people in Bukhara, but the structure of Bukharan education limited those scholars' effectiveness in teaching and hindered intellectual progress.[79]

Bīgī also pointed out what he interpreted as the negative influence of Bukhara on Kazan education. He highlighted the use of the *munāẓara*, or debate, as a teaching tool. Like Fayḍkhānov before him, he argued that Kazan Muslim *munāẓaras* rapidly descended into shouting, sophistry, and nonsense, and that nothing useful was learned.[80] He concluded his account by observing that the students of Bukhara, despite having hundreds of madrasas and millions of rubles in charitable endowments at their disposal, gained little in the way of useful education. He laid the blame for this squarely at the feet of the Bukharan 'ulamā'.[81]

Allen Frank has read Bīgī's account as a veiled critique of Kazan Muslim society mapped onto Bukhara.[82] The portrayals of the wealthy abdicating their social responsibility can easily be read as part of a larger protest of the privileged behavior of the prominent Machkaran 'ulamā' families. However, the text also reveals how the relative positions of Kazan and Bukhara had changed since the 1860s, at least in the eyes of some of Kazan's 'ulamā'. Two points are especially noteworthy. The first is the implicit contrast between Russia's rapidly developing infrastructure and Bukhara's, which Bīgī portrays as having changed little in centuries. The second is Bīgī's highlighting of the marginal position of Kazan's Muslims in Bukharan society. Such marginalization, while perhaps unremarkable to a native Bukharan, would have been infuriating to a Kazan Muslim like Bīgī, who had grown up in a society in which Kazan Muslims ran factories and trading houses in Bukhara and other Central Asian towns and enjoyed cultural and educational experiences in Istanbul, Cairo, and Paris. The poor treatment or simple neglect of Kazan Muslims in Bukhara was to Bīgī an inversion of the proper order of things. Russia had embraced new technologies and ideas. Bukhara had not and had suffered for it. In doing so, it had forfeited its claim to cultural supremacy over the Muslims of Kazan.

Writing in 1908, Muḥammad Dhākir Hādī offered an even harsher assessment of Bukharan education and its relationship to Kazan. The titular hero of his novella *Reverend Jihānshāh* embodies the worst aspects of Bukharan training. The village in which Jihanshah is posted has five mosques and a small army of mullās, madrasa directors, and shaykhs, but most of the residents are illiterate.[83] This pitiful situation is directly connected to Jihānshāh himself. The son of a peasant, he decides to become an imam because his father told everyone that he should and because, by the age of twelve, he had figured out that an imam's work was much easier than a peasant's.[84] Jihānshāh's father contacts and bribes a local imam to take Jihānshāh under his wing. Informed that poor boys who stay put never rise above the level of junior teacher, young Jihānshāh moves from madrasa to madrasa and finally sets out for Bukhara.[85] He returns several years later, in time for the election of the new village imam. He bursts into the room in his brightly colored Bukharan robes and wins the election.[86]

Hādī's *Reverend Jihānshāh* is Bukharan cynicism and corruption transplanted to the Volga-Ural region. It is also a brutal attack on the ʿulamāʾ gentry of the mid-1800s. Jihānshāh's choice of careers is motivated not by his love of learning or his wish to serve Muslim society, but by his desire to wear fancy clothes, treat himself to sugar with his tea, and convince people to give him money.[87] He goes through the motions of education without attaining knowledge of Islamic law, theology, or any other academic discipline. All he learns is how to forge contacts with men more powerful than himself and to dazzle ignorant Muslims with his pretty clothes and Bukharan credentials. Hādī does not fault Jihānshāh for taking this path. In an education system that promotes the well-born, the wealthy, and the well-connected over the talented but poor, Jihānshāh has no choice. Nonetheless, his ignorance casts a long shadow across his village, trapping his congregation in the same corrupt system than had warped him.

The denigration of Holy Bukhara was not limited to traveler accounts and novels. In 1907, the Orenburg journal *The World and Life* (*Dunya wa Maʿīshat*, soon to be *Dīn wa Maʿīshat*) published an issue devoted to Russian Turkestan. It included an article on the medieval history of the region and a second critiquing the work of the Turkestan Commission and its connection to the severe economic problems besetting the region.[88] It also included an article on the dangers of consuming *nospay*, an opium-based narcotic. Though this article did not specifically mention Bukhara, Central Asia, or Turkestan, it characterized *nospay* as a distinctly Asiatic problem (inherited from the Persians, the Japanese, the Chinese, and/or the Indians), and the article itself was situated among articles and photographs pertaining to

Turkestan.[89] These three articles characterized the journal's treatment of Central Asia through 1907–1908. The casual reader would have encountered the region only as it related to medieval history and the failures of Russian colonial policy. Other post-1905 Kazan and Orenburg journals and newspapers offered similar treatments of Bukhara. Poet ʿAbdullāh Tūqāyev, when writing in 1906 about ʿAbdarrashīd Ibrāhīmov's recent trip to Tokyo, asked: "Will Bukhara's smoke rein there [in Japan] as well? Tell me, will that Islam that is Bukharan-ism become known there?"[90] A caricature in the youth journal *Yālt Yūlt* portrayed "the Sart madrasa director." The first frame showed the director at madrasa during day, sitting with his students in a circle on the floor, poring over books. The second frame showed the director by night enjoying food and drink while ogling an underage dancing boy.[91]

Volga-Ural newspapers across the political spectrum offered similar portrayals of the other conquered Central Asian states. They praised Samarkand and Urgench sources of great ancient and medieval literature, architecture, and religious life while portraying them as impoverished, stagnant, and victimized in the present. Kazan Muslim journalists constructed an exotic and orientalized image of Central Asia that allowed them to reverse the historical relationship between it and their native region. Instead of being supplicants seeking enlightenment from Bukhara or Khorezm, Kazan Tatars now cast themselves as the enlighteners, magnanimously offering Central Asian Muslims the knowledge and skills required to join the modern world.

To rewrite the relationship between Kazan and Bukhara, early twentieth-century writers needed to replace the older image of Bukhara as a place of knowledge and prestige with a new one of Bukhara as a once-glorious society fallen into decadence and decay. Placing Kazan Muslims ahead of the Bashkirs and the Kazakhs required much less effort because many Kazan ʿulamāʾ had always seen themselves as culturally superior to these peoples. Kazan Tatars had settled among the Bashkirs since the mid-1700s and among the Kazakhs since the late 1700s, but the descendants of these settlers did not fully assimilate to their new society. Historian Qurbān ʿAlī Khālidī, when writing about the *chala Kazakhs*, a population of mixed Kazakh–Kazan Tatar–Central Asian descent living in the steppe, emphasized the Kazan Tatar (Nogay) heritage of this community.[92] In Semipalatinsk, as late as the 1860s, it was relatively easy for Kazan Tatars to retain a distinct identity because restrictions were placed on how Kazakhs who had not submitted to Russia could interact with the town's Russian subjects.[93] This had changed by the 1880s, when most of the local Kazakhs had become Russian subjects, and impoverished herders began to settle in the city in large numbers. However, ethnic separation remained, as the Kazan Tatars and the Kazakhs lived in separate urban quarters and maintained separate mosques.[94]

Early twentieth-century Muslim reformers from inner Russia often made little effort to represent Kazakhs in a positive manner. ʿAbdarrashīd Ibrāhīmov, in his 1907 memoir, recalled how, upon arriving in a Kazakh aul, he was mobbed by its inhabitants, who groped him, tore apart his luggage, and proceeded to devour his provisions in front of him.[95] ʿAbdullāh Tūqāyev presented a different approach to the Kazakhs. In a letter to Aḥmad Ūrmānchiyev in May 1911, he described his recent trip to the steppe to treat his advancing tuberculosis: "I'm drinking kumis. I'm eating meat. The weather's good. From now on, I am beginning to fortify my strength and my spirit."[96] Kamāladdīn Ḥusmaddīnov, recalling what appears to be the same trip, describes how he and Tūqāyev lodged with Kazakh acquaintances, bought butter from Kazakh women to bake flatbread, went fishing, and marveled at how Kazakh parents permitted their children to run about naked.[97] Despite being surrounded by Kazakhs, Tūqāyev, in his letters, managed to render them completely invisible.

Ibrāhīmov and Tūqāyev represented two different but interrelated approaches to the Kazakhs: castigating and ignoring. Whether Kazan Muslim writers found the Kazakhs quaint, boorish, or simply not worth mentioning, the Kazakhs' mobile pastoralist way of life, in the Kazan Muslim view, set them significantly behind the Kazan Tatars in terms of cultural achievement. Emerging narratives of Tatar and Turkic history enabled Kazan Muslims to fantasize about their medieval Mongol and Qipchaq ancestors, but like Russian and European ethnographers, they understood mobile pastoralism as a phase through which a people passed on their way to a more advanced way of life. It was the Kazakhs' misfortune to have stalled in their mobile pastoralist phase, and it was this misfortune that made them vulnerable to the land-grabbing tendencies of Russian officials and Slavic settlers. This view formed the foundation for a third stereotype: Kazakhs as the victims of colonialism and progress.

Kazan Muslim views on Bashkirs resembled their views on Kazakhs. Like the Kazakhs, Bashkirs were portrayed as a people left behind while the rest of the world progressed. ʿUlamāʾ and officials who worked among the

Bashkirs in the 1890s and early 1900s lamented their lack of education, poor hygiene, and extreme poverty.[98] In fiction and in calls for reform, Bashkirs were perpetually cast as hopelessly ignorant and easily exploited. Bashkir nomads were portrayed in early twentieth-century Muslim literature as willing to sell their land for a bag of flour or a bottle of vodka.[99] Bashkirs were also depicted as the people most likely to be taken advantage of by corrupt, dishonest imams and shaykhs or by opportunistic Tatars.[100] It is not coincidental that Hādī described the amoral Reverend Jihānshāh as imam of the "Bashkir Mosque" in a village inhabited by "Kazan Tatars, Bashkirs, new Bashkirs or people who came from elsewhere and were registered as Bashkirs, [. . .] and mostly Bashkirs."[101] Hādī's repetition of the term "Bashkir" was intended to emphasize to his readers the extreme ignorance of Jihānshāh's congregation.

Unlike Kazakhs, Bashkirs presented a peculiar conundrum for Kazan Muslims. On the one hand, they lived within the geographic space that Kazan Muslims had long defined as part of their own, they were Muslims, and their language was closer to the Tatar-Turki vernacular than languages of the Kazakhs or the peoples of Central Asia. On the other hand, they had enjoyed an existence as a separate social estate until the 1860s, many of them continued to follow a nomadic way of life, and they were not well represented in Kazan 'ulamā' circles. An unpleasant truth underlay these differences: the Bashkirs were what remained of the Muslim population that had lived in the South Urals before the Kazan Tatars had settled in the region. Although some Bashkir families worked their way into the Kazan 'ulamā' networks, the politics of key South Urals Muslim cultural centers such as Orenburg, Seitov, Ufa, Cheliabinsk, and Istarlībāsh were dominated by members of the Kazan Tatar settler 'ulamā' and their descendants.

As visions of a Kazan-based Tatar nation emerged in the early 1900s, Tatar nationalists included Bashkirs and their land in the Tatar nation.[102] At times, they also included the Bashkirs to add regional coloring to their fiction, as 'Abdalmajīd Ghafūrī did in his 1914 story "Altınchāch."[103] But Kazan Muslim reformers rarely engaged directly with the Bashkirs, nor did they include much in their writings that addressed the Bashkirs' primary concern: their loss of land.

The intensity of Kazan Tatar chauvinism varied from place to place. In Kazan, where Kazakhs and Bashkirs were few, discrimination and derogatory remarks came more easily. At the time of the 1916 Revolt, the Kazan newspaper *Yūldız* showed no qualms about lumping all the peoples of

Turkestan and the steppe together under the label of inorodtsy.[104] By contrast, in Orenburg, Tatars, Bashkirs, and Kazakhs lived side by side, and periodicals gave more space to Bashkir and Kazakh issues. Nonetheless, the articles published in Orenburg still focused on land loss, colonial policy, and poverty, effectively reinforcing the image of the Bashkirs and Kazakhs as helpless victims of colonialism and modernity. In addition to Tatar-language writings, Russian-fluent Kazan Tatar reformers could draw on a wealth of Russian ethnographic research on the Bashkirs, the Kazakhs, and the peoples of Central Asia. Much of this research confirmed Kazan Tatar claims that Bashkirs, Kazakhs, and Central Asians were backward peoples.

In portraying the Muslim peoples of Russia, Kazan's Muslims held unfair advantages over many of the empire's other Muslim societies. Russian officials in Tashkent managed Muslim publishing much more closely than did those in Kazan and Orenburg.[105] The Kazakhs lacked their own publishing houses and had to send their books to Orenburg or Kazan for publication.[106] Only the Caucasus and Crimea boasted Muslim publishing centers outside the Kazan Tatars' sphere of influence. Imperial policy also favored the Kazan Tatars in liberal politics. Kazan Tatars were far more likely to live in provinces with zemstvos than were Central Asians, Kazakhs, or Caucasian Muslims. Even before the disenfranchisement of the steppe oblasts and Turkestan in 1907, Kazan Tatars were overrepresented in the State Duma compared with the rest of Russia's Muslims. They accounted for nine of the twenty-three seats held by Muslim deputies in the first duma and thirteen of thirty-four seats in the second duma. In the third they accounted for eight of eleven seats. In the fourth duma, all four Muslim deputies were Kazan Tatars.[107] Kazan Tatars were similarly overrepresented in the "all-Russian" Muslim organization *Ittifāq al-Muslimīn*. This predominance enabled Kazan Tatars to shape discourses on Islam and the relative backwardness of Russia's various Muslim peoples more thoroughly than the Kazakhs, Central Asians, or Bashkirs could hope to.

Conclusion

Jadidism as it evolved in the Volga Basin can only be understood against the background of Russia's conquest of Central Asia in the 1860s and how that conquest intersected with longer-term developments in the Machkaran network. The full integration of the Kazakh steppe and Central Asia into the empire made possible the rise of transregional commercial firms, especially in meat and animal byproducts, that were based in places such as Orenburg, Malmyzh, and Troitsk but boasted offices from Tashkent to Berlin. Such firms provided employment to ever-growing ranks of madrasa graduates as the Machkaran-sponsored madrasas continued to expand their enrollments. The overall spirit of the 1860s–1890s was one of optimism. With more capital circulation through the Kazan Muslim society than ever before, young men imagined themselves as upwardly mobile, whether that meant gaining an appointment to a major urban mosque or entering the commercial world. Ambitious students gravitated toward certain madrasas, believing that affiliation with the right school and patron would set them on the road to success.

Three madrasas stood at the center of this new maelstrom: Chistopol, Tūntār, and Lakeside. Each differed in the specifics of its structure and internal culture, but all shared deep connections to the Machkaran network, all boasted large student bodies, and all were tightly woven into global commercial relations and intellectual cultures. As their students traveled to distant commercial outposts, read foreign newspapers, and corresponded with Russian orientalists, they imagined themselves as part of a world that reached well beyond the bounds of Bulghar historiography. They became increasingly aware of European colonialism and imperialism as a threat to the Islamic world, but at the same time, they engaged in their own forms of economic and cultural imperialism, from their business endeavors in Central Asia and their school building in the steppe to their appropriation of Russian orientalist rhetoric to set themselves above other Muslim groups within the empire. In a way, Kazan Tatar Jadidism repeated the Kazan Tatar colonization of the South Urals but did so on a much larger canvas and in a more subtle manner. Whereas eighteenth-century settlers physically populated the Urals, the Jadids strove to achieve cultural and economic dominance in the steppe and Central Asia. One major obstacle to this, of course, was that the Russian government was trying to achieve the same.

Notes

1. GAOO f. 153, op. 1, del. 259, l. 74ob-76.

2. E. V. Burlutskaya, "Deevy: Vekovaya dinastiia orenburgskikh predprinimatelei," *Kupechestvo Orenburga* (2 vols.), ed. E. V. Birlutskaya (Orenburg: Izdatel'stvo OGPU, 2016), 1:15.

3. Burhān Sharaf, "ʿAbdalghanī Ḥusaynovnıng tarjama-i ḥāle ham Ḥusaynovlar firması tārīkhı," *Ghanī Bāy: Tarjama-i ḥāle, khatiralare, anıng ḥaqqında khatiralar* (Orenburg: Tipografiia gaz. "Vakt," 1913), 11.

4. Azade-Ayşe Rorlich, *The Volga Tatars: A Profile in National Resilience* (Stanford, CA: Hoover Institute, 1986); Mustafa Tuna, *Imperial Russia's Muslims: Islam, Empire, and European Modernity, 1788–1914* (Cambridge: Cambridge University Press, 2015); Christian Noack, *Muslimscher Nationalismus im Russischen Reich: Nationsbildung und Nationalbewegung bei Tataren und Bashkiren, 1861–1917* (Stuttgart: Franz Steiner Verlag, 2000); James H. Meyer, *Turks across Empires: Making Muslim Identity in the Russian Ottoman Borderlands* (Oxford: Oxford University Press, 2014).

5. Adeeb Khalid, *The Politics of Muslim Cultural Reform: Jadidism in Central Asia* (Berkeley: University of California Press, 1998); Adeeb Khalid, "What Jadidism Was and What It Wasn't: The Historiographical Adventures of a Term," *Central Eurasian Studies Review* 5, no. 2 (2006); Paolo Sartori, "Ijtihād in Bukhara: Central Asian Jadidism and Local Genealogies of Cultural Changes," *Journal of the Economic and Social History of the Orient* 59 (2016): 193–236.

6. Devin DeWeese, "It Was a Dark and Stagnant Night ('Til the Jadids Brought the Lights): Clichés, Biases, and False Dichotomies in the Intellectual History of Central Asia," *Journal of the Economic and Social History of the Orient* 59 (2016); Jeff Eden and Paolo Sartori, "Moving Beyond Modernism: Rethinking Cultural Change in Muslim Eurasia (19th–20th Centuries)," *Journal of Social and Economic History of the Orient* 59 (1-2) (2016): 1–36.

7. *Khösäen Fäezkhanov: Tarikhi-dokumental' jyentyk*, ed. Raif Märdanov (Kazan: n.p., 2006), 433–35, 480–82.

8. Rizaeddin Fäkhreddin, *Asar: Öchenche häm dürtenche tom*, ed. Ilshat Gyimadiev, Ramil Mingnullin, and Sirina Bahavieva (Kazan: Rukhiyat, 2009), 217–18; Rizaeddin Fäkhreddin, *Asar: Ikenche tom*, ed. Ilshat Gyimadiev, Ramil Mingnullin, and Sirina Bahavieva (Kazan: Rukhiyat, 2009), 95, 130–31. Riḍā'addīn bin Fakhraddīn's parents considered sending him to study with Muḥammad Dhākir, but at the time that Ghilmān received his appointment as imam of Minglebay village in 1868 and left Muḥammad Dhākir's madrasa, Riḍā'addīn bin Fakhraddīn was only ten—too young, in his parents' opinion, to be left in Chistopol alone. Instead, he was sent to Tuben Shāl village's madrasa in 1869 and eventually to Kizlāu Madrasa outside of Chistopol. (Rizaeddin Fäkhreddin, "Tärjemäi ḥälem" *Rizaetdin Fakhretdin: Fänni-biografik jyentyk*, ed. Raif Märdanov et al. [Kazan: Rukhiyat, 1999], 14–15.)

9. Fäkhreddin, *Asar: Öchenche häm dürtenche tom*, 219; Gayaz Iskhaqyi, "Tärjemäi khälem," *Gayaz Iskhaqyi: Tarikhi-dokumental' jyentyk*, ed. Söläyman Räkhimov, Zöfär Mökhämmätshin, and Ayrat Zahidullin (Kazan: Jyen, 2011), 41–42.

10. Ravil Amirkhan, "Zakir Ishan Kamalov i Tatarskoe prosveshchenie," *Gasyrlar avazy/ Eko vekhov* 1, no. 2 (2001), accessed July 16, 2018, http://www.archive.gov.tatarstan.ru/magazine/go/anonymous/main/?path=mg:/numbers/2001_1_2/05/05_1/&searched=1.

11. Fäkhreddin, *Asar: Öchenche häm dürtenche tom*, 217–18.

12. Iskhaqyi, "Tärjemäi khälem," *Gayaz Iskhaqyi*, 38.

13. *Marthiyya-i Dāmallā Muḥammad Dhakir Khaḍrat al-Chistawī* (Kazan: Tipo-litografiia Imperatorskago Universiteta, 1895), 6.

14. Iskhaqyi, "Tärjemäi khälem," *Gayaz Iskhaqyi*, 39.

15. Ibid., 40–41.

16. Ibid., 41.

17. Ibid., 41–42.

18. Ibid., 38.

19. Ibid., 45.

20. Ibid., 49.

21. Fäkhreddin, *Asar: Öchenche häm dürtenche tom*, 218.

22. Fatimai Farida, "Fatimai Farida khanymnyng üz kuly belän yazylgan köndälek däftär," *Millät analary: Tarikhi-dokumental' häm biografik jyentyk*, ed. A. Kh. Mäkhmütova (Kazan: Jyen, 2012), 486–93.

23. R. Mukhammetdinov, "Ismail Gasprinskii," *Tatarskie intellektualy: istoricheskie portrety*, ed. R. M. Mukhammetshin (Kazan: Magarif, 2005), 62; Fäkhreddin, "Ismägyil' bäk Gasprinskii," *Ismägyil' Gasprinskii: Istoricheskо-dokumental'nyi sbornik*, ed. Söläyman Räkhimov (Kazan: Jyen, 2006), 190.

24. Fäkhreddin, "Ismägyil' bäk Gasprinskii," *Ismägyil' Gasprinskii*, 192.

25. Sirri Hakan Kirimli, "National Movements and National Identities among the Crimean Tatars" (PhD diss., University of Wisconsin-Madison, 1990), 13–14.

26. Ismägyil' Gasprinskii, "Russkoe Musul'manstvo: mysli, zametki, i nabliudeniia musul'manina," *Ismägyil' Gasprinskii*, 50–85.

27. Rizaeddin Fäkhreddin, "Ismägyil' bäk Gasprinskii," *Ismägyil' Gasprinskii*, 194.

28. Gyilman Kärmiov, "Kosusyi tarikhybyz wä bashtan kichkännär," *Fatikh Kärimi, Fänni-biografik jyentyk*, ed. Mirkasyim Gosmanov (Kazan: Rukhiyat, 2000), 19; *Islam na Evropeiskom vostoke: Entsiklopedicheskii slovar'*, ed. R. A. Nabiev (Kazan: Izdatel'stvo "Magarif," 2004), 324.

29. Il'dus Zagidullin, *Islamskie instituty v Rossiiskoi imperii: Mecheti v evropeiskoi chasti Rossii i Sibiri* (Kazan: Tatarskoe Knizhnoe Izdatel'stvo, 2007), 143.

30. Fäkhretdin, "Tärjemäi khälem," *Rizaetdin Fakhretdin*, 9.

31. Ibid., 13.

32. Gyilman Kärimov, "Khosuşyi tarikhybyz wä bashtan kichkännär," *Fatikh Kärimi, Fänni-biografik jyentyk*, 18.

33. Ibid.

34. Ibid.

35. Ibid., 19.

36. "1885 g., dekabria 17. Korrespondent gazety 'Terjuman-Perevodchik' pod psevdonimom 'O.S.E.' o prichenakh otsustviia v g. Ufe medrese," in *Modernizatsionnye protsessy v tatarsko-musul'manskom coobshchestve v 1880-e–1905 gg.: dokumenty i materialy*, ed. I. K. Zagidullin (Kazan: Institut istorii im Sh. Mardzhani, 2014), 23–24.

37. Ismägyil' Rämi and Räis Dautov, *Ädäbi Süzlek* (Kazan: Tatar kitap näshriyaty, 2001), 179–80; Kamil Mutigyi, "Mäshhür Gabdullah Äfände Tukayev khakynda khätirälärem," *Tukay turynda istäleklär*, ed. Ibrahim Nurullin and Rif Yakupov (Kazan: Tatarskoe knizhnoe izdatel'stvo, 1986), 31.

38. Mutigyi, "Mäshhür Gabdullah Äfände Tukayev khakynda khätirälärem," *Tukay turynda istäleklär*, 31.

39. Rämi and Dautov, *Ädäbi Süzlek*, 23–24.

40. Ibid., 112.

41. Sharaf, "ʿAbdalghanī Ḥusaynovnıng tarjama-i ḥāle ham Ḥusaynovlar firması tarīkhı," *Ghanī Bāy*, 9–11

42. Ibid., 12. An account of the Ḥusaynovs' trading activities is also given in Tuna, *Imperial Russia's Muslims*, 133–36. While Tuna mentions the brothers' trade with the Kazakhs, he places it in the context of Russia's trade with Europe rather than Russia's conquests and growing influence in Asia.

43. Ibid., 12.
44. Ibid.
45. Ibid.
46. Ibid., 16–17.
47. Ibid., 18–19.
48. "ʿAbdullāh Būbī, 'Yaushevlar kem?'" K(P)FU-ORRK No. 208 T, l. 169.
49. "Mozaffarov, Mökhämmätkämal Mozaffar-ulı," *Baltach Entsiklopediase*, ed. Garifjan Mökhämmätshin (Kazan: PPK Idel-Press, 2006), 223–24.
50. "Mustafa Fayḍullinnan Muḥammadkamāl Muzaffarovga," K(P)FU-ORRK No. 1156T, 28–44ob, 48–125ob.
51. "6 Yanvar 1904, Mustafa Fayḍullinnan Muḥammadkamāl Muzaffarovga," K(P)FU-ORRK No. 1156T, 126.
52. "Fäyzullin, Säetgäräy Mostafa-ulı," *Baltach Entsiklopediase*, 325–26; "5 Yanvar 1914, Sayyidgaray Fayḍullinnan Muḥammadkamāl Muzaffarovga" K(P)FU-ORRK 1148T, 196.
53. "Khosuṣyi tarikhybyz wä bashtan kichkännär," *Fatikh Kärimi*, 19.
54. Ibid., 19–20.
55. "1898 yıl May 21-nda, Ismāʿīl bek Gasprinskiiga. Bakchasarayga," *Ghanī Bāy*, 112–13.
56. "(Qazaq muʿtabärennan Qıpchaq bāy Asimovka), 1898 yıl, Gīnwar 13. Qazalyga Orenburgtan," *Ghanī Bāy*, 38–39; "1898 yıl, Fevral'. Irgizga Orenburgtan," *Ghanī Bāy*, 66–67; "(Kashshafaddīn Shahidullinga) 1898 yıl May 4. Irgizga," *Ghanī Bāy*, 109–10; "1898 yıl May 26. Aqmasjidka," *Ghanī Bāy*, 119–20.
57. "Aḥmad Bāy Ḥusaynovga, 1898 yıl, Gīnwar 31. Qazānga. Orenburgtan," *Ghanī Bāy*, 45–46.
58. L. Deviatykh, *Iz istorii Kazanskogo kupechestva*, 93–95, 134–40; *Modernizatsionnye protsessy v tatarsko-musul'manskom soobshchestve v 1880-e – 1905 gg.: dokumenty i materialy*, ed. I. K. Zagidullin (Kazan: Institut istorii im Sh. Mardzhani, 2014), 28, 30, 52; "ʿAbdullāh Būbī, 'Yaushevlar kem?'" K(P)FU-ORRK 208T 169–70; "Ushbu waqfnāma" K(P)FU-ORRK 332T, 1–8; QurbānʿAlī Khalīdī, "History of Semipalatinsk," *Materials for the Islamic History of Semipalatinsk, Two manuscripts by Aḥmad-Walī al-Qazānī and Qurbānʿalī Khālidī*, trans. and ed. Allen J. Frank and M. G. Gosmanov (Berlin: Das Arabische Buch, 2001), 73.
59. Fäkhreddin, *Asar: Öchenche häm dürtenche tom*, 368.
60. Rämi and Dautov, *Ädäbi süzlek*, 272–73.
61. Fäkhreddin, *Asar: Ikenche tom*, 80.
62. R. Sh. Zaripov, *Gali Ishan, Ishmi Ishan häm Tüntär mädräsäse* (Kazan: Iman, 2002), 11; "Iz vedomosti o sostoianii medrese g. Kazani za 1905 god," *Medrese Kazani: XIX-nachalo XX vv. Sbornik dokumentov i materialov*, ed. L. V. Gorokhova (Kazan: Natsional'nyi arkhiv Respubliki Tatarstan, 2007), 127.
63. Zaripov, *Gali Ishan*, 11.
64. Gabdulla Bubyi, "Bubyi mädräsäseneng qısqa tarikhı," *Bertugan Bubyilar häm Izh-Bubyi mädräsäse: tarikhi-dokumental' jyentyk*, ed. Raif Märdanov, Ramil Mingnullin, and Söläyman Räkhimov (Kazan: Rukhiyat, 1999), 34–35.
65. NART f. 41, op. 11, del. 1, l. 114ob-15.
66. "Kasimiia," *Tatarskaia Entsiklopediia*, ed. M. Kh. Khasanov (Kazan: Institut Tatarskoi Entsiklopedii, 2006), 3:257; "Salikhov, Mukhammetkasim Abdulgallamovich," *Tatarskaia Entsiklopediia* 5:221; Rämi and Dautov, *Ädäbi Süzlek*, 152–53; "Medrese 'Apanaevskoe,'" *Islam na Evropeiskom vostoke*, 195–96.

67. Fäkhreddin, *Asar: Öchenche häm dürtenche tom*, 248.
68. "Medrese 'Apanaevskoe,'" *Islam na Evropeiskom vostoke*, 196.
69. Iskhakyi, "Tärjemäi khälem," *Gayaz Iskhakyi*, 49–52.
70. Zahir Bigiev, "Mawarannahrda säyäḥät," *Zahir Bigiev: Zur gönahlar*, ed. Räis Dautov (Kazan: Tatar kitap näshriyaty, 1991), 290–94.
71. Ibid., 293.
72. Ibid., 289.
73. Ibid., 331.
74. Ibid., 335.
75. Ibid.
76. Ibid., 336.
77. Ibid., 334–36.
78. Ibid., 335–36.
79. Ibid., 338.
80. Ibid., 337
81. Ibid., 337.
82. Allen J. Frank, *Bukhara and the Muslims of Russia: Sufism, Education, and the Paradox of Islamic Prestige* (Leiden: Brill, 2012), 162–69.
83. Zakir Hadi, "Jihansha Khäzrät," *Zakir Hadi: Saylanma Äsärlär*, ed. M. Kh. Gaynullin (Kazan: Tatarskoe knizhnoe Izdatel'stvo, 1957), 142.
84. Ibid., 142.
85. Ibid., 146–54.
86. Ibid., 154.
87. Ibid., 143.
88. "Ūrtā Aziya tārīkhī," *Dunya wa Maʿīshat* 7 (1907): 110–11; Imām Muḥammad as-Sadīq al-ʿUthmānī al-Qargalī, "Turkistan Komisiyasına raddiyya," *Dunya wa Maʿīshat* 7 (1907): 113–14.
89. A. Sh., "Waq, yaki Nospay," *Dunya wa Maʿīshat* 7 (1907): 109–10.
90. Gabdulla Tukay, "Yaponiyane möselman idächäk golama närädä?" *Gabdulla Tukay: Äsärlär* (6 vols.), ed. R. M. Kadyirov and Z. G. Mökhämmätshin (Kazan: Tatar kitap näshriyaty, 2011), 1:98.
91. "Sārt mudarrise kundez dareskhānada/Sārt mudarrise kich bāchakhānada," *Yālt-yūlt* 100 (1915): 8.
92. Qurbān ʿAlī Hājjī Khālid-ulī, *Tawārīkh-i khamsa-i sharqī* (Kazan: Urnek, 1910), 385–91.
93. N. Abramov, "Gorod Semipalatinsk," NBRK-ORK No. 58, 190b.
94. *Materials for the Islamic History of Semipalatinsk*, 14–31.
95. Gabderashit Ibrahimov, *Tärjemäi khälem*, ed. F. Äkhmätov-Urmanche (Kazan: Iman, 2001), 57.
96. Gabdulla Tukay, "Äkhmät Urmanchiyevka, [1911, May 5, Asterkhannan Kazanga], *Gabdulla Tukay*, 5:222.
97. Kamaletdin Khisametdinov, "Berge bulgan chaklar," *Tukay turynda istäleklär*, 29.
98. Muḥammadsalim Umetbaev, "Bogateet ili bedneet narod?: Analiz sotsialno-ekonomicheskie usloviia zhizni russkogo, bashkirskogo i drugikh narodov, 1897," UFITs-RAN f. 22, op. 1, del. 1, l. 116–23.
99. Bakhtiyār Bakhtigārāy-ulī, "Jīr ṣātū: Bāshqūrtlar tūrmishīnnān" (Orenburg: n.p., 1915), 2–9.

100. Ishān Muḥammad Ḥarīth Aydarov (al-Qargalī), *Ishānnarga Khiṭāb!* (Sterlitamak: Tipografiia T-va "Nur," 1911), 2; Fatikh Kärimi, "Nuretdin Khälfä," *Fatīkh Kärimi: Murza Qızı Fatyima*, 62–64.

101. Zakir Hadi, "Jihanshah Ḥäzrät," 140–41.

102. A. Ḥakīmov, *Bāshqūrtlar* (Orenburg: Karīmov, Ḥusaynov wa Sharkāsı, 1908), 3.

103. Mäjit Gafuri, "Khan kyzy Altynchach," *Mäjit Gafuri: Äsärlär*, vol. 3 (Kazan: Tatarstan kitap näshriyaty, 1981), 258.

104. "Inorodtsilarnī jiyu ḥaqqinda," *Yūldiz* 1677 (1916): 1.

105. Khalid, *Politics of Muslim Cultural Reform*, 117–27.

106. Zh. Shalgynynbai, *Istoriia kazakhskoi knizhnoi kultury (XIX v.-1917 g.—1991-2001 gg.)* (Almaty: Baspalar uyı, 2009), 33–45.

107. *Musul'manskie deputaty gosudarstvennoi dumy Rossii, 1906–1917 gg.: Sbornik dokumentov i Materialov*, ed. L. A. Yamaeva (Ufa: "Kitap," 1998), 276–313.

7

FUNDAMENTALISM, NATIONALISM, AND SOCIAL CONFLICT

Introduction

In Fatīḥ Amirkhan's 1910 novel, *Reverend Fatḥullāh*, the titular character, an early twentieth-century imam resurrected into a Tatar-Muslim society fifty years in the future, begs his son, Aḥmad, for a dream interpretation manual. Aḥmad finally relents and takes Fatḥullāh to the city's Old Book Museum, a building filled with shelf after shelf of Sufi handbooks and Hanafi law books. Fatḥullāh gazes in bliss at shelves full of copies of *Mukhtaṣar al-Qudūrī* and *Mukhtaṣar al-Wiqāya*, not realizing that he is not in a library, but rather a book graveyard.[1] These books have been warehoused in the museum because, in Amirkhan's imagined 1958, no one reads them. These future Kazan Muslims have not ceased to be Muslim. In fact, they take Islam quite seriously, as Fatḥullāh discovers to his chagrin whenever he commits a moral transgression. Nor has Islam become a private matter. Instead, it permeates everything from the legal system to the theater. However, Amirkhan's Muslims have jettisoned Sufism, munāẓaras, madhhab commentaries, and speculative theology (kalām). Fatḥullāh has been dragged against his will into the most Muslim of Muslim societies, complete with skyscrapers, Islamic courts, and flying sharīʿa police. For him, the embodiment of nineteenth-century Kazan Muslim morals and tastes, it is a waking nightmare.

Salafi Theology, Balanced Reform, and Nationalism in the Volga-Ural Region

Religious reform and national awakening have long composed two pillars of the Jadid narrative. Studies of the Jadids in the Volga-Ural region position Islamic legal reform and especially the promotion of ijtihād (original legal reasoning) over taqlīd (adherence to established precedents) as part of Jadid programs.[2] However, most of these studies give greater attention to the emergence of modern national identities among Russia's Muslim peoples.[3] In the historiography of the Volga-Ural region, the relationship between Islamic legal reform and national awakening has been portrayed as an evolutionary one: calls for change began in the "religious" sphere and proceeded to the political sphere.[4] Although this model makes space for Islam, it discusses Islam in terms of "modernization," "secularization," and/or "desacralization."[5] This reinforces a sense of rupture between the Muslim intellectual culture before and after the 1880s and creates a dichotomy between "traditional" and "modern" ways of thinking and being that is rooted in a shift from a "religious" to a "secular" and/or "national" discursive framework.

In fact, when Tatar-language texts on Islam and those on nation are arranged by date, there is no clear evidence of one retreating before the other. On the contrary, discourses on both increased in sophistication from the 1880s to the 1910s. Nor are admonitions to be conscientious Muslims replaced by calls to be model citizens of a nation. Rather, references to Islam and nation occur in tandem; rituals and symbols meant to invoke the nation were often paired with those meant to invoke Islam. Moreover, the Islam invoked was not "individualized,"[6] but rather very public and woven into the fabric of community life. Only in a society in which Islamic law regulated interpersonal relations and public behavior could the performance of ijtihād have any meaning.

An understanding of the relationship between Islamic discourses and national ones requires a dissection of the rather murky category of "religion" itself. Volga-Ural reformers did not make broad assertions about the place of Islam; rather they made very deliberate interventions into specific branches of the Islamic sciences: jurisprudence (*fiqh*) and speculative theology (kalām). Their interventions into each of these fields was methodologically different, but they had the same goal: breaking the monopoly of the highly educated and socially well-positioned over Islamic knowledge and making that knowledge accessible to all Muslims. The nation, a community of purported equals united by language, culture, history, and faith, made the ideal vehicle for pursuing this goal.

The antiauthoritarian streak among certain of Kazan's ʿulamāʾ was an outcome of the economic success and the rapid expansion of Muslim education. Shaykh Muḥammad Dhākir al-Chistāwī could accept six hundred boys into his madrasa, but it was unlikely that he could secure gainful employment for so many. The more sons of peasants and poor imams that poured into the madrasas, the more obvious the limits of Kazan ʿulamāʾ society became. If Russian Muslim identity and education policy became useful for reimaging the relationship between Kazan Tatars and the other Muslims of the empire, ijtihād, tawhīd, and Tatar nationalism became weapons for contesting social and economic privilege within Kazan Tatar society.

The term Salafism has been applied to a range of movements across the history of Islam, including the followers of Muḥammad ibn ʿAbdalwahhāb, the "Islamic modernists" of nineteenth- and early twentieth-century Egypt, and nineteenth-century South Asian reform movements such as the *Ahl al-Hadith*.[7] In attempting to more clearly define Salafism and reconstruct its genealogy, historians have highlighted several stances that characterize Salafi thought. In questions of doctrine (*ʿaqīda*), Salafis stress the oneness of God (tawhīd) and insist on a literal (rather than allegorical) reading of passages in the Qurʾān relating to the aspects of God. As a result, they reject speculative theology (kalām), by which scholars apply logic and philosophy to interpret Qurʾānic passages concerning the nature of God and his attributes.[8] They also reject the discipleship to Sufi shaykhs, veneration of saints and their graves, witchcraft, veneration of sacred trees and springs, and any other practice by which Muslims attributed divine powers to someone or something other than God, for they view such acts as a denial of God's oneness.[9]

In their practice of Islamic jurisprudence, many Salafi movements elevate the exercise of independent legal reasoning (ijtihād) by well-educated jurists and, in some cases, by all Muslims based on the Qurʾān and the hadiths. They contrast ijtihād with taqlīd, the practice of following legal precedents set down by the great scholars of the Islamic legal schools (madhhabs), and characterize the latter as "blind following" of erroneous rulings by jurists who distorted the pure Islamic law of the early Muslim community.[10]

In matters of doctrine and jurisprudence, Salafis claim to have returned to the beliefs and practices of the first three generations of Muslims and the urge their fellow Muslims to do the same. They believe that this claim makes them "pure" in their practice of Islam as non-Salafi Muslims are not, and they seek to "purify" Muslim society by spreading their modes of interpretation, often through education (*tarbiyya*), and anyone who achieves an adequate level of education may gain authority within their ranks.[11] Salafism's legitimacy is bolstered by its heavy privileging of texts; its adherents constantly reference Qur'ānic passages and hadiths to support their views.[12]

Until recently, the term Salafism has not been widely applied in historical studies of Volga-Ural Muslim society in the late 1800s and early 1900s. "Modernism" has provided the lens through which Islamic reform across the Russian empire is presented.[13] Recently, Devin DeWeese has called attention to the "Salafist" aspects of Jadid programs in pre-1917 Russia and Central Asia based on their calls for returns to the Qur'ān and hadiths as the sole sources in legal interpretations, their promotion of ijtihād, their rejection of syncretic practices, and their idealization of the early generations of Muslim society.[14] DeWeese's analysis is hampered somewhat by the fact that he draws much of his evidence from secondary sources rather than from the writings of the Jadids themselves; these secondary writings often do not devote much space to discussions of the fields of theology and jurisprudence, which are where parallels between Jadidism and early Salafi movements must be sought. Nonetheless, his proposal to reposition the Jadids vis-à-vis the Wahhabis and twentieth-century Salafism merits serious consideration.

Volga-Ural reformers of the 1880–1910s, in terms of their promotion of ijtihad and calls to reinterpret the Qur'ān and hadiths through the application of rational thought, most resemble the views of the "balanced reformers" or "enlightened Salafis" of Egypt, such as Jamaladdīn al-Afghānī and Muḥammad 'Abduh, with whom they proudly associated themselves. These balanced reformers' inconsistent views on Islamic theology, their interest in unifying Muslims across sectarian divides, and their preoccupation with normalizing Western technologies and ideas for use in Islamic societies have led historians of Salafism to exclude them from the ranks of the Salafis, for whom literalists' theology, boundary-drawing, and vocal rejection of the West are defining components of their program.[15]

That said, like the balanced reformers of Egypt, Volga-Ural reformers displayed Salafi-ish behaviors. They favored literal readings of Islamic theology, a return to the Qur'ān and hadiths for resolving legal questions, and the application of ijtihād. If they had not yet adopted the term "*takfīr*," they did try to exclude those who did not share their interpretation of Islam from the community of believers.[16] Volga-Ural reformers, even as they introduced a wide range of vernacular texts on law and doctrine, placed a great value on the ability to speak and read fluently in Arabic, the key that would allow believers to interact directly with the sacred texts.[17] They also shared the Salafis' democratic attitude concerning who could put themselves forward as an authority on the faith.[18]

Other factors, especially Volga-Ural reformers' willingness to look to the West for models of high culture and social organization and to accept aspects of western scientific and social scientific thought as universal, distinguish them from mid-twentieth-century Salafi movements and put them more in sympathy with the balanced reformers of the late 1800s. Also, their promotion of increasingly local forms of ethno-nationalism by the 1910s and their willingness to engage in politics through Duma elections, multi-ethnic parties, and civic organizations do not fit neatly with globalist and political quietist tendencies that often characterize twentieth-century Salafism.[19]

Given these differences, it is anachronistic and misleading to label Volga-Ural reformers as Salafis. It also transforms their movements into purely derivative ones and ignores their local specificity. It is most accurate to say that Volga-Ural reformers, with some variation among individuals, combined the Salafist theology with the balanced reformers' approach to jurisprudence and notions of nation, socialist utopia, uplift of the masses, and vanguard of revolution imbibed from Russian political writings. This combination of ideologies could be mutually reinforcing, especially when deployed against privilege and authority. Volga-Ural reformers did not wish simply to give the average Muslim political autonomy or material comfort. They sought the democratization of Islamic law and theology. In this sense, while they were not Salafis, they shared certain goals, views, and strategies and belonged to an intellectual lineage that was akin to that of the Salafi movements that had emerged by the mid-1900s.

Constructing Enemies: The Reformers of the Late 1880s and 1890s

Starting in the 1880s, a new kind of literature appeared in Volga-Ural Muslim society: the novel. Students at Chistopol and Lakeside madrasas first encountered this genre in the form of early Ottoman experiments in prose writing, such as Namık Kemal's *Awakening* (1874), and the growing corpus of nineteenth-century Russian novels. French and British fiction gradually became accessible through Turkish and Russian translations.

Mūsā Aqyeget's *Reverend Ḥusamaddīn* (1886) is considered the first effort at writing a Tatar novel. However, Aqyeget's tale of a young teacher from the generic village of N., who collects money to buy new textbooks for his maktab and finds true love, is both less memorable and less typical of the tone of early Tatar prose fiction than Muḥammad Ẓāhir Bīgī's novel, *Great Sins* (1889).[20] Borrowing stylistically from the works of Fyodor Dostoyevsky and Victor Hugo, *Great Sins* portrays the moral failings of Kazan Muslim society through lurid depictions of murder, infanticide, and criminality.[21] Written shortly after Bīgī's arrival at Lakeside Madrasa, *Great Sins* is a distinctly Kazan-ian novel. With some knowledge of the landmarks of the pre-1917 city, it is still possible to retrace the steps of the novel's characters. For Muslim readers in the 1880s and 1890s, Bīgī's characters were recognizable social types: the wealthy merchant, the merchant's young wife, and the rural imam's son sent to study with a prominent madrasa director. But from the opening of the novel, everything goes wrong. The merchant's wife, Māhrūi, emotionally abandoned by her husband, who is constantly out of town on business, is drawn into a liaison with another merchant and ends up pregnant by him. She resolves to keep the child, and when it is born, she turns it over to an old woman to foster. Shortly afterward, her lover turns up dead, and she is arrested for his murder. To avoid having to deal with an illegitimate addition to his family, the lover's brother pays the old woman to drown Māhrūi's baby.

In the meantime, ʿAbdalʿallām, a rural imam's son, arrives at a prestigious madrasa in Kazan. Unable to cope with the stress of studying, he takes up drinking. When the director catches him with a glass of vodka, he is expelled from the madrasa. Too ashamed to return home, ʿAbdalʿallām retreats to the poorest part of the city, where he becomes a thief and killer-for-hire.

In *Great Sins*, Bīgī purports to portray the genteel world of the nineteenth-century Kazan merchants and ʿulamāʾ. Rather than foregrounding pious shaykhs, generous merchants, and a culture of polite deference, Bīgī offers a vision of society wallowing in its own corruption. Māhrūi's husband is so busy making money that he cannot be bothered to worry about his wife. The brother of Māhrūi's lover is so obsessed with protecting the good name of his family that he is willing to murder his brother and newborn nephew. ʾAbdalʾallām struggles desperately to gain entry to the ranks of the prominent ʿulamāʾ and is morally and psychologically broken by an indifferent educational system. At the end of the novel, Māhrūi and her wealthy husband slip quietly out of Kazan and head for Siberia, leaving a scandal and a dead baby behind them. ʿAbdalʿallām escapes from prison with a band of criminals and heads to St. Petersburg to find new victims. No one has profited from the growing wealth of Kazan Muslim society. Those who succeed in scrambling to the top of society become entrapped by their wealth. Those who fail are destroyed.

Bīgī's harsh moral critique of Kazan Muslim society was repeated in other works. In 1902, ʿAyaḍ Isḥāqī, a rural imam who quit his post, published *The Hat-Making Girl*, the tale of an impoverished girl who earns her living sewing the quilted, embroidered hats so popular among nineteenth-century Kazan Muslims. She is seduced by the shopkeeper's son, disgraced, and forced into a life of prostitution.[22] In 1901, Shākir Muḥammadev, a madrasa-educated manager at Aḥmad Ḥusaynov and Bros. Co., penned "Under the Leaves, or Makarja Fair," a tale of ignorant and morally corrupt Muslim merchants.[23] The new Kazan Muslim prose did not make a generalized protest of colonialism or backwardness. Its authors hailed from a specific socioeconomic group. They were shop clerks, middle managers, rural imams, and teaching assistants subsisting on the fringes of the large scholarly networks, men who felt their careers were not commensurate with their education, talent, and ambition. In their writings, they aired their grievances against those who they imagined as the authors of their woes: the nouveau riche businessmen and the powerful, multigenerational ʿulamāʾ families.

For these disgruntled young men, the madrasa and its teachers were natural targets for criticism. The madrasa had been their main social world through early childhood, adolescence, and young adulthood, where they had been instilled with the idea that the young deferred to the old and the lesser to the greater with the understanding that patrons would intervene on behalf of their clients and teachers on behalf of their students. In the madrasa, class and social connections did not matter, because everyone was able to pursue knowledge, and the most talented and hardworking would prevail in public demonstrations of skill, as young Isḥāqī, the son of a humble village imam, had caught the eye of Chistopol's Shaykh Muḥammad Dhākir.

Outside the walls of the madrasa, however, life was quite different. Prestigious postings were few and far between. This had already been a problem in the 1860s and 1870s. By the 1890s, as madrasa enrollments continued to expand, unemployment had become more common. There was simply no way that even a madrasa director as powerful as Shaykh Muḥammad Dhākir could guarantee ideal employment for all of his students. There was still employment to be had, especially for muezzins, junior teachers, village imams, and students who were willing to turn their back on Islamic intellectual pursuits to enter the business world. But this was clearly not what many late nineteenth- and early twentieth-century prose writers wanted. This was especially the case for young men who graduated from Machkara-network madrasas such as Chistopol, Lakeside, and Tūntār. They had chosen these madrasas specifically because they strove to rise above their parents' station, join the ranks of the "great" ʿulamāʾ, and command social and moral authority.

The madrasa graduates of the 1880s and 1890s were systematic thinkers. Their philosophy and logic-heavy education, intended to prepare then to carry out public debates over speculative theology, had conditioned them to gather data, weigh the merits of competing evidence, draw analogies, and formulate conclusions. Those who attended well-financed, well-connected madrasas would have been familiar with discussions of failed governance in the Muslim world, expanding European power, and perceived crisis in the Turkish and Arabic-language press. Those with fluency in Russian would also have been aware of liberal and socialist discourses on Russia's social, political, and economic backwardness. For those who traveled abroad to Istanbul, Cairo, Mecca, or Paris, knowledge gleaned through reading was reinforced by personal contact with Ottoman and Arab reformers and dissidents.[24] Kazan's madrasa students stood at the confluence of multiple discourses on progress, backwardness, and crisis, and they began to map those discourses onto their own society. Increasingly, their failure to achieve their career goals was not a function of their individual lack of talent, will, or luck. Rather, it was symptomatic of structural failures within Kazan Muslim society. These structural failures were endemic in the larger spheres that Kazan Muslim society occupied: the Russian empire and the Muslim world. By the late 1890s, they had determined that the only cure for these failures was the reconstruction of Kazan Muslim intellectual culture.

Early Tatar novelists soon narrowed their social critique from elites' morality in general to the injustices of Muslim scholarly culture. They began to launch vicious attacks on the culture of munificence, dignity, and deference on which relations between powerful shaykhly families and their clients were constructed. In *A Student and a Shakird* (1898), Fatīḥ Karīmī portrays a shaykh's disciples as uncultured buffoons in stained clothing. They are rude to everyone around them, know nothing about Islam despite years of study at the madrasa, and are shown racing about the deck on an opium-fueled rampage.[25] The shaykh himself is portrayed as kind but narrow minded and provincial, unable to conceive that Karīmī 's narrator could wear European clothes but still be a faithful Muslim.[26] The wealthy disciple who presents the narrator with a book opposing Gasprinskii's new method proves illiterate.[27] In another of Karīmī 's stories, "The Junior Teacher Nūraddīn," an ignorant, morally repulsive young man seeks to marry the imam Gainaddīnovs's daughter solely to gain a house and a teaching post.[28] Another of Karīmī's stories, "Jihāngīr Studies at a Village Madrasa," presents Aḥmadshāh, a bumbling, but well-intentioned village imam who is utterly oblivious to the fact that he does not know how to teach.[29]

Karīmī's fiction dispensed with all pretense of civility. His 'ulamā' characters, the beneficiaries of late nineteenth-century scholarly culture, were crude caricatures who lacked any redeemable qualities. In a later edition of *A Shakird and a Student*, Karīmī alluded to the hostility that the book's first edition had raised. He argued that its readers were not yet sophisticated enough to understand that he was not deriding all imams and shaykhs, but only the "bad" ones.[30] However, in his readers' defense, there was nothing in the novel to suggest that Karīmī's critique of Kazan's 'ulamā' was not general. Karīmī drew the battle lines clearly. There were only two kinds of people in the world: those who supported the established way of doing things and those who wished to overturn the system. Karīmī portrayed the former as delusional, stupid, or villainous. This approach left no room for people to disagree or pose questions about the merits of his critique. It was also deliberately offensive to anyone economically, socially, or emotionally invested in the social order that had emerged during the nineteenth century.

Isḥāqī, in his apocalyptic novel, *Extinction after Two Hundred Years* (1904), made an even more pointed attack on 'ulamā' culture. In *Extinction,* Isḥāqī lays out a speculative history in which Kazan's Muslim Bulghar population ceases to exist within two centuries. The novel borrowed liberally from the first volume of Marjānī's depiction of Tatar history in *Mustafād al-Akhbār* and played a significant role in popularizing Kazan-centered Tatar national identity among madrasa students.[31] However, it also singled out nineteenth-century elite Muslim culture, with its wealthy merchants, nepotistic scholarly networks, and lavish parties, as instrumental in the downfall of "Bulghar" society. At the center of this destructive, self-absorbed elite were the 'ulamā' and *ishan*s (shaykhs), who exploited and deliberately misled less educated Muslims.[32]

Isḥāqī, who at the time dabbled in socialist revolutionary political philosophies, presented the 'ulamā' as a distinct class ('ulamā' *ṣınıfı*) readily identifiable by its members' parasitic behavior, obscurantism, and opposition to change.[33] This understanding of the ʿulamāʾ as a class of exploitative gentry-clergy would have been foreign to nineteenth-century Kazan Muslims. It was an import from Russian Marxist thought. But it was a potent one, especially for young people who existed on the margins of the powerful scholarly networks and for those who had succeeded professionally but watched their friends and classmates fail to find employment and patrons.

Redefining the ʿulamāʾ as a clerical class gave disgruntled madrasa graduates a clear adversary. It also set up a broader imagined conflict between the keepers of arcane knowledge and the average Muslim. The former, under the guise of guiding the latter, intentionally restricted access to Islamic legal and doctrinal knowledge by transmitting it in foreign languages and complicating it with commentaries and convoluted philosophy. Karīmī's and Isḥāqī's effort to break the "ʿulamāʾs" monopoly over knowledge was facilitated by the spread of literacy, Islamic education, and vernacularization that had begun in the late 1700s, but they blatantly ignored these longer-term changes and wrote as though Kazan Muslim culture had existed unchanged for hundreds of years and as if their goal of raising popular knowledge of Islamic law and doctrine was novel. Their fetishizing of mathematics, astronomy, geography, and history as "European" or "universal" sciences similarly ignored the fact that these subjects had already been taught effectively in the madrasas for generations.

Karīmī's and Isḥāqī's attacks on Muslim education and intellectual culture were never truly about the effectiveness of madrasa education. They were about power. By leveling accusations of incompetence and irrelevance against powerful madrasa directors and shaykhs, they attempted to strip them of their social authority. By championing the "European" sciences, they appropriated the most persuasively powerful culture of their day to support their position. By setting themselves up as defenders of the common Muslim, they sought to usurp the position of the powerful shaykhly and scholarly families as community leaders. The fringes of the Machkaran network had rebelled against the core.

Constructing a New Islam

While late nineteenth-century reformers reimagined the ʿulamāʾ as a closed class that used their control of Islamic knowledge to wield control over common Muslims, they also began to make assertions about the nature of

Islam itself. Near the end of *A Student and a Shakird*, a wealthy Sufi disciple offers Karīmī's narrator a book and proposes that he follow the way (madhhab) of Reverend ʿArīfūllah, a Kazan imam who opposes education reform. The narrator responds that he follows only one way (madhhab), that of the Prophet Muhammad.[34] The anonymous author of the poetry collection *Read!* proclaims that he "is in agreement with the way (madhhab) of the Muslim community (*ahl as-sunna wāl-jamāʿa*)."[35] The implication in both works is that there is only one "way," only one Islam. According to both authors, that Islam was to be found in the Qurʾān and hadiths. Arabic grammar, logic, and philosophy had been intended as tools to assist Islamic scholars in interpreting the texts, but instead they had become ends in themselves. Islamic scholars no longer studied the Qurʾān and the hadiths or learned Arabic as a functional language. Instead, they obsessed over lines they had memorized out of books on logic, philosophy, grammar, guides to Ḥanafī jurisprudence, and in some cases, their own teachers' writings. Sunni Islam had become divided not only among the four legal schools (the Ḥanafī, Shafīʿī, Malikī, and Ḥanbalī), but also among factions loyal to individual Sufi masters and legal scholars.

Karīmī and Isḥāqī argued that Sufi leaders, syncretic practices, classical philosophy, and intense loyalty to a single teacher separated a believer from true Islam. They adopted an uncompromising view of those who disagreed with them: the only true Muslims were those who shared their point of view. Karīmī, Isḥāqī , and other reformers in the Volga-Ural region were by no means followers of Muḥammad ibn ʿAbdalwahhāb, but the resemblance between their assertions of the unity of Islam and those of the Wahhabis was not lost on their opponents, who openly compared the two movements.[36]

By the late 1890s and early 1900s, Volga-Ural reformers increasingly argued that Islam was supposed to be easy to understand. It was fractious, madhhab-bound Muslim scholars who had complicated the faith with their law commentaries, grammars, ancient philosophy, legal schools, and Sufi lineages. By returning Islam to its roots, the reformers believed that they were not only returning Islam to the common Muslims, but also empowering those Muslims to wrest control of their society from a small group of wealthy exploiters. Education reform as it was implemented by reformist members of the Machkaran networks by the 1890s and early 1900s was designed to destroy the imagined divide between the ʿulamāʾ and the uneducated. By reducing the amount of time needed to teach children to read in their native language, teachers could devote more time to teaching foreign languages and other subjects.[37] Native-language literacy opened the way for children to acquire knowledge through a growing Turki-language published literature on religion, accounting, geography, and astronomy. Until the 1880s, these subjects had been accessible only in Arabic and Persian. As Karīmī suggested in *A Shakird and a Student*, native-language literacy could also be a stepping stone to learning foreign languages more rapidly.[38] For reformers, even Russian-language lessons, which were introduced into reformed madrasas in the 1890s, served to undermine the authority of the scholarly elite. Russian fluency enabled Muslims to communicate directly with Russian officials without having to work through intermediaries. It also gave access to the world of Russian literary, philosophical, political, and scientific writings.

Karīmī scoffed at his opponents' concern that widespread literacy in Turki would lead to the translation of the Qur'ān into the vernacular and that chaos would ensue, but for scholars who did not share his views, that was the logical result of encouraging all Muslims to read the sacred text and draw their own conclusions.[39] Kazan scholars had already dealt with the dilemmas posed by popular literacy in the early nineteenth century. Their solution has been to take on the role of spiritual guides and mediators, providing education, prescribing appropriate readings, and adhering strictly to the Ḥanafī madhhab. Even some reformers feared the outcome of not regulating what Muslims read. In 1890, a contributor to *Terjuman* proposed the appointment of a Muslim specialist to the Russian censorship committee. The author argued that the state censor lacked the expertise to differentiate between reliable and unreliable books on Islam and, therefore, approved many "religious" books for press that were full of nonsense and misled Muslims.[40]

In general, however, the reformers favored breaking down hierarchies of religious and intellectual authority rather than reinforcing or coopting them. Amid the flood of literature on Islamic law, theology, and morality in the first half of the nineteenth century, scholars such as Qūrṣāwī and Ūtiz-Īmānī reasserted the limitations on ijtihād and advocated the practice of taqlīd, provided that the decisions followed did not contradict the Qur'ān and hadiths. The reformers of the late 1800s were far less cautious.

'Abdullāh, 'Ubaydullāh, and Mukhlīsa Būbī were the grandchildren of Muḥammad Raḥīm bin Yūsuf's student, Ni'matullāh.[41] Unlike Karīmī and Isḥāqī, who chose to become writers rather than licensed imams, the Būbī brothers were licensed as imams in their native village and, together with their sister, ran the village's maktab and madrasa. In 1904, ʿAbdullāh Būbī, the most prolific writer of the siblings, published a series of pamphlets entitled *Truth*. He argued that many intelligent Muslims of his own day had adopted the views and beliefs of their parents and grandparents and in doing so had unwittingly embraced error.[42] Būbī argued that the Islamic revelation had been sent not only for the Prophet's companions and the first Muslims, but also for all humankind across time. It was therefore incumbent on all Muslims in all times and places to return to the revealed texts and interpret them in the context of their own day.[43] He argued that the Ḥanafī legal commentaries of the past were not infallible or eternal because they could only interpret the Qurʾān and hadiths for their own time. As human civilization changed, Muslims scholars needed to return to the Qurʾān and the hadiths and adapt their interpretations. One example he raised of the historically contingent nature of Islamic legal interpretation was clothing. He conceded that pants were not mentioned in the Qurʾān and the hadiths because no one in early Muslim society wore them. However, they were widely worn in the early 1900s. Thus, an early Muslim and a twentieth-century Muslim would necessarily possess a different understanding of the specifics of permissible clothing, although both would agree on the need to cover the body.[44]

Būbī further developed his views on legal interpretation in *Has the Time for Ijtihād Ended or Not?* (1909). He noted that one of the common arguments for limiting or forbidding ijtihād was the prevention of divergent opinions on a single issue. However, he argued, divergence of opinion had been inherent in Islamic legal life from the earliest days of the Hanafī legal school; even some of Abū Ḥanīfa's own students had disagreed with him.[45] Early Muslims had embraced the idea of using human reason to interpret the law. However, later Muslims fell under the influence of the Jews and the Christians and decided that it was preferable to follow the interpretations of past jurists, even when those decisions lacked a sound evidentiary basis. As different Muslims chose to follow the decisions of different early jurists, once-unified Islam was divided into factions and legal schools.[46]

According to Būbī, in addition to dividing Islam, the preference for following established legal decisions over formulating new ones led to "blind imitation" (*suqur taqlīd*), when Muslims began to apply past scholars' decisions without analyzing or understanding them. Muslims also began to follow the proclamations of their teachers and shaykhs without considering the evidence supporting those proclamations. As a result, what was permissible was made forbidden and what was forbidden was made permissible.[47] Islamic law, as it was practiced in nineteenth-century Kazan, had become unmoored from the Qur'ān and the hadiths and thus from the values and priorities of the faith.

Būbī's views on using human reasoning to reinterpret the Qur'ān and striving to bring happiness (*sa'ādat*) to Muslim society were heavily influenced by Muḥammad 'Abduh. Būbī also cited Ottoman liberal reformer and writer Ahmed Midhat as an important influence.[48] Like 'Abduh, Būbī promoted ijtihād as a tool for adapting Islam to the conditions of the twentieth century and restoring the strength and unanimity that had characterized the early Muslim community. Būbī shared Qūrṣ āwī's and Ūtiz-Īmānī's concern over the dissemination of legal decisions that were based on faulty evidence or contradicted the Qur'ān and hadiths. However, Būbī's views on the madhhabs and the following of established legal precedent (taqlīd) differed starkly from those of the early nineteenth-century legal scholars. Where they saw stability, Būbī saw stagnation.

Mūsā Bīgīev, a son-in-law of Shaykh Muḥammad Dhākir and younger brother of novelist Muḥammad Ẓāhir Bīgī, also called for an overhaul of Islamic law in Kazan. Bīgīev attended Lakeside Madrasa and went to Bukhara in 1895. There he read Euclid, Pythagoras, Archimedes, Descartes, and Bacon and translated treatises on mathematics from Russian into Turkish. Upon returning to Russia, he was determined to pursue a career in mathematics.[49] When his faulty knowledge of Latin made it impossible for him to attend St. Petersburg University, he traveled to Istanbul to enroll in the Ottoman engineering school.[50] There, he met novelist Mūsā Aqyeget, who encouraged him to give up engineering and devote his energies to the Islamic sciences. Bīgīev dropped out of engineering school and set out on a journey across the Islamic world.[51] He studied at madrasas in India, Mecca, Medina, Syria, and Egypt. While in Egypt, he studied at al-Azhar. Parts of Bīgīev's *History of the Qur'ān* appeared in 'Abduh's journal *al-Manār*.[52]

By the time Bīgīev returned to Russia in 1904, he was convinced that in every part of the Muslim world Islamic education was broken.[53] Whereas Būbī divided his energies between restructuring Islamic legal education and critiquing Islamic legal culture among the Kazan Tatars, Bīgīev, in his early works, focused primarily on reinventing juridical training at the madrasa. He encouraged students to exercise reason in their studies. To this end, in 1907 he translated the poetry collection *Unnecessary Necessity* by eleventh-century rationalist Abū 'Alā' al-Ma'arrī, from Arabic into Tatar.[54]

Bīgīev also began to write textbooks and law guides to replace the standard texts of the nineteenth-century madrasa. In *Arabic Literature*, he criticized the nineteenth-century madrasa curriculum. On the one hand, he claimed that it was full of books of Arabic grammar, theology, and Greek philosophy that were incomprehensible to students and in some cases led them to erroneous conclusions.[55] On the other hand, he argued that the curriculum offered little or nothing in the way of hadith studies, tafsīrs, explanations of the rules relating to basic Islamic rituals and obligations, history, arithmetic, or the natural sciences, things Bīgīev believed to be vital for gaining a basic understanding of Islam.[56]

Bīgīev, like Būbī, saw rationalism as the salvation of Islam and the element that distinguished "progressive" societies from "backward" societies. However, he did not advocate the simple importation of European knowledge and curricula into the madrasa. Instead, he called on Muslims to recover rationalist thinkers from the Arab-Islamic intellectual heritage. He acknowledged that some of these authors' ideas may have been "borrowed" from other civilizations, but he argued that Arab Muslim authors put their own mark on those ideas and made them authentically Muslim.[57] Reviving the rationalist strain in Islamic thought, Bigiev believed, would lead to a revolution in religious and political thought. He also sought to reform the teaching of Islamic jurisprudence. In his *Rules of Jurisprudence* (1910), he defined for students Islamic jurisprudence, which included the fields of doctrine, ethics, ritual, women's issues, social relations, and punishments.[58] In order to assist students in navigating these fields, he first identified and explained the fourteen sources of the law.[59] He then went on to enumerate and explain 193 rules to follow when resolving a legal question.

The information that Bīgīev offered in *Rules of Jurisprudence* was not original or innovative. The book presented the basic foundations and method of the Ḥanafī madhhab. Bīgīev's innovation lay in his presentation of the material. He gathered concepts that had been scattered across multiple books and presented them in one 232-page volume composed in the Turki-Tatar language. Like *Arabic Literature*, *Rules of Jurisprudence* was designed to systematize and rationalize Islamic legal education. Bīgīev defined and explained new words and concepts in simple language. He tailored the knowledge to the abilities of his imagined students rather than demanding that the preteen and teenage students rise to the level of overly difficult or mature material.

Calibrating Islamic legal and theological knowledge to meet the needs of specific age groups and grade levels was also embraced by ʿAbdullāh Būbī's brother, ʿUbaydullāh. In *Turki Reading*, a primer for the maktab, he introduced his young readers to the concept of divine love by drawing a comparison between a mother's relationship with her child and God's relationship with human beings. By moving from the child's love for his/her mother to explaining that God was the creator of the child, the mother, and everything else that made up the child's immediate world, ʿUbaydullāh reduced the complicated concepts of creation, divine power, and divine love to something that five-year-old children could comprehend.[60]

Mūsā Bīgīev and the Būbī brothers' efforts to reform Islamic law by emphasizing rational thought stood at the extreme end of a spectrum of education and legal reform in Kazan Muslim society from the late 1880s to the 1910s. Other scholars focused on vernacularizing the madrasa curriculum rather than overhauling it, translating popular textbooks such as *Mukhtaṣar Qudūrī*, *Mukhtaṣar al-Wiqāya*, and *ʿAyn al-ʿIlm* into Turki.[61] Some scholars translated or composed books for emphasizing hadith studies in the classroom.[62] By providing biographies of hadith transmitters, Bārūdī used hadith studies to improve students' reading skills in Arabic.[63] Others focused on improving methods for teaching Arabic. ʿAbdullāh Būbī penned at least three different textbooks for teaching the Arabic language through Turki.[64] Other authors published Turki-language books of catechism and doctrine for children and a general readership.[65] Some scholars sought to historicize Islam with new textbooks on the life of the Prophet Muḥammad and the history of the faith.[66] By the early 1900s, maktab and madrasa teachers could choose from a growing variety of vernacular-language textbooks and teaching methods.

Literalist Theology and the Limits of Rationalism

While reformers promoted the use of reason for resolving Islamic legal questions, their approach to theology was very different. This approach was already evident in *Doctrine*, a theology textbook published in 1894, which explained in straightforward vernacular Turki that God was unique and without equals or intermediaries. The author patiently explained that God could indeed see and hear but needed no eyes or ears (in the way human beings imagined them) to do so. How precisely this was accomplished was beyond the reader's ability to comprehend and no allegorical or metaphorical readings were required to clarify what was meant by the words sight or hearing; the reader was to take the matter of God's hearing and the inability to conceive of how God actually heard (or saw or spoke) on faith.[67] Aḥmad Hādī Maqsūdī's textbook on theology, also titled *Doctrine*, echoed this view, informing his readers that God's attributes were "beyond the ability of the human mind to comprehend." It was enough to be able to list them and to believe that they existed.[68]

These literalist presentations of God's attributes were not in keeping with theology as it was practiced in and around Kazan in the 1800s. Kazan's Muslim scholars hailed from the Māturīdī school of theology, which enjoyed popularity among Sunni Muslim scholars in South Asia, Central Asia, and the Ottoman empire. Māturīdī theologians placed especial value on the use of reason to resolve theological questions. Debates over speculative theology (kalām) were a centerpiece of intellectual and social life among Kazan ʿulamāʾ and provided an opportunity for scholars to put their knowledge and reasoning skills on public display. Yet theology was precisely the field in which supposedly reason-loving reformers waged a fierce war against reason.

ʿAbdullāh Būbī, in the foreword to his translation of Muḥammad ʿAbduh's *The Unity of Theology* into Tatar-Turki, proposes why reformers rejected the use of reason in matters of theology. He claims that the "old books of doctrine" were full of "discussions." When students saw that there were as many as fifteen different discussions of proofs relating to the divine attributes, they became confused and began to doubt. Encounters with these overly complicated, contradictory discussions and disputes caused many educated young people to abandon the faith. The cure that Būbī prescribed for this confusion was the composition of new books of doctrine that replaced multiple discussions of proofs with unambiguous statements on the nature of God and his attributes. He put forward ʿAbduh's *Risāla at-Tawḥīd* as an ideal model of this new kind of doctrinal textbook.[69] In Būbī's foreword, one can detect the same impulse toward simplification that reformers applied to jurisprudence. He took the same stance toward theological madhhabs that he took toward legal ones: all madhhabs were divisive and useless; Islam needed "new," "strong" answers.[70]

Ḍiyaʾ al-Kamālī, the founder of Ufa's Madrasa-i ʿAliyya, offers a fuller discussion of tawḥīd in his *The Philosophy of Islam*. He includes a discussion of the difference between tawḥīd (unity of God) and various forms of *shirk* (polytheism) and identifies tawḥīd as the foundation of Islam.[71] For an understanding of the philosophical discussions of the proofs of tawḥīd, he refers his readers to the numerous existing works of speculative theology.[72] However, in his discussion of the divine attributes only a few pages later, he dismisses earlier scholars' efforts to classify and analyze God's attributes, asking his readers "if it is impossible to measure the depth of the sea with an axe handle, is it possible to measure with knowledge and classify the eternal perfection of God?"[73]

Dhākir al-Qadīrī studied in Bukhara, Mecca, Madina, and Cairo before returning to Russia in 1906 and writing for the St. Petersburg journal *at-Tilmīdh*. From 1907 to 1909, he taught philosophy and Arabic literature at Ḥusayniyya Madrasa before taking a similar job at Madrasa-i ʿAliyya in Ufa, where he remained until 1913.[74] In the foreword to his *Lessons in the Science of Speculative Theology*, Qadīrī reveals himself as a strong supporter of Muḥammad ʿAbduh, going so far as to claim that *Risāla at-Tawḥīd* was the only textbook appropriate for teaching Islamic doctrine to early twentieth-century students.[75] *Lessons* appeared in print two years before Būbī's translation of *Risāla al-Tawḥīd* and was intended as a companion book for students reading *Risāla* in Arabic. However, *Lessons* stands on its own as an expression of Qadīrī's views on theology. *Lessons* begins with a lengthy history of the evolution of speculative theology in Islam, a process that he claims tore apart the early Muslim community. This bloody factionalism is temporarily ended when Abū al-Ḥasan al-Ashʿarī, the founder of the Ashʿarī school (madhhab) of theology, advocated an intermediary position between those theologians who promoted the application of reason to resolve theological questions and those who rejected it. For Qadīrī, however, this moment, which marked the beginning of rise of the Ashʿarī school as a major theological school of the Sunni Muslim world, was not a victory but merely a respite. Although the Ashʿarī school placed bounds on the use of reason, it still permitted reason-based interpretation of the Qurʾān and the hadith for resolving theological questions, and over the succeeding centuries, Islamic theology grew into a complicated field riddled with disputes. Even the school's founder, Abū al-Ḥasan, recognized the monster he had created. According to Qadīrī, Abū al-Ḥasan eventually abandoned his own school for that of the Ḥanbalīs, who opposed any application of reason or logic in the field of theology.[76] In the centuries that followed, Ashʿarī theology gradually drew to itself all the intellectual resources of the Muslim world, leaving other fields of intellectual inquiry to stagnate. Educated Muslims dedicated their lives to tedious debates over arcane points of theology while the world passed them by.[77]

Qadīrī's history of speculative theology presented in *Lessons* ties together multiple threads of reformist thought. Like Būbī and Kamālī, he simultaneously advocated the application of reason in jurisprudence and literalist readings of the sacred texts in matters of theology. This seeming contradiction can be explained by the fact that he saw theological disagreements as dangerously divisive without providing visible benefit, whereas the reconsideration of matters within the realm of jurisprudence could allow for the normalization of new technologies, goods, and practices into Muslim society.[78]

Volga-Ural reformers' literalist approach to theology served multiple purposes. Literalism in discussions of the divine attributes made theology readily explicable to less educated Muslims. As Lauzière has argued, it also set limits on the disorder that could be loosed through ijtihād by declaring theology, and thereby the core tenets of Islam, unassailable.[79] This strategy was meant to avert the bitter doctrinal conflicts that had plagued the early Islamic community. Finally, devaluing speculative theology, the discipline at the heart of public dispute and reputation building in the Kazan Muslim community, amounted to an attack on the legitimacy and authority of the region's powerful ʿulamāʾ families. In this way, the theological writings of Qadīrī, Būbī, and Kamālī and the social protest novels of Karīmī and Isḥāqī served the same purpose. All these authors branded speculative theological debate and adherence to madhhab as markers of social privilege. Even as they warned of the evils of theological conflict, they showed no qualms about stirring up social conflict.

Responses to Reform

Efforts at reforming Islamic legal and theological instruction provoked mixed responses in Kazan Muslim educated society. Discussions of the language of instruction, the reliability of textbooks, and the role of philosophy in the curriculum had a decades-long history in the Volga-Ural region, but the fact that some reformers made no secret of their interest in European ideas on education and knowledge made their proposed reforms hotly contested. Maktab and madrasa teachers found it necessary to clarify that they wanted neither to transform Kazan's Muslim culture into a

European one nor to eliminate Islam from law and education. The teachers' society of Jīnālstānī Madrasa in Agerje village, Kazan province, began their handbook on pedagogy with a discussion of how their views on education reform were supported by the Qur'ān and the hadiths and were therefore compatible with Islam.[80] In *A Student and a Shakird*, Karīmī tries to justify and normalize the adoption of technologies and organizational methods from Europe by differentiating between form and function. Using the metaphor of transportation, he argued that performing the hajj was important, but whether one arrived in Mecca on a cart or a train was not.[81] Likewise, he emphasized that it was important that all Muslims studied and understood Islamic law and doctrine. Any education method was fine, so long as it achieved that goal.[82] 'Abdullāh Būbī addressed these concerns more specifically in *Must Progressive Science and Knowledge Be Atheist?*, in which he discussed the relationship between the spiritual and material aspects of God's creation. He firmly dismissed allegations by European writers that Islam hindered progress and the development of science.[83] As he saw it, art, science, and intellectual life could only exist because of the spiritual side of creation.[84]

Some scholars took an openly hostile stance toward the reformers' proposed changes to Islamic legal theory, theology, and education. In a correspondence with Muḥammadiyya Madrasa director Bārūdī about imam appointments in the 1890s, Ishmuḥammad Dīnmuhammadov, the director of Tūntār Madrasa, harshly criticized those who called for wider practice of independent legal reasoning and new interpretations of Islamic law. Dīnmuhammadov argued that if following the legal opinions of Abū Hanīfa, the founder of the Hanafī school, was evil, then the protection of God must itself be evil. He pointed out that those who claimed that the era of ijtihād was not at an end believed that there was no need to follow any authority at all.[85] Dīnmuḥammadov's critique of Bārūdī's stance on legal theory eventually descended into vicious personal insults, with Dīnmuḥammadov calling Bārūdī the son of a soldier and the grandson of a *kumgan*-making peasant.[86] The remarks targeted Bārūdī's unscholarly origins—his father had been a cobbler's apprentice before becoming a wealthy merchant and his grandfather had been a soldier—to question his abilities as a jurist and teacher. They also illustrate how charged, bitter, and personal the conflict over legal theory, theology, and teaching methods had become.

In the face of such conflict, other scholars assumed a more conciliatory tone. An anonymous writer, in a pamphlet entitled *Truth*, called for Kazan's teachers to end their fights over education methods. He claimed that four conditions led to the decline of Islam: (1) a society of people who did not act on the knowledge they possessed; (2) a society of people who took actions out of ignorance; (3) a society of people who did not pass on the knowledge they possessed; (4) a society of people who prevented teaching. He identified the fourth condition as the most shameful.[87] He implied that, by fighting among themselves, Kazan ʿulamāʾ impeded the educational process and endangered the future of Islam regardless of what kind of education they favored.

Objections to changing the madrasa curriculum were not purely a matter of nostalgia or desire for social harmony. They were also about standardization and stability. With no central administration for organizing Islamic education, the use of a "traditional" set of texts guaranteed the transmission of the same body of knowledge across generations and among different parts of the region. There was also the matter of legitimacy. The authority attributed to the textbooks used in the Ḥanafī madrasas was derived, in part, from their perceived antiquity. ʿAbdullāh Būbī's rejection of the legal formulas set out in *Mukhtaṣar al-Wiqāya* or Mūsā Bīgīev's conceit that he could write a better Arabic grammar book than al-Jūrjānī, whose *al-Awāmil al-Miʾah* had been used to teach Arabic to madrasa students for hundreds of years, struck some as reckless arrogance. In the eyes of some scholars, Būbī and Bīgīev overestimated their abilities and, by encouraging others to follow them in their deviance, threatened to throw Russia's Muslims into chaos.[88] The results of their reform projects confirmed their critics' fears rather than allayed them.

The New Madrasas and Their Graduates

In 1889, the Ḥusaynov family opened Ḥusayniyya Madrasa in Orenburg. In 1891, Bārūdī opened Muḥammadiyya Madrasa in Kazan. In 1906, Ḍiyāʿ al-Kamālī opened Madrasa-i ʿAliyya in Ufa. From the 1890s to the early 1900s, Būbī Madrasa, Madrasa-i Shamsiyya in Tūntār village, ʿUthmāniyya Madrasa in Ufa, and Rasūliyya Madrasa in Troitsk enacted extensive curricular and administrative reforms.[89]

While there was not a single model of madrasa reform, there were certain characteristics that many of the reformed madrasas shared. In the classroom, they moved away from the munāẓara format (assigning students reading and meeting to discuss them) to an instructor-centered model in which students spent more time at lessons being lectured to by the teacher.[90] Open-ended study was replaced with rigid programs divided into grade levels and instructional hours.[91] In the classrooms and the dormitories, students were sorted by age. Lessons were organized around academic subjects rather than books. With more classroom hours at their disposal, reformed madrasa directors expanded the amount of time devoted to mathematics, natural sciences, native-language reading and writing, and the Russian language.

The fate of legal and theological training in the reformed madrasas was complex. Persian language and classical philosophy were stigmatized by reformers as antiquated and impediments to students' learning; they were either reduced or eliminated from the curriculum. Speculative theology was replaced with courses in "doctrine" (*ʿaqīda*), which presented a list of statements of faith rather than reasoned arguments. Reformers tended to view Arabic language, Qurʾānic and hadith studies, and jurisprudence as crucial to reinvigorating Islam. These subjects were retained, but they were often taught from newly published Turki-language textbooks. Reformers, subscribing to the belief that subjects could be learned more quickly if they were taught "rationally," reduced the number of classroom hours devoted to these subjects.

Studies of Jadid education reform have emphasized the introduction of "secular" subjects (mathematics, natural sciences, etc.) as a destabilizing factor in the new madrasas.[92] However, the structural changes to the madrasa were much more destabilizing. In the eighteenth and nineteenth centuries, the madrasas had been sites for establishing social connections across generations. By studying with a teacher or shaykh, a student became a member of his network. For the student, this meant gaining a patron and protector. For the ʿulamāʾ collectively, this system provided a means of judging the quality of younger colleagues. It was still very much in force in the early 1900s, when ʿAbdalmajīd Ghafūrī proudly identified himself as a student of Naqshbandi Shaykh Zaynullāh Rasūlev on the cover of one of his early books of poetry.[93] Ghafūrī, as a young poet and ex-madrasa student, was unknown, but Rasūlev was a widely respected spiritual leader. Ghafūrī could borrow his master's reputation until he established his own.

The new system of grade levels, instructional hours, and age cohorts obliterated intergenerational ties. Repeated assertions that one person could not possibly teach all academic subjects led madrasa directors to hire more teachers who could be assigned to teach specific subjects. The mass-production of textbooks that included prepared exercises and pedagogical instructions enabled directors to hire junior teachers and teaching assistants with limited teaching experience. The addition of designated dormitories, cafeterias, libraries, orphanages, theaters, endowments, and other facilities to madrasas necessitated the hiring of support staff. In the 1800s, madrasa directors had been teachers and mentors to their students. In the reformed madrasas of the early 1900s, they became administrators.

Those directors and sponsors dedicated to overhauling Islamic law and theology believed that the most effective way to spread their ideas was to produce as many likeminded teachers and imams as rapidly as possible. The new madrasas were designed to process students en masse. Students enrolled, were issued uniforms, and over the next six to ten years, were ushered from class to class until they finished their program of study and graduated. The reformers tried to recruit and retain students from varied backgrounds. Scholarships and patronage by wealthy merchants made education at the new madrasas available to boys from poor families.[94] Some urban madrasas offered special dormitories for orphans.[95] Madrasa directors maximized their influence over these boys and young men by providing lodgings for them. By 1905, half of Kazan's madrasa students came from outside the city and lodged in dormitories, far from their villages and families.[96] At the new madrasas, students were exposed daily to reformers' rhetoric on the decline of the Muslim world, the power of ijtihād, and the evils of speculative theology. They read Muslim newspapers and writings on Islamic reform from Russia and abroad. They also studied the Russian language, which was supposed to prepare them to take an active role in provincial life and guide Muslims in becoming part of a liberalizing Russian society.

The new madrasas were in effect educational factories designed to provide teachers and imams who would spread reformers' views on law and theology across Russia and Central Asia. In 1910 alone, Izh-Būbī Madrasa enrolled 64 students in its summer training program for teachers.[97] In 1905, Muḥammadiyya enrolled around 300 students. Between 1903 and 1916, Ḥusayniyya's student population fluctuated between 200 and 500.[98] By the early 1900s, a single reformed madrasa could produce between 50 and 200 graduates per year. By 1905–1906, between 1,380 and 1,500 boys were enrolled in Kazan's twelve madrasas (reformed and unreformed).[99] By contrast, the total number of licensed muezzins, imams, and madrasa directors employed in all of inner Russia in 1908 was 8,300.[100] For reformers, this large student population was not necessarily a problem. As ʿAbdalghanī Ḥusaynov had articulated in 1898, excess graduates would go out to towns and villages in other regions, open schools, train more students, and transform Islam across the empire.

In practice, however, matters unfolded very differently. Students at reformed madrasas internalized their teachers' messages about the decline of Islam and the need for renewal. They also internalized their teachers' views that Islamic law and doctrine should be straightforward and that anyone who said otherwise was acting out of ignorance or self-interest. They learned the Russian language, which enabled them to read Russian political literature and to interact with Russian university and gymnasium students. At the same time, they struggled with a set of unfortunate circumstances beyond the walls of the madrasa. The reformed madrasas' prodigious output worsened an already-flooded employment market. Students from network core families could rely on their social connections, but orphans, peasants' sons, and the sons of rural imams, who enrolled in large numbers due to the scholarships and charity offered by the reformed madrasas, faced great difficulty in obtaining employment.[101] Despite grand visions of opening schools across the empire, Kazan's reformers lacked effective mechanisms for placing their graduates. Reformed madrasa graduates in 1907 faced the same dilemma as their colleagues in the 1880s and 1890s: frustrations and shattered expectations when the best job their madrasa education could secure them was a posting in a remote village.

Some students decided that they did not want to be licensed imams. Their decision was determined not only by the difficulty of gaining such employment, but also by the education they had received from their teachers and from their reading and social contacts outside the madrasa. Taking to heart Karīmī's and Isḥāqī's critique of the "ʿulamāʾ" as exploiters of common Muslims, they were repulsed by the idea of living off community charity, especially in poor villages, where resources were limited.[102] They sought ways to guide their fellow Muslims without having to gain a posting and a license.

The disdain that reformers cultivated in their students for seniority, shaykhly prestige and the established Islamic intellectual culture transformed early twentieth-century madrasa classrooms into battlefields. The struggles were most intense in the reformed madrasas, where students interpreted reformers' encouragement to question the established social and intellectual authorities as a license to reject all kinds of authority, including that of their teachers. At Muḥammadiyya, the students organized underground newspapers and circles to pressure their teachers to enact further reforms of Muslim education.[103] There, student protests and civil disobedience led to mass expulsions by 1904.[104] It did not help that reformed madrasa directors were often the beneficiaries of the very social-scholarly networks that they pushed students to challenge: Muḥammadiyya's director, Bārūdī was an Ūtamishev in-law, Ḥusayniyya was staffed with teachers from Tūntār and Chistopol, and Izh-Būbī had strong ties to Machkara. This made it easy for students to cast their teachers and sponsors as their enemies. For example, at Ḥusayniyya in 1907, students publicly alleged misappropriations of the madrasa's endowment (waqf) funds and physical and psychological abuse of their classmates by members of the endowment management council and the madrasa administration.[105]

For their part, the older generation of reformers showed no desire to include their restless students in discussions of politics and reform. When, during the 1905 Revolution, the First All-Russian Muslim Union met on a riverboat in Nizhnii Novgorod, the older participants left port an hour ahead of schedule in hopes of preventing the madrasa students from attending. The students and younger activists commandeered a smaller boat and pursued them on the river until the union's organizers gave in and permitted them to board the riverboat on the condition that they remain silent through the meeting.[106] In provincial towns, students organized their own political groups and newspapers and repeated their demands that curricula be changed, dormitory living conditions improved, and students' voice in madrasa governance increased. In autumn of 1905, the conflicts inside of the madrasas overflowed into the city streets. In Kazan, Muslim students joined protests across the city and issued new demands. In at least one case, a group of armed students were accused of accosting their teacher.[107]

Friction between the upper levels of Muslim society and its middling ranks was not limited to the madrasas. A similar struggle was underway in the large Muslim trading companies and manufacturing concerns, spearheaded by the *prikazchiks*, a category of workers that included shop clerks, bookkeepers, floor managers, and overseers of shepherds and cattle hands. In 1905, the prikazchiks of all Orenburg's trading houses formed a mutual support organization and demanded defined working hours, mandatory lunch breaks, and vacation time.[108] Many Muslim prikazchiks were madrasa educated. Madrasa graduates sometimes drifted between prikazchik jobs and educational work. The prikazchik, together with the junior teacher (*khalfa*, *muʿallim*) became a recurring character in Tatar literature. In ʿAlīaskar Kamāl's play *The First Theater*, an elderly merchant, Ḥamza Bāy, goes to the barbershop and ends up behind a long line of "snot-nosed shop boys" (*qızıl awız kibetchelar*). Ḥamza, as a wealthy merchant, tries to cut to the front of the line, only to be told that he should come back another day, because he, a "rich man," can get a haircut whenever he wants, whereas the prikazchiks, the "rich men's employees" (*bay keshese*) can only come on Fridays when they get their day off. Ḥamza storms out in a rage and goes home without a haircut.[109] This scene is in keeping with the tone of the entire play, in which all Ḥamza's social inferiors—his children, his prikazchik son-in-law, and his household servants—repeatedly ignore or defy him.

The 1905 Revolution magnified the social conflicts between madrasa students and the directors, shaykhs, and businessmen who mentored and/or employed them. In the wake of the 1905 revolution, reformed madrasa graduates became the face of political radicalism in Kazan Tatar communities. Clad in European dress, spouting socialist rhetoric, and singing violence-tinged revolutionary songs, these young men seemed alien and threatening. Parents who had sent their sons to the reformed madrasas lamented that they no longer recognized their own children.[110] Opponents of education reform faulted reformist teachers for creating a generation of students who were disrespectful of their elders, dismissive of the Islamic legal tradition, and committed to imitation (taqlīd) of European culture.[111]

In some ways, the graduates of the reformed madrasas were very much their teachers' students. Like their teachers, they firmly believed that Islam was in a state of crisis and required serious change. That change would be accomplished by rejecting speculative theology and the madhhab commentaries and returning to the Qurʾān and the hadiths to create the basis for a new Islam that could meet the demands of the twentieth century. The graduates of the reformed madrasas envisioned a future that was at once Muslim, high-tech, and egalitarian. Fatīḥ Amirkhan, in his novel *Reverend Fatḥullāh*, presents a futuristic Tatar-Muslim society in which crimes were tried in an Islamic court before a committee of Muslims knowledgeable in Islamic law, and in which offenders would be sent to a Muslim monastery for reeducation.[112] In this society, the post of imam still exists, but factional and school divisions have been eliminated. Kazan Muslims' unity of belief has become such that they maintain a single, gigantic mosque for all 150,000 of the town's Muslims. To explain why this is so, one character asks: "What would be the use in splitting them in two?"[113] Amirkhan's fictional Muslim society manages to integrate science and technology while preserving Islam as a source of law and order, personal morality, community identity, and unity.

The graduates of the reformed madrasas, like their teachers, emphasized sincerity in faith and adherence to the basic obligations of Islam. For them, treating the poor humanely was more important than whether one chose to wear a turban or a European suit. In the short story "Those Who Are Not Fasting," Amirkhan criticizes Muslims who avoided observing the Ramadan fast. In Tūqāyev's satirical poem "The Haymarket, or the New Severed Head," the supposedly devout residents of Kazan demonstrate their ignorance, cynicism, and cowardice by calling on a circus wrestler to save a fellow Muslim and his family from a demon.[114] In Amirkhan's play, "The Youth," the character ʿAzīz asserts that "there is no Islamic society [here], because here in Kazan, with its population of 30,000 Tatars, 20 Tatar brothels find patronage; half of all profits earned by the bars come from Tatars, and only half the zakāt donations ever get paid."[115]

True Muslims appealed to Islamic law to improve people's lives while bad Muslims abused Islamic law and their authority within the community to improve their own lot, oppress their coreligionists, and abdicate responsibility for the less fortunate members of their community. The graduates of the reformed madrasas wished to make Islam a matter of personal conscience not to remove it from the public sphere, but to reinforce its place there. Correct knowledge of Islam would contribute to a stronger, more cohesive society as all community members strove to properly practice their faith.

The Youth and Tatar Nationalism

In the wake of the 1905 Revolution, madrasa students, recent graduates, and dropouts began to emerge as a recognizable and outspoken social group. Their distinguishing feature, aside from their madrasa education and often their lack of gainful employment, was their age. They tended to range from their midteens to their midtwenties. In provincial towns and larger villages, they organized musical evenings and mutual support groups. They connected with one another across provinces through periodicals produced by and targeted at people like themselves. Such journals took up matters such as living conditions in the madrasa dormitories, directors' teaching philosophies and disciplinary methods, and the bleak employment market for madrasa graduates.[116]

These young men identified as a generational cohort more strongly than any generation of ʿulamāʾ before them. They imagined the injustices they faced as committed not just by their socioeconomic betters, but by their elders: their teachers, their madrasa directors, and, ultimately, their parents. They imagined themselves at once as the victims of the ignorant, self-interested older generation and as history's designated heirs to that generation's authority. As a song circulated among the students at Izh-Būbī Madrasa put it:

> Indeed, we are your blood! We are your soul!
> We are your goodness! Please, fathers!
> Take us into your embrace, fathers
> And tears will flow from our eyes.
> The day will come, fathers, when all the old people will die,
> And the world will belong to us.[117]

As with the Jadids of Central Asia, youth was central to the madrasa students' and recent graduates' identity. They imagined that their youth freed them from the past and enabled them to see their community's sins and shortcomings with a clarity and detachment that their parents and teachers could not. They believed that youth gave them a purity of intention that their elders, complicit in the relationships and conventions of the "old days," lacked. As those destined to inherit the future, they imagined young people to be more invested in social change; youth lent them moral authority. As Khalid has noted for Central Asia, this was a fundamental inversion of the prevailing notions of what granted moral authority in Volga-Ural Muslim society—age; patient, contemplative study; affiliation with long-established Sufi lineages; and a lifetime of charitable acts.[118] Students and junior teachers existed at the bottom of the scholarly and social ladder; they were people who might one day become authoritative but represented at best unrealized potential. For most of Kazan's Muslims, the proposition that these young people should lead the community would have seemed absurd.

Young reformers' antiestablishment tendencies did not mesh well with the narratives of community history and organization that had evolved during the nineteenth century. Bulghar historiography was structured around hierarchies of pious men. These men did not simply serve as examples of how to live; within the framework of the Bulghar histories, their piety legitimized the social status and authority enjoyed by shaykhs and teachers living in the 1800s and 1900s. Sufi lineages (silsila) served a similar function. Shaykhs such as ʿAlī at-Tūntārī commanded respect not only for their own deeds but also because they could claim membership in chains of authority that purportedly reached back to towering figures such as Khwaja Aḥrār, Aḥmad Sirhindī, Bahaʾaddīn an-Naqshbandi, and finally the Prophet Muḥammad himself.[119] There were implicit hierarchies within this culture between greater and lesser scholars and shaykhs and between shaykhs and their disciples, the vast majority of whom would never attain social, educational, or spiritual equality with their masters. Thus, for the Youth, shaykhly prestige was something that could only be obtained, if at all, through age and long service. Also, the culture of elected-ness and deference inherent in Sufism in the Volga-Ural region was incompatible with the Youth's visions of a society in which all knowledge was accessible to all Muslims.

Marjānī's history of Kazan provided the Youth with an alternative narrative. For Marjānī, *Mustafād al-Akhbār* was a demonstration of how to reconcile Islamic and non-Islamic knowledge, but for the Youth, the first volume of the work provided a compelling story of a Kazan Tatar nation. That story was reduced to a set of symbols and poignant moments in Isḥāqī's novel *Extinction after Two Hundred Years* and it was in this format rather than in Marjānī's history that most students encountered it.[120] If the Sufi-based world of Bulghar historiography presented a hierarchy with the "scholars" at the top and everyone else at the bottom, the nation offered a vision of a community of equal members. For madrasa students, that equality extended beyond membership in the nation to participation in upholding Islamic law and morality. It was every Tatar's obligation not only to learn his native language and customs but also to learn and properly practice his faith.

In the Youth's literature, the fate of the Tatar national homeland and that of Islam became inextricably entwined. In the opening verses of *Love of the Nation*, a poetic cycle that launched Youth poet Ghafūrī to popularity among the Volga-Ural region's madrasa students, Ghafūrī ties his calls for cultural reform to the landscape of the Volga River basin, lamenting that "In these days, nothing remains in my hands, not Astrakhan, not Bulghar, not my Kazan."[121] Linking together notions of nation with older Muslim concepts of the House of War (Dar al-Ḥarb) and the conquest of Muslim lands by non-Muslims, he writes that "my religion has died in the dust of the world; all I have left is my faith" and "today, I have no designated homeland; my place has gone over to my enemies."[122] In "A Poem Recited by a Tatar Student upon Seeing the Minaret of Kazan's Khan Mosque," Ghafūrī again links nation and faith. The narrator imagines how Tatars and Turks once gathered to pray in Kazan's preconquest mosque and how Muslims once wielded great military and cultural power in the world. The recurring symbol of the nation is the Khan's Mosque, invoked repeatedly in the refrain. Indeed, as the poem passed into the oral culture of madrasas, it was often renamed "The Khan's Mosque."[123]

The new literature on the Tatar nation borrowed freely from Bulghar historiography but told a very different story. If the Bulghar histories were generally about the construction of a Muslim community, Tatar national literature was about a Muslim community's decline and destruction; it was written to evoke a sense of crisis and dissatisfaction with the existing order. Tūqāyev, in his poem "The Evening Prayer" (1906), invoked the lost glory of the Tatar nation's past with references to Suyumbika (the last queen of Kazan before the Russian conquest), Genghis Khan, and the khanates of Qasim, Kazan, and Astrakhan.[124] Wāqıf Jalāl in *Sādā-i Madanīyāt* (1908) lamented how Kazan and Bulghar had been lost to the Russians and the rose gardens of the khans had fallen to ruins.[125] An anonymous student's song circulating in Kazan in early 1900s struck a similar tone:

> We are children of the Tatars,
> Where is our khan's city?
> It has all ended; it is all finished
> Whatever will we do now?[126]

Another song from a village madrasa outside Kazan characterized the nation as a sickly person in need of aid:

> My nation, you are unfortunate,
> When I think about it, it burns.
> The strength has gone out of your arms,
> How did you fall into the state?
> You are like an orphaned child,
> Your countenance has grown sallow [. . .]
> How did you fall into the state?[127]

According to the Youth's narrative of Tatar nationalism, such aid would come from the members of the nation. If Bulghar histories highlighted the efforts and experiences of extraordinary men and women, Tatar national poetry and song called on all Muslims, regardless of origin or class, to pursue education and service to the national-confessional community. Not everyone could become a shaykh, but anyone could aspire to be a national citizen. For most Youth writers, any true national citizen was, of necessity, a good Muslim.

Youth writers imagined the Tatar nation as a community of equals, but they also believed that national citizens could only achieve such equality once they achieved "consciousness" of their identity, their unjust lot in society, and what needed to be done to change that lot. Such consciousness would be achieved through education, whether in the classroom or by attending theatrical performances and public lectures and reading the appropriate books and newspapers. The Youth themselves would lead the rest of the nation's citizens in this education.

The Youth acquired the concepts of consciousness, uplift, and intelligentsia primarily from their exposure to Russian-language political and literary discourses. (As Russian-language instruction took root in larger madrasas by the early 1900s, Russian literary culture pushed aside the Ottoman literature and periodicals that had been important in the formative experiences of madrasa students in the 1870s–1890s.) However, as with other constructs and genres that they had borrowed, the Youth understood and applied the concept of *intelligent* within the social and cultural context of the Volga-Ural region. First, "*intelligenty*" were defined in opposition to the "ʿulamāʾ" in Youth discourses. The ʿUlamāʾ, as the Youth used the term, was meant to conjure images of privilege, exclusivity, self-interest, and investment in the established order. The intelligenty, by contrast, were conceived of as a loose group of facilitators rather than as a permanent, closed class of elites. Unlike their ʿulamāʾ foils, they sought social and cultural revolution rather than stability. Once that revolution had been achieved, the need for the intelligenty would wither away, or rather the need to serve and nurture the nation would have become the preoccupation of all citizens.

Second, whereas becoming an influential member of the ʿulamāʾ required belonging to a powerful family, gaining the proper social connections, and obtaining a posting and government-issued license, there were no such requirements for becoming an intelligent; One required only education, moral purity, and dedication. In their professional lives, intelligenty could be shop clerks, teachers, journalists, newspaper editors, or factory workers. This model of servants of the nation who came from all walks of life harmonized well with the Kazan reformers' vision of a Muslim society in which all members could engage directly with the Qur'ān and hadiths and thereby take an active role in constructing and sustaining a proper Islamic community. It also offered the possibility of a more flexible enforcer of Islamic morality. Intelligenty, unfettered from daily administrative duties to mosque, maḥalla, and state, had more freedom in choosing where and how they intervened in social discourses and educated people on morality, faith, and social responsibility. The Youth did not propose an order in which administrative, educational, and judicial responsibilities were removed entirely from the hands of imams. Rather, they sought to divide those responsibilities among a larger base of educated people and to allow people who were not licensed imams to take part in conversations of Islamic law and community management. They also questioned the ability of licensed imams to act in the best interest of the Muslim community as their licensing process made them "bureaucrats" in the service of the imperial government.[128]

Despite presenting themselves as benevolent saviors, the Youth, like their reformist teachers, were often anything but polite in their engagement with those who did not share their point of view. In the press, Youth writers waged war against prominent scholars, accusing them of vice and moral failings.[129] In daily life, they treated with rank disrespect anyone who questioned their views and methods. Their views of the Russian autocracy echoed the most radical end of the Russian political spectrum. The contributors to the newspaper *Tāng Yūldızı* openly called for the popular overthrow the "bureaucratic" government.[130] Unpublished songs that circulated among the madrasa students adapted the "Marseillaise" into Tatar, called for the overthrow of the "blood-sucking" government, and cheerfully imagined the emperor being crushed with stones, burned to ash, or devoured by dogs.[131] Youth writers were scarcely kinder to the common folk of the nation they claimed to be saving, often painting them as dupes of the powerful or as uneducated "dark people" (*qara muzhiklar; qara khalıq*). They did not hesitate to employ tactics such as harassment, defamation in the press, protests, and boycotts to intimidate their opponents. One of the protagonists of Fatīḥ Amirkhan's unfinished play *The Youth* (1909) summed up the Youth's program: If Muslims did not wish to follow the intelligentsia's lead, the intelligentsia would "smash their teeth in."[132]

With such attitudes, the Youth provoked anxiety in other members of Muslim society. Critics called them revolutionaries (*inqilābiyyūn*;

revoliutsionarlar) and Wahhabis, highlighting their combination of disrespect for their elders, literalist theological views, and violent rhetoric. Others challenged their moral purity and Islamic orthodoxy, focusing especially on their use of theater, musical performance, and mixed-gender socializing to spread their views. The Youths' critics believed these activities violated Islamic law and threw the Youth's moral integrity into question. As an anonymous contributor to *Dīn wa Maʿīshat* remarked concerning the Youth's popular education tactics, "What's next? National bars and national brothels?"[133] Debates over the permissibility of music and theater in a Muslim society illustrate the diversity of Islamic legal thought in early twentieth-century Kazan. Not only did scholars take a variety of positions for and against musical performance, but the performers themselves often came from Islamic scholarly backgrounds. Actor and drama troupe leader ʿAbdullāh Qarīyev began his career as a Qurʾān reader. So too did popular singer Kāmil Mutiʿī, who attended al-Azhar and wrote a multivolume Tatar-language commentary on the Qurʿān.[134]

Conclusion

In the 1880s and 1890s, a small group of scholars from the Machkaran network began to promote a new approach to Islamic law and theology. They broke with previous generations of legal scholars in that they questioned the reliability of the accepted Ḥanafī law books, called on their colleagues to return to the core Islamic texts, and viewed ijtihād as a force for creativity and reform rather than as a source of potential discord and instability. This was not the first Islamic reform or revival movement to unfold in the Volga-Ural region, but it was in some ways the most radical. By challenging accepted practices and precedents and encouraging their students to do the same, scholars and writers such as Mūsā Bīgīev, Fatīḥ Karīmī, ʿĀlimjān Bārūdī, and ʿAbdullāh Būbī mentored a generation of madrasa-educated young people who rejected not only the madhhab system, but also the very foundations and hierarchies on which Kazan Muslim educated society was built.

These young people did not reject Islam itself, but rather the monopoly over socioeconomic influence and Islamic knowledge exercised by the powerful scholarly families and networks of the nineteenth century. They sought to create a society in which such knowledge was available to all and in which talent, hard work, and moral purity were rewarded over wealth and social connections. The concept of the Tatar nation provided them a means of articulating their vision for a future of Kazan Muslims in which all Muslims became agents in upholding Islamic morality and the well-being of the community.

There was much that the reformist teachers shared with their younger students: hostility toward the madhhabs, a love of rationalism, a thirst for social justice, and the firm belief that Islamic law could and should be comprehensible to all Muslims. Those scholars who still placed value in the madhhabs tended to highlight these similarities across the two generations. However, the Youth were much more unconventional than their teachers were in the methods by which they promoted these ideas. The Youth's turn to radical politics and their rejection of the culture of intergenerational deference complicated the relationship between them and their teachers. For teachers, alliance with their students could amount to complicity in the Youth's antiauthoritarian, rhetorically violent subculture. Given the Youth's contempt for authority based on age, such alliances sometimes became impossible. Such was the case with Muḥammad Ẓarīf Amirkhan, the liberal imam of Kazan's Ninth Mosque (and son of historian Ḥusayn Amirkhanov), and his twenty-year-old son, Fatīḥ. Fatīḥ, who printed underground newspapers and repeatedly organized his classmates at Muḥammadiyya against their teachers, had defied madrasa director Bārūdī one time too many. Muḥammad Ẓarīf, a colleague and good friend of Bārūdī, could no longer bear the embarrassment of having to answer for his son's chronic disrespect for his elders. In October 1906, as Fatīḥ prepared to leave for Moscow, tensions reached a breaking point, and father and son began to shout at each other. The fight ended with Muḥammad Ẓarīf calling Fatīḥ a scoundrel and throwing him out of the house.[135] Like other of Kazan's reformist imams and madrasa directors, neither Muḥammad Ẓarīf nor Bārūdī seems to have considered how their own rejection of established intellectual, legal, and political authorities had shaped Fatīḥ.

Notes

1. Fatikh Ämirkhan, "Fätkhulla Khäzrät," *Fatikh Ämirkhan: Äsärlär dürt tomda* (4 vols.), ed. Zöfär Rämiev (Kazan: Tatar Kitap näshriyaty, 1985), 2:84–91.

2. Azade-Ayşe Rorlich, *The Volga Tatars: A Profile in National Resilience* (Stanford, CA: Hoover Institute, 1986), 49–51; Ahmet Kanlıdere, *Reform within Islam: The Tajdid and Jadid Movement among the Kazan Tatars (1809–1917): Conciliation or Conflict?* (Istanbul:

Eren, 1997); Adeeb Khalid, "What Jadidism Was and What It Wasn't: The Historiographical Adventures of a Term," *Central Eurasian Studies Review* 5, no. 2 (2006): 5.

3. Rorlich, *Volga Tatars*, 104–41; James H. Meyer, *Turks across Empires: Making Muslim Identity in the Russian Ottoman Borderlands* (Oxford: Oxford University Press, 2014); Aidar Khabutdinov, *Ot obshchiny k natii: Tatary na puti ot srednevekov'ia k novomu vremeni* (Kazan: Tatarskoe knizhnoe izdatel'stvo, 2008), 88–200.

4. Rorlich, *Volga Tatars*, 104; Khalid, "What Jadidism Was," 5.

5. "Secularization" seems to be the preferred term among those historians who argue that "scientific," rational, non-Islamic-based forms of knowledge and identity replaced Islamic ones. (For a recent example of this view, see Mustafa Tuna, *Imperial Russia's Muslims: Islam, Empire, and European Modernity, 1788–1914* [Cambridge: Cambridge University Press, 2015], 174–94.) "Desacralization" is preferred by those historians who argue that Islam remained relevant to reformers but was reimagined in response to European rationalist and empirical thought. (See Agnés Nilüfer Kefeli, *Becoming Muslim in Imperial Russia: Conversion, Apostasy, and Literacy* [Ithaca, NY: Cornell University Press, 2014], 213–32; and Khalid, "What Jadidism Was," 5.)

6. Kefeli, *Becoming Muslim*, 218.

7. Roel Meijer, "Introduction," *Global Salafism: Islam's New Religious Movement*, ed. Roel Meijer (New York: Columbia University Press, 2009), 4–8.

8. Henri Lauzière, *The Making of Salafism: Islamic Reform in the Twentieth Century* (New York: Columbia University Press, 2016), 34, 36; Bernard Haykel, "On the Nature of Salafi Thought and Action," *Global Salafism*, ed. Meijer, 38–41.

9. Haykel, "On the Nature of Salafi Thought," *Global Salafism*, 39–41.

10. Ibid., 42–45.

11. Meijer, "Introduction," *Global Salafism*, 4; Haykel, "On the Nature of Salafi Thought," *Global Salafism*, 36.

12. Haykel, "On the Nature of Salafi Thought," *Global Salafism*, 36.

13. Jeff Eden and Paolo Sartori, "Moving Beyond Modernism: Rethinking Cultural Change in Muslim Eurasia (19th–20th Centuries)," *Journal of Social and Economic History of the Orient* 59 (1-2) (2016): 2–14.

14. Devin DeWeese, "It Was a Dark and Stagnant Night ('Til the Jadids Brought the Lights): Clichés, Biases, and False Dichotomies in the Intellectual History of Central Asia," *Journal of the Economic and Social History of the Orient* 59 (2016): 74–82.

15. Haykel, "On the Nature of Salafi Thought," *Global Salafism*, 45–47; Lauzière, *Making of Salafism*, 38–40.

16. Haykel, "On the Nature of Salafi Thought," *Global Salafism*, 40.

17. Ibid., 34–35.

18. Ibid., 36.

19. Meijer, "Introduction," *Global Salafism*, 13–14; Haykel, "On the Nature of Salafi Thought," *Global Salafism*, 47–51.

20. Musa Ak'eget, "Khisametdin menla," *Karurmanny chykkan chakta*, ed. A. G. Yakhin (Kazan: Mägarif, 2001).

21. Zahir Bigiev, "Gönah-i Kaba'ir," *Zahir Bigiev: Zur gönahlar*, ed. Rais Dautov (Kazan: Tatarstan kitap näshriyaty, 1991), 254–88.

22. Muḥammad ʿAyāḍ al-Isḥāqī, *Kalapushche qiz* (Kazan: Tipografiia B. L. Dombrovskago, 1902).

23. Shakir Mökhämmädev, "Yafrak asty yaki Mäkärjä yarminkäse," *Sh. Mökhämmädev: saylamna äsärlär*, ed. M. Gaynullin (Kazan: Tatknigoizdat, 1958), 57–98.

24. Gabderashit Ibrahimov, *Tärjemäi khälem* (Kazan: "Iman" näshriyatı, 2001), 96–99; A. G. Khayrutdinov, *Musa Dzharullakh Bigiev* (Kazan: Fan, 2005), 15–16; Yu. Aqchūra-ulı, *Dāmallā ʿAlīmjān al-Bārūdī: Tarjama-i ḥāle* (Kazan: Sharaf Matbuʿasī, 1907), 59.

25. F. K., *Ber shakīrd ila ber student* (Kazan: Tipografiia B. L. Dombrovskago, 1899), 13.

26. Ibid.,10–11.

27. Ibid., 36.

28. Fatikh Kärimi, "Nuretdin khälfä," *Fatikh Kärimi: Murza Kyzy Fatyima, Saylanma äsärlär*, ed. M. B. Gaynetdinov (Kazan: Tatarstan kitap näshriyaty, 1996), 58.

29. Fatikh Kärimi, "Jihangir mäkhdümneng awıl mäktäbendä uquyi (Tornaly awylynyng mäktäbendä) (1898)," http://kitap.net.ru/karimi.php.

30. Fatikh Kärimi, "Ber shäkird ilä ber student," *Fatikh Kärimi: Murza Kyzy Fatyima*, 30.

31. Muḥammad ʿAyāḍ al-Isḥāqī, *Ike yūz yıldan sūng inqirāḍ* (Kazan: Lito-Tipografiia I. N. Kharitonova, 1904).

32. Ibid., 6–10.

33. Ibid., 2–3, 25.

34. F. K., *Ber shakīrd ila ber student*, 36.

35. *Uqigiz: Taqī gajaptan dakhī gajap* (Orenburg: Tipografiia M. F. G. Karimova, 1904), 4.

36. Muḥammad Akhmarov, "Wahhābīlar kemnar?" *Dīn wa Maʿīshat*, 46 (1910): 731–34; 47 (1910): 747–50; 1 (1911): 6–8; 2 (1911): 21–23; 3 (1911): 38–40; Muḥammad Akhmarov, "Wahhābīlar ham tawaṣṣul," *Dīn wa Maʿīshat* 6 (1911): 90–92; 7 (1911): 103; 8 (1911): 121–22.

37. F. K., *Ber shakīrd ila ber student*, 34.

38. Ibid., 24.

39. Ibid., 27–28.

40. "1890 g., fevral'ia 9. Gazeta 'Terjuman-Perevodchik' o neobkhodimosti dlia musul'manskikh religioznykh izdanii dukhovnoi tsenzury: K voprosu o tatarskoi pechati," *Modernizatsionnye protsessy v tatarsko-musul'manskom soobshchestve v 1880-e – 1905 gg.: dokumenty i materialy*, ed. I. K. Zagidullin (Kazan: Institut istorii im Sh. Mardzhani, 2014), 44–45.

41. A. Makhmutova, "G. Bubi," in *Tatarskie intellectualy: istoricheskie portrety*, ed. R. M. Mukhammetshin (Kazan: Mägarif, 2005), 173.

42. ʿAbdullāh Būbī, *Ḥaqīqat, yakhud tuğrılıq: berenche juze* (Kazan: Lito-Tipografiia I. N. Kharitonova, 1904), 2–3.

43. Ibid., 4–5.

44. Ibid., 12.

45. ʿAbdullāh Būbī, *Zamān-i ijtihād munqarīḍmı degelme?* (Kazan: Elektro-Tipografiia "Milliat", 1909), 3.

46. Ibid., 3–4.

47. Ibid., 4.

48. Būbī, *Ḥaqīqat, yakhūd tuğrılıq: berenche juze*, 5.

49. Khayrutdinov, *Musa Dzharullakh Bigiev*, 14–15.

50. Ibid., 15.

51. Ibid., 15; Gabdullah Battal-Taymas, *Musa Yarulla Bigi: Tormyshy, eshchänlege wä äsärläre* (Kazan: "Imān," 1997), 5.

52. Khayrutdinov, *Musa Dzharullakh Bigiev*, 16, 18.

53. Mūsā Bīgīev, “Mutarjimnan ber-ike sūz,” *al-Luzūmiyyāt*, trans. and ed. Mūsā Bīgīev (Kazan: Tipografiia Sharaf, 1907), 2; Mūsā Bīgīev, *Adabiyyāt ʿarabiyya ila ʿulūm islamiyya* (Kazan: I. N Kharitonova,1909), 5.

54. Bīgīev, “Mutarjimnan ber-ike sūz,”*al-Luzūmiyyāt*, 3.

55. Bīgīev, *Adabiyyāt ʿarabiyya*, 2–4.

56. Ibid., 4.

57. Ibid., 6–7.

58. Mūsā Bīgīev, *Qawāʿid fiqhiyya* (Kazan: Elekto-tipografiia “Urnek,” 1910), 2.

59. Ibid., 4–5.

60. ʿUbaydullāh Muḥammad Fayzī Niʿmatullin, *Qirāʾat Turki: berenche juze* (Kazan: Tipo-Litografiia nasl. M. Chirkovoi, 1899), 2–3.

61. *Mukhtaṣar al-Wiqāya tarjamase turkicha*, trans. Shihābaddīn bin Mullā ʿAbdalʿazīz Imānlībāshī (Kazan: Tipografiia T. D. Brat. Karimovykh, 1901); *Mukhtaṣar al-Qudūrī tarjamase*, trans. Abū ʿAbdalaḥād Shaykh al-Islām bin Asādullāh Ḥamidullāh (Kazan: Tipografiia T. D. Brat. Karimovykh, 1904); *Kitāb tarjama-i ʿAyn al-ʿIlm* (Kazan: Qazqn Universitetining Ṭabiʿkhana, 1886).

62. Sälim Gyilajetdinov, “Keresh süz,” *Meng dä ber hadis shäreḥe* (Kazan: Rannur, 2005), 5; Rizaeddin Fäkhreddinov, *“Jawāmiʿ al-Kalim” Shärḥe*; *Akhadis Mutajiba*, ed. Ilshat Gyimadiev (Kazan: Rukhiyat, 2005).

63. Mullā ʿAlīmjān al-Bārūdī, *Al-kitāb ath-thānī min al-arbaʿīnāt al-mustasalsila* (Kazan: Elektro-tipografiia “Milliat,” 1908).

64. Mullā ʿAbdullāh al-Makhdūmī ibn ʿAbdalʿallām, *Mukālama ʿarabiyya* (Kazan: Tipo-Litografiia M. Chirkovoi, 1898); ʿAbdullāh Būbī, *Ṣarf ʿarabī* (Kazan: Tipo-Litografiia V. Z. Eremeev, n.d.); ʿAbdullāh al-Makhdūmī, *Mukhtaṣar naḥw ʿarabī* (Kazan: Tipografiia Torgovago Dom Brat’ev Karimovykh, 1900).

65. ʿAbdarrashīd Ibrahimov, *ʿIlm ḥāl*, 5 vols. (Kazan: Lito-Tipografiia I. N. Kharitonova, 1913); Aḥmad Ḥādī Maqsūdī, *Jamāʿat* (Kazan: Lito-Tipografiia I. N. Kharitonova, 1910); Aḥmad Ḥādī Maqsūdī, *Rūza, zakāt* (Kazan: Lito-Tipografiia I. N. Kharitonova, 1911).

66. Muḥammad Shākir bin Muḥammad Zākir Sulāymānī, *Tārīkh-i Islām*, 4 vols. (Kazan: Lito-Tipografiia T. D. “Br. Karimovykh,” 1908–1910); Mullā Sabīrjān Mullā ʿAbdalbadīʿ-ulı, *Sīrat an-Nabī ʿalayhi as-salām* (Kazan: Elektro-Tipografiia “Milliat,” 1910); Sunʿatullāh Bīkbūlātov, *Khaḍrat Muḥammad (ṣallā ʿalayhi wa sallam)* (Kazan: Elekto-tipografiia “Maarif,” 1914); Fatīḥ Karīmī, *Mukhtaṣar Tārīkh-i Islām* (Orenburg, n.d.); Yaʿqub Mamishev, *Tārīkh-i Islām: Anbiyāʾ qismı* (Kazan: Tipografiia T. D. “Br. Karimovykh,” 1910); Dhākir Shākir-ulı, *Tārīkh-i muqaddas* (Kazan: Shamsaddīn Ḥusaynov warithasī, 1912).

67. Burḥānaddīn ibn Mullā Jamāladdīn al-Bāghishī, *ʿAqāʾid ahl sunnat wa jamāʿat* (Kazan: Vyatcheslav, 1894), 1–5.

68. Aḥmad Ḥādī Maqsūdī, *ʿAqāʾid: ʿIbadāt Islāmiyya Majmūʿasınıng bereche jüze* (Kazan: Lito-Tipografiia I. N. Kharitonova, 1910), 9–10.

69. ʿAbdullāh Būbī, “Mutarjimdan ber sūz,” *Tawḥīd*, trans. ʿAbdullāh Būbī (Kazan: Elekto-tipografiia “Urnek,” 1911), 2–4.

70. Ibid., 2.

71. Zyiaetdin Kamali, “Filosofiia islama (Falsafa islāmiyya),” *Zyiaetdin Kamali*, ed. and trans. L. I. Almazova (Kazan: Tatarskoe knizhnoe izdatel’stvo, 2010), 230–31.

72. Ibid., 232.

73. Ibid., 235.

74. "Kadyri, Zakir," *Tatarskaia entsiklopediia*, ed. M. Kh. Khasanov (Kazan: Institut Tatarskoi Entsiklopedii, 2006), 3:12.

75. Ḍākir al-Qadīrī, *ʿIlm-i kalām dareslare* (Ufa: n.p., 1910), 3–4.

76. Ibid., 14–15.

77. Ibid., 16.

78. This stance is consistent with that of balanced reformers such as Muḥammad ʿAbduh who advocated reform in the late 1800s and early 1900s (Lauzière, *Making of Salafism*, 41).

79. Ibid., 47.

80. *Uṣūl Tadrīs: Madrasalarda muʿällimnara maslak mustaqīm uzara taʿlīm itmak ṭarīqnı bayān iden kitap* (Kazan: Tipografiia B. L. Dombrovskago, 1899), 3.

81. F. K. *Ber shakīrd ila ber student*, 38.

82. Ibid., 38.

83. ʿAbdullāh Būbī, *Taraqqī funūn wa maʿārif dīnsezlege mawjūbmı?* (Kazan: Lito-Tipografiia I. N. Kharitonova, 1902), 3.

84. Ibid., 4.

85. "Bārūdīga khāt," K(P)FU 1615 T, 2.

86. Ibid., 3. A *kumgan* is a vessel that hold water and is kept near the toilet for the purpose of performing ablutions.

87. *Ṭughriliq* (Kazan: Tipografiia T-go d. Br. Karimovykh, 1904), 1.

88. See, for example, "Mūsā Bīgīev jinābларına ber-ike sūz," *Dīn wa Maʿīshat* 14 (1909): 219–20; "Mūsā Bīgīev jinābларına ber-ike sūz," *Dīn wa Maʿīshat* 15 (1909): 231–33.

89. *Mädräsälärdä kitap kishtäse: mäshhür mägrifät üzäkläre tarikhınnan* (Kazan: Tatarstan kitap näshriyatı, 1992); Muḥammad Najib ibn Shamseddin, "Tüntär awılında märkhüm ostazlar shaykh Gali wa shaykh Shamseddin 'Mädräsä-i Shamsīyaneng echkä eshlärenä qarağan waqıtlı qanunnamä," in R. Sh. Zaripov, *Gali Ishan, Ishmi Ishan häm Tüntär mädräsäse* (Kazan: Iman, 2002); *Ufada berenche masjid jamīʿ khuḍurındagı Madrasa-i ʿUthmāniyyaning mufaṣṣal program* (Ufa: Tūrmish Matbuʿasī, 1917).

90. Gabdulla Bubyi, "Bubyi mädräsäseneng qısqa tarikhı," *Bertugan Bubyilar häm Izh-Bubyi mädräsäse: tarikhi-dokumental' jyentyk*, ed. Raif Märdanov, Ramil Mingnullin, and Söläyman Räkhimov (Kazan: Rukhiyat, 1999), 34–35.

91. Ibid., 36–57; *Ufada berenche masjid jamīʿ khuḍurındagı Madrasa-i ʿUthmāniyyaning mufaṣṣal programı*, 4; Muḥammad Najīb ibn Shamseddīn, "Tūntār awılında mārkhūm ostazlar shaykh Gali," Zaripov, *Gali Ishan*, 22–25; Madina Rakhimkulova, *Medrese "Khusainiia" v Orenburge* (Orenburg: n.p., 1997), 18–24; *Madrasa-i Muḥammadiyya programması*, 1331 h./1913 m. (Kazan: Elektro-Tipografiia "Milliat," 1913), 8, 24–25.

92. Mustafa Tuna, "Madrasa Reform as a Secularizing Process: A View from the Russian Empire," *Comparative Studies in Society and History* 53, no. 3 (2011): 540–70.

93. ʿAbdalmajīd bin Nūrghanī al-Ghafūrī al-Qazānī, "Wa an min al-shiʿr al-ḥikmāt," *Sibir timer yulı* (Orenburg: Tipografiia M. F. G. Karimova, 1904), cover.

94. Madina Rakhimkulova, *Medrese "Khusainiia" v Orenburge*, 7–9; Yarulla Moradi, "Tukayev Ural'skida," *Tukay turynda khätirälär*, ed. Ibrahim Nurullin and Rif Yakupov (Kazan: Tatarskoe knizhnoe izdatel'stvo, 1986), 35.

95. Ravil Amirkhan, "Mökhämmädiia mädräsäse," *Mädräsälärdä kitap kishtäse: mäshhür mägrifät üzäkläre tarikhınnan* (Kazan: Tatarstan kitap näshriyaty, 1992), 18.

96. *Medrese Kazani: XIX-nachalo XX vv. Sbornik dokumentov i materialov*, ed. L. V. Gorokhova (Kazan: Natsional'nyi arkhiv Respubliki Tatarstan, 2007), 124–30.

97. Bubyi, "Bubyi mädräsäseneng qısqa tarikhı," *Bertugan Bubyilar*, 47. These summer courses were offered in addition to the madrasa's regular program of study.

98. Rakhimkulova, *Medrese "Khusainiia," v Orenburge*, 13.

99. *Medrese Kazani*, 124–30; "Işlāḥ-i madāris," *Azat* 9 (1906): 2.

100. Il'dus Zagidullin, *Islamskii instituty v rossiiskoi imperii: Mecheti v evropeiskoi chasti Rossii i Sibiri* (Kazan: Tatarskoe Knizhnoe Izdatel'stvo, 2007), 143.

101. G. Ibrahimov, "Shakīrdlar ah-zarı," *al-Işlāḥ* 33 (1908): 6–7; *Medrese Kazani*, 143.

102. Ibid., 143.

103. Ibrahim (Alushev), "Fatikh Ämirkhan turında istäleklär," *Fatikh Ämirkhan turında istäleklär* (Kazan: Tatarstan kitap näshriyatı, 2005), 10.

104. Fatikh Ämirkhan, "Rizvan Alushiga, 1904 el, fevral', Kazan," *Fatikh Ämirkhan*, 4:226.

105. Mullā Sh. Q., *Waqf Pārāzitī* (Orenburg: Karīrimov, Ḥuysanov wa sharkatī, 1907).

106. Galimjan Ibrahimov, "Tatarlar arasında revolutsiia khäräkätläre," *Galimjan Ibrahimov: äsärlär sigez tomda*, 9 vols., ed. S. Kh. Alishev (Kazan: Tatar kitap näshriyaty, 1984), 7:360–61.

107. *Medrese Kazani*, 131–32.

108. "Iz Orenburga," *Orenburgskii listok* 13 (1905): 3.

109. Galiäskär Kämal, "Berenche teatr," *Galiäskär Kämal: Äsärlär öch tomda* (3 vols.), ed. Bäyan Gyizzät (Kazan: Tatarstan kitap näshriyaty, 1978), 1:75.

110. "Shakīrd ham yāshlar," *al-Işlāḥ* 31 (1908): 8.

111. "Taraqqīparwar fidā'ī yaki 'anqā' shamālī," *Dīn wa Ma'īshat* 5 (1909): 74; "'Ulamā' kirāmgā achiq khāt," *Dīn wa Ma'īshat* 11(1909): 174.

112. Fatikh Ämirkhan, "Fatkhulla Khäzrät," *Fatikh Ämirkhan*, 2:22–23.

113. Ibid., 40.

114. Gabdulla Tukay, "Pechän Bazary, yakhud yanga kisekbash," *Gabdulla Tukay: Äsärlär* (6 vols.), ed. R. M. Kadyirov and Z. G. Mökhämmätshin (Kazan: Tatar kitap näshriyaty, 2011), 1:268–83.

115. Fatikh Ämirkhan, "Yashlär," *Fatikh Ämirkhan*, 2:281.

116. The content of Amirkhan and Tuqayev's journal *al-Işlāḥ*—which was begun at Kazan's Muḥammadiyya Madrasa in 1905 as an underground publication, was legalized in 1907, and continued to appear until 1909—gives a sense of the students' grievances.

117. From the notebooks of Najīb Sibghatullin, teacher at Izh-Būbī Madrasa, NART f. 41, op. 11, del. 2, l. 67ob.

118. Adeeb Khalid, *The Politics of Muslim Cultural Reform: Jadidism in Central Asia* (Berkeley: University of California Press, 1998), 105.

119. Ḥusayn Amirkhan, *Tawārīkh-i Bulghāriyya* (Kazan: Vyatcheslav, 1883), 50–51; "Hadha fī bayān silsila Mu'inaddīn Chīstī wa as-Sayyīd 'Abdalqadīr al-Gīlānī wa ash-Shaykh Muḥammad Baha'addin Naqshbandī al-Bukhārī," IIaLI, F. 39, op. 1. del. 4461, l. 99–112; "Silsila," K(P)FU-ORRK No. 4204T, l. 2–6.

120. Danielle Ross, "The Nation That Might Not Be: The Role of Iskhaqi's Extinction after Two Hundred Years in the Popularization of Kazan Tatar National Identity among the 'Ulama Sons and Shakirds of the Volga-Ural Region, 1904–1917," *Ab Imperio* 3 (2012): 341–69.

121. 'Abdalmajīd Ghafūrī, "Tātār millāteneng lisān ḥāl ila shikayatı," *Millāt maḥabbate nām ash'irı* (Kazan: Elektro-tipografiia Sharaf, 1907), 3.

122. Ibid., 4.

123. ʿAbdalmajīd Ghafūrī, "Ber Tātār shakīrdınıng Qazanda mashhūr khān masjideneng manarasını kūrgāndā inshād itādege shigri dır," *Millāt maḥabbate nām ashʿirı*, 34–35.

124. Gabdulla Tukay, "Kichke Azan," *Gabdulla Tukay*, 1:134–35.

125. Wāqıf al-Jalālī, "Sūz bashı," *Sādā-i Madaniyyāt berenche juze* (Astrakhan: Tipografiia "A. N. Umerova i Ko., 1908), 3–4.

126. Untitled shakīrd song, 1909, collected and translated by the Kazan Gendarmerie, NART f. 199, op. 1, del. 773, c l. 171a.

127. "Dahī da shıgır budır," student notebook from Arskii Raion. (This manuscript is held in the private archive of the author.)

128. "'Kto ustraivaet revolutsiiu?,' *Tāng Yūldizī*, 21 July 1906, Russian translation ordered by the Kazan gendarmerie," NART f. 199, op. 1 del. 551, l. 10–10ob.

129. Gabdulla Tukay, "Piala bash," *Gabdulla Tukay*, 1:118; Näjib Dumavi, "Dinne ashap beterä yazgan ishan wa mullalar khakynda," *Näjip Dumavi: Tormısh säḥifläre: Shigri äsärlär häm proza*, ed. Zöfär Rämiev and Rezedä Ganiyeva (Kazan: Tatarstan kitap näshriyaty, 1985), 48–49; Sägyit Rämiev, "Ḥäzrätlär eshe," *Sägyit Rämiev: Tang Vakyty*, ed. Shäykhi Sadretinov (Kazan: Tatarstan kitap näshriyaty, 1980), 18–20.

130. "Revoliutsiia ham duma," *Tāng Yūldizī* 1 (1908), 1.

131. "Marsel'eza o podniatii rabochago naroda protiv pravitel'stva, From the confiscated papers of Izh-Būbī teacher Fatīḥ Fayḍullin," F. 41, op. 11, del. 2, l. 72; "Notebook 4, confiscated from Izh-Būbī teacher ʿAbdarraḥīm Muḥammadov Salīmıch," F. 41, op. 11, del. 2, l. 75ob-81ob.

132. Fatikh Ämirkhan, "Yashlär," *Fatikh Ämirkhan*, 2:295. This line alludes to the Tatar folk saying "Food that is meant to be eaten will smash one's teeth to get into one's mouth" (*Keräsä rizıq teshlärne sındırıp kerä*) and suggests the historical inevitability of the reforms that the Youth championed.

133. "Reformatorlar ḥaqqında," *Dīn wa Maʿīshat*, 1 (1912): 11; Taraqqīparwar fidāʾī yaki ʿanqāʾ shamālī," *Dīn wa Maʿīshat* 5 (1909), 74.

134. Muḥammadkamīl al-Mutiʿī Tuḥfatullin, *Tatarcha qurʾān tafsīre* (Kazan: Elektrotipografiia "Maarif," 1914); Guzal Safullina, "Khasan-gata Gabashi v diskussii o dzvolennosti muzyki v Islame," *Islam i Muzyka*, ed. Guzal Saifullina (Kazan: Tatarskoe kinzhnoe izdatel'stvo, 2015), 43.

135. Fatikh Ämirkhan, "Rizvan Alushiga, 1906 yıl, 24 oktiabr', Mäskäü," *Fatikh Ämirkhan*, 4:232.

8

AT WAR WITH THE TATAR KINGDOM

ISHMUḤAMMAD DĪNMUḤAMMADOV'S SCHOLARLY CAREER HAD STARTED OUT WELL enough. As a young man, he became a student and disciple of 'Alī Ishān at-Tūntārī. After 'Alī 's death, he continued to study and teach in Tūntār under the supervision of 'Alī's son-in-law, Shamsaddīn bin Raḥmatullāh.[1] In 1876, Shamsaddīn died, and Dīnmuḥammadov became the director of Tūntār Madrasa, one of the most prominent madrasas of the Machkara network.

Then the intellectual terrain of the Machkara network began to shift. In the 1880s and the 1890s, a new generation of young scholars emerged from the Chistopol and Lakeside madrasas. Dīnmuḥammadov was not opposed to Muslims learning to speak Russian; he sent his son, 'Abdalḥay, to study at a Russian-Tatar school in Malmyzh and then to a teachers' school in Slobodsk in Viatka province.[2] Nor was he opposed to women's education. Numerous girls received their education at Tūntār Madrasa. However, Dīnmuḥammadov could not stomach the new scholars' rejection of the Ḥanafī commentaries and theological debates on which he and his teachers had built their careers. Nor did he trust their new rationalist interpretations of the Qur'ān and the hadiths and their promotion of ijtihād as the cure for all of society's ills.

This new way of doing Islamic law was brought into Tūntār by Muḥammad Najīb Shamseddīnov, the son and grandson of Dīnmuḥammadov's teachers, who opened Madrasa-i Shamsiyya in 1894.[3] By the early 1900s, political radicalism spread among the students of Dīnmuḥammadov's madrasa, and they began to sing antigovernment songs behind his back.[4] Then, in 1902, this new Islamic legal and educational culture invaded his family life when his daughter, Faṭīma, and his son-in-law and former student, Sayyidgārāy Fayḍullin, implemented "reformed" pedagogical methods at their maktab in Shoda village.[5]

Dīnmuḥammadov's growing frustration reflected the broader tensions straining Kazan's 'ulamā' in the early 1900s. Network politics and factionalism had long been a reality, but literalist theology, the overhaul of the madrasas, and the political and social activism of the Youth presented a new kind of conflict. This conflict tore through the Machkaran network, dividing the network's families against one another and pitting parents against their children. With the growth of the periodical press and the Youth culture of rebellion and dissent, the old rules of engagement were no longer respected. Age and experience carried no weight. Deference was ridiculed. The public display of scholarly accomplishment in the munāẓara was rejected as a show of vanity.

As older madrasa-educated Muslims like Dīnmuḥammadov grappled with these changes and conflicts, Russian officials, still reeling from the 1905 Revolution, turned their attention to the questions of how to instill loyalty to the empire and prevent separatist and antigovernment activities. In the 1860s, some officials had questioned the usefulness of "fanatic" Tatars as imperial agents. In Kazan province after 1905, a new conflict emerged between Kazan's Muslims and Russian officials over who had the right to "enlighten" Russia's Muslim population. Reformist teachers, the Youth, and their opponents found themselves in the middle of this conflict.

A Scholarly Conflict

What became a confrontation between the Russian government and Kazan's Muslim community began as a quarrel between two madrasa directors: Ishmuḥammad Dīnmuḥammadov of Tūntār Madrasa and 'Abdullāh Būbī of Izh-Būbī Madrasa. Both traced their scholarly lineages back to Machkara Madrasa, and they moved in the same social circles.[6] Būbī called for the reinterpretation of Islamic law through ijtihād. Dīnmuḥammadov believed in strict adherence to the Ḥanafī madhhab. In 1907, Tūntār Madrasa's students began to transfer to Izh-Būbī, drawn by Būbī's reputation as a legist and the politically charged atmosphere of the school.[7] Some students returned to Tūntār and spread radical socialism and revolutionary propaganda.[8] Dīnmuḥammadov, already angered by Būbī's legal scholarship, immediately blamed Būbī for spreading revolutionary sentiments among his students.

In 1910, Dīnmuḥammadov cornered Būbī at a gathering of the Machkaran 'ulamā'. As the two drank tea, he warned Būbī that he had best stop teaching as he did. Būbī protested that there was nothing harmful in his teaching methods and encouraged Dīnmuḥammadov to visit Izh-Būbī Madrasa to see situation for himself. Dīnmuḥammadov refused and left Būbī with an ominous warning: if he did not change his teaching methods, he would be changing other things.[9]

The Pan-Islamic Panic, 1908–1910

The escalating conflict between Būbī and Dīnmuḥammadov coincided with rising Russian official tensions over the loyalty of the empire's Muslim subjects. Anti-Muslim sentiments flowed from multiple points of origin within the imperial bureaucracy. Russia's prime minister, P. A. Stolypin, viewed ethnic separatism as a fundamental threat to the empire. His antiseparatist rhetoric sharpened as he turned to conservative elements in Russian society to gain support for his governmental reform projects. Kazan's provincial branch of the Ministry of Internal Affairs (Ministerstvo Vnutrenikh Del; hereafter, MVD) was overwhelmed by the output of the Arabic-script commercial publishers and bombarded by complaints about revolutionaries and antigovernment radicals in the Muslim quarters and villages. Without adequate bilingual staff or officers knowledgeable about local Muslim communities, police and gendarme officers were either unable to penetrate Muslim society or found themselves chasing red herrings.

The Young Turk Revolution and Stolypin's antiseparatism agenda brought to a head tensions that had been brewing in the ministries as well as among Russian conservatives since 1905. In December 1908, less than four months after the start of the Young Turk Revolution, an article appeared in the newspaper *Russkaia zeml'ia* decrying what the author called "Pan-Islamic" and "Young Turk" propaganda in the Volga-Kama region. The article identified the culprits behind this propaganda as the Tatar schools funded by wealthy Muslim merchants and the teachers who staffed these schools. Since this harmful ideology had become enmeshed in the Tatar-Muslim schools, it had become a cancer, infecting not only Muslim elites but also all levels of society.[10]

The article's author was not alone in his concern about reformed madrasas and their teachers. On almost the same day as the article appeared, an anonymous Muslim submitted a complaint to the Kazan MVD calling for the arrest of the "new method" teachers in his village. He explained the politics of Volga Muslim society simply: "The [supporters of the] new form, the so-called *usul-zadit [jadid]*, are from the red parties. The [supporters of the] old form, the so-called *usul-kadim*, are with the white party."[11] This delineation of Muslim politics harmonized well with official priorities as they had been in the wake of 1905, when the MVD had cracked down on radical socialism. But by late 1908, the lens through which Russian officials viewed Volga-Ural Muslim society shifted from a political one to an ethnic-confessional one.

This new trend gained momentum through 1909. In January, Muslim opponents of madrasa reform had changed the language of their complaints against the "new method" teachers and the radical youth. Petitions to the Spiritual Assembly accused young imams and new method teachers in Mamadysh uezd of spreading Islam among the Votiaks. According to the writer, these young imams intended not only to lead the Votiaks away from the Christian faith but also to convince them that the imperial government needed to be reorganized or done away with. According to the author, the impetus for this activity came from the "new method," which he characterized as a set of political ideas imported from the Ottoman empire.[12]

In the following months, a definition of "Pan-Islamism" appeared in the Kazan Gendarme Administration's agents' information log. It explained:

> Many think that the Muslims are burning with the desire to call for holy war against Christendom. [. . .] But in fact, they have a plan that is much more dreadful, and that plan is for the unification of all Muslims to struggle against the political and economic rule of Christian Europe in the East. That idea is Pan-Islamism. Each of us knows that in recent years throughout the Muslim world some sort of quiet stirrings have been noticed, and few know their true character. On the surface, it would seem that those stirrings pose no danger, and that they emerged as a result of the dissatisfaction of the younger generation with the old traditions of the Muslims. It is correct that many things in Islam displease the pan-Islamists. They talk about the misunderstandings of the old Muslims concerning many points of Shariat and about the intolerability of the despotism of Muslim rulers. But the field of activity of the pan-Islamists are not limited to this. They go further, saying, "The old traditions and the despotism of the caliphate and the shaykhs held back Muslim development, and thanks to that, they created the possibility for the Europeans to become masters of the Muslims of the East. It is now necessary to bring all of that to an end." It follows logically from here that in all Muslim states constitutions should be established, and then it will be possible to fight European power in the East [. . .] the goal of pan-Islamism in Russia is, before all else, the preservation of the nationality of the Muslims, to hold their way of life within a purely Muslim framework, so that by such a path it will be possible to resist the assimilative influence of the Russians.[13]

The entry went on to discuss how the Pan-Islamists of Russia hoped to form a Muslim Union with the Turks, but noted that they were nowhere near achieving that end, as pan-Islamists could not agree among themselves as to what such a union might look like.[14] To cloak their true separatist intentions while simultaneously working toward their goal of overthrowing the government, the pan-Islamists had forged a union with Russia's Kadet (Constitutional Democratic) party and joined the Kadets in "spreading constitutional propaganda" among the empire's Muslim population in order to "increase people's hatred toward the government."[15]

This report did not simply represent the idiosyncrasies of Kazan's police force. It was part of an official policy dictated to provincial MVD and gendarme offices by their superiors in St. Petersburg. Stolypin himself took a leading role in defining what the relationship between Muslims and the imperial government should be and how those Muslim intellectuals who did not share his view of Russian statehood (*gosudarstvennost'*) had transgressed.[16]

From late 1908 to early 1911, the intellectual and cultural life of the Volga-Ural Muslim community went from a relatively obscure interest of local ethnographers, educators, and missionaries to a threat to the future of the Russian state. However, the official origins of these definitions displayed a variety of contradictions. Stolypin and his subordinates determined that Muslim discourses, publications, and gatherings posed a direct threat, but they struggled to describe with any degree of precision the nature of the movements under suspicion. These movements were simultaneously "pan-Islamic" and "pan-Turkic," at once "Tatarizing" and "drawing together" with the Ottoman Turks. They involved madrasas, Russian Muslims living in Turkey and Egypt, those Muslims who tempted baptized inorodtsy away from Christianity, Russian Muslim publishers, and pilgrims returning from Mecca.[17]

Official paranoia in the ranks of the MVD cannot alone be blamed for the sweeping, all-encompassing description appearing in Stolypin's report. MVD officials reproduced rhetoric previously published by Russian Muslim writers themselves and especially by ʿAbdarrashīd Ibrāhīmov in his *1001 Hadiths*, *The Islamic World*, and *Ulfat*. This emphasis on Ibrāhīmov was not entirely out of place. Ibrāhīmov had taken a leading role in organizing the Muslim Unions in 1905–1906, and he had been a prolific writer in the early 1900s. He also represented one of the most outspoken advocates of a transnational "Muslim" identity to emerge out of the 1905 Revolution. In 1905, even as he organized the Muslim Congresses, he called for Muslims in Russia and beyond to unite along confessional lines.[18] However, Ibrāhīmov represented only one voice in Kazan Muslim society. There was no single clearly articulated vision of Muslims' future within Russia.

Another factor that confounded the MVD's quest to define and stamp out "pan-Islamism" was the ministry's means of carrying out investigations. When seeking information, police and gendarme officials turned to a variety of sources in the Volga basin. These groups included the Ministry of Popular Enlightenment, the zemstvos, the Russian press, the orientalists of Kazan University, the Kazan Provisional Committee on Printing Affairs, and Muslim subjects themselves. The new official interest in the Muslim community of Kazan became a moment for various groups to air pent-up grievances against various factions of Kazan Muslim educated society.

School inspectors complained about the way in which Kazan's Muslims persistently resisted zemstvo and the Ministry of Education efforts to promote Russian culture in Muslim schools: "The Tatar-Mohammadans of Kazan uezd make up a very large part (up to 30 percent) of the population. But despite more than three hundred years of living side by side with the Russian population, it is impossible to say that they have grown closer to them. They live an absolutely separate life, rejecting en masse the influence of the broader cultural idea that would unite them with the rest of the population of the uezd and would make them useful cultural workers in the widening of Russian state life."[19]

This concern over the separate nature of Kazan's Muslim community flowed into a second question: Who had the duty to lead the empire's Muslims to enlightenment and modernity? For the school inspector who contributed the report cited above, the answer to that question was clear:

> It is not hard to guess what kind of light and education they [reformist teachers] can bring to the Muslim masses, not having the most elementary general-educational knowledge. In that spirit, they educate the people in the same way that they themselves were educated, strengthening and developing in them hatred, fanaticism and revulsion toward people of other faiths.
>
> If there is someone, for example in the Kazan uezd zemstvo, working in the center of the Tatar population, what we might call the Tatar kingdom, before all else, the duty lies before them to establish education among the Tatars and lead them out of the darkness and confusion in which they continue to languish. The guiding of the Tatars to general-cultural education and to general cultural work should be declared to be the most important state (*gosudarstvenniaia*) goal, and it should be set forth as one of the main duties of the zemstvo.[20]

The conservative Russian newspapers added their voices to the discussion. An article published in *Kolokol* in 1911 pointed out: "The welfare and peace of the Russian state is now threatened not only by the Jewish revolution. Laziness, shortsightedness, the liberalism of the agents of power in the provinces and the lack of attention on the part of central government has permitted the growth in Russia of the so-called Young Muslim movement. Oral pan-Islamic propaganda that is regulated by no one and lack of attention and strict censorship of the Muslim press has permitted the unchecked spread [of such propaganda] among Russia's Muslim population by the actors and supporters of revolution."[21]

By 1909 and 1910, there was a growing awareness in the Volga-Ural Muslim communities of the Russian government's pan-Islamic anxieties. Muslims tapped that anxiety when they wrote to denounce rivals for funding and sponsorship, misbehaving youths, and fellow jurists with whom them disagreed over legal opinions and teaching methods. They petitioned the Spiritual Assembly, the MVD, and various governors:

> In the Muslim schools in the city of Troitsk, they teach our young people by the new method, which goes against the bases of our Muslim religion. As people educated by the preexisting methods, we are not won over by these new ideas, which bring harm to our religion and our government. [. . .] On our city of Troitsk, a schism has occurred and two absolutely opposing parties have suddenly appeared. One is purely Muslim, educated in the old religious manner, worshiping just as our ancestors did. The other, armed with the seeds of some kind of innovations, which, not desiring to listen to voices of advice, caused harm every step of its way to us followers of the pure, traditional Muslim faith, to those of us who have been brought up to respect the law and ruling power, and to reject the new ideas put about by the extreme left parties that seek not to strengthen the state, but to overthrow it.[22]

All these groups agreed on two points: (1) Since 1905, certain elements in Muslim society had run amuck; and (2) it was the duty of the imperial government to bring these elements back under control before they caused irreparable harm to imperial society. However, on other matters, their views diverged radically. The eclectic collection of petitions, newspaper articles, letters and reports submitted to the police and the gendarmerie from 1909–1914 helped to focus the investigation on particular groups ("new method" teachers, liberals, socialists, publishers, Duma deputies) and institutions (madrasas, mosques, printing houses) in Kazan Muslim society, but it also complicated the MVD's struggle to define movements in the Muslim community because each petitioner focused on his own specific conflicts and described those conflicts his own terms.

The result of the MVD's effort to define dangerous political behavior in the Muslim community was the homogenization of the way in which political disloyalty among Muslims was measured, investigated, and prosecuted. "Pan-Islamism" became the catch-all term for any political activity involving Muslims that questioned or rejected the authority of the imperial government, including participation in liberal politics, formation of organizations not under the direct control of the government, socialism, ethno-national separatism, anticolonial sentiments, and the desire to overthrow the government. By 1910, Muslims who worked for social and political reform through the dumas and the zemstvos were subjected to the same level of police scrutiny as their more outspoken socialist coreligionist.

Pan-Islamism: From Theory to Reality

By early 1909, the MVD's new interest in Muslim political life, fueled by Russian conservatives and Muslim opponents of legal, theological, and educational reform, began to make itself felt in the Volga-Ural region. The first to feel the effects of this new policy were those individuals and groups who had taken the most overtly antigovernment course since 1905. In Kazan, the police shut down Gaynān Vaisov's "House of Learning" and independent spiritual assembly, an organizational structure that had operated outside of the Spiritual Assembly hierarchy and entirely without official permission since its reestablishment in 1906.[23] The headquarters of the Kazan newspaper *Bayān al-Ḥaqq* was shut down for several days and searched for having printed several articles by Vaisov's followers.[24]

Around the same time, historian Muḥammad Mūrād ar-Rāmzī was taken into custody for making anti-government and anti-Russian statements in his two-volume history, *The Kingdom of the Tatars*.[25] The full print run of his book was confiscated from the publishing house where it had been awaiting distribution among local bookstores.[26] Upon closer scrutiny, Nikolai Katanov, invited from Kazan University to serve as a linguistic specialist to the MVD, determined that Rāmzī had not made any specific threats against the imperial government or the person of the emperor. Rāmzī was released, but by that time, the gendarmerie had already destroyed all the copies of his book they had confiscated.[27]

By 1908, ʿAbdarrashīd Ibrāhīmov had left Russia, but his *1001 Hadiths* was still in circulation. Initially reported to the OMSA by several imams for antiautocratic statements hidden among its commentary, the book became a recurring nightmare for the MVD. In addition to changing titles as it was transcribed from one report to another and thus confusing provincial MVD officials, a rumor circulated that *1001 Hadiths* had been approved by the imperial censors in 1905 and that it had therefore been published legally.[28] After following numerous false leads concerning the book's origins, one MVD official proposed that all copies of *1001 Hadiths* be confiscated from stores, publishing houses, and purchasers and destroyed. However, thousands of copies had been sold, often to imams who had assumed they were purchasing a hadith collection and not a political tract. Also, officials discovered that there were, in fact, several books published under the title *1001 Hadiths*, only one of which had been written by Ibrāhīmov. Gendarme officials in Kazan quickly determined that it would be impossible to arrest every purchaser of *1001 Hadiths* and that too much time had elapsed between the commission of the crime and its discovery to arrest the publishers or the readers.[29]

Būbī Madrasa on Trial

In 1909, Izh-Būbī Madrasa appeared on a list of madrasas considered worthy of gendarme attention.[30] It continued to appear in MVD reports in 1910 as one of several madrasas suspected of promoting pan-Islamism. However, ʿAbdullāh Būbī was unaware of this longer investigation. When in 1910 a school inspector arrived at his madrasa, he assumed that Dīnmuḥammadov had reported the school to the police. Būbī treated the inspector to a carefully orchestrated tour of the madrasa grounds, and the inspector left without any apparent complaints. Būbī continued to view Dīnmuḥammadov as his primary enemy.[31] However, disaster came from a different direction.

Since 1905, Izh-Būbī village had experienced tensions between the young and mature members of the community. Village resident Shahīd Appakov owned a store and rented rooms to Izh-Būbī Madrasa students and guests. One day in 1910, as he was walking past the madrasa, he overheard a group of Izh-Būbī students singing revolutionary songs. As their elder, he ordered them to desist. Instead of complying, the students treated him with disdain and promised to boycott his store. The next day, students ceased buying goods from Appakov's store and frightened away his tenants. Appakov took the matter to ʿAbdullāh Būbī. According to Appakov, Būbī shrugged his shoulders and claimed to know nothing about it.[32] Frustrated by what he interpreted as Būbī's complicity in his students' misbehavior, Appakov reported the incidents to the police.[33] The report was passed on to the Kazan gendarme, who added it to the other complaints they had received about Izh-Būbī Madrasa, its antiautocratic teachers, and its radical students.

On midnight of January 30, 1911, the police raided the residences of two of Izh-Būbī Madrasa's teachers and those of three of its teaching assistants. Based on the material they found, they arrested one teacher.[34] They also began a search of Izh-Būbī village that lasted for three days, starting with the madrasa facilities and expanding to the houses of the village and finally to several neighboring villages. With the teachers confined to their quarters and the police turning the village upside down, the students were left to themselves. Some milled about outside the school singing the "Marseillaise" and other revolutionary songs. Others rushed to burn their notebooks and illegal pamphlets before the police could find them.[35] The parents of one of the younger local students were puzzled and horrified when their son returned home from school and asked them to help him burn his school notebooks and homework in the household stove.[36] According to one police official, the air was filled with smoke and ashes from the burning of books. Following the search, ʿAbdullāh Būbī, his brother ʿUbaydullāh, two of the madrasa's senior teachers, four of its junior teachers, and three of its teaching assistants were placed under arrest.[37] The madrasa's entire library was confiscated.

With the arrest of the Izh-Būbī Madrasa teaching staff, the MVD and Kazan Muslim educated society collided at an unprecedented level, for the incident involved a well-regarded Machkara-network family and one of the most prominent madrasas of the early 1900s. That collision sent shockwaves through Kazan Muslim society. Called on to testify against the school's staff, the residents of Izh-Būbī village were divided against one another. Some willingly joined the upcoming prosecution, using the moment to vent long-held hostilities against ʿAbdullāh Būbī and his students. Others closed ranks around the Būbī siblings. Still other residents reacted with shock. This was the case with many local parents, who were informed that their sons were entangled in an antigovernment conspiracy, and for peasants of Izh-Būbī village, who suddenly had the police searching their houses.

ʿAbdullāh Būbī's reformist colleagues and their Youth students rallied to the defense of Izh-Būbī's teachers. Initially, Tatar newspapers launched attacks on imams and madrasa directors who were known monarchists, had opposed 1880s–1890s education reforms, or had protested the reformers' overhaul of Islamic law and theology. They accused these groups of having loosed the police on Izh-Būbī Madrasa out of spite and narrow-minded self-interest. The Youth launched a particularly vicious press campaign against those who were perceived to have aided the MVD.

The Būbī brothers' supporters viewed the police raid as a revelation of the Russian government's true agenda for its Muslims. That agenda was cultural assimilation or destruction. A report for *Waqt* noted that, during interrogation, the suspects and witnesses were permitted to converse only in Russian, despite their native language being Tatar.[38] Poet ʿAbdullāh Tūqāyev characterized the Izh-Būbī raid as direct attack on the Tatar nation: "Before my eyes everything has gone dark. I've lost all hope for our national life and for my own dreams." He foresaw in the closing of Izh-Būbī Madrasa the impending doom of all Muslim libraries, schools, and presses in the empire. He vowed that if indeed it came to pass that the government closed every Muslim press and journal, he would rend his clothing and go out into the streets barefoot.[39]

The raid on Izh-Būbī Madrasa and the seizure of the madrasa's library sent tremors through Muslim educated circles across the Volga-Ural region. The gendarme hoped to use the library collection to track down additional pan-Islamists. However, most of the collection was in Tatar, and the gendarme had a limited number of translators. In the rush to follow up on the Izh-Būbī raid, gendarme officials resorted to a new tactic. The inclusion of an author's works in the Izh-Būbī collection was by itself enough to merit police investigation.[40] Though 1911 and 1912, Muslim writers found themselves under surveillance or arrested. Historian-jurist Riḍāʾaddīn bin Fakhraddīn had his apartment searched and his research notes and manuscripts seized.[41] Poet Saghīt Rāmīev was investigated because of his popularity among the madrasa youth. Some of the investigated writers held distinctly antiautocratic views. Others were simply unfortunate enough to have had their books purchased for the madrasa library.

The Izh-Būbī Madrasa raid flooded Kazan's police with oral and written material. But when most of this material had been gathered, identified, and translated, officials faced the challenge of building a case against the Izh-Būbī teachers and, in the process, defining what crime they had committed. Since 1909, the MVD had worked to compile a definition of pan-Islamism as it pertained to Russia's Muslims. But once the translators analyzed the seized materials, they confessed that, while there was ample evidence of antigovernment sentiment at Izh-Būbī Madrasa, including the promotion of socialism, antiautocratic propaganda, and Tatar nationalism, they could find little to support the existence of the pan-Islamism as it was defined in MVD reports.

A notable voice among the translators was orientalist Nikolai Katanov, who analyzed many of the confiscated texts. Gendarme officials pressed Katanov for a more "pan-Islamic" reading of the material, but Katanov refused to read into the texts meanings that he did not believe were there. When it became clear that Katanov would not be moved, gendarme officials questioned whether Katanov's true loyalties were to the empire or to his friends in Kazan's Muslim community. Katanov was put under police surveillance.[42] Similar suspicion spread to Katanov's colleague and friend, Gaynaddīn Akhmarov, who had assisted him with the translations.[43]

The texts and translators proved more cooperative than the prosecution's witnesses. Though many people in Izh-Būbī village and beyond took the madrasa teachers' side, ʿAbdullāh Būbī had made enemies, and there was no lack of voices to bear witness against him: imams whom he had publicly insulted or from whom he had stolen pupils, students' parents who were horrified at the idea that their children had been singing revolutionary songs instead of Qurʾānic verses, and shopkeepers and landlords who had chastised the Izh-Būbī students and suffered financially as a result. But these testimonies were fraught with problems. Witness accounts contradicted one another and related stories that were not be confirmed by the existing physical evidence.

Moreover, witnesses came to the police interrogations with their own expectations. They told a story of how revolutionary chaos had engulfed their village. Young people sang violent songs, conducted themselves in a criminal manner, and treated their elders with scathing disrespect. Their teachers and imams, who ought to have been sources of guidance and discipline, appeared to encourage the students' bad behavior. Witnesses appealed to their interrogators, and more broadly to the imperial government, to restore order. Those who were more politically savvy employed terms such as "radical," "nationalist," "anti-Russian," and "anti-government" in describing the political views of the Izh-Būbī teachers.[44] A theme that recurred in the statements of several peasant witnesses was the Būbī brothers' promise that "new method" education would one day enable the Muslims of Kazan to establish their own "Tatar kingdom."[45]

The one word that many witnesses failed to use spontaneously, however, was "pan-Islamism." When pressed by the interrogators, some claimed never to have heard the term previously and expressed confusion as to what pan-Islamism was. After receiving an explanation of the term, some conceded that if political radicalism and socialism were pan-Islamism, then maybe there had been pan-Islamism in their village.[46] Others appropriated the new term with more certainty but failed to identify other tell-tale signs of the movement such as the collection of money to be sent to the Ottoman empire or the preaching of brotherhood among Muslims. Grasping that the MVD wanted to find pan-Islamists, these latter witnesses were willing to call the Izh-Bubi teachers by whatever name necessary for the police to remove them from the village.[47]

In the year before the Izh-Būbī case to came to trial, both the Tatar press and supporters of the madrasa worked to have the teachers exonerated. The Muslim newspapers ran articles vindicating the teachers and cursing the prosecution witnesses as national traitors and collaborators with a reactionary government.[48] Imams who had volunteered to serve as witnesses and specialists were lampooned in poems and caricatures. Dīnmuḥammadov, who had taken a prominent role in the case, was singled out for especial ridicule and harassment in the Tatar press. Tūqāyev led the way in this endeavor, dubbing Dīnmuḥammadov first "Ishmī the Donkey" and then "Ishmī Ishan."[49] At least one group of Dīnmuḥammadov's opponents denounced him to the MVD as a threat to the Muslim community.[50] In response to such abuse, Dīnmuḥammadov's supporters called on the MVD to defend him. The petition highlighted the way in which Youth writers had succeeded in transforming the word ishān from a term of prestige into a derogatory label: "Word reached me that our akhund is writing about Dinmukhammetov in various newspapers and calling him an 'ishan.' Among other things, Dinmukhammetov is an honest person. He never strays from the Qur'ān and the shariat, he teaches our children in the old way, and he has never made any pretensions of being an ishan. This label has been hung on him unfairly and that is why I have sent a petition to the governor-general to ask him to defend this elderly mullā."[51]

Taking a less legal approach to aiding the Izh-Būbī teachers, an anonymous group of Muslims wrote a letter to the *rotmistr* of the gendarme, offering him twenty thousand rubles if he would release the teachers. When he refused to be moved by bribes, the same group sent a second letter threatening to kill him.[52]

The residents of Izh-Būbī village who had volunteered to testify for the prosecution began to recant. One witness claimed not to have understood the questions initially asked of him, which had supposedly been delivered in "literary Russian" instead of a simpler conversational style. Another admitted that he was under tremendous pressure from his neighbors, who had given him the choice of recanting or leaving the village.[53]

The prosecution did not lose all its witnesses and specialists. Those most committed to ridding the Muslim community of radical antigovernment elements refused to be intimidated. Dīnmuḥammadov, facing threats of violence, refrained from appearing in public when he went to Sarapul for the trial and requested that he be provided with a police escort when he had to go out into the street.[54] However, the main problem for the prosecution was that the witnesses who were stubborn enough not to be intimidated by threats and criticism proved equally impervious to the prosecution's efforts to shape their testimony. The MVD had called on them to testify on pan-Islamism, but they had come to see a destabilizing force in their community dismantled. Either unaware of this gap in mutual understanding, or perhaps having exhausted its alternatives, the prosecution proceeded to put these witnesses on the stand.

The trial of ʿAbdullāh and ʿUbaydullāh Būbī began in May of 1912. Muslim members of Kadet Party hired Duma deputy V.A. Maklakov to lead the Būbī brothers' defense.[55] His fees and those of the other defense lawyers, more than fifteen thousand rubles, were paid by Būbī Madrasa's merchant sponsors.[56] The Tatar press continued to level accusations of anti-Muslim bias against the Kazan MVD and against the Stolypin administration in St. Petersburg. In an article in *Waqt*, ʿĀlimjān Ibrāhīmov accused the gendarme of fabricating all the antigovernment songs and writings that it claimed to have confiscated from the madrasa. Given that level of official corruption, he argued, how could a Muslim expect to receive a fair trial? The MVD would achieve its ends one way or another.[57]

On May 28, 1912, the first day of the trial, more than six hundred people gathered in front of Sarapul's courthouse. Among them was a correspondent from the Kazan newspaper, *Yūldiz*, sent to cover the trial. The police barred his entrance. With the all the arguments, local intriguing, and threats swirling around the case, the prosecutor decided to hold the trial in closed sessions.[58] Meanwhile, on the other side of the doors, Maklakov was less than thrilled with the men he had been paid to defend. In a private discussion with ʿAbdullāh Būbī, he told the madrasa director that his antigovernment writings had made him physically ill.[59] Maklakov conceded that he could not defend Būbī's political opinions but only his right to hold them. He constructed his defense around two basic points. First, ʿAbdullāh Būbī had not published the texts that were being used as evidence against him. While publishing and distributing antigovernment material was a punishable crime, thinking antigovernment thoughts and writing them in texts produced for personal consumption was not. Second, in relation to the writings and antigovernment activities of his staff and students, Būbī had no knowledge of any of these and could not be accountable for other people's transgressions.[60]

Once the trial began, the prosecution faced problems as well. Its Muslim witnesses and specialists were, for the most part, the same people who had come forward in 1911 to testify against Izh-Būbī Madrasa. However, in the intervening year, prosecutors had failed to build a rapport with these witnesses. Once the Muslim witnesses took the stand, their own direct examiners treated them with open contempt. Dīnmuḥammadov, appearing in long, flowing robes and a turban with an escort of his students, clearly hoped to impress the court officials with the authority and majesty of Kazan's ʿulamāʾ. Recognizing his linguistic limitations, he brought one of his Russian-fluent students to interpret. But as soon as he took the stand, the prosecutors dismissed the student-interpreter and called on their own translator. Dīnmuḥammadov protested to no avail. The questioning began. Dīnmuḥammadov accused the state translator of mistranslating his answers. Appakov, a shopkeeper from Izh-Būbī village, faced similar treatment. When asked about pan-Islamism, he began to relate the story of how the Izh-Būbī students had boycotted his store. The questioner cut him off and repeated the question. Frustrated, Appakov asked when someone would be punished for damaging his business. He was told to be silent.[61]

In the confrontations between the prosecutors and their own witnesses, the disconnect between the MVD and its Muslim allies became clear. Dīnmuḥammadov and Appakov saw themselves as loyal subjects of the empire. By lending their support and testimony to the trial, they envisioned themselves taking part in restoring order and upholding the imperial system against the threat posed by ʿAbdullāh Būbī and his students. By mobilizing imperial authority against their rivals, they also defended their own positions within the Muslim community. Moreover, Dīnmuḥammadov, through his dress and behavior, positioned himself as the professional and intellectual equal of the state bureaucrats with whom he and generations of Kazan ʿulamāʾ before him had labored to bring imperial order to Russia's Muslim territories. But to the gendarme and prosecution officials, he was a Muslim, distinguished by his foreign language and alien faith, traits that made him innately inferior to the Christian and ethnic Russian officials in charge of questioning him. In their eyes, Dīnmuḥammadov posed only slightly less danger to Russian society than ʿAbdullāh Būbī because he had yet to embrace revolutionary politics. His political reliability was undercut by his persistence in preserving the "fanatical" curriculum of the nineteenth-century madrasa.[62]

Despite the setbacks faced by the prosecution, the Būbī brothers were convicted under the first part of article 102: belonging to an association that plotted to overthrow the government or disrupt the line of succession to the throne.[63] The conviction appears to have been based largely on written statements made by ʿAbdullāh Būbī himself, particularly in his multivolume work, *Ḥaqīqat,* where he had vented his frustration with the imperial government's post-1905 reactionary turn: "The Russian government took Kazan from us, destroyed our khanate, forcibly baptized us, and took away all our rights. And that is why the government is our most evil enemy. No one, and most especially, no Muslim, should do anything to help the Russian government. On the contrary, everyone should try to destroy its power. The stronger the government becomes, the more it oppresses us and our religion."[64]

Būbī, in his own memoirs, made no effort to deny his guilt. Rather, he lamented the suffering of his brother, ʿUbaydullāh, whom he considered innocent of wrongdoing. ʿAbdullāh Būbī was sentenced to six months imprisonment and ʿUbaydullāh to two months.[65] After their release, the brothers departed with their families for Kulja in western China. There, they opened a primary school to serve Kulja's community of Volga-Ural Muslim merchants and immigrants.[66]

In Kazan, the conviction of the Būbī brothers sent a new wave of indignation through Muslim educated society. In a speech to the State Duma, Sadraddīn Maqṣūdī asserted that, between 1911 and 1912, seventy Muslim schools had been closed under orders from the Ministry of Education and one hundred and fifty teachers and writers had been searched and/or arrested by the Ministry of Internal Affairs. In Kazan province alone, twenty imams had been dismissed from their posts. Newspapers, publishing houses, and community-run libraries had been shut down.[67] The source of the figures Maqṣūdī offered is not clear, and the numbers may have been inflated, but his protest reflected a broader reality: the relationship between Kazan's ʿulamāʾ and the provincial bureaucracy was in shambles.

Conclusion

The pan-Islam investigations of 1908–1912 revealed the degree to which developments outside and within Kazan Muslim society had reshaped the relationship between the Kazan 'ulamā' and the imperial government. For Russian officials, memories of 1905, growing Russian nationalism, and a suspicion toward Islam that had been growing since the mid-1800s made alliance with the 'ulamā' increasingly fraught. For Kazan's 'ulamā', new ethno-national identity and consciousness of European colonialism across the Muslim world made even tolerating the Russian government increasingly problematic.

Notes

1. UFITs-RAN f. 7, op. 1 del. 12(sa) s. 12ob; R. Sh. Zaripov, *Gali Ishan, Ishmi Ishan häm Tüntär mädräsäse* (Kazan: Iman, 2002), 9–10.
2. "Dinmökhämmätov Gabdelkhay Ishmökhämmät-uly: Mägrifätche, zhurnalist, yazuchy," *Baltach entsiklopediiase*, ed. Garifjan Mökhämmätshin (Kazan: PPK Idel-Press, 2006), 139.
3. Zaripov, *Gali Ishan*, 11.
4. Ibid., 13.
5. "Fäyzullin Säetgäräy Mostafa Uly: Din eshleklege," *Baltach Entsiklopediiase*, 325.
6. Gabdulla Bubyi, "Bubyi mädräsäseneng kyska tarikhy," *Bertugan Bubyilar häm Izh-Bubyi mädräsäse: tarikhi-dokumental' jyentyk*, ed. Raif Märdanov, Ramil Mingnullin, and Söläyman Räkhimov (Kazan: Rukhiyat,1999), 61.
7. Ibid., 42.
8. R. Gazizov, "Uyan shäkird, yoqlamaghyl!" *Mädräsälärdä kitap kishtäse: mäshhür mägrifät üzäkläre tarikhınnan* (Kazan: Tatarstan kitap näshriyatı, 1992), 172.
9. Gabdulla Bubyi, "Bubyi mädräsäseneng kyska tarikhy," *Bertugan Bubyilar*, 61.
10. NART f. 199, op. 1, del. 722, l. 14–15.
11. Ibid., 18.
12. NART f. 199, op. 1, del. 771, l. 37.
13. Ibid., 48.
14. Ibid., 48ob.
15. Ibid., 49.
16. NART f. 1370, op 1, del. 3, l. 77.
17. Ibid., 78.
18. "Natsionalizm/Millayat, Qawmiyat," *Ulfat* 1 (1905): 3.
19. NART 199, op. 1, del. 771, l. 237.
20. Ibid., 238.
21. NART f. 199, op. 1, del 857, l. 204.
22. NART f. 1370 op. 1 del 3. p. 188–188ob.
23. NART f. 41. op. 13, del. 3, p. 4–6ob.

24. Fatikh Ämirkhan, "Ismägyil Aitovka, 1908, 8 mart, Kazan," *Fatikh Ämirkhan turynda istäleklär*, vol. 4 (Kazan: Tatarstan kitap näshriyaty, 2005), 244.
25. NART f. 199, op. 1, d. 773, l. 29–34ob.
26. N. Garaeva, "M. Ramzi," *Tatarskie intellectualy: istoricheskie portrety*, ed. R. M. Mukhammetshin (Kazan: Mägarif, 2005), 58.
27. Zeki Velidi Togan, *Hâtiralar: Türkıstan ve dığer müsülman doğu türklerının mıllî varlik ve kültür mücadelelerı* (Istanbul: n.p., 1969), 68.
28. NART f. 199, op. 1 d. 722, l. 75ob–76.
29. NART f. 199, op. 1, del. 792, l. 130, 46–146ob, 255.
30. NART f. 92, op. 2, del. 8777, l. 58ob; NART f. 199, op. 1 d. 675 l. 19ob.
31. Gabdulla Bubyi, "Bubyi mädräsäseneng kyska tarikhy," *Bertugan Bubyilar*, 61.
32. NART f. 41, op. 11, del. 1, l. 83–83ob; del. 3, l. 68 ob.
33. Gabdulla Bubyi, "Bubyi mädräsäseneng kyska tarikhy," *Bertugan Bubyilar*, 70.
34. "Būbī madrasa ḥaqqinda tafsilat," *Kazan mukhbīra* 441 (1911): 3.
35. Mökhämmät Mähdiev, "Bubi Mädräsäse," *Mädräsälärdä kitap kishtäse: mäshhür mägrifät üzäkläre tarikhynnan* (Kazan: Tatarstan kitap näshriyaty, 1992), 51.
36. NART f. 41, op 11, del. 1, l. 83–83ob, 106.
37. "Būbī madrasa ḥaqqinda tafsilat," *Kazan mukhbīra* 441 (1911): 3.
38. Ibid.
39. Gabdulla Tukay, "Sägyit Rämievkä, 1911, 4 Mart," *Gabdulla Tukay*, 5:105.
40. NART f. 41, op.11, del. 1, l. 119.
41. NART f. 41, op. 6, del. 1, l. 174.
42. NART f. 199, op. 1, del. 2086, l. 110.
43. NART f. 199, op. 1, del. 792, l. 112–112ob.
44. NART f. 41, op. 11, del. 1, p. 62–62a, 72, 74, 79
45. NART f. 41, op. 11, del. 10, l. 30ob, 189, 193.
46. NART f. 41, op. 11, del. 10, l. 13ob-14.
47. NART f. 41, op. 11, del. 1, p. 81, 100, 104–6; del. 10, l. 1–5.
48. "Musul'man āzīflarī wa pānislāmizm," *Yūldiz* 777 (1911): 1; "Būbī eshlare ḥaqqinda," *Yūldiz* 837 (1912): 1–2.
49. Gabdulla Tukay, "Kushmyi ishäk jyrlyi," *Gabdulla Tukay: Äsärläre* (6 vols.), ed. R. M. Kadyirov and Z. G. Mökhämmätshin (Kazan: Tatar kitap näshriyaty, 2011), 2:161; Tukay, "Kushmyi ishan khilkasendä," *Gabdulla Tukay: Äsärläre*, 2:159; Tukay, "Shigriyät häm näser," *Gabdulla Tukay: Äsärläre*, 2:180–81; Tukay, "Awyl jyrlary (berenche költä)," *Gabdulla Tukay: Äsärläre*, 1:258–59; Shäekhzadä Babich, "Hatif wa Tatar," *Zänggär Jyrlar*, ed. Galimjan Gyil'manov (Kazan: Tatarstan kitap näshriyaty, 1990), 49–50; Äminä Töḥfätullina, "Khatyn-kyz dikkätenä," *Ömet yoldyzlary: XIX yöz akhyry häm XX yöz bashy tatar khatyn-kyz yazuchylary äsärläre*, ed. Mökhämmät Gaynullin (Kazan: Tatarstan kitap näshriyaty, 1988), 192–93; Fatikḥ Ämirkhan, "Fatkhulla Ḥäzrät," *Fatikḥ Ämirkhan: Äsärlär dürt tomda* (4 vols.), ed. Zöfär Rämiev (Kazan: Tatar Kitap näshriyaty, 1985), 2:72–75.
50. NART 199, op. 1, d. 771, l. 301–2ob.
51. NART f. 1370 op. 1, del. 3, l. 184.
52. TsGIARB f. 187, op. 1, d. 412, l. 147.
53. Ibid., 153ob.
54. "Būbī eshlare ḥaqqinda," *Yūldiz* 839 (1912): 1.
55. Gabdulla Bubyi, "Bubyi mädräsäseneng kyska tarikhy," *Bertugan Bubyilar*, 67.
56. Ibid., 82.

57. Galimjan Ibrahimov, "Tentü wa khäbeslär nätijäse," *Galimjan Ibrahimov: äsärlär sigez tomda*, vol. 6, ed. S. Kh. Alishev (Kazan: Tatarstan kitap näshriyaty, 1984), 71–74.
58. "Būbī eshlare ḥaqqinda," *Yūldız* 839 (1912): 1.
59. Gabdulla Bubyi, "Bubyi mädräsäseneng kyska tarikhy," *Bertugan Bubyilar*, 61.
60. Ibid., 78.
61. Ibid., 74–75.
62. NART f. 199, op. 1 del. 771, l. 238ob.
63. NART f. 41, op. 11, d. 3, l. 800b; for the precise definition of this article and article 100, to which it is directly related, see *Das neue russische Strafgesetzbuch (Ugolovnoje Uloženje) Allerhöchst bestätigt am 22. März 1903*, trans. O. S. Bernstein (Berlin: J. Guttentag, 1908), 39.
64. NART f. 41, op. 11, del. 1, l. 111 ob.
65. "Būbī eshlare ḥaqqinda," *Yūldiz* 839 (1912): 2.
66. Gabdulla Bubyi, "Bubyi mädräsäseneng kyska tarikhy," *Bertugan Bubyilar*, 85–89; A. Makhmutova, "G. Bubi," *Tatarskie intellektualy*, 172–89.
67. Sadrī Maqsūdov, "G. Dumada dakhīliyya ministerlıghının ismetası qaralghan waqtta deputat Sadraddīn Afande Maqsūdovning suilagan notighī," *Waqt* 955 (1912): supplement 1–2.

9

AN EMPIRE WITHOUT RUSSIANS

Introduction

With the start of World War I, the Ministry of Internal Affairs scaled back its investigations of pan-Islamism and pan-Turkism in the Volga-Ural region. It redirected its resources toward hunting for German spies and Zionists. This shift came too late to salvage the working relationship between the government and its old Muslim allies. By 1914, Russian nationalism coupled with concerns over revolutionary groups at home and anti-colonial sentiments abroad diminished imperial bureaucrats' willingness to work with Muslim community leaders. The growth of official personnel, state institutions, and Russian civil society organizations in the provinces made governmental cooperation with non-Russian elites less necessary to the running of the empire. Russian officials could maintain order, collect revenue, and provide basic services without Muslim interlocuters. For the Kazan ʿulamāʾ, the price of cooperation with the imperial state had become too high. An increasing number of them believed that the Russian government's vision for its non-Russian and non-Christian subjects was either assimilation or acceptance of permanently inferior status to Russian Christians.

However, the parting of the ways between the Russian state and the Kazan Tatar ʿulamāʾ did not entirely sweep away two hundred years of colonizing the eastern and southern borderlands. Territorial expansion and the assimilation of new people to the empire formed the foundations of both the Russian empire and Kazan's ʿulamāʾ. As Russian mapping expeditions, missionaries, and frontier officials had claimed new lands and attempted to reconstruct them in the image of the empire, so networks of imams, shaykhs, and merchants had sought to construct well-ordered, pious, profitable communities in the imperial borderlands. It was in this mission of "taming" the frontier, whether in the name of empire or Islam, that eighteenth-century bureaucrats and 'ulamā' had found common ground.

As the old allies had grown apart, neither had abandoned their identity as tamers and enlighteners. But by the second half of the nineteenth century, they found themselves working at cross purposes. As Russian missionaries and the Ministry of Education attempted to instill loyalty among the Volga-Ural region's non-Russians through shared Russian language and Christian faith, the 'ulamā' continued to expand their own educational institutions. While the 'ulamā' were not solely responsible for the apostasy of baptized inorodtsy to Islam, the expansion of madrasas, Sufi networks, and circulation of Tatar mystical texts created an atmosphere in which such conversions became possible, and the post-1905 Tatar press adopted a celebratory tone when announcing new inorodtsy converts. Tatar imams, teachers, and shaykhs crossed ethnic lines and imperial boundaries despite official efforts to contain them. The Būbī trial brought to a head a conflict that had been in the making since the 1860s: the Kazan Tatars' greatest sin was not that they refused to assimilate to Russian culture, but that they persisted in carrying out an enlightenment and empire-building project that interfered with the Russians' own.

By 1917, the full impact of the Kazan 'ulamā''s long participation in the colonial project became clear. It gave them a sense of superiority over the other Muslims of the empire. As the imperial system began to collapse, the Kazan 'ulamā' rushed in to fill the vacuum.

Life after the Empire: February–May 1917

Despite their difficult relationship with the imperial government, Russia's Muslim Duma deputies were caught off guard by the protests and soldiers' munity in Petrograd in February 1917. Zaki Validi Togan recalled how he and fellow deputy Mustafa Chokaev wandered through the streets of the capital city amid the disorder. They passed a group of protestors hanging the overcoats of slain policemen from the lampposts. A truck drove by them, heading from Tauride Palace, bearing away General Dmitri Pisarev and Prince Kochubei while workers on the street corner lobbed dirty snowballs at them. On Nevskii Prospect, someone had broken into a government warehouse and begun selling the weapons inside. Validi bought himself a pistol.[1]

Within a week of the mutiny, Muslim representatives from Kazan, Crimea, the Caucasus, and the Kazakh steppe began making their way to Petrograd or contacted the Muslim Duma deputies to demand a general meeting of Russia's Muslims.[2] In Kazan, which was a regional center for recruitment and mobilization for ten of the empire's central and eastern provinces, the garrisons received by telegram news of the soldiers' uprising in Petrograd. They mutinied three days later, arresting their officers, and electing a Provisional Military Committee of the Garrisons.[3] Two thousand of Kazan's Muslim residents held a meeting in the city's Bolshoi Theater. Discussions of religious freedom and national-cultural institutions quickly turned to military matters. The soldiers declared that the Tatars needed their own regiments, a demand that resulted in the creation of a committee for the city's Muslim soldiery. The committee established relations with the Provisional Military Committee and Kazan's Workers'-Soldiers' Soviet and contacted Muslim soldiers in the surrounding provinces.[4]

While the soldiers organized military affairs, the Muslim Duma deputies attempted to control the message that the Muslim press sent regarding the war. When the newspaper *Liberty* (*Irek*) published several articles calling for Russia to pull out of the war, some of those deputies sent word to ʿAbdarrakhmān Fakhreddīnov, son of historian Rizaʾaddīn bin Fakhreddīn, ordering the Youth activists in Kazan to stop writing against the war. Fakhreddīnov was warned that if the antiwar articles persisted, the offending writers would be arrested.[5] Sadraddīn Maqsūdī made a speech at the union of the Kadet Party, promising that "30 million Muslims stand behind continuing the war until total victory is achieved." When making this pronouncement, he seems to have ignored the uprisings that had broken out across Central Asia in summer 1916 in response to the conscription of the region's Muslim men. Apparently, the response to Maqsūdī's prowar message was so negative that Validi felt compelled to explain it to the Petrograd Muslim Society several days later: "Maqsūdī spoke from the mistaken assumption of the main party in Russia—the Kadet Party, of which he is a member. 30 million Muslims did not swear allegiance to the Kadets and no one gave Sadrī Bāy the right to come forward and made such a claim. Sadrī Bāy knows just as well as the rest of us that no one in Russia wants to continue the war."[6]

Maqsūdī's attempt to single-handedly articulate a Muslim stance on the war reflected the broader Kazan ʿulamāʾ tendency to speak for the other Muslim populations of the empire without consulting them. Kazan's

Muslim leaders struggled to acknowledge that Muslims outside of inner Russia, Crimea, and South Caucasus were capable of participating in imperial politics. This problem again came to the fore when the Duma's Muslim faction met to plan an All-Russian Muslim Union of six hundred delegates to be held in Moscow in May. When it was suggested that seats at the congress should be allotted in proportion to the size of the empire's various Muslim populations, ʿAyāḍ al-Isḥāqī rejected the proposal, arguing that "there is no point in calling up all sorts of random, uneducated people [for the sake maintaining equal representation of ethnic groups]. You need to invite the Kazanians. More than half of the delegates should be from Kazan."[7]

In April, a Muslim council convened in Tashkent in preparation for the Moscow union the following month. Maqsūdī pushed the Turkestani attendees to accept the creation of a single ethno-confessional, extraterritorial Muslim community within an emerging democratic Russia. The plan favored the Kazan Tatars, both because it provided them with a framework for politically unifying the geographically disparate Volga-Ural Muslim community, and also because it allowed Kazan to fully realize its role of guiding, and in essence speaking for, other Muslim communities. The representatives from Turkestan and the Kazakh steppe rejected the proposal in favor of a national-territorial model.[8]

The All-Russian Muslim Union convened in Moscow in May 1917. The head of the Provisional Central Muslim Bureau (which had organized the union) was Ossetin Aḥmad Tsalikhov, but six of the bureau's twelve members (ʿAyāḍ al-Isḥāqī, Ibrāhīm Akhtiyamov, Ḥasanʿaṭā ʿAbashī, Ilyās Alkīn, Fatīḥ Karīmī, and Mūsā Bīgīev) hailed from Kazan's ʿulamāʾ networks. The seventh (and only female) member of the bureau, Salīma Yaqūpova, was a scion of a Kazan Muslim merchant family living in Tashkent. She had studied at Kazan University before the revolution.[9] The Muslims of Crimea, the Caucasus, the steppe, and sedentary Central Asia were represented by the bureau's remaining five members (Aḥmad Tsalikhov, Jaʿfar Sayyid Aḥmad, Khalil Dosmuḥammadov, Abdullāh Khojaev, and ʿAlīmardān Topchibashev).

The preponderance of Kazan Tatars in the central bureau reflected the Kazan ʿulamāʾ's view of the rest of Russia's Muslims as people in varying states of backwardness. It also undermined their ability to provide effective leadership. Rather than listening to the grievances of their coreligionists, they projected their own vision of postrevolutionary order onto the other

Muslim regions of Russia. Their indifference to the concerns of the non-Kazan delegates bordered on callousness. In an especially egregious episode, a representative from Semirech'e demanded that the congress's participants turn their attention to the devastation caused by the 1916 Uprising and the ongoing violence between Russians and Muslims in Central Asia and the Kazakh steppe. The Turkestani participants supported this petitioner and argued that that the congress had the obligation to intervene in some way or, at the very least, to discuss the issue. However, Isḥāqī quickly shut down the discussion of the revolt, arguing that the representatives simply did not have time to discuss all the requests that had been sent to the congress.[10] The Bashkir delegates were similarly silenced. They had formed a commission and submitted a report concerning the land ownership and settlement on Bashkir land. All they managed to get printed in the minutes of the congress was their official protest that the agricultural section had promised to let them read their report and then did not permit them to do so.[11]

These clashes between the Kazan delegates and participants from the other Muslim regions foreshadowed the divisions over the future political organization of Muslims across the former empire. Tsalikhov advocated for Isḥāqī's plan for the formation of a Muslim National Council. According to this plan, each Muslim region would enjoy control over designated local affairs while the National Council would provide unified leadership to all Muslims across a democratic Russia.[12] The proposed constituency of the council made clear who would be leading Russia's Muslims. Ten of the council's twenty-seven positions were allocated to the Turko-Tatars of Inner Russia—that is, to the Kazan Tatars. Turkestan was to receive seven seats, the North and South Caucasus five seats, and Crimea two. The council would convene in Kazan.[13]

The Turkestani and Caucasian participants in the congress pushed to reduce the Kazanian influence on the National Council. Khojaev suggested that the National Council should be increased to thirty members—one for every million Muslims in Russia—and that seats be apportioned by population. Under this model, he argued, Turkestan should have ten representatives and the Caucasus six.[14] Isḥāqī scoffed that perhaps Khojaev wanted to grant the Caucasian Muslims six and a half delegates, as there were 6.5 million of them. Participants from other regions joined in the fray, demanding greater representation for their ethnic groups even as Isḥāqī fought to keep power concentrated in Kazan. One delegate accused Isḥāqī of turning the congress into an autocracy.[15]

Isḥāqī prevailed in having his proposal for a National Council of thirty members with ten Volga-Ural Muslims approved. However, Tsalikhov, Bīgīev, and Maqṣūdī's plan for a unified Russian Muslim nation was defeated in favor of the creation of individual federal states that would one day join a multiethnic democratic Russian state. At the end of the congress, delegates departed for their home regions with instructions to hold regional congresses in preparation for the second All-Russian Muslim Congress in August. In fact, few delegates from Turkestan, the Caucasus, Crimea, or even the south Urals bothered to attend the July congress in Kazan. They organized locally instead. Kazan Muslims' effort to unite all the empire's Muslims under their leadership had failed.

Losing the South Urals: The July Congresses

Three congresses opened in Kazan in July 1917: the All-Russian Muslim Soldiers' Congress, the second All-Russian Muslim Congress, and the Union of All-Russian Muslim ʿUlamāʾ. On July 22, the delegates of the All-Russian Muslim Union gathered in one of Kazan's theaters to celebrate what they dubbed the first "National Autonomy Day." The entire auditorium joined ʿĀlimjān Bārūdī, now mufti of Orenburg, in reciting the opening verse of the Qurʾān, after which the audience departed from the hall for a few minutes. When they returned, two flags had been raised on stage: on one side, the red "banner of revolution" and on the other, the "banner of Islam," a bow and arrows against a green background. The audience clapped and began to sing the "Marseillaise" in Tatar.[16]

The three congresses foreshadowed the three groups that would play a major role in the construction of the Tatar autonomy: the National Council (*Millī Shūrā*), the Military Council (*Ḥarbī Shūrā*), and the ʿulamāʾ. Despite the all-Russian Muslim pretensions of the three July meetings, most of the organizers and attendees came from the Volga-Ural region. Of 280 people who attended the ʿUlamāʾ Union, only 43 came from other regions of the empire.[17]

In nine days, the delegates of the All-Russian Muslim Congress declared into existence a national-cultural autonomous entity consisting of the Muslims of "Inner Russia and Siberia." With this population in mind, they put together a Muslim faction for the upcoming elections to Russia's Constituent Assembly.[18] They created a new National Council (*Millī Shūrā*), which was in turn charged with organizing a National Parliament (*Millī Majlīs*) in

Ufa. They laid out the principles by which the parliament would be elected and set plans for creating a school system, a treasury, a tax-collection system, and an administrative structure for Muslim institutions.[19] At the same time, the ʿUlamāʾ Union proposed the founding of digest on Islamic law to provide standardized guidelines to village imams tasked with resolving civil disputes. The delegates of the All-Russian Muslim Soldiers' Congress passed a motion to initiate the formation of Tatar national regiments.[20]

While the "All-Russian Muslim" delegates celebrated their Inner Russian Muslim Autonomy, the Bashkirs convened a congress (*quraltai*) in Orenburg. Delegates met in the city's caravanserai, a "property of the Bashkir nation."[21] The gathering included three hundred Muslim soldiers who welcomed the opening of the Bashkir union with a musical performance and took part in speeches and demonstrations in front of the Ural Hotel.[22] Taking their lead from the resolution passed at the All-Russian Muslim congress in Moscow, the Bashkir delegates declared into existence the autonomous state of Bashqortistan. Like the delegates in Kazan, those in Ufa showed special interest in two issues: mobilization of their coethnics for the elections to the Constituent Assembly and the creation of national regiments. However, the Bashkir delegates were much more direct in explaining their goals. In a telegram to Kazan, they explained: "An even more difficult task stands before the Bashkir people: the war for the autonomy of Bashqortistan, which will answer the domestic and economic interests of the Bashkir people and represents the only road to the liberation of their native land of Bashqortistan from centuries of economic oppression."[23]

The declaration of autonomous Bashqortistan was the last in a series of defections from the Kazan Tatars' vision of all-Russian Muslim unity. It was the most painful. Kazan claims to authority over Turkestan, the Caucasus, and the Kazakh steppe had been tenuous at best, but the South Urals had been an integral part of Kazan Muslim lands since the mid-1700s. The region featured in the sacred geographies of the Bulghar histories of the 1800s and in the Tatar national histories of the early 1900s. As far as Kazan's Muslims were concerned, Orenburg and Ufa provinces belonged to them.

On August 25, the Second Bashkir Union convened in Ufa. Its members issued a declaration that the Kazan-based proposal for the creation of a national-cultural autonomy for Muslims within a resurrected Great Russian state could only harm the Bashkir people by leaving decisions about local policy (especially land policy) in the hands of an All-Russian legislative body that would have the power to revoke Muslims' autonomous status at any time.[24] Instead, they proposed to excise the Bashkir-majority regions of Orenburg, Ufa, Perm', Samara, and Cheliabinsk provinces and combine them into a federal autonomous Ural Republic.[25] They ended their protocol with a direct blow to the Kazan movement for a single Muslim autonomy:

> If thirty million Muslims, with the exception of two million of them, that is a certain part of the Volga Tatars, are all in favor of federation, then the Bashkirs' joining of this majority does not represent a division, but, on the contrary, an act of union. It is that very Tatar Kadet movement that is divisive, and we summon them to join the federalists, that is, to join with us, the Bashkirs. From a religious-national point of view, we consider this to be their obligation. We, the Bashkirs, see our national and political goals as follows: we, brothers in faith and blood with Crimea, the Caucasus, Turkestan, the Kazakhs, the Turkmens, and others, took the side of the federalists and united. Only the Tatars, upholding the Kazan-ian platform, have diverged from all the Muslims.[26]

The Kazan national organizations reacted immediately to the Bashkirs' defection. Hādī Āṭlāsov tried to delegitimize the Bashkirs' actions by invoking the imperial language of backwardness and progress. He told the Bashkirs that, although they held more territory than Germany or Austria, they had not reached the level of advancement necessary to build an autonomous or independent state.[27] Speaking for Bashqortistan, Sharif Manatov countered with that fact that Tatar "help" usually took the form of giving Bashkir lands away to the Russians. That being the case, Bashkirs would be better off on their own.[28]

The feud between Kazan and the Bashkirs died down after August but reignited in November when the National Assembly of the Inner Russian-Siberian Muslim Autonomy met in Ufa. The initial meeting of the assembly was postponed to November 20 due to bad weather and poor conditions on the road.[29] When the delegates finally arrived, the supporters of the Bashkir autonomy barred them from entering Ufa's theater. The assembly finally met in a small shop. The floor above them housed local soldiers, whose carousing created a racket that lasted through the entire meeting.[30]

A few days before the National Assembly convened, the Bashkir Council had responded to the Bolsheviks' "Declaration of the Rights of Nations" by publicly declaring an autonomous Bashkir Ural Republic. When the National Assembly's delegates heard this, several pushed for Kazan's Muslims to follow the Bashkirs' example and declare their own autonomous

Volga Republic.[31] From this point, the delegates no longer spoke of "Russian Muslims," but rather of the "Turko-Tatar" or "Tatar" nation.

On December 8, autonomous Bashqortistan convened a new union in Orenburg. The leaders of the Bashkir Council announced their intent to lay claim to all majority-Muslim regions of Orenburg, Perm, Ufa, and Samara provinces as part of their federal autonomous state. They continued to encourage Muslims in Kazan to abandon the National Council's project of "extraterritorial" cultural autonomy in favor of territorial autonomy and federalism.[32] Emboldened by the Bashkirs, the Territorialist Faction within the National Assembly began to call for the formation of a territorial-based autonomy around Kazan. Isḥāqī, seeing that the cause of extraterritorial autonomy and unitarism was lost, proposed that Turkism and territorial autonomy did not have to contradict one another. The territorialists and the extraterritorialists could come to a solution that would please both sides.[33] Speaking on behalf of the Territorialist Faction of the Assembly, ʿĀlimjān Ibrāhīmov proposed that both factions of the National Assembly (Territorialists and Turkists) should nominate three representatives to send to Orenburg to negotiate with the Bashkirs.[34] Once these representatives had been selected, the National Assembly approved ten resolutions on the creation of a Turko-Tatar federal autonomous state.[35] The resolutions called for the reorganization of the Russian Empire as a "federal republic" and for the creation of a South Urals-Volga State as a member state of that federation. The South Urals-Volga State would include those regions of Kazan, Ufa, and Orenburg *guberniias* in which "Turko-Tatars" made up the majority. They promised to respect the rights of other nations within the new state's borders but forbid the formation of smaller states within the boundaries of the South Urals-Volga State, although they promised to reach out to the Bashkir Assembly and coordinate with them in the establishment of a single autonomous state for all Muslims of the Volga basin and the South Urals. They also resolved to continue pursuing the national-cultural autonomy project for the benefit of those Turko-Tatars located outside the borders of the new state. The Bashkir Assembly's response was simple and direct: the Bashkirs needed their own state.[36]

The Endgame

While the National Assembly and the Bashkir Assembly faced off over territorial claims, a second conflict unfolded in Kazan. In the wake of October, the Kazan Workers-Peasants' Soviet, which was dominated by the

Bolsheviks, attempted to assert authority over the city. It was challenged by the National Council and the Muslim Military Council. On January 8, 1918, when the Military Council held its second congress, two Bolshevik representatives attended. They congratulated the congress's attendants on the convening of Russia's new Constituent Assembly, then complained that Petrograd had received little news from Kazan in the past weeks. The only news that had reached party leaders was that "some partyless people" had taken it into their own hands to build themselves a government. Ilyās Alkīn, head of the Military Council, respond that the Kazan Muslim "government building" project was the work of a body of popularly elected officials, many of whom belonged to Russia's major political parties. He argued that while these ministers went about the constructive task of building a government, Kazan's Bolshevik-dominated Soviet had occupied itself with compiling lists of people to arrest.[37]

Within days after this confrontation, the Military Council published a proposal for the creation of a territorial autonomous state. It included within its borders portions of Ufa, Kazan, Perm, Samara, Viakta, Orenburg, and Simbirsk provinces. Ethnic "Tatars" made up 51 percent of the population of just under 7 million. Ethnic Russians made up the next largest group, at almost 39 percent. No distinction was made between Tatars and Bashkirs.

The Kazan Soviet and other Bolshevik personnel in the city tried to win over the Military Council to the Bolshevik side. In February, Mirsaid Sultan-Galiev published an article in the Bolshevik paper *Banner of Revolution* (*Znamia revoliutsii*) reiterating Bolshevik support for national self-determination but arguing that such self-determination should be carried out by the "will of the proletariat" and not by "secret vote." But this article did little to reconcile the Bolsheviks and the Military Council.

In late February 1918, a series of events ended the Kazan Soviet's efforts at reconciliation. In late 1917, an exclusively Tatar army division had been formed and was stationed in Finland. The members of this division demanded to be posted closer to their home territory and succeeded in obtaining permission to relocate. The Kazan Soviet contacted the People's Commissar of Military Affairs and demanded that the relocation be stopped as the soldiers might be manipulated by counterrevolutionary elements. This exchange of telegrams was intercepted by the All-Russian Muslim Military Council, the leaders of which publicized the conflict at the second All-Russian Muslim Soldiers' Congress. On February 23, forty-five railcars of Muslim soldiers arrived in Kazan. They were met by the Muslim Military Council.[38]

The conflict over the arrival of the "Finland division" exacerbated existing conflicts between the Military Council and the Soviet and within the Military Council itself. The left wing of the Military Council walked out of the congress and joined forces with the Bolsheviks to form the Commissariat of Muslim Affairs. The pro-Bashkir faction of the Military Council soon joined the new commissariat. With the establishment of the Commissariat, an order from Petrograd called for the transformation of the "Russian" army into a "socialist" army. The Muslim military organizations responded immediately, proposing the creation of a "Muslim socialist" army, but the newly formed Commissariat of Muslim Affairs informed them that the new army was only opened to "politically conscious" socialists. The Military Council and the Bolshevik-allied Muslim Commissariat found themselves at an impasse. The Muslim Commissariat called for the Military Council to remove its "commissars" from those jurisdictions which the Muslim Commissariat claimed for itself. The Military Council responded by promising to officially declare a Middle Volga-South Urals State on March 1.[39]

On the night of February 27, 1918, the Kazan Soviet sent out agents to arrest the leadership of the All-Russian Muslim Military Council and the Muslim National Council.[40] The Bolshevik-allied organizations in Orenburg had previously undertaken a similar operation against the Bashqortistan government.[41] The arrest of the Military Council leadership sent shockwaves through the Old Tatar Quarter of Kazan. By morning on February 28, people began to gather in the streets, and the quarter descended into disorder and violence. Supporters of the Military Council went to the house of Warriors of God leader Gaynān Vaisov to demand he surrender to them the weapons his followers had stockpiled. When Vaisov, a Bolshevik supporter, refused, he was shot dead in front of his family.[42]

The Kazan Soviet brought out its own troops and surrounded the urban quarter with artillery. Several members of the Soviet suggested firing on the quarter until the disorder was put down, but the Commissariat of Muslim Affairs recommended a more conciliatory approach. The Soviet used the Bolshevik Muslim socialist committee, a group that included Mullanur Vakhitov and Sultan-Galiev, to appeal to the Muslim soldiers to cease their riot and recognize the Soviet's authority. The Soviet promised to recognize the soldiers' national concerns. The soldiers capitulated. The Idel-Ural Autonomous State fell without fight. By March 28, Petrograd sent a unit of Baltic sailors to reinforce the pro-Bolshevik divisions in Kazan. On April 12, the National Administration in Ufa was closed, its members arrested, and its treasury confiscated. The next day the Bolshevik government in Petrograd disbanded the Turko-Tatar Autonomous Administration. On April 24, the Moscow branch of the Muslim Military Council was liquidated, and a month after that, the National Council was closed.

The Bolsheviks held a conference to discuss the future of the Muslims of the Volga-Ural region. The conference resolved to create two republics, one for Kazan Tatars and one for Bashkirs. The Tatars were granted Kazan, the Bashkirs Ufa, and the Kazakhs Orenburg. Over the next years, borders shifted and cities changed hands, but the effect of this policy remained. The relatively uniform culture that Kazan 'ulamā' had fostered across Muslim communities in central and eastern Russia since the late 1600s was to be replaced by a set of Soviet national cultures.

Notes

1. Zaki Validi Togan, *Vosponinaniia* (Moscow: Moskovskaia tipografiia No. 12, 1997), 112–13.
2. Ibid., 114.
3. I. G. Gizzatullin, *Musul'manskie voennye organizatsii (1917–1921 gg.)* (Kazan: Fän, 2002), 46–47.
4. Ibid., 48–49.
5. Galimjan Ibrahimov, "Böek oktyabr' revoliutsiiase häm proletariat diktaturasy," *Galimjan Ibrahimov: Äsärlär sigez tomda*, vol. 7, ed. S. Kh. Alishev (Kazan: Tatarstan kitap näshriyaty, 1984), 65–66.
6. Togan, *Vospominaniia*, 115.
7. Ibid.
8. Ibid., 119; Gabdelbari Battal-Taymas, *Min ber yaktylyk ezlägän idem*, ed. Älfiyä Sibgatullina (Kazan: Tatarstan kitap näshriyaty, 2003), 30; Gabdulla Bubyi, "Bubyi mädräsäseneng kyska tarikhı," *Bertugan Bubyilar häm Izh-Bubyi mädräsäse: tairikhi-dokumental' jyentyk*, ed. Raif Märdanov, Ramil Mingnullin, and Söläyman Räkhimov (Kazan: Rukhiyat, 1999), 88.
9. Ismägyil' Rämi and Räis Dautov, *Ädäbi Süzlek* (Kazan: Tatarskoe Knizhnoe Izdatel'svto, 2001), 359.
10. *Butūn rūsiya muslimnarīning 1917-nchı yilda 1–11 māyda Maskaūda būlghān gumūmī isyīzdīnıng prūtākūllarī* (Petrograd: Amanet, 1917), 64–66.
11. Ibid., 325.
12. Ibid., 96–99.
13. Ibid., 397, 446.
14. Ibid., 435–38.
15. Ibid., 445.

16. "Butūn rūsiya muslim soldatlarī isyīzdī," *Bizning tāwish* 11 (1917): 2.

17. *ʿUlamāʾ Ittifāghī: Berenche nadwasī* (Kazan: Tipo-litografiia T. D. "Br. Karimovykh," 1917), 49–58.

18. "Yāngī kābīnītning yūlī," *Bizning tāwish* 15 (1917): 1–2.

19. *Natsional'naia Avtomoniia* (Ufa: Sharykh, 1917), trans. and republished in Tamurbek Davlatshin, *Sovetskii Tatarstan: Teoriia i praktika leninskoi natsional'noi politiki* (Kazan: Zhyen, 2005), 402–18.

20. "Muhīm ber majlīs," *Bizning tāwish* 13 (1917): 1.

21. *Natsional'no-gosudarstvennoe ustroistvo Bashkortostana (1917–1925 gg): Dokumenty i materialy v 4-kh tomakh* (4 vols.), ed. B. Kh. Yuldashbaev (Ufa: "Kitap," 2002), 1:136.

22. "Bāshkirdlar namaishī," *Waqt* 22 (1917): 4.

23. *Natsional'no-gosudarstvennoe ustroistvo Bashkortostana*, 1:139.

24. *Khitābnāma: Ikenche gumūmī bāshqūrt isyīzdī khaqqinda* (Belebei: n.p., 1917), 3–4.

25. Ibid., 4–5.

26. Ibid., 11–12.

27. Ibid., 14.

28. Ibid., 23.

29. "14 nuyabr 1917," *Bizning tāwish* 44 (1917): 1–2.

30. "Millāt majlīse," *Bizning tāwish* 50 (1917): 1; "Milliat Medzhlise," *Izvestiia Vserossiiskago Musul'manskago Boennago Shuro* 1 (1917): 1; "Bashkirskaia avtonomiia," *Izvestiia Vserossiiskago Musul'manskago Boennago Shuro* 2 (1917): 3.

31. "Millāt majlīse," *Bezneng tawısh* 50 (1917): 1–2.

32. *Natsional'no-gosudarstvennoe ustroistvo Bashkortostana*, 1:190.

33. "8 dikābr 1917," *Bizning tāwish* 53 (1917): 1–3.

34. Ibid.

35. Ibid.

36. "Bashqirdistan Avtonomiiase" *Bezneng tawısh* 65 (1918): 1–2.

37. "Musulman gaskirilare sezdin soviet taraturgha uylī ikan," *Bizning tāwish* 67 (1918): 1.

38. *Mirsäet Soltangaliev: Saylanma khezmätlär*, ed. I. G. Gizzatullina and D. R. Sharafutdinov (Kazan: "Gasyr," 1998), 664.

39. Mirsäet Soltangaliev, "Zapis soobshcheniia Kommissariatu po delam musul'man vnutrennei Rossii po priamomu povodu o sobytiiakh proiskhodivshikh v Kazani v fevrale-marte 1918 goda," *Mirsäet Soltangaliev*, 116.

40. "Prikaz No. 1: Revoliutsionanogo shtaba Kazanskogo soveta R.S.K.D.," in Rämzi Väliyev, *Bolak arty respublikasy* (Kazan: Tatarstan kitap näshriyaty, 1999), 118–19.

41. Togan, *Vosponinaniia*, 148–50.

42. Svetlana Malysheva and Lilia Zaripova, "Uravnenie so mnogimi neizvestnymi, ili o tom, kak byl ubit Sardar Vaisov," *Tatarstan* 5–6 (1992): 39.

CONCLUSION

Islam in Russia

For more than two hundred and thirty years, the Kazan ʿulamāʾ built and maintained a network of Muslim institutions, scholars, and holy men that stretched from one end of the Russian empire to the other. Through this process, they created a new geography composed of towns, villages, holy sites, and landscapes that they identified as their own, a shared textual culture, and a loose hierarchy of scholarly and shaykhly families who provided moral and intellectual leadership. The building of a Kazan Muslim world in the middle of the Russian empire did not in occur in isolation from the construction of the empire. Nor was it a result of the Russian government "permitting" Islam to exist on its territory and grateful Muslims committing themselves to serve the imperial state. Rather, it came about because of dovetailing interests. Russian officials needed settlers, merchants, interpreters, and mediators. Kazan Tatar peasants, merchants, and ʿulamāʾ sought free land, new business opportunities, and souls to shepherd and convert.

At the ideological level, the relationship between the Russian government and the Kazan Tatars was always complicated. Even when the relationship was at its friendliest, some Russians questioned the wisdom of accommodating Muslims rather than converting them to Christianity. Some Muslims, for their part, expressed such discomfort with living and serving under a non-Muslim ruler that they emigrated to lands beyond Russia's borders. At its lowest points, the partnership between Kazan Tatars and their Russian rulers disintegrated into suspicion, accusations, and persecution. From the 1680s to the 1910s, Russia had no consistent policy toward the Kazan Muslims, much less toward Islam in general. Nor did Kazan Tatars hold a unified opinion on the Russian government. Significant collaborations between Russian officials and members of the Kazan ʿulamāʾ occurred simultaneously with harsh anti-Muslim legislations. Periods of greater religious tolerance were still riddled by conflicts between the state and its Muslims and among Kazan's Tatars themselves. The happy, post-Catherinian era of ʿulamāʾ in service to "prophet and tsar" never existed as such. Neither did the dark period of mass persecution of Islam that supposedly preceded it.

Kazan Tatars served their Christian rulers because that was the only avenue to resources and power in the Russian autocratic state and had been since the 1552 conquest. From the 1550s to the 1680s, Muslim aristocrats who chose to remain in the Volga Basin integrated into the Muscovite-Russian state with minimal difficulty. It was only in the late 1600s that this situation changed. Laws aimed at assimilating or dissolving Kazan's Muslim aristocracy stripped that society of its last political center and marginalized the old landowning class. However, it proved a windfall for the ʿulamāʾ, who assumed many of the responsibilities of the aristocrats. Far from languishing under Russian rule, the Kazan ʿulamāʾ flourished.

The Mutuality of Empire

From the 1680s to the 1910s, the relationship between Russia and the Kazan ʿulamāʾ was one of unintended consequences. The use of Muslims as settlers and intermediaries facilitated Russia's eastward expansion at a time when Russia lacked either a cadre of specialists in Turkic languages and Islamic cultures or a large pool of Slavic settlers willing and able to migrate east. However, it also created transregional networks of Muslim scholars and educators who embraced the mission of pacifying and civilizing the peoples of Russia's south and east. The seeds of the Russian government's real and imagined crises in the late 1800s and early 1900s—the non-Russian apostacies, Kazan Tatar fanaticism, pan-Islamism, and perceived Tatar influence over other Muslim populations—were planted in the mutually executed colonization of the South Urals, western Siberia, and the northern Kazakh steppe. The "Tatar kingdom" was built into the DNA of the Russian empire because of the roles that Kazan Tatars had been given or had assumed in the eighteenth-century expansion.

The Caucasian wars, Russian officials' growing awareness of British discourses on the perils of Islam, and emerging Russian nationalist sentiments made the privileged position that Kazan Tatars held in the Russian expansion increasingly untenable. During the nineteenth century, the Russian government replaced Tatar mediators with professionalized cadres of ethnic Russian and inorodtsy officials. However, this did not neutralize Kazan Tatars' sense of superiority and mission. They continued to settle along Russia's expanding frontier and establish diaspora communities, and they attempted to "enlighten" their new Muslim neighbors, even as the Russian government enacted laws to stop them. They embraced the elements of Russian culture and institutions that they found useful but stubbornly resisted efforts by Russia's ministries to exert control over their community institutions. They resented being compared with the empire's other Muslims because their experience of Russia's expansion had conditioned them to think of themselves as more culturally advanced Muslims who were better equipped to work with the imperial government than were other conquered populations.

Empire and Nation

Through the Russian expansion, Kazan Tatar scholarly networks constructed a new zone of Muslim culture inside Russia, a new sacred geography, and a new history. As they became enmeshed in the Eurasian commodities trade from the late 1700s, they also acquired a new material culture. The ʿulamāʾ replaced the aristocracy, and Islamic literature pushed aside the older Chinggisid traditions. Wherever they went, Kazan Tatars, and especially the Kazan ʿulamāʾ, took this culture with them. Early twentieth-century reformers may have ridiculed *Kisekbash* and *Baqirghān kitabi*, but the circulation of these and other Turkic-language works created a shared culture and identity among the many Kazan Tatar enclaves that appeared across Russia in the 1700s and 1800s. This Muslim identity did not exist alongside a developing national identity. It created the foundation for an ethno-national identity. The geographical boundaries of the Tatar nation as it was envisioned in the early 1900s were not the boundaries of the Kazan khanate, but those defined in the Bulghar histories. Those boundaries, in turn, were set in the process of constructing the Russian empire. Kazan Tatars' visions of nationhood, whether of a unified community of Russian Muslims led by the Kazanians or of a regional community who shared the same language, literary tradition, and history, were definitively shaped by Kazan Tatars' role in the Russian expansion.

Islam and Modernity

Kazan Tatars did not shift from a "traditional" society to a "modern" one in the 1860s or the 1880s. With Russia's ongoing eastward and southward expansion, the expansion of printing, and the rise of the commodities trade among Russia, China, and South Asia, Muslim society in the Volga-Ural region was in a constant state of geographic, cultural, and economic change from the 1600s to the early 1900s. Increasing exposure to Russian and western European culture in the nineteenth century did not lead to abandonment of Islamic culture, but to its popularization and politicization. Even as the concepts of "worldly" and "universal" knowledge versus "Islamic" knowledge entered the Kazan Muslim intellectual world, Islam remained central, not only as a source of personal morality and spiritual guidance, but also as a foundation of personal status law, interpersonal relations, and economic interactions. Early twentieth-century reformers called for the reconsideration of specific aspects of Islamic law and theology but continued to regard Islam as critical to education, civil law, public morality, and national identity. In 1918, the case of the Kazan Tatars was one of a society that adopted a national identity without removing religion from education, governance, and public life. However, once incorporated into the Soviet project, Kazan Tatar society would be set on a different course of evolution.

GLOSSARY

ʿaqīda Islamic doctrine or creed

fatwā a nonbinding Islamic legal ruling

fiqh Islamic jurisprudence; the process by which Muslim jurists derive Islamic law

imām a Muslim prayer leader

ishān [see "shaykh"]

ijtihād the process of formulating an Islamic legal ruling through independent interpretation of the primary sources of the law

kalām Islamic speculative theology through the application of philosophy

khanaqah a lodge in which a Sufi shaykh and his disciples gather

madrasa a school offering instruction in the Islamic sciences

muezzin one who gives the call to prayer; he is often also responsible for the upkeep of the mosque

mufti a Muslim legal scholar considered qualified to formulate original legal decisions; in the Volga-Ural region, the head of the Orenburg Muslim Spiritual Assembly

mullā in the Volga-Ural region, a title used by Muslims to indicate a person of great learning; also used in the Russian and Tatar languages to refer to the head of a mosque or a Muslim legal scholar

qāḍī A Muslim judge; in the case of the Volga-Ural region, one of several Muslim legal specialists elected to assist the mufti.

shaykh a Sufi teacher and spiritual leader

taqlīd adherence to an established Islamic legal precedent

tawḥīd the oneness of God

ʿulamāʾ the plural of the Arabic *ʿalīm* (scholar); used to refer to Islamic scholars collectively.

waqf a Muslim charitable endowment

zakāt a charitable contribution that every Muslim who is able must make annually; it should equal 1/40 of the value of a Muslim's annual income and accumulated wealth

BIBLIOGRAPHY

Archival Sources

Gosudarstvennyi Arkhiv Orenburgskoi Oblasti (GAOO)
Fond 6 (Orenburg District Court)
Natsionalnyi Arkhiv Respubliki Tatarstan (NART)
Fond 41 (Kazan District Court)
Fond 199 (Gendarmerie)
Fond 1370 (Personal archive of Fatīḥ Karimi)
Rossiskii Gosudarstvennyi Arkhiv Drevnikh Aktov
Fond 126: Mongol'skie dela
Tsentral'nyi Gosudarstvenyi Istoricheskii Arkhiv Respubliki Kazakhstan (TsGIARK)
Fond 487 (Semipalatisk Customs House)
Tsentral'nyi Istoricheskii Arkhiv Respubliki Bashkortostan (TsIARB)
Fond 187 (Gendarmerie)
Ufimskii Federal'nyi Issledovatel'skii Tsentr—Rossisskaia Akademiia Nauk (UFITs-RAN)
Fond 7 (Personal archive of Rizaeddin Fakhreddinov)
Fond 22 (Personal archive of Mukhammatsalim Umetbaev)

Manuscript Sources

Institut Iazyka, Literatury i Isskustva im. G. Ibragimova, Tatarstan (IIaLI)
f. 39, op. 1, del. 2768, p. 269 — "Ismāʿīl al-Qıshqārī marthiyyasī."
f. 39, no. 3442, pp. 35ob-42ob. — "Risāla-i Dāmallā Ḥabībullāh al-Ūrıwī."
f. 39, op. 1. del. 3772 — "Shah-i Aḥmad bin Batirshah ham Fatḥullāh bin Ḥabībullāh, "Tūntār madrasase daftare."
f. 39, op. 1, del. 3772, p. 29 — "Qasīda Madaḥa Shaykhinā wa Ustādhinā Ustādh al-Kull Ishān ʿAlī Muḥammad at-Tūntārī."
f. 39, op. 1. del. 4461, l. 99–112 — "Hadha fī bayān silsila Muʿinaddīn Chīstī wa as-Sayyīd ʿAbdalqadīr al-Gīlānī wa ash-Shaykh Muḥammad Bahaʾaddin Naqshbandī al-Bukhārī."
f. 39, op. 1, del. 5942 — "ʿAbdaljabbār bin Mullā ʿAbdalḥakīm ham Bahāʾaddīn bin Mullā Sirājaddīn, Machkara madrasase daftare, 1854."
Kazanskii (Povolzh'skii) Federal'nyi Universitet—Otdel' Rukopisei i Redkikh Knig (K(P)FU-ORRK)
No. 29 gotv — "Yunys Oruvi, Shärḥ 'Färaiz al-Sijävendi'."
No. 205T — "Taṣawwuf kitābī."
No. 208T, pp. 160–70 — "ʿAbdullāh Būbī, 'Yaushevlar kem?'"
No. 332T — "Ushbu waqfnāma."
No. 399T — "Shirdānī."
No. 615AR — "Shihābaddīn al-Marjānī, *Wafayāt al-Aslāf*." 6 vols.

No. 749AR, pp. 460b-480b — "Marjānī madrasase niẓāmnāmasī."
No. 1148T, p. 196 — "5 Yanvar 1914, Sayyidgaray Fayḍullinnan Muḥammadkamāl Muzaffarovga."
No. 1156T, p. 126. — "6 Yanvar 1904, Mustafa Fayḍullinnan Muḥammadkamāl Muzaffarovga."
No. 1156T, pp. 28–440b — "Mustafa Fayḍullinnan Muḥammadkamāl Muzaffarovga."
No. 1156T, pp. 48–1250b — "Mustafa Fayḍullinnan Muḥammadkamāl Muzaffarovga."
No. 1265T, p. 41 — "ʿAbdarraḥīm Ūtiz-Imānī al-Bulghārī, 'Manẓūm.'"
No. 1615T — "Bārūdīga khāt."
No. 4199T — "Dastān-i Tārīkh (1740s)."
No. 4174 — "Protokol tsenzurnago komiteta pri Kazanskom Universitete uchrezhdennago 1822 goda."
No. 4175 — "Po otnoshenniiu bibliotekra universiteta s prepovozhdenii raznyikh knig' dlia khraneniia."
No. 4204T — "Silsila."
Natsionalnaia Biblioteka Respubliki Kazakhstan—Otdel' Redkikh Knig (NBRK-ORK)
No. 58 — N. Abramov, "Gorod Semipalatinsk."
No. 450 — "Sobranie dokumentov otnosiashchikhsia do aziatskoi torgolvli. Vypiski iz arkhiva generala S. A. Khruleva."
Natsionalnaia Biblioteka Respubliki Tatarstan—Otdel' Rukopisei i Redkikh Knig (NBRT-ORRK)
No. 499T — "Machkara dāmallāsınā khātı."
No. 828T — "Muḥammad Najīb at-Tūntārī — *Tūntūr āwilī.*"
No. 962T — "Wālī Āpānāev belan Naʿima Ūtamishevning aerilshūlarī turinda dokument (1870)."
St. Peterburgskii otdel Instituta Vostokovedeniia Rossiiskoi Akademii Nauk
B 749 — "Tawārīkh-i Bulghāriyya Husmaddīn al-Bulghārī."
Personal Archive of the Author
"Dahī da shıgır budır"

Published Primary Sources

Abramof, N. "Semipalatinsk." *Journal of the Royal Geographic Society of London* 32 (1861): 555–59.

Abū Nāsr ʿAbd al-Nasīr al-Qūrsāwī. *Kitāb al-Irshād lil-ʿIbād.* Kazan: Lito-tipografiia I. N. Kharitonova, 1903.

Akhmarov, Muḥammad. "Wahhābīlar ham tawaṣṣul." *Dīn wa Maʿīshat* 6 (1911): 90–92; 7 (1911): 103; 8 (1911): 121–22.

———. "Wahhābīlar kemnar?" *Dīn wa Maʿīshat.* 46 (1910): 731–34; 47 (1910): 747–50; 1 (1911): 6–8; 2 (1911): 21–23; 3 (1911): 38–40.

Amirkhanov, Ḥusayn. *Tawārīkh-i Bulghāriyya.* Kazan: Vyatcheslav, 1883.

Aqchūra-ulı, Yu. *Dāmallā ʿAlīmjān al-Bārūdī: Tarjama-i ḥāle.* Kazan: Sharaf Matbuʿasī, 1907.

Argınbay Isḥāq Ḥajjī ilä Ḥajjge Üskä ulinīnī Troitskī Ishān Zaynullāh khäḍrätkä chigharghān madkhiyalarī. Kazan: Matbuʿa Karīmiyya, 1911.

"Arkhiv Grafa Igel'stroma." *Russkii arkhiv* 4 (1886): 341–71.

Babich, Shäekhzadä. *Zänggär Jyrlar.* Edited by Galimjan Gyil'manov. Kazan: Tatarstan kitap näshriyaty, 1990.

Badavām. Kazan: Tipografiia B. L. Dmobrovskago, 1907.
Bakhtiyār Bakhtigārāy-ulī, "Jīr ṣātū: Bāshqūrtlar tūrmishīnnān." Orenburg: n.p., 1915.
Baldāt-i Qazanda sabākh kitapkhanäsīning asmā'-i kutūbdir. Kazan: Knigoizdatel'stvo Sabakh, 1906.
Barudi, Galimjan. *Qyzylyar säfäre*. Kazan: "Iman" näshriyatı, 2004.
al-Bārūdī, Mullā ʿAlīmjān. *al-Kitāb ath-thānī min al-Arbaʿinat al-mustasalsila*. Kazan: Elektro-tipografiia "Milliat," 1908.
"Bashkirdlar namaishı." *Waqt* 22 (1917): 4.
"Bashkirskaia avtonomiia." *Izvestiia Vserossiiskago Musul'manskago Voennago Shuro* 2 (1917): 3.
"Bashqirdistan Avtonomiiase." *Bizning tāwish* 65 (1918): 1–2.
Battal-Taymas, Gabdelbari. *Mīn ber yaqtylyk ezlägän idem*. Edited by Alfiya Sibgatullina. Kazan: Tatarstan kitap näshriyaty, 2003.
Battal-Taymas, Gabdulla. *Musa Yarulla Bigī: Tormıshı, eshchänlege wa äsärläre*. Kazan: "Imān" näshriyatı, 1997.
Bayazitov, ʿAtaʾullāh. *Islām Kitābı*. Kazan: n.p., 1880.
Bertugan Bubyilar häm Izh-Bubyi mädräsäse: tarikhi-dokumental' jyentyk. Edited by Raif Märdanov, Ramil Mingnullin, and Söläyman Räkhimov. Kazan: Rukhiyat, 1999.
Bigiev, Mökhämmätzahir. "Gönah-i Kabaʾīr." In *Zahir Bigiev: Zur gönahlar*, edited by Rais Dautov. Kazan: Tatarstan kitap näshriyaty, 1991.
Bigiev, Mūsā. *Adabiyyāt ʿarabiyya ila ʿulūm islamiyya*. Kazan: I. N Kharitonova, 1909.
———. *Qawāʾid fiqhiyya*. Kazan: Elekto-tipografiia "Urnek," 1910.
———. *Zakāt*. Petrograd: Tipografiia Mukhammadalima Maksudova, 1916.
Bīkbūlātov, Sunʿatullāh. *Khaḍrat Muḥammad (ṣallā ʿalayhi wa sallam)*. Kazan: Elekto-tipografiia "Maarif," 1914.
Būbī, ʿAbdullāh. *Ḥaqīqat, yakhūd tughrılıq: berenche juze*. Kazan: Lito-Tipografiia I. N. Kharitonova, 1904.
———. *Ṣarf ʿarabī*. Kazan: Tipo-Litografiia V. Z. Eremeev, n.d.
———. *Taraqqī funūn wa maʿārif dīnsezlege mujībmı?* Kazan: Lito-Tipografiia I. N. Kharitonova, 1902.
———. *Zamān-i jtihadd munqariḍmı degelme?* Kazan: Elektro-Tipografiia "Milliat," 1909.
"Būbī madrasa ḥaqqinda tafsilat." *Kazan mukhbīra* 441 (1911): 3.
"Būbī eshlare ḥaqqinda." *Yūldiz* 837 (1912): 1–2.
"Būbī eshlare ḥaqqinda." *Yūldiz* 839 (1912): 1.
Burḥānaddīn ibn Mullā Jamāladdīn al-Bāghishī. *ʿAqāʾid ahl sunnat wa jamāʿat*. Kazan: Vyatcheslav, 1894.
Butūn rūsiya muslimnarīning 1917-nchı yilda 1–11 māyda Maskaūda būlghān gumūmī isyīzdīnıng prūtākūllarī. Petrograd: Amanet, 1917.
"Butūn rūsiya muslim soldatlarī isyīzdī." *Bizning tāwish* 11 (1917): 2.
Chitkä ber dudı shıgre. Kazan: n.p., n.d.
Ḍākir al-Qadīrī. *ʿIlm-i kalām dareslare*. Ufa: n.p., 1910.
Ḍalik faḍl Allāh yuʿtihi man yashāʾ wa Allāh ḍū al-faḍl al-ʿaẓīm. Istanbul: Evner Baytan Kitabevi, n.d.
Das Buch der Dschingis-Legende (Däftär-i Čingiz-nāmä). Translated and edited by Mária Ivanics and Mirkasym Usmanov. Szeged: Department of Altaic Studies, 2002.
Das neue russische Strafgesetzbuch (Ugolovnoje Uloženje) Allerhöchst bestätigt am 22. März 1903. Translated by O. S. Bernstein. Berlin: J. Guttentag, 1908.
Dobrosmyslov, A. I. *Materialy po istorii Rossii: Sbornik ukazov i drugikh dokumentov, kasaiushchikhsia upravleniia i ustroistva Orenburgsako kraia, 1734, Tom 1*. Orenburg, 1900.

Dokumenty stavki E.I. Pugacheva, povstancheskikh i uchrezhdenii. Edited by P. V. Ovchinikov. Moscow: Nauka, 1975.

"8 dikābr 1917." *Bizning tāwish* 53 (1917): 1–3.

XVIII yöz tatar ädäbiyatı: Proza. Edited by M. Äkhmätzhanov. Kazan: G. Ibrahimov isemendäge Tel, ädäbiyat häm sängat' instituty, 2012.

F. K. *Ber shakīrd ila ber student.* Kazan: Tipografiia B. L. Dombrovskago, 1899.

Fäkhreddin, Rizaeddin. *"Jawāmi' al-Kalim."* In *Shärkhe,* edited by Ilshat Gyimadiev. Kazan: Rukhīyat näshrīyatı, 2005.

———. *Asar: berenche tom.* Edited by Raif Märdanov and Ramil Mingnullin. Kazan: Rukhiyat, 2006.

———. *Asar: ikenche tom.* Edited by Ilshat Gīmadiev, Ramil Mingnullin, and Sirina Bahavieva Kazan: Rukhiyat, 2009.

———. *Asar: öchenche häm dürtenche tom.* Edited by Liliya Baybulatova, et al. Kazan: Rukhiyat, 2010.

Fatīḥ Ämirkhan turında istäleklär. Kazan: Tatarstan kitap näshriyaty, 2005.

Fatikh Ämirkhan: Äsärlär dürt tomda. 4 vols. Edited by Zöfär Rämiev. Kazan: Tatarstan Kitap näshriyaty, 1985.

Fatikh Kärimi, Fänni-biografik jyentyk. Edited by Mirkasyim Gosmanov. Kazan: Rukhiyat, 2000.

Fatikh Kärimi: Morza Kyzy Fatyima, Saylanma äsärlär. Edited by M. B. Gaynetdinov. Kazan: Tatarstan kitap näshriyaty, 1996.

"14 nūyābr 1917." *Bizning tāwish* 44 (1917): 1–2.

Fuks, Karl. *Karl Fuks, o Kazani, Kazanskom krae: Trudy, dokumenty, vosponinaniia, issledovaniia.* Kazan: Izdatel'stvo "Zhien," 2005.

Gabderäkhim Utyz-Imäni äl-Bolghari: Shigyrlär, poemalar. Edited by Änvär Shäripov. Kazan: Tatarstan kitap näshriyaty, 1986.

Gabdessäläm Möfti: Khäter däftäre, tärjemäi Gabdessäläm Möfti, Säfärnamäi shahzadä Alexander. Edited by Masgud Gaynetdin. Kazan: Iman, 2002.

Gabdrakhim Utyz-Imiani al-Bulghari. Translated and edited by Ramilia Adygamova. Kazan: Tatarskoe Knizhnoe Izdatel'stvo, 2007.

Gabdulla Tukay: Äsärlär. 6 vols. Edited by R. M. Kadyirov and Z. G. Mökhämmätshin. Kazan: Tatar kitap näshriyaty, 2011.

Galiäskär Kämal: Äsärlär öch tomda. 3 vols. Edited by Bäyan Gyizzät. Kazan: Tatarstan kitap näshriyaty, 1978.

Ghafūrī, 'Abdalmajīd. *Millät maḥabbate nām ash'ārı.* Kazan: Elektro-tipografiia Sharaf, 1907.

al-Ghafūrī al-Qazānī, 'Abd al-Majīd bin Nūr Ghanī. *Sibir timer yulī yakī aḥwāl-e millāt* Orenburg: Tipografiia M. F. G. Karimova, 1904.

Mäjit Gafuri: Äsärlär. 4 vols. Kazan: Tatarstan kitap näshriyaty, 1981.

Galimjan Ibrahimov: Äsärlär sigez tomda. 9 vols. Edited by S. Kh. Alishev. Kazan: Tatarstan kitap näshriyaty, 1984.

Gayaz Iskhaqyi: Tarikhi-dokumental' jyentyk. Edited by Söläyman Räkhimov, Zöfär Mökhämmätshin and Ayrat Zahidullin. Kazan: Jyen, 2011.

Ḥakīmov, A. *Bāshqūrtlar.* Orenburg: Karīmov, Ḥusaynov wa Sharkāsı, 1908.

Ibrahimov, 'Abdarrashīd. *'Ilm ḥāl.* 5 vols. Kazan: Lito-Tipografiia I. N. Kharitonova, 1913.

Ibrahimov, G. "Shakīrdlar ah-zarī." *al-Iṣlāḥ* 33 (1908): 6–7.

Ibrahimov, Gabderäshit. *Tärjemäi khälem.* Edited by F. Äkhmätov-Urmanche. Kazan: "Iman" näshriyaty, 2001.

Imām Muḥammad as-Sadīq al-ʿUthmānī al-Qargalī. "Turkistan Komisiyasına raddiyya." *Dunya wa Maʿīshat* 7 (1907): 113–14.
"Inorodtsilarnī jiyu ḥaqqinda." *Yūldız* 1677 (1916): 1.
Ishān Muḥammad Ḥarīth Aydarov (al-Qargalī). *Ishānnarga Khiṭāb!* Sterlitamak: Tipografiia T-va "Nur", 1911.
"Iṣlāḥ-i madāris." *Azat* 9 (1906): 2.
Islam na evropeiskom vostoke: Entsiklopedicheskii slovar'. Edited by R. A. Nabiev. Kazan: Izdatel'stvo "Magarif," 2004.
An Islamic Biographical Dictionary of the Eastern Kazakh Steppe, 1770–1912. Qurbān ʿAlī Khālidī. Edited by Allen J. Frank and Mirkasyim A. Usmanov. Leiden: Brill, 2005.
Ismägyil' Gasprinskii: Istorichesko-dokumental'nyi sbornik. Edited by Söläyman Räkhimov. Kazan: Jyen, 2006.
Istoriia Kazani v dokumentakh i materialakh XIX veka: Obrazovanie: vysshee, srednee, nachal'noe, kniga 4. Kazan: Tatarskoe knizhnoe izdatel'stvo, 2012.
Istoriia Tatarii v Materialakh i dokumetakh. Moscow: Institut istorii (Akademiia nauk SSSR), 1937.
Istoriia Tatarskoi ASSR. 2 vols. Edited by N. I. Vorob'ev et al. Kazan: Institut iazyka, literatury i istorii (Akademiia Nauk SSSR), 1955.
al-Jalālī, Wāqif. *Sādā-i Madanīyat, berenche juze*. Astrakhan: Tipografiia "A. N. Umerova i Ko.," 1908.
Karīmī, Fatīḥ. *Mukhtaṣar Tarīkh-e Islām*. Orenburg: n.p., n.d.
Kärimi, Fatikh. "Jihangir mäkhdümneng awıl mäktäbendä uquyi (Tornaly awylynyng mäktäbendä) (1898)." Accessed July 16, 2018. http://kitap.net.ru/karimi.php.
Katanov, N. F., and I. M. Pokrovskii. "Otryvok iz odnoi tatarskoi letopisi o Kazani i Kazanskom khantsve." *Izvestiia obshchestva arkheologii, istorii, i etnografii pri Kazanskom Universitete* 21, no. 4 (1905): 303–48.
Kazakhskie chinovniki na sluzhbe Rossiiskoi imperii: Sbornik dokumentov i materialov. Almaty: Qazaq universitetı, 2014.
Kazakhsko-russkie otnosheniia v XVIII-XIX vekakh [1771–1867 gody]: Sbornik dokumentov i materialov. Alma-Ata: Nauka,1964.
Kazanskaia Tatarskaia Uchitel'skaia shkola, 1876–1917: Sbornik dokumentov i materialov. Edited by L. V. Gorokhova. Kazan: Izdatel'stvo Gasyr, 2005.
Kharlampovich, K.V. "Izvestiia G. Gmelina o Kazani i o kazanskikh inorodtsakh." *Izvestiia Obshchestva arkheologii, istorii i etnografii pri Imperatorskom Kazanskom universitete* XIX v.1-6. 1903.
Karurmanny chykkan chakta. Edited by A. G. Yakhin. Kazan: Mägarif, 2001.
Khitābnāma: Ikenche gumūmī bāshqūrt isyīzdī khaqqinda. Belebei: n.p., 1917.
Khösäen Fäezkhanov: Tarikhi-dokumental' jyentyk. Edited by Raif Märdanov. Kazan: Rukhiyat, 2006.
Kitāb Shamʿ aḍ-Ḍiyāʾ fī tadkira qaum ahl aḍ-ḍīyāʾ. Kazan: Vyacheslav, 1883.
Kitāb tärjemä-i ʿAyn al-ʿIlm. Kazan, 1886.
al-Maʿarrī, Abū al-ʿAlāʾ. *al-Luzūmiyyāt*. Translated and edited by Mūsā Bīgīev. Kazan: Tipografiia Sharaf, 1907.
Madrasa-i Muḥammadiyya Programması. 1913 m./1331 h. Kazan: Elektro-tipografiia Milliat, 1913.
Mäjlisi. *Säyfelmölek*. Edited by Farit Yakhin. Kazan: Tatarstan kitap näshriyatı, 2007.
al-Makhdūmī, ʿAbdullāh. *Mukhtaṣar naḥw ʿarabī*. Kazan: Tipografiia Torgovago Dom Brat'ev Karimovykh, 1900.

al-Makhdūmī, Mullā ʿAbd Allāh bin ʿAbd al-ʿAllām. *Mukālama ʿarabiyya.* Kazan: Tipo-Litografiia M. Chirkovoi, 1898.
Mamishev, Yaʿqūb. *Tarīkh-e Islām: Anbiyāʾ qismı.* Kazan: Tipografiia T. D. "Br. Karimovykh," 1910.
Maqsūdī, Aḥmad Ḥādī. *ʿAqāʾid.* Kazan: Lito-Tipografiia I. N. Kharitonova, 1910.
——. *Jamaʿat.* Kazan: Lito-Tipografiia I. N. Kharitonova,1910.
——. *Rūza, zakāt.* Kazan: Lito-Tipografiia I. N. Kharitonova, 1911.
Maqsūdov, Sadrī. "G. Dumada dakhīliyya ministerlıghınıng ismetası qaralghan waqtta deputat Sadraddīn Afande Maqsūdovning suilagan notighī." *Waqt* 955 (1912): supplement 1–2.
Marthiyya-i Dāmallā Muḥammad Dhakir Khaḍrat al-Chistawī. Kazan: Tipo-litografiia Imperatorskago Universiteta, 1895.
Materials for the Islamic History of Semipalatinsk: Two manuscripts by Aḥmad-Walī al-Qazānī and Qurbānʿalī Khālidī. Translated and edited by Allen J. Frank and M. G. Gosmanov. Berlin: Das Arabische Buch, 2001.
Materialy po istorii Bashkirskoi ASSR. 5 vols. Moscow: Izd-vo Akademii Nauk SSSR, 1960.
Materialy po istorii Bashkortostana, Tom 6: Orenburgskaia ekspeditsiia i bashkirskie vosstaniia 30-kh godov XVIII v. Edited by N. F. Demidova. Ufa: "Kitap," 2002.
Medrese Kazani: XIX-nachalo XX vv. Sbornik dokumentov i materialov. Edited by L. V. Gorokhova. Kazan: Natsional'nyi arkhiv Respubliki Tatarstan, 2007.
Millät Analary: Tarikhi-dokumental' häm biografik jyentyk. Edited by A. Kh. Mäkhmütova. Kazan: Jyen, 2012.
"Millāt majlīse." *Bizning tāwish* 50 (1917): 1.
"Milliat Medzhlise." *Izvestiia Vserossiiskago Musul'manskago Voennago Shuro* 1 (1917): 1.
Mirsäet Soltangaliev: Saylanma khezmätlär. Edited by I. G. Gizzatullina and D. R. Sharafutdinov. Kazan: "Gasyr," 1998.
Muḥammad ʿAyāḍ al-Isḥāqī. *Ike yüz yıldan sūng inqirāḍ.* Kazan: Lito-Tipografiia I. N. Kharitonova, 1904.
——. *Kalapushche qiz.* Kazan: Tipografiia B. L. Dombrovskago, 1902.
Muḥammad Shākir bin Muḥammad Zākir Sulāymānī. *Tārīkh-i Islām.* 4 vols. Kazan: Lito-Tipografiia T. D. "Br. Karimovykh," 1908–1910.
"Muhīm ber majlīs." *Bizning tāwish* 13 (1917): 1.
Mukhtaṣar al-Qudūrī tarjamase. Translated by Abū ʿAbdalaḥād Shaykh al-Islām ibn Asadullāh Ḥāmidullāh. Kazan: Tipografiia T. D. Brat. Karimovykh, 1904.
Mukhtaṣar al-Wiqāya tarjamase turkicha. Translated by Shihābaddīn bin Mullā ʿAbdalʿazīz Imānlībāshī. Kazan: Tipografiia T. D. Brat. Karimovykh, 1901.
Mullā Sh. Q. *Waqf Pārāzitī.* Orenburg: Karīrimov, Ḥuysanov wa sharkatī, 1907.
Mullā Ṣabirjān Mullā ʿAbd al-Badīʿ-ulı. *Sīrat an-Nabī ʿalayhi as-salām.* Kazan: Elektro-Tipografiia "Milliat," 1910.
"Mūsā Bīgīev jinābларına ber-ike sūz." *Dīn wa Maʿīshat* 14 (1909): 219–20.
"Mūsā Bīgīev jināblarına ber-ike sūz." *Dīn wa Maʿīshat* 15 (1909): 231–33.
"Musulman āzīflarī wa pānislāmizm." *Yūldiz* 777 (1911): 1.
"Musulman gäskeriläre sezdın soviet taraturgha uylī ikän." *Biznng tāwish* 67 (1918): 1.
Musul'manskie deputaty gosudarstvennoi dumy Rossii, 1906–1917 gg.: Sbornik dokumentov i Materialov. Edited by L. A. Yamaeva. Ufa: Kitap, 1998.
Näjip Dumavi: Tormısh säḥifläre: Shigri äsärlär häm proza. Edited by Zöfär Rämiev and Rezedä Ganiyeva. Kazan: Tatarstan kitap näshriyaty, 1985.

"Natsionalizm/Millayat, Qawmiyat." *Ulfat* 1 (1905): 3.
Natsional'no-gosudarstvennoe ustroistvo Bashkortostana (1917–1925 gg): Dokumenty i materialy v 4-kh tomakh. 4 vols. Edited by B. Kh. Yuldashbaev. Ufa: "Kitap," 2002.
Nepliuev, I. I. *Zapiski Ivana Ivanavicha Nepliueva (1693–1773).* St. Petersburg, 1893.
Niʿmatullin, ʿUbaydullāh Muḥammad Fayzī. *Qirāʾat Turkī: berenche jüze.* Kazan: Tipo-Litografiia nasl. M. Chirkovoi, 1899.
Ocherki Mardzhani o vostochnykh narodakh. Translated and edited by A. N. Yuzeev. Kazan: Tatarskoe knizhnoe izdatel'stvo, 2003.
Ömet yoldızları: XIX yöz akhırı häm XX yöz bashı tatar khatın-qız yazuchıları äsärläre. Edited by Mökhämmät Gaynullin. Kazan: Tatarstan kitap näshriyaty, 1988.
Onytyrga mömkin tügel: Tatarstan Respublikasynyng fol'klor muzykasy däülät amsamble repertuarynnan. Edited by A. F. Fayzrakhmanov. Kazan: n.p., 2013.
Pis'ma Nikolaia Ivanovicha Il'minskago. Kazan: n.p., 1895.
Pis'mo Batyrshi Imperatritse Elizavete Petrovne. Edited by G. B. Khusainov. Ufa: UNTsRAN, 1993.
Polnoe Sobranie Zakonov Rossiskoi Imperii. St. Petersburg: n.p., 1830.
Pugachvshchina, tom pervyi: iz arkhiva Pugacheva. Edited by S. G. Golubtsov. Moscow: Gos. Izdat, 1926.
Qayyum Nasīrī: Saylanma Äsärlär dürt tomda. 4 vols. Edited by Khujiäkhmät Makhmutov. Kazan: Tatarskoe Knizhnoe Izdatel'stvo, 2005.
Qurbān ʿAlī Ḥājjī Khālid-ulī. *Tawārīkh-i khamsa-i sharqī.* Kazan: Urnak, 1910.
ar-Rāmzī, M. M. *Talfīq al-Akhbār wa Talqīḥ al-Athār fī Waqāʾiʿ Qazān wa Bulġār wa Mulūk al-Tatār.* Orenburg: n.p., n.d.
"Reformatorlar ḥaqqında." *Dīn wa Maʿīshat* 1 (1912): 11.
"Revoliutsiia ham duma." *Tāng Yūldizī* 1 (1908): 1.
Rizaetdin Fäkhretdin: Fänni-biografik jyentyk. Edited by Raif Märdanov et al. Kazan: Rukhiyat, 1999.
"Sārt mudarrise kundez dareskhānada/Sārt mudarrise kich bāchakhānada." *Yālt-yūlt* 100 (1915): 8.
Sägyit Rämiev: Tang Vakyty. Edited by Shäykhi Sadretinov. Kazan: Tatarstan kitap näshriyaty, 1980.
Säyakhätnamälär. Edited by Raif Märdanov. Kazan: "Millī kitap," 2011.
Sayyid Ahmad Khan. "Asbab-e-Baghawat-e-Hind." *Writings and Speeches of Sir Syed Ahmad Khan.* Bombay: Nachiketa, n.d.
Sh. Mökhämmädev: saylamna äsärlär. Edited by M. Gaynullin. Kazan: Tatknigoizdat, 1958.
Shākir-ulı, Dhākir. *Tārīkh-i muqaddas.* Kazan: Shamsaddīn Ḥusaynov warithasī, 1912.
"Shakīrd ham yāshlar." *al-Iṣlāḥ* 31 (1908): 8.
Sharaf, Burhān. "ʿAbdalghanī Ḥusaynovnıng tarjama-i ḥāle ham Ḥusaynovlar firması tārīkhı." *Ghanī Bāy: Tarjama-i ḥāle, khatiralare, anıng ḥaqqında khatiralar.* Orenburg: Tipografiia gaz. "Vakt," 1913.
Sharaf, Shaḥr. *Marjānī.* Kazan, Magārif, 1915.
Shihābaddīn al-Marjānī. *Qism al-Awwal min Kitāb Mustafād al-Akhbār fī aḥwāl Qazān wa Bulghār.* Kazan: Tipo-Litografiia Imperatorskago Universiteta, 1897.
———. *Qism ath-Thānī min Kitāb Mustafād al-Akhbār fī aḥwāl Qazān wa Bulghār.* Kazan: Tipo-Litografiia Imperatorskago Universiteta, 1900.
Sobornoe Ulozhenie Alekseia Mikhailovicha 1649 goda. St. Petersburg: Sinodal'naia Tipografiia, 1907.

Sulaymānī, Muḥammad Shākir ibn Muḥammad Zākir. *Tārīkh-i Islām.* 4 vols. Kazan: Lito-Tipografiia T. D. "Br. Karimovykh," 1908–1910.
Tājaddīn Yalchigul. *Risāla-i ʿAzīza.* Kazan: Elektro-tipografiia "Umid," 1912.
"Taraqqīparwar fidāʾī yaki ʿanqāʾ shamālī." *Dīn wa Maʿīshat* 5 (1909): 74.
Tatar khalyk ijaty: Tarikhi häm lirik jyrlar. Edited by I. N. Nadirov. Kazan: Tatarskoe knizhnoe izdatel'stvo, 1988.
Tawḥīd. Translated by ʿAbdullāh Būbī. Kazan: Elekto-tipografiia "Urnek," 1911.
Tooke, William. *View of the Russian Empire.* 2 vols. New York: Arno Press, 1970.
Torgovlia i diplomatiia: Dokumenty o rossiisko-sredneaziatskikh otnosheniiakh, 1723–1725 gg. Edited by I. M. Vasil'ev. Ufa: Gilem, 2012.
Ṭughriliq. Kazan: Tipografiia T-go d. Br. Karimovykh, 1904.
Tuḥfatullin, Muḥammadkāmil al-Mutiʿī. *Tatarcha qurʾān tafsīre.* Kazan: Elektro-tipografiia "Maarif," 1914.
Tukay turynda istäleklär. Edited by Ibrahim Nurullin and Rif Yakupov. Kazan: Tatarskoe knizhnoe izdatel'stvo, 1986.
al-Tüntäri, Mökhämmätnäjip. "Mökhämmätnäjip khäzrät yazması." *Gasyr awazy/Ekho vekhov* 1–2 (2003).
Tuqayev, Muḥammad Shākir. *Tarīkh-i Istärlibash.* Kazan: n.p., 1899.
Ufada berenche masjid jamīʿ khuḍurındagı Mädräsä-i ʿUṯmanīyanıng mufaṣṣal programması. Ufa: Tūrmish Matbuʿasī, 1917.
ʿUlamāʾ Ittifāghī: Berenche nadwasī. Kazan: Tipo-litografiia T. D. "Br. Karimovykh," 1917.
"ʿUlamāʾ kirāmgā achiq khāt." *Dīn wa Maʿīshat* 11 (1909): 174.
Uqigiz: Taqqī ʿajabtan dakhī ʿajab. Orenburg: Tipografiia M. F. G. Karimova, 1904.
"Urta Aziya tarīkhī." *Dunya wa Maʿīshat* 7 (1907): 110–11.
Uṣūl Tadrīs: Mädräsälärdä muʿallimnara maslak mustaqīm uzara taʿlīm itmak ṭarīqnı bayān iden kitāb. Kazan: Tipografiia B. L. Dombrovskago, 1899.
Validov, Dzhamaliutdin. *Ocherki istorii obrazovannosti i literatury Tatar.* Kazan: Izdatel'stvo "Iman," 1998.
Valikhanov, Chokan. "O Musul'manstve v stepi." In *Smert' Kukotai Khana.* Semei: Mezhdunarodnyi klub Abaia, 2001.
Vel'iaminov-Zernov, V. V. *Issledovanie o Kasimovskikh tsariakh i tsarevichakh.* 4 vols. St. Petersburg: Tipografiia imperatorskoi akademii nauk, 1866.
Validi Togan, Zaki. *Vosponinaniia.* Moscow: Moskovskaia tipografiia No. 12, 1997.
Velidi Togan, Zeki. *Hâtiralar: Türkıstan ve dığer müsülman doğu türklerının mıllī varlik ve kültür mücadelelerı.* Istanbul: n.p., 1969.
Vitevskii, V. N. *I .I. Nepliuev: vernyi sluga svoego otechestva, osnovatel' Orenburga i ustroitel' Orenburgskago kraia.* Kazan: n.p., 1891.
Vozzvaniia i perepiska vozhakov Pugachevskogo dvizheniia v Povolzh'e i Priural'e. Edited by Mirkasyim Usmanov. Kazan: Izdatel'stvo Kazanskogo Universiteta, 1988.
"Yāngī kābīnītning yūlī." *Bizning tāwish* 15 (1917): 1–2.
Zahir Bigiev: Zur gönahlar. Edited by Räis Dautov. Kazan: Tatar kitap näshriyaty, 1991.
Zakir Hadi: Saylanma Äsärlär. Edited by M. Kh. Gaynullin. Kazan: Tatarskoe knizhnoe izdatel'stvo, 1957.
Zhizn' i deiatel'nost' P. I. Rychkova. Orenburg: OOO "Izdatel'stvo Orenburgskaia Kniga," 2011.
Zyiaetdin Kamali. Edited and translated by L. I. Almazova. Kazan: Tatarskoe knizhnoe izdatel'stvo, 2010.

Secondary Literature

Algar, Hamid. *Mīrzā Malkum Khān: A Study in the History of Iranian Modernism*. Berkeley: University of California Press, 1973.

———. "Shaykh Zaynullah Rasulev: The Last Great Naqshbandi Shaykh of the Volga-Ural Region." In *Muslims in Central Asia: Expressions of Identity and Change*, edited by Jo-Ann Gross. Durham: University of North Carolina Press, 1992.

———. *Religion and the State in Iran, 1785–1906: The Role of the Ulama in the Qajar Period*. Berkeley: University of California Press, 1969.

Allworth, Edward. *The Modern Uzbeks: From the Fourteenth Century to the Present: A Cultural History*. Stanford, CA: Hoover Institute, 1990.

Alternative Modernities. Edited by Dilip Parameshwar Gaonkar. Durham, NC: Duke University Press, 2001.

Amirkhan, Ravil. "Zakir Ishan Kamalov i Tatarskoe prosveshchenie." *Gasyrlar avazy/Eko vekhov* 1, no. 2 (2001). Accessed July 16, 2018. http://www.archive.gov.tatarstan.ru/magazine/go/anonymous/main/?path=mg:/numbers/2001_1_2/05/05_1/&searched=1.

Arsharuni, A., and Kh. Gabidullin. *Ocherki Panislamizma i Panturkizma v Rossii*. Riazan: n.p., 1931.

Azamatov, Danil' D. "The Muftis of the Orenburg Spiritual Assembly in the 18th and 19th Centuries: The Struggle for Power in Russia's Muslim Institution." In *Muslim Culture in Russia and Central Asia from the 18th to the Early 20th Centuries*, vol. 2, edited by Anke von Kugelgen et al., 355–86. Berlin: Klaus Schwarz Verlag, 1998.

———. "Russian Administration and Islam in Bashkiria (18th–19th centuries)." In *Muslim Culture in Russia and Central Asia from the 18th to the Early 20th Centuries*, vol. 1, edited by Anke von Kugelgen et al., 91–112. Berlin: Klaus Schwarz Verlag, 1996.

Babadzhanov, B. M. *Kokandskoe khanstvo: Vlast', politika, religiia*. Tokyo/Tashkent: NIHU Program Islamic Area Studies Center at the University of Tokyo/Institut vostokovedeniia Akademii nauk Respubliki. Uzbekistan, 2010.

Baltach Entsiklopediase. Edited by Garifjan Mökhämmätshin. Kazan: PPK Idel-Press, 2006.

Bennigsen, Alexandre, and Chantal Lemercier-Quelquejay. *Islam in the Soviet Union*. London: n.p., 1967.

———. *Les mouvements nationaux chez les musulmans de Rusie: Le "sultangalievisme" au Tatarstan*. Paris: n.p., 1960.

———. *La presse et le mouvement national chez les musulmans de Rusie avant 1920*. Paris: n.p., 1964.

Berman, Marshall. *All That Is Solid Melts into Air: The Experience of Modernity*. New York: Penguin, 1982.

Bibliograficheskii slovar' otechestvennykh tiurkologov: dooktiabrskii period. Edited by A. N. Kononov. Moscow: Glavnays redaktsiia vostochnoi literatury, 1974.

Biktimirova, T. A. *Stupendi obrazovaniia do Sorbonny*. Kazan: Tatarskoe Knizhnoe Izdatel'stvo, 2011.

Brower, Daniel R. "Islam and Ethnicity: Russian Colonial Policy in Turkestan." In *Russia's Orient: Imperial Borderlands and People, 1700–1917*, edited by Daniel R. Brower and Edward J. Lazzerini, 115–37. Bloomington: Indiana University Press, 1997.

Burbank, Jane, and Frederick Cooper. *Empires in World History: Power and Politics of Difference*. Princeton, NJ: Princeton University Press, 2010.

Bustanov, Alfrid K. "The Bughlar Region as a "Land of Ignorance": Anti-Colonial Discourse in Khvārazmian Connectivity." *Journal of Persianate Studies* 9 (2006): 183–204.

———. "Soviet Islam Reconsidered: Zainap Maksudova and the Study of Tatar Literature (Peresmotr kontseptsii sovetskogo islama: Zainap Maksudova i izuchenie tatarskoi literatury)." In *Islam v multikulturnom mire*, edited by Denis Brilev, 482–88. Kazan: Kazanskii Universitet, 2014.

Campbell, Elena I. *The Muslim Question and Russian Imperial Governance*. Bloomington: Indiana University Press, 2015.

Carrère d'Encausse, Hélène. *Islam and the Russian Empire: Reform and Revolution in Central Asia*. Berkeley: University of California Press, 1988.

Cavender, Mary W. *Nests of the Gentry: Family, Estate, and Local Loyalties in Provincial Russia*. Newark: University of Delaware Press, 2007.

Chakrabarty, Dipesh. *Provincializing Europe: Postcolonial Thought and Historical Difference*. Princeton, NJ: Princeton University Press, 2000.

Chamberlain, Michael. *Knowledge and Social Practice in Medieval Damascus, 1190–1350*. Cambridge: Cambridge University Press, 1994.

Chatterjee, Partha. *The Nation and Its Fragments: Colonial and Post-Colonial Histories*. Princeton, NJ: Princeton University Press, 1993.

Chuloshnikov, A. P. *Vosstanie 1755 g. v Bashkirii*. Moscow: n.p., 1940.

Cooper, Frederick. *Citizenship between Empire and Nation: Remaking France and French Africa, 1945–1960*. Princeton, NJ: Princeton University Press, 2014.

———. *Colonialism in Question: Theories, Knowledge, History*. Berkeley: University of California Press, 2005.

Crews, Robert D. *For Prophet and Tsar: Islam and Empire in Russia and Central Asia*. Cambridge, MA: Harvard University Press, 2009.

Dabashi, Hamid. *The World of Persian Literary Humanism*. Cambridge, MA: Harvard University Press, 2012.

Davletshin, Tamurbek. *Sovetskii Tatarstan: Teoriia i praktika leninskoi natsional'noi politiki* Kazan: Zhyen, 2005.

DeLong-Bas, Natana J. *Wahhabi Islam: From Revival to Reform to Global Jihad*. Oxford: Oxford University Press, 2004.

Deviatykh, L. *Iz istorii Kazanskogo Kupechestva*. Kazan: Titl-Kazan', 2005.

DeWeese, Devin. "It was a Dark and Stagnant Night ('til the Jadids Brought the Lights): Clichés, Biases, and False Dichotomies in the Intellectual History of Central Asia." *Journal of the Economic and Social History of the Orient* 59 (2016): 37–92.

Donnelly, Alton. *The Russian Conquest of Bashkiria, 1552–1740: A Case Study in Imperialism*. New Haven, CT: Yale University Press, 1968.

Dudoignon, Stéphane A. "Qadîmiya as a Historiographical Category: The Question of the Communal Unity as Seen by 'Reformists' and 'Traditionalists' among the Muslims of Russia and Central Asia in the Early Twentieth Century." In *Reform Movements and Revolutions in Turkistan: 1900–1924: Studies in Honour of Osman Khoja*, edited by Timur Kocaoğlu, 159–77. Haarlem, Netherlands: Sota, 2001.

Eden, Jeff, and Paolo Sartori. "Moving Beyond Modernism: Rethinking Cultural Change in Muslim Eurasia (19th–20th Centuries)." *Journal of Social and Economic History of the Orient* 59, nos. 1–2 (2016): 1–36.

Eighteenth-Century Renewal and Reform in Islam. Edited by Nehemia Levetzion and John O. Voll. Syracuse, NY: Syracuse University Press, 1987.

Evtuhov, Catherine. *Portrait of a Russian Province*. Pittsburgh, PA: University of Pittsburgh Press, 2011.

Fischer, George. *Russian Liberalism: From Gentry to Intelligentsia*. Cambridge, MA: Harvard University Press, 1958.

Fisher, Alan W. *The Russian Annexation of Crimea, 1772–1783*. Cambridge: Cambridge University Press, 1970.

Fitzpatrick, Anne L. *The Great Russian Fair: Nizhnii Novgorod, 1840–90*. New York: Palgrave Macmillan, 2016.

Frank, Allen J. *Bukhara and the Muslims of Russia: Sufism, Education, and the Paradox of Islamic Prestige*. Leiden: Brill, 2012.

———. "Islam and Ethnic Relations in the Kazakh Inner Horde: Muslim Cossacks, Tatar Merchants, and Kazakh Nomads in a Turkic Manuscript, 1870–1910." In *Muslim Culture in Russia and Central Asia from the 18th to the Early 20th Centuries*, vol. 2, edited by Anke Kügelgen et. al., 211–42. Berlin: Klaus Schwarz, 1996.

———. *Islamic Historiography and 'Bulghar' Identity among the Tatars and Bashkirs of Russia*. Leiden: Brill, 1998.

———. "Muslim Cultural Decline in Imperial Russia: A Manufactured Crisis." *Journal of the Economic and Social History of the Orient* 59, nos. 1–2 (2016): 166–92.

———. *Muslim Religious Institutions in Russia: Islamic World of Novouzenek District and the Kazakh Inner Horde, 1780–1910*. Boston: Brill, 2001.

———. "Tatarskikh mulli sredi kazakhov i kirgizov v XVIII-XIX vekakh." In *Kul'tura, isskustvo tatarskogo naroda: istoki, traditsii,vzaimosviazi*, edited by M. Z. Zakiev et al. Kazan: n.p., 1993.

Frank, Andre Gunder. *The 19th Century: Global Economy in the Continuing Asian Age*. Edited by Robert A. Denemark. London: Routledge, 2015.

———. *ReOrient: Global Economy in the Asian Age*. Berkeley: University of California Press, 1998.

Friedman, Yohanan. *Shaikh Ahmad Sirhindi: An Outline of His Thought and a Study of His Image in the Eyes of Posterity*. Montreal: n.p., 1971.

Gabdrafikova, Liliia. *Tatarskoe burzhuaznoe obshchestvo*. Kazan: Tatarskoe Knizhnoe Izdatel'stvo, 2015.

Gainullin, M. Kh. *Tatarskaia literatura i publitsistika nachala XX veka*. Kazan: Tatarskoe knizhnoe izdatel'stvo, 1966.

———. *Tatarskaia literatura XIX veka*. Kazan: Tatarskoe knizhnoe izdatel'stvo, 1975.

Garipova, Rozaliya. "The Protectors of Religion and Community: Traditionalist Muslim Scholars of the Volga-Ural Region at the Beginning of the Twentieth Century." *Journal of Economic and Social History of the Orient* 59 (2016): 126–65.

Geraci, Robert P. *Window on the East: National and Imperial Identities in Late Tsarist Russia*. Ithaca, NY: Cornell University Press, 2001.

Giddens, Anthony. *Modernity and Self-Identity: Self and Society in the Late Modern Age*. Stanford, CA: Stanford University Press, 1991.

Gilajetdinov, Salim. "Keresh süz." In *Meng dä ber hadis shärekhe*. Kazan: Rannur, 2005.

Gizzatullin, I. G. *Musul'manskie voennye organizatsii (1917–1921 gg.)*. Kazan: Fän, 2002.

Global Salafism: Islam's New Religious Movement. Edited by Roel Meijer. New York: Columbia University Press, 2009.

Gvozdikova, I. M. *Bashkortostan Nakanune i v gody krest'ianskoi voiny pod predvoditel'stvom E. I. Pugacheva*. Ufa: "Kitap," 1999.

Hämäläinen, Pekka. *The Comanche Empire.* New Haven, CT: Yale University Press, 2008.
Hamamoto, Mami. "Tatarskaia Kargala in Russia's Eastern Policies." In *Asiatic Russia: Imperial Power in Regional and International Contexts*, edited by Tomohiko Uyama, 32–52. New York: Routledge, 2012.
Hamburg, G. M. *Boris Chicherin and Early Russian Liberalism.* Stanford, CA: Stanford University Press, 1992.
Hanioglu, M. Sukru. *Young Turks in Opposition.* Oxford: Oxford University Press, 1995.
Hatch, Nathan O. *The Democratization of American Christianity.* New Haven, CT: Yale University Press, 1991.
Haykel, Bernard. *Revival and Reform in Islam: The Legacy of Muhammad al-Shawkani.* Cambridge: Cambridge University Press, 2003.
Hourani, Albert. *Arabic Thought in the Liberal Age, 1798–1939.* Cambridge: Cambridge University Press, 1983.
Hunter, Dard. *Papermaking: The History and Technique of an Ancient Craft.* London: A. A. Knopf, 1947.
Islam i Muzyka. Edited by Guzal Saifullina. Kazan: Tatarskoe kinzhnoe izdatel'stvo, 2015.
Istoriia Kazakhstana s drevneishikh vremen do nashikh dnei. 5 vols. Almaty: Atamura, 1997.
Jersild, Austin. *Orientalism and Empire: North Caucasus Mountain Peoples and the Georgian Frontier, 1845–1917.* Montreal: McGill-Queens Press, 2002.
Johnson, Paul E. *A Shopkeeper's Millennium: Society and Revivals in Rochester, New York, 1815–1837.* New York: Hill and Wang, 2004.
Jones, Robert E. *Provincial Development in Russia: Catherine II and Jacob Sievers.* New Brunswick, NJ: Rutgers University Press, 1984.
Kanlidere, Ahmet. *Reform within Islam: The Tajdid and Jadid Movement among the Kazan Tatars (1809–1917): Conciliation or Conflict?* Istanbul: Eren, 1997.
Karimullin, A. G. *U istokov tatarskoi knigi: ot nachala vozniknovenniia do 60-kh godov XIX veka.* Kazan: Tatarskoe knizhnoe izdatel'stvo, 1992.
Keddie, Nikki R. *Sayyid Jamāl ad-Din "al-Afghānī": A Political Biography.* Berkeley: University of California Press, 1972.
Kefeli, Agnès. "The Tale of Joseph and Zulaykha on the Volga Frontier: The Struggle for Gender, Religious, and National Identity in Imperial and Postrevolutionary Russia." *Slavic Review* 70, no. 2 (2011): 373–98, doi: 10.5612/slavicreview.70.2.0373.
Kefeli, Agnès Nilüfer. *Becoming Muslim in Imperial Russia: Conversion, Apostasy, and Literacy.* Ithaca, NY: Cornell University Press, 2014.
Kemper, Michael. "Imperial Russia as Dar al-Islam? Nineteenth-Century Debates on Ijtihad and Taqlid among the Volga Tatars." *Islamic Law and Society* 6 (2015): 95–124.
———. "The North Caucasian Khalidiyya and 'Muridism': Historiographical Problems." *Journal of the History of Sufism* 5 (2006): 111–26.
———. *Sufis und Gelehrte in Tatarien und Baschkirien, 1789–1889: Der islamische Diskurs unter russischer Herrschaft.* Berlin: Schwarz, 1998.
Khabutdinov, Aidar. *Instituty rossiiskogo musul'manskogo soobshchestva v Volgo-Uralskom regione.* Moscow: Izdatel'stvo "Mardzhani," 2013.
———. *Ot obshchinay k natii: Tatary na puti ot srednevekov'ia k novomu vremeni.* Kazan: Tatarskoe knizhnoe izdatel'stvo, 2008.
Khairutdinov, A. G. *Musa Dzharullakh Bigiev.* Kazan: Fan, 2005.
Khalid, Adeeb. *The Politics of Muslim Cultural Reform: Jadidism in Central Asia.* Berkeley: University of California Press, 1998.

———. "What Jadidism Was and What It Wasn't: The Historiographical Adventures of a Term." *Central Eurasian Studies Review* 5, no. 2 (2006): 3–7.

Khasavnekh, A. A. *Filosofsko-eticheskie motivy v sufiiskoi poezii Abdulmanikha Kargali.* Kazan: Izdatel'stvo AN RT, 2015.

Khodarkovsky, Michael. *Russia's Steppe Frontier: The Making of a Colonial Empire, 1500–1800.* Bloomington: Indiana University Press, 2004.

Kim, Kwangmin. *Borderland Capitalism: Turkestan Prodce, Qing Silver, and the Birth of an Eastern Market.* Stanford, CA: Stanford University Press, 2016.

Kirimli, Sirri Hakan. "National Movements and National Identities among the Crimean Tatars (1905–1916)." PhD diss., University of Wisconsin-Madison, 1990.

Kirmse, Stefan B. "Law and Empire in Late Tsarist Russia: Muslim Tatars Go to Court." *Slavic Review* 72, no. 4 (2013): 778–801.

Knysh, Alexander. "Sufism as an Explanatory Paradigm: The Issue of the Motivations of Sufi Resistance Movements in Western and Russian Scholarship." *Die Welt des Islams* 42, no. 2 (2002): 139–73.

Konanov, A. N. *Biobibliograficheskii slovar' otechesvennykh tiurkologov: dooktiabr'skii period.* Moscow: Nauka, 1989.

Kupechestvo Orenburga. 2 vols. Edited by E. V. Birlutskaya. Orenburg: Izdatel'stvo OGPU, 2016.

Laffan, Michael. *The Makings of Indonesian Islam: Orientalism and the Narration of a Sufi Past.* Princeton, NJ: Princeton University Press, 2011.

Lauzière, Henri. *The Making of Salafi Islam: Islamic Reform in the Twentieth Century.* New York: Columbia University Press, 2016.

Lazzerini, Edward. "Ismail Bey Gasprinskii and Muslim Modernism in Russia, 1878–1914." PhD diss., University of Washington, 1973.

Le Donne, John. *The Russian Empire and the World, 1700–1917: The Geopolitics of Expansion and Containment.* Oxford: Oxford University Press, 1996.

Legal Pluralism and Empires, 1500–1850. Edited by Lauren Benton and Richard J. Ross. New York: New York University Press, 2013.

Levi, Scott Cameron. *The Indian Diaspora in Central Asia and Its Trade, 1550–1900.* Leiden: Brill, 2002.

———. *The Rise and Fall of Khoqand, 1709–1876: Central Asia in a Global Age.* Pittsburgh, PA: University of Pittsburgh Press, 2017.

Lieven, Dominic. *Empire: The Russian Empire and Its Rivals.* New Haven, CT: Yale University Press, 2001.

Lincoln, Bruce W. *In the Vanguard of Reform: Russia's Bureaucratic World, 1825–1855.* DeKalb: Northern Illinois University Press, 1982.

Mädräsälärdä kitap kishtäse: mäshhür mägrifät üzäkläre tarikhınnan. Kazan: Tatarstan kitap näshriyatı, 1992.

Mähdiev, M. S. *Ijtimagyi häm estetik fikerneng tatar ädäbiyatı üseshenä yogyntysy.* Kazan: Kazan universitety näshriyaty, 1977.

Makhmutova, Al'ta. *Pora i nam zazhech' zariu svobody! Dzhadidizm i zhenskoe dvizhenie.* Kazan: Tatarskoe Knizhnoe Izdatel'stvo, 2006.

Malysheva, Svetlana, and Lilia Zaripova. "Uravnenie so mnogimi neizvestnymi, ili o tom, kak byl ubit Sardar Vaisov." *Tatarstan* 5–6 (1992).

Mardin, Şerif. *The Genesis of Young Ottoman Thought.* Syracuse, NY: Syracuse University Press, 2000.

Martin, Janet. "Muscovite Frontier Policy: The Case of the Khanate of Kasimov." *Russian History* 19, nos. 1–4 (1992): 169–79.

Martin, Terry. *The Affirmative Action Empire: Nations and Nationalism in the Soviet Union, 1923–1939*. Ithaca, NY: Cornell University Press, 2001.

Martin, Virginia. *Law and Custom in the Steppe: The Kazakhs of the Middle Horde and Russian Colonialism in the Nineteenth Century*. London: Routledge, 2001.

Mashkina, Olga. "The Pulp and Paper Industry Evolution in Russia: A Road of Many Transitions." In *The Evolution of Global Paper Industry, 1800–2050*, edited by Juha-Antti Lamberg, Jari Ojala, Mirva Peltoniemi, and Timo Särkkä. London: Springer, 2012.

Metcalf, Barbara D. *Islamic Revival in British India: Deoband, 1860–1900*. Princeton, NJ: Princeton University Press, 2014.

Meyer, James H. "Speaking Sharia to the State: Muslim Protesters, Tsarist Officials, and the Islamic Discourses of Late Imperial Russia." *Kritika: Explorations in Russian and Eurasian History* 14, no. 3 (2013): 485–505.

———. *Turks across Empires: Making Muslim Identity in the Russian Ottoman Borderlands*. Oxford: Oxford University Press, 2014.

Millward, James A. *Eurasian Crossroads: A History of Xinjiang*. New York: Columbia University Press, 2007.

Modernizatsionnye protsessy v tatarsko-musul'manskom soobshchestve v 1880-e – 1905 gg.: dokumenty i materialy. Edited by I. K. Zagidullin. Kazan: Institut istorii im Sh. Mardzhani, 2014.

Moosa, Ebrahim. *What Is a Madrasa?* Chapel Hill: University of North Carolina Press, 2015.

Mostashari, Firouzeh. *On the Religious Frontier: Tsarist Russia and Islam in the Caucasus*. London: I. B. Tauris, 2006.

Mukerji, Chandra. *Modernity Reimagined: An Analytic Guide*. New York and London: Routledge, 2017.

Multiple Modernities. Second printing. Edited by Shmuel N. Eisenstadt. London: Routledge, 2017.

Nafigov, R. I. *Formirovanie i razvitie peredovoi tatarskoi obshchestvenno-politicheskoi mysli*. Kazan: Tatarskoe knizhnoe izdatel'stvo, 1964.

Naganawa, Norihiro. "Maktab or School? Introduction of Universal Primary Education among the Volga-Ural Muslims." In *Empire, Islam and Politics in Central Eurasia*, edited by Kimitaka Matsuzato, 65–97. Sapporo, Japan: Slavic Research Center, 2007.

———. "Molding the Muslim Community through the Tsarist Administration: Mahalla under the Jurisdiction of Orenburg Muhammadan Spiritual Assembly after 1905." *Acta Slavica Iaponica* 23 (2006): 101–23.

Noack, Christian. *Muslimscher Nationalismus im Russischen Reich: Nationsbildung und Nationalbewegung bei Tataren und Bashkiren, 1861–1917* Stuttgart: Franz Steiner Verlag, 2000.

Noda, Jin. *The Kazakh Khanates between the Russian and Qing Empires: Central Eurasian International Relations during the Eighteenth and Nineteenth Centuries*. Leiden: Brill, 2016.

Offord, Derek. *Nineteenth-Century Russia: Opposition to Autocracy*. New York: Longman, 1999.

Perdue, Peter C. *China Marches West: The Qing Conquest of Central Eurasia*. Cambridge, MA: Harvard University Press, 2005.

Pickett, James Robert. "The Persianate Sphere during the Age of Empires: Islamic Scholars and Networks of Exchange in Central Asia, 1747–1917." PhD diss., Princeton University, 2015.
Pietsch, B. M. *Dispensational Modernism*. Oxford: Oxford University Press, 2015.
Pomeranz, Kenneth. *The Great Divergence: China, Europe, and the Making of the Modern World Economy*. Princeton, NJ: Princeton University Press, 2009.
Rakhimkulova, Madina. *Medrese "Khusainiia" v Orenburge*. Orenburg: n.p., 1997.
Rämi Ismägyil' and Räis Dautov. *Ädäbi süzlek*. Kazan: Tatarstan kitap näshriyaty, 2001.
Robinson, Francis. *The 'Ulama of Farangi Mahall and Islamic Culture in South Asia*. London: C. Hurst, 2001.
Romaniello, Matthew P. *The Elusive Empire: Kazan and the Creation of Russia, 1552–1671*. Madison: The University of Wisconsin Press, 2012.
Rorlich, Azade-Ayşe. *The Volga Tatars: A Profile in National Resilience*. Stanford, CA: Hoover Institute, 1986.
Ross, Danielle. "Muslim Charity under Russian Rule: *Waqf*, *Sadaqa*, and *Zakat* in Imperial Russia." *Islamic Law and Society* 24, nos. 1–2 (2017): 77–111.
———. "The Nation That Might Not Be: The Role of Iskhaqi's Extinction after Two Hundred Years in the Popularization of Kazan Tatar National Identity among the '*Ulamā*' Sons and Shakirds of the Volga-Ural Region, 1904–1917." *Ab Imperio* 3 (2012): 341–69.
Rostislavov, Dmitri Ivanovich. *Provincial Russian in the Age of Enlightenment: The Memoir of a Priest's Son*. Translated by Alexander M. Martin. De Kalb: Northern Illinois University Press, 2002.
Russia's Great Reforms, 1855–1881. Edited by Ben Eklof, John Bushnell, and Larissa Zakharova. Bloomington: Indiana University Press, 1994.
Sanders, James E. *Contentious Republicans: Popular Politics, Race, and Class in Nineteenth-Century Colombia*. Durham, NC: Duke University Press, 2004.
———. *The Vanguard of the Atlantic World: Creating Modernity, Nation, and Democracy in Nineteenth-Century Latin America*. Durham, NC: Duke University Press, 2014.
Sartori, Paolo. "Ijtihād in Bukhara: Central Asian Jadidism and Local Genealogies of Cultural Change." *Journal of the Economic and Social History of the Orient* 59 (2016): 193–236.
———. *Visions of Justice: Sharia and Culture in Russian Central Asia*. Leiden: Brill, 2017.
Scharf, Claus. "Noble Landholding and Local Administration in the Guberniia Reform of Catherine II: Arguments from the Middle Volga." In *Reflections on Russia in the Eighteenth Century*, edited by Joachim Klein et al. Köln: Bohlau Verlag, 2001.
Schimmelpennick van der Oye, David. *Russian Orientalism: Asia in the Russian Mind from Peter the Great to the Emigration*. New Haven, CT: Yale University Press, 2010.
Senenov, Vladimir, and Vera Semenova. *Gubernatory Orenburgskogo Kraia*. Orenburg: Orenburgskoe knizhnoe izdatel'stvo imeni G. P. Donkovtseva, 2014.
Shalgynynbai, Zh. *Istoriia kazakhskoi knizhnoi kultury (XIX v.-1917 g.—1991-2001 gg.)*. Almaty: Baspalar uyı, 2009.
Shaw, Stanford J., and Ezel Kural Shaw. *History of the Ottoman Empire and Modern Turkey*. 2 vols. Cambridge: Cambridge University Press, 1977.
Smith, David. *Hinduism and Modernity*. Oxford: Blackwell Publishing, 2003.
Spannaus, Nathan. "The Decline of the Akhund and the Transformation of Islamic Law under the Russian Empire." *Islamic Law and Society* 20, no. 3 (2013): 202–41.

——. "Formalism, Puritanicalism, Traditionalism: Approaches to Islamic Legal Reasoning in the 19th-Century Russian Empire." *The Muslim World* 104 (2014): 354–78.

——. "Islamic Thought and Reformism in the Russian Empire: An Intellectual Biography of Abu Nasr Qursawi (1776–1812)." PhD diss., McGill University, 2013. "The Ur-Text of Jadidism: Abū Naṣr Qūrsāwī's *Irshād* and the Historiography of Muslim Modernism in Russia." *Journal of the Economic and Social History of the Orient* 59 (2016): 93–125.

Steinwedel, Charles. *Threads of Empire: Loyalty and Tsarist Authority in Bashkiria, 1552–1917.* Bloomington: Indiana University Press, 2016.

Stoler, Ann Laura. *Carnal Knowledge and Imperial Power: Race and the Intimate in Colonial Rule.* Berkeley: University of California Press, 2002.

Subrahmanyam, Sanjay. *Penumbral Visions: Making Polities in Early Modern South Asia.* Ann Arbor: University of Michigan Press, 2001.

Sunderland, Willard. *Taming the Wild Field: Colonization and Empire on the Russian Steppe.* Ithaca, NY: Cornell University Press, 2004.

Suny, Ronald Grigor. *Looking Toward Ararat: Armenia in Modern History.* Bloomington: Indiana University Press, 1993.

Tatarskaia entsiklopediia. Edited by M. Kh. Khasanov. Kazan: Institut Tatarskoi Entsiklopedii, 2006.

Tatarskie intellektualy: istoricheskie portrety. Edited by R. M. Mukhammetshin. Kazan: Magarif, 2005.

Tensions of Empire: Colonial Cultures in a Bourgeois World. Edited by Frederick Cooper and Ann Laura Stoler. Berkeley: University of California Press, 1997.

Tolz, Vera. *Russia's Own Orient: The Politics of Identity and Oriental Studies in the Late Imperial and Early Soviet Periods.* Oxford: Oxford University Press, 2011.

Tuna, Mustafa. *Imperial Russia's Muslims: Islam, Empire, and European Modernity, 1788–1914.* Cambridge: Cambridge University Press, 2015.

——. "Madrasa Reform as a Secularizing Process: A View from the Russian Empire." *Comparative Studies in Society and History* 53, no. 3 (2011): 540–70.

Usmanov, M. A. *Tatarskie istoricheskie istochniki XVII-XVIII vv.* Kazan: Izdatel'stvo Kazanskogo Universiteta, 1972.

Väliev, Rämzi. *Bolak arty respublikasy.* Kazan: Tatarstan kitap näshriyaty, 1999.

van der Veer, Peter. "The Global History of 'Modernity.'" *Journal of the Economic and Social History of the Orient* 41, no. 3 (1998): 285–94.

——. *Imperial Encounters: Religion and Modernity in India and Britain.* Princeton, NJ: Princeton University Press, 2001.

Vasiliev, Alexei. *The History of Saudi Arabia.* New York: New York University Press, 2000.

Veselovskii, B. B. *Istoriia Zemstva za sorok let'.* 4 vols. St. Petersburg: Izdatel'stvo O. N. Popovoi, 1909–1911.

Voll, John Obert. *Islam Continuity and Change in the Modern World.* Syracuse, NY: Syracuse University Press, 1994.

Werth, Paul W. *At the Margins of Orthodoxy: Mission, Governance, and Confessional Politics in Russia's Volga-Kama Region, 1827–1905.* Ithaca, NY: Cornell University Press, 2001.

Wheeler, Geoffrey. *The Modern History of Soviet Central Asia.* London: Praeger, 1964.

White, Richard. *The Middle Ground: Indians Empires, and Republics in the Great Lakes Region, 1650–1815.* Cambridge: Cambridge University Press, 2010.

Zagidullin, Il'dus. *Islamskie instituty v Rossiiskoi imperii: Mecheti v evropeiskoi chasti Rossii I Sibiri.* Kazan: Tatarskoe Knizhnoe Izdatel'stvo, 2007.

Zaman, Muhammad Qasim. *Islamic Thought in a Radical Age: Religious Authority and Internal Criticism*. Cambridge: Cambridge University Press, 2012.
———. *The Ulama in Contemporary Islam: Custodians of Change* Princeton, NJ: Princeton University Press, 2010.
Zaripov, R. Sh. *Gali Ishan, Ishmi Ishan häm Tüntär mädräsäse*. Kazan: Iman, 2002.
Zelkina, Anna. *In Quest for God and Freedom: The Sufi Response to the Russian Advance in the North Caucasus*. London: Hurst and Company, 2000.
Zenkovsky, Serge A. *Pan-Turkism and Islam in Russia*. Cambridge, MA: Harvard University Press, 1967.
Zobov, Iu. S. "Nachal'nyi etap formirovaniia tatarskogo naseleniia Orenburzh'ia (40–50-e gg. XVIII v.)" In *Tatary v Orenburgskoi krae*, edited by I. M. Gabdulgafarova. Orenburg: Dimur, 1991.

INDEX

A Compendium of News on the Affairs in Kazan and Bulghar, 131–35, 198
A Student and a Shakird, 177–78, 180, 181, 189
ʿAbashī, Ḥasanʿatā, 156, 232
ʿAbdalʿallām b. Niʿmatullāh, 104, 154
ʿAbdalʿallām b. Salīḥ, 156
ʿAbdalʿallām's Madrasa. *See* Lakeside Madrasa
Abdalḥamīd bin Ūtagan, 98
ʿAbdalkarīm ash-Shirdānī, 24, 88
ʿAbdalkarīm's Madrasa. *See* Lakeside Madrasa
ʿAbdalkhalīq al-Qūrṣāwī, 99, 100, 105
Abdalqayyūm an-Naṣīrī, 126, 127
ʿAbdannaṣīr b. Sayfalmulūk al-Jabalī, 115
Abdarraḥīm b. ʿUthmān Ūtiz-Īmānī al-Bulghārī, 73–75, 79, 85, 87–88, 135, 183
Abdassalām bin Ḥasan al-Qarile, 33
Abdassalām bin Ūtamish, 98
Abdrakhmanov, Ḥusayn, 33, 42
Abdrakhmanov, Manṣūr. *See* Mullā Manṣūr b. ʿAbdarraḥman
ʿAbdrakhmānov, Quddus, 155
Abdrazakov, Muḥammad, 55–56
ʿAbduh, Muḥammad, 173, 183, 186, 187
ʿAbdullāh al- Chirtūshī, 96–97, 99, 102, 104, 106, 142, 154
ʿAbdullāh b. Muslīm, 38
Abdullin, Yanısh, 35
Abdulmecid (Sultan), 119
Abdulov, Abdey, 39
Ablai Khan, 40, 41
Abode of Islam, 23–25, 88, 119
Abode of War, 24–25, 88, 108
Abū ʿAlāʾ al-Maʿarrī, 184
Abū al-Ḥasan al-Ashʿarī, 187–88
Abū Ḥanīfa, 24, 189
Abu'l-khayr Khan, 24–25, 32, 40
Abū'n-Nāṣr al-Qūrṣāwī, 86–87, 98–100, 115–16, 135
Abylai Tashi, 22
Adventures of Seyyid Bat.t.āl Ghāzī, 133
ʿAfīfa bint ʿAlī at-Tūntārī, 103
Agerje village, 189
Aḥmad b. Khālid al-Manggarī, 143
Aḥmad Ḥusaynov & Bros. Co., 150–51
Aḥmad, Jaʿfar Sayyid, 232
Akay, 29, 30
Akchurina, Zuhra, 146
Akhtiyamov, Ibrāhīm, 232
akhund, 32–36, 40, 42–44, 52, 59, 66, 77, 98, 123, 127, 142, 152, 222
al-Afghanī, Jamāladdīn, 173
al-ʿAṣr al-Jadīd. See *The New Century*
al-Awāmil al-Miʾah, 190
al-Azhar, 148, 183, 202
Alexander I, 64, 71
Alexander II, 102, 120
Alexei Mikhailovich, 22, 23
ʿAlī al-Jurjānī ,157
ʿAli al-Qārī, 79
ʿAlī bin Sayfullāh at-Tūntārī, 102–4, 107, 116, 143, 151, 198
ʿAlī Ishān. *See* ʿAlī bin Sayfullāh at-Tūntārī
al-Iṣlāḥ, 149
Aliyev, Batırshah, 35–37, 53, 83
al-Kamālī, Ḍiyaʾ, 186
Alkīn, Ilyās, 232
Allāhyār Sūfī, 88
All-Russian Muslim Soldiers' Congress, 234, 238
All-Russian Muslim Union (1917), 232
Almambet Khan, 40
al-Manār, 183
Almat b. Sarmakay, 29–30
Almat village, 28–30
al-Qadīrī, Dhākir, 187–88
Amir Haydar, 115–16
Amirkhan, Fatīh, 170, 195–96, 203
Amirkhan, Muḥammad Ẓarīf, 203

Amirkhanov, Ḥusayn, 23, 57, 105, 135, 203
Anatolia, 10, 33, 98
Anna Ioanovna, 40
Āpānāev Madrasa. *See* Lakeside Madrasa
Āpānāev, ʿAbdalkarīm b. Mūsā, 100
Āpānāev, ʿAbdullāh, 100–1
Āpānāev, Munāsib, 100
Āpānāev, Mūsā b. Ismaʿīl, 98–100
Āpānāev, Muzaffar, 100
Āpānāev, ʿUbaydullāh b. Mūsā, 100
Āpānāev, Walī, 101
Āpānāev, Yūsuf, 99–100
Appakov, Shahīd, 218, 224
Aqyeget, Mūsā, 174, 183
Arab, 7, 87, 132, 146, 177, 184,
Arabic language, 6, 11, 24, 55, 76, 78, 79, 85, 105, 106, 108, 110, 117, 122, 126, 127, 145, 156, 157, 173, 180, 181, 184, 185, 187, 190, 191
Arabic script, 54, 55, 67, 78, 116, 212
Armenians, 5
Arsk, 33
Arslanov, Kinzia, 39
Ashıt village, 98, 115
Ashıtbāshı village, 100
Asiatic Press, 54, 56, 59, 116, 126
Astrakhan, 5, 24, 84, 89, 98, 198, 199
Āṭlāsov, Hādī, 236
at-Tilmīdh, 187
Austria, 1, 236
ʿAwāʾrif al-Zamān, 88
ʿAyn al-ʿIlm, 185
Ayshuaq Khan, 63, 66

Badavām, 80–81
Bahaʿaddīn al- Marjānī, 115–16
Bahaʾaddīn an-Naqshbandi, 198
Bāimurād's Madrasa. *See* Lakeside Madrasa
Bakchasarai, 145
Baltic, 5, 28, 37, 39, 240
Baltic Germans, 5, 41
Bārūdī, ʿĀlimjān, 108, 154, 156, 185, 189, 190, 194, 202–3, 234,
Bashkir Uprising of 1704–1708, 24
Bashkir Uprising of 1735–1740, 27, 33–35, 42,
Bashkirs, 1, 22, 23, 27–32, 35–38, 41, 43, 57, 65, 73, 82–84, 88, 89, 160–63, 233, 235–240
Bashqortistan, 235–37
Bayān al-Ḥaqq, 217
Bayazitov, ʿAtaʾullah, 127, 142–43
Beresin, I. I., 117
Bestuzhev-Riumin, K. N., 128
Bībī Ḥabība bint ʿAbdannaṣīr, 115
Bībī Ḥubayda bint ʿAbdannaṣīr, 115
Bigashev, Adil, 39
Bīgī, Muḥammad Ẓāhir, 156–58, 175–76, 183
Bīgīev, Mūsā, 143, 156, 183–85, 190, 202, 232, 234
Bikchurin, Mirsalim, 66
Bolsheviks, 237–39
Būbī, ʿAbdullāh, 104, 108, 154, 181–86, 188–90, 202, 211–12, 218–25
Būbī, Mukhlīsa, 181
Būbī, ʿUbaydullāh, 154, 181, 185, 219, 220, 223, 225
Bugelma, 152
Bukhara, 22, 24, 25, 27, 32, 33, 38, 42, 56, 62–65, 73–75, 79, 88, 98, 99, 101, 102, 107, 108, 115, 116, 119, 122, 129, 132, 134, 140, 143, 149, 150, 156–60, 183, 187
Bulghar (city and khaganate), 84, 88, 105, 128, 131–34, 198, 199
Bulghar historiography, 83, 105, 127, 131, 133–134, 136, 141, 155, 164, 197–99, 235, 244
Bulghar identity, 83, 90, 127, 132, 134, 135, 178
Burashev, Abu'l-Ghazi, 54, 55
Burbank, Jane, 5
Burındıq village, 32

Cairo, 107, 120, 148, 156, 158, 177, 187
Catherine II, 4, 21, 38–44, 56, 58, 64
Caucasian wars, 88, 243
Caucasus, 5, 88, 132, 163, 231–36
Central Asia, 5, 8, 10, 12, 13, 25, 27, 31, 33, 39, 41, 59, 72, 107–9, 119, 134, 140, 141, 146, 150, 151, 153, 154, 156, 157, 159, 160, 162–64, 173, 186, 192, 197, 231–33
chala Kazakhs, 160
Chawchak, 70
Cheliabinsk, 1, 38, 162, 236
Cheremises, 27

China, 1, 9, 12, 40, 70, 72, 84, 99, 149, 151, 225, 245,
Chistopol, 100, 104, 142, 143, 154
Chistopol Madrasa, 142–45, 147, 149, 152, 154–56, 164, 174, 177, 194, 210
Chuvashes, 22, 29
Constitutional Democratic Party, 214, 223, 231, 236
Cooper, Frederick, 5
Cossacks, 29, 37, 38, 41, 89
Crimean khanate, 41, 44
Crimean War, 119, 120, 146

Dagestan, 98
Damascus, 107, 120
Delhi, 119
Deoband, 119
DeWeese, Devin, 8, 173
Dīn wa Ma'īshat, 159, 202
Dīnmuḥammadov, Abdalḥay, 210
Dinmuḥammadova, Faṭīma, 151, 210
Dīnmuḥmmadov, Ishmuḥammad, 103, 151, 189, 210–12, 218, 222–25
Diyarbakir, 98
Dosmuḥammadov, Khalil, 232

Egypt, 7, 120, 172, 173, 183, 214
'Eid al-Adhā, 71, 100
Elizabeth Petrovna (Empress Elizabeth), 75
Extinction after Two Hundred Years, 178–79, 198

Fakhreddīnov, Abdarrakhmān, 231
Farudaddin 'Attar, 79, 133
Fatḥullāh b. al-Ḥusayn al-Ūriwī, 56–57
Fawz an-Najāt, 55
Fayḍkhān b. Khiḍrkhān, 42, 56
Fayḍkhānov, Ḥusayn, 13, 116–23, 125–31, 134, 136, 142, 143, 158
Fayḍullin, Maḥmūdgaray, 151
Fayḍullin, Mustafa, 151
Fayḍullin, Sayyidgaray, 151, 210
Fayḍullina, Faṭīma, 151
Finland, 9, 238–39
First All-Russian Muslim Union, 194
First Theater, 195

Florio Beneveni, 25
France, 9, 72, 75, 76, 136
Frank, Allen, 8, 52, 83, 114, 158
Fuks, Karl, 82

G. 'A. Ḥamidullin Co., 150
Gabdrakhimov, Gabdessalam, 51, 53, 61–67
Gainin volost', 35
Galikeevs, 154
Gasprinskii, Ismail, 8, 142, 145–48, 152–56, 178
Georgians, 5
Ghafūrī, 'Abdalmajīd, 162, 191, 198–99
Gīzzatannisa' bint 'Abdalghafūr, 102, 103
Great Comet of 1680, 21
Great Reforms, 114, 120, 123, 146
Great Sins, 175–76
Grigor'ev, V. V., 117

Ḥabībullāh b. al-Ḥusayn al-Ūriwī, 56, 59–61
habitas, 109
Hādī, Muḥammad Dhākir, 158–59, 162
hadith, 11, 76–79, 82, 86, 87, 99, 102, 122, 129, 158, 172, 173, 180–85, 187, 189, 191, 195, 201, 210, 214, 217, 218
Haft-i Yak, 54
Ḥakīmov Trading House, 151
Hanafī madhhab, 85, 102, 106, 108, 122, 144, 170, 182, 189
Ḥarbī Shūrā, 234, 236. *See* Muslim Military Council
Has the Time for Ijtihād Ended or Not?, 182
Ḥasan bin Ḥamid al-Qūrṣāwī, 100, 105, 143
Hat-Making Girl, 176
Hatt-i Humayun, 119
Haymarket Mosque, 100
History of Kazan (*Qazān tārīkhī*), 129
History of the Qur'ān, 183
Hui, 70
Ḥusayniyya Madrasa, 152, 154, 190, 194
Ḥusaynov, 'Abdalghanī, 140, 149, 150, 152, 153, 193
Ḥusaynov, Aḥmad, 149, 150, 152, 153
Ḥusaynov, Karimov, and Co., 152

Ḥusaynov, Maḥmūd 149, 150
Ḥusaynov, Muḥammad ʿAlī, 149–50
Ḥusmaddīn bin Sharafaddīn al-Bulghārī, 83, 133
Ḥusmaddīnov, Kamāladdīn, 161

Ibrahīm b. Khūjāsh, 72, 98, 100
Ibrāhīmov, Abdarrashīd, 160, 161, 214, 217, 218
Ibrāhīmov, ʿĀlimjān, 7, 223, 237
Idel-Ural Autonomous State, 239
Igel'strom, Osip, 41–44, 53, 56
ijtihad, 86–87, 106, 171–73, 181, 182–83, 188, 189, 192, 202, 210–11
Ili Valley, 70
Ilyāsī, ʿAbdarrakhmān, 156
imams, 2, 24, 25, 28, 29, 33, 34, 35, 36, 38, 43, 44, 55–58, 60–67, 72, 73, 76, 78, 79, 89, 97, 98, 100–4, 106, 110, 115, 116, 121, 143, 147, 152, 159, 162, 170, 172, 176–78, 180, 181, 189, 192, 193, 195, 201, 203, 211, 213, 217–19, 221, 222, 225, 229, 230, 235
India, 41, 71, 72, 75, 79, 102, 107, 119, 121, 183
Indian merchants, 5
Indonesia, 7
Inner Russian Muslim Autonomy, 234–35
inorodtsy, 116, 117, 123, 163, 214, 230, 243
intelligenty, 200
Iran, 7, 22, 33, 72, 99, 119
Irgiz, 153
Irka Mullā, 22–23
Irytysh, 1
Isāghūjī, 79, 106
Isḥāqī, ʿAyad, 143–45, 149, 156, 176, 178, 180–81, 188, 232–34, 237
Ishbūlāt Mullā, 24
Islamic jurisprudence, 11, 13, 102, 106–8, 110, 122, 157, 171–74, 180, 184, 186, 188, 191
Islamic law, 3, 7, 8, 36, 39, 58, 75, 79, 81, 83, 85, 86, 87, 97, 105, 106, 116, 117, 125, 127, 135, 145, 147, 152, 154, 159, 171, 172, 174, 179, 181, 183, 185, 189, 192, 193, 195, 196, 198, 201–3, 210, 211, 219, 235, 245
Islamic World, 214
Ismāʾīl bin Āpānāy, 99
Istanbul, 1, 103, 107, 119, 148, 156, 158, 177, 183
Istarlībāsh Madrasa, 33, 42, 101, 121, 124
Istarlībāsh village, 33, 102, 104, 105, 162
Itkulov, Ishmen, 39
Ittifāq al-Muslimīn, 163
Ivan the Terrible, 21
Izh-Būbī Madrasa, 13, 154, 155, 192, 194, 197, 211, 212, 218–22, 224
Izh-Būbī village, 104, 218–22, 224

Jadidism, 4, 109, 141–42, 148, 156, 170, 171, 173, 191, 212
Jaʿfar ibn ʿAbdi, 73
Jahāngīr Khan, 101
Jalāl, Wāqıf, 199
Jalāladdin Saʾdi, 79, 133
Jamiʿ, 79
Jīnālstānī Madrasa, 189
jiyen, 101

Kaban Lake, 100, 155
Kabir, Amir, 119
Kabul, 42, 56, 73, 79
Kache village, 24
Kadermat, 28
Kadets. *See* Constitutional Democratic Party
Kakre Elga, 28
Kalmyks, 22, 40, 41
Kama River, 22, 212
Kamāl, ʿAliaskar, 156, 195
Kamalov, Ibrāhīm, 145
Kankaev, Bakhtiyar, 39
Karakalpaks, 26
Karamzin, N. I., 128
Karīmī, Fatīḥ, 149, 152, 177–78, 180–81, 188–89, 202, 232
Karīmov, Ghilmān, 143, 147, 148–49, 152, 165
Karkarinsk oblast', 1
Katanov, Nikolai, 217, 221
Katkov, Mikhail, 145
Kazakh Junior Horde, 24, 25, 40, 61, 65, 66
Kazakh Middle Horde, 40
Kazakh steppe, 2, 6, 13, 37, 39, 87, 89, 90, 102, 105, 107, 119, 122, 141, 150, 151, 153, 163, 231–33, 235, 243

Kazakhs, 1, 24–27, 32, 40–44, 49, 56, 58, 59, 61, 62, 64, 65, 70, 71, 72, 82, 88–90, 101, 114, 122, 132, 140, 150, 155, 160–63, 236, 240
Kazalinsk, 150, 153
Kazan Ecclesiastical Academy, 117, 126
Kazan khanate, 2, 3, 10, 23, 129, 130, 131, 134, 244
Kazan Russian-Tatar Teachers' School, 124, 125
Kazem-bek, A. K., 117
Kemal, Namık, 174
Kemper, Michael, 8, 86
khalfa, 144, 195
Khalfin, Ibrāhīm, 55, 56, 59
Khalid, Adeeb, 109, 142, 197
Khālidī, Qurbān ʿAlī Khālidī, 160
Khiva, 9, 27, 28, 64, 79, 88, 132, 140, 149
Khojaev, Abdullāh, 232, 233
Khorezm, 160
Khūjāsh's Madrasa. *See* Lakeside Madrasa
Khusainov, Ḥabībullāh. *See* Ḥabībullāh b. al-Ḥusayn al-Ūriwī
Khusainov, Mukhametdzhan, 42–44, 53–67, 73, 88, 101, 115
Khvol'son, D., 118
Khwaja Aḥrār, 198
Khwaja Naṣreddīn, 133
Kiakhta, 70
Kichui River, 28
Kiev, 1
Kirch's Comet. *See* Great Comet of 1680
Kirdas village, 26
Kirilov, Ivan, 27–32, 35, 44
Kirov oblast', 97
Kisekbāsh kitābi. See *The Severed Head*
Kliuchevskii, V. O., 128
Knali River, 31
Kolokol, 215
Kraishen apostacies, 103, 116, 117, 230
Külbuye Madrasa. *See* Lakeside Madrasa
Kulja, 70, 225
Kurmanov, Maral, 88

Laish uezd, 99
Lakeside Madrasa, 100, 145, 148, 155–57, 164, 174–75, 177, 183, 210
Lauzière, Henri, 188
Lessons in the Science of Speculative Theology, 187
Limkov, Roman, 25
Love of the Nation, 198

Machkara, 12, 13, 96–99, 101, 102, 104, 105–7, 109–11, 115, 141–46, 148, 149, 151–56, 158, 163, 164, 177, 179, 180, 194, 202, 210, 211, 219
madhhabs, 24, 86, 102, 106, 108, 170, 180, 181, 184, 186–88, 195, 202, 203, 211
Madina, 33, 187
madrasa, 1, 2, 6, 11, 12, 26, 32–35, 42, 51, 58, 61, 71, 73, 74, 76–79, 82, 96–110, 115–17, 119–27, 129, 131, 133, 141–52, 154–60, 164, 172, 174–79, 181–203, 210–14, 216, 218–25, 230
Madrasa-i ʿAliyya, 186, 187, 190
Madrasa-i Shamsiyya, 190, 210
Maḥmūdov, Muḥammad ʿAlī, 125
majun, 72
Makhmud-Garay Mustafin Fayzullin and Co., 151
Maklakov, V. A., 223
maktab, 44, 77, 78, 109, 124, 147, 154, 175, 182, 185, 188, 210
Maktubāt al-Imām al-Rabbānī, 73
Malmyzh, 96, 97, 98, 101, 102, 104, 141, 151, 152, 154, 164, 210
Mamadysh uezd, 213
Manatov, Sharif, 236
Mangyshlak, 64
Maqṣūd b. Yūnus, 25, 26, 31
Maqṣūd Yunusov. *See* Maqṣūd b. Yūnus
Maqṣūdī, Aḥmad Hādī, 156, 186
Maqṣūdī, Ṣadraddīn, 156, 225, 231, 234
Marjānī Madrasa, 154
marthiyya, 3
Marxism, 2, 7
Maʿsūd b. Afaq, 33
Mawarannahr, 157
Mawlīd b. Mustafa, 38
Mecca, 24, 33, 34, 65, 99, 177, 183, 187, 189, 214,
Mella Tursunjan's madrasa, 115
Menzele River, 31

Menzelinsk, 22, 28, 30
Middle Volga-South Urals State, 239. *See also* Idel-Ural Autonomous State
Miliutin Cadet Corps, 145
Millī Shūrā. *See* Muslim National Council
Ministry of Education, 120, 124, 215, 225, 230
Ministry of Internal Affairs, 56, 58, 123, 212–25, 229
mirza, 22, 28
Mishars, 28, 29, 31, 36–39, 57, 73, 89, 116
modernity, 2, 5–10, 13, 29, 72, 141–42, 160, 163, 171, 215, 244
Mordvins, 27
Morning Star (*Chulpan*), 120
Moscow, 1, 21, 22, 54, 72, 118, 145, 152, 203, 232, 235, 240
muʿāllim. *See* khalfa
mudarris, 34, 78
mufti, 44, 51, 53, 55–67, 73, 75, 87, 88, 101, 115, 121, 234
Muḥammad ʿAlī Yūnusov Co., 150
Muḥammad Dhākir ibn ʿAbdalwahhāb Kamālov aṣ-Ṣaṣnawī al-Chistāwī, 100, 104, 142–47, 149, 172, 176, 183
Muḥammad ibn ʿAbdalwahhāb, 180
Muḥammad Karīm b. Muḥmmad Raḥīm al-Qazānī, 104
Muḥammad Mūrād ar-Rāmzī, 217
Muḥammad Najīb Shamsaddīnov at-Tūntārī, 103, 108, 143
Muḥammad Raḥīm bin Yūsuf, 97, 98, 100, 102, 104, 106, 181
Muḥammadev, Shākir, 176
Muḥammadiyya Madrasa, 154, 190, 194
Muḥsin b. Yūnus, 25
Mukhtaṣar al-Qudūrī, 106, 170, 185
Mukhtaṣar al-Wiqāya, 106, 170, 185, 190
Mullā Ismāʿīl bin Bikmuḥammad, 34
Mullā Manṣūr b. ʿAbdarraḥman, 32, 33, 42
Mullā Mūrād Affair, 60, 87
Mullā Nadir b. Urazmet, 28, 29, 30, 31
munāẓara, 106, 158, 170, 190
muridizm, 88
Murtaḍa bin Qutlıghısh as-Simetī, 33, 115
Muscovy, 6, 22, 23, 28
Muslim Military Council, 234, 239
Muslim National Council, 233, 239
Must Progressive Science and Knowledge Be Atheist?, 189
Mustafād al-akhbār fī aḥwāl Qazān wa Bulghār. See *A Compendium of News on the Affairs in Kazan and Bulghar*
Mutiʿī, Kāmil, 148, 149, 202
Muzaffarov, Muḥammad Kamāl, 151
MVD. *See* Ministry of Internal Affairs

Nadir Urazmetov. *See* Mullā Nadir b. Urazmet
Nadir village, 28, 30
Naqshbandi, 1, 42, 56, 96, 101, 102, 143, 191, 198
National Assembly of the Inner Russian-Siberian Muslim Autonomy, 236, 237
nationalism, 2, 13, 172, 174, 199, 220, 226, 229
Nepliuev Military School (Nepliuev Cadet Corps), 82
Nepliuev, I. I., 33, 37, 40, 128
New Century, 148–49
Newton's Comet. *See* Great Comet of 1680
Nicholas I, 120
Niʿmatullāh b. Munāsib, 104, 181
1916 Uprising, 233
Nizhnii Novgorod, 57, 60, 62, 150, 151, 194
Nogay horde, 22
nospay, 72, 159
Nowruz, 101
Nurali Khan, 41–43, 61

October Manifesto, 148
Odessa, 1
Oka River, 22
Omsk, 89
1001 Hadiths, 214, 217–18
Orenburg, 4, 12, 27–30, 32– 37, 39, 40, 42, 43, 45, 53, 54, 59, 61– 67, 75, 82, 84, 89, 102, 120, 128, 140, 149–54, 159, 160, 162–64, 190, 234–40
Orenburg Muslim Spiritual Assembly (OMSA), 4, 12, 44, 52–63, 65, 67, 87, 90, 116, 121, 123, 142, 148, 213, 216, 217
Orsk, 151
Ottoman empire, 7, 44, 118, 119, 121, 142, 144, 146, 149, 156, 174, 177, 183, 186, 200, 213, 214, 222

Pakistan, 7
pan-Islamism, 212–26, 229, 243
pan-Turkism, 214, 229
Paris, 150, 156, 158, 177
Pavel I, 55, 56, 61, 64, 71
Perm', 236
Perovskii, 153
Persian language, 6, 55, 76, 78, 79, 102, 105, 106, 107, 117, 132, 133, 181, 191
Peter I, 25
Peter the Great. *See* Peter I
Philosophy of Islam, 186
Pir'ali Khan, 64
Pisarev, Dmitri, 230
prikazchik, 194–95
Provisional Central Muslim Bureau, 232
Provisional Military Committee and Kazan's Workers'-Soldiers' Soviet, 231, 238
Provisional Military Committee of the Garrisons, 231
Pugachev, Emil'ian, 38–39
Pugachev's Revolt, 38–39, 53

qāḍī, 44, 61
qadim, 4
Qaltay village, 38
Qaraqay b.'Uthmān, 38
Qarghalı. *See* Seitov Sloboda
Qarīyev, 'Abdullāh, 202
Qasim Khanate, 22, 23, 24, 199
Qāsimiyya Madrasa. *See* Lakeside Madrasa
Qing, 40, 70, 72
Qıshqār Madrasa, 99, 107–9, 121, 125, 148, 154
Qıshqār village, 104
Qiṣṣa-i Yūsuf. See *The Tale of Joseph*
Qur'ān, 11, 30, 43, 54, 55, 76–79, 82, 85, 86, 107, 116, 122, 129, 158, 172, 173, 180–83, 187, 189, 191, 195, 201, 202, 210, 221, 222, 234, 235
Qūrṣā village, 99, 100, 104

Radlov, V. V., 123–26
Rafīq b. Tayyib al-Qūrṣāwī, 33
Raḥmatullāh b. Maqṣūd b. Yūnus, 25
Ramadan, 9, 62, 63, 75, 82, 100, 196
Rāmīev, Saghīt, 220
Rāmīevs, 154
Rasūlev, Zaynullāh, 1, 2, 191
Rasūliyya Madrasa, 190
Razin, Stepan, 22
Reverend Fatḥullāh, 170, 195–96
Reverend Ḥusamaddīn, 174
Reverend Jihānshāh, 159, 162
Riḍā'addīn bin Fakhraddīn, 73, 108, 110, 143, 149, 220
Rifā'a T.aht.āwī, 120
Risāla at-Tawḥīd. See *The Unity of Theology*
Rogorvik, 28
Romania, 1
Rostov-na-Donu, 157
Rules of Jurisprudence, 184
Rumiantsev, A. I., 31, 32
Russian Archaeological Society, 117
Russkaia zeml'ia, 212
Russkoe Musul'manstvo, 146

Sa'adaddīn at-Taftāzānī, 157
Saba uezd, 55
Saba village, 31
Sabachay village, 116
Sādā-i Madanīyāt, 199
sadaqa, 82
Sa'di, 133
Sadıqov, Sabit, 55
Safar b. Yūnus, 25
Sa'īd Aitov-Khalevin, 31, 33
Salafism, 8, 172–74
Saliḥov, Muḥammad Qāsim 'Abdal'allām-ulı, 155
Samara, 236
Samarkand, 27, 73, 79, 116, 152, 153, 157, 160
Sarapul, 223
Saratov, 57–60, 84, 88, 129
Sarmakay, 28
Sartori, Paolo, 142
Ṣaṣna village, 101
Saudi Arabia, 7
Saymanov, Ḥarīth, 155
Sayyid Ahmad Khan, 119
Sayyid Ja'far, 23
Sazly Elgan River, 31
Second All-Russian Muslim Congress, 234
secularization, 8, 10, 11, 110, 141, 171, 191

Seitov Sloboda, 33–36, 42, 45, 61, 63, 65, 73, 140, 149, 162
Semipalatinsk, 1, 70, 71, 160
Semirech'e, 150, 233
Seshma River, 28, 30
Sevastopol, 145
Severed Head, 81
Shah Walīullāh, 73
Shah-i Aḥmad b. Abū Yazīd, 104
Shamsaddīn b. Raḥmatullāh, 103, 107, 210
Shamsiyya, 79
Sharḥ al-ʿAqāʾid Nafīsa al-Jadīda, 99
shaykh, 1, 2, 4, 11, 56–58, 60, 65, 67, 71–74, 77, 78, 80, 82, 85, 87, 88, 96, 97, 99–105, 115, 121, 143–47, 159, 162, 172, 175–79, 182, 183, 191, 193, 195, 198, 200, 229, 230, 242
Shibanid, 22
Shihābaddīn al-Marjānī, 13, 59, 72, 75, 99, 103, 115–18, 121–36, 143, 144, 147, 178, 198
Shirghāzī Khan, 101
Shnor, Johann Karl, 43
Shoda village, 152, 210
Shūrā, 149
Siberia, 2, 12, 21, 27, 30, 35, 37, 40, 41, 44, 84, 89, 105, 107, 126, 132, 146, 151, 170, 175, 198, 234, 236, 243
Siberian doroga, 35
silsila, 3, 83, 105, 198
Simbirsk, 145
Simbirsk guberniya, 116, 238
Simet village, 32, 33
Sirhindī, Aḥmad, 73, 74, 198
Sivas, 98
Socialist Revolutionary, 1, 143, 178
Sok River, 28
Solov'ev, M. S., 128
Song of Sayfalmulūk, 51, 53, 81, 115
Spannaus, Nathan, 52, 86
Speranskii, Mikhail, 89
St. Petersburg, 38, 43, 52, 54, 58, 59, 62, 118, 127, 176, 187, 214, 223
St. Petersburg University, 117, 122, 128, 142, 183
Statute on the Siberian Kazakhs, 89
Stolypin, P. A., 212, 214, 223
Sufi, 1, 2, 3, 9, 11, 33, 55, 57, 74, 77, 79–83, 85, 87, 88, 96, 97, 99, 101, 105, 135, 152, 170, 172, 180, 197, 198, 230
Suleymanov, Gabdulvakhid, 102
Sullam al-ʿUlūm, 79, 106
Sultan-Galiev, Mirsaid, 238, 239
Sviaga River, 28, 30, 34, 61
Syr Darya River, 150, 153
Syria, 24, 183

Taikara (Princess), 62, 64
Taininsk volost', 27
Tājaddīn b. Bāshir, 96
Tājaddīn Yālchīgūl-ulı, 83
Tale of Joseph, 80
Tāng majmūʿası, 149
Tāng yūldızı, 149, 201
Tanzimat, 120
taqlid, 87, 171, 172, 181, 182, 183, 195
Taranchis, 70, 71
Tārīkh-nāme-i Bulghār, 83
tarkhans, 28, 102
Tashkendi merchants, 70, 72
Tashkent, 64, 70, 141, 153, 163, 164, 232
Tāshkichū village, 33, 35, 104, 115
Tatishchev, V. N., 30, 32, 42
Tauride Palace, 230
Tawārīkh-i Bulghāriyya (attributed to Ḥusmaddīn bin Sharafaddīn al-Bulghārī), 83, 84, 131, 133
Tawārīkh-i Bulghāriyya (by Ḥusayn Amirkhanov), 23, 105, 135
tawḥid, 172
Tāwısh, 149
Tenishev, Safar, 22
Teptiar, 49, 61, 62, 65
Tergulov, Ibrāhīm, 125
Terjuman, 8, 142, 146–48, 149, 181
Tevkelev, A. I., 32, 36, 40, 42
Tevkelev, Salimgarey, 102, 121
Thabāt al-ʿAjizīn, 55, 88
Thabāt al-ʿAjizīn, 88
theology, 7, 11, 13, 35, 83, 86, 87, 102, 106, 107, 110, 143, 157, 159, 170–74, 177, 181, 184–89, 191, 192, 195, 202, 211, 219, 245
Tilyachev, Mullā Abūbakr, 39
Timachev, Adigut, 39

Time of Troubles, 21
Tobolsk, 37, 84
Tolstoy, Dmitri, 123–26
Topchibashev, ʿAlīmardān, 232
Troitsk, 1, 38, 43, 143, 154, 164, 190, 216
Tsalikhov, Aḥmad, 232
Tsalikhov, Aḥmad, 232, 233
Tsouroukhaitou, 70
Tuḥfatullin, Mutiʿullāh, 148
Tūntār Madrasa, 103, 107, 109, 151, 152, 154, 164, 177, 189, 194, 210, 211
Tūntār village, 102, 103, 104, 140, 151, 190, 210
Tūqāyev, Abdullāh, 149, 160, 161, 199, 220, 222
Tūqāyev, Muḥammad Ḥarīth, 101, 102, 121, 124, 127
Tūqāyev, Niʿmatullāh b. Bīktimir, 101
Turgai, 1, 88, 150, 155
Turkestan, 117, 146, 150, 159, 160, 163, 232–36
Turkestan Wilayate Gazetası, 107
Turkey, 7, 9, 214
Turki Reading, 185
Turkish language, 55, 117, 156, 174, 177, 183
Turkistan (city), 27, 153

Ufa, 4, 22, 25, 27, 29, 30, 32–34, 38, 39, 41, 44, 59, 61, 66, 69, 82, 84, 116, 124, 125, 148, 153, 162, 187, 190, 235–38, 240
ʿulamāʾ, 3, 4, 6, 9, 10, 12, 13, 21, 23, 25–27, 29, 31–44, 51–54, 58–67, 75–86, 88, 90, 97, 98, 102–5, 110, 114–21, 123–25, 131–34, 141–43, 145, 146, 148, 151–53, 155–62, 171, 172, 175–80, 186, 190, 191, 193, 197, 200, 211, 224–26, 229, 230–35, 240, 242–44
Ulfat, 214
Union of All-Russian Muslim ʿUlamāʾ, 234
Unity of Theology, 186, 187
Unnecessary Necessity, 184
Urals, 1, 2, 6, 12, 13, 21, 25–38, 40, 42, 44, 52, 59, 67, 123, 132, 151, 152, 154, 162, 164, 234, 235, 237, 239, 243
Uralsk, 38, 65, 148
Uralsk Madrasa, 148
Urayev, ʿAbdassalām b. Urāz Muḥammad, 33, 35, 36, 37
Urgench, 22, 64, 160
Ūri village, 24, 25, 56, 57, 58, 60
Ūrmānchiyev, Aḥmad, 161
us.ūl-e jadīd, 142
Usayev, Kanzafar, 39
Ustav o Sibirskikh Kirgizakh. *See* "Statute on the Siberian Kazakhs"
Ūtamishev, ʿAbdullāh, 98–99
Ūtamishev, Ismāʿīl, 99, 107–10, 154
Ūtamishev, Mūsā, 98–99
Ūtamisheva, Naʾīma, 101
ʿUthmāniyya Madrasa, 190
Ūtiz-Īmānī. *See* Abdarraḥīm b. ʿUthmān Ūtiz-Īmānī al-Bulghārī
Uvarov, A. S., 118

Vaisov, Gaynān, 217, 239
Vakhitov, Mullanur, 239
Validi Togan, Zaki, 156, 230–31
Valīdov, Jamāladdīn, 7, 108–9
Valikhanov, Chokan, 89
Vambery, Armin, 157
Vel'iaminov, Zernov, V. V., 117
Vernyi, 119
Viakta guberniya, 97, 98, 104, 154, 210
Vitevskii, V. N., 128
Volkonskii, Grigori, 65, 66
Voronezh, 145
Votiaks, 27, 213

Wafayāt al-Aslāf, 128
Wahapov, Murtaḍa, 145
Wahapova, Faṭīma-i Farīda, 145, 149
Wahhabis, 180, 202
Waqt, 149, 220, 223

Yabınchı village, 115
Yaik, 61
Yākhin, Tayyib, 125
Yālt-Yūlt, 149, 160
Yanbulat village, 99
Yanga Sala village, 33
Yanga Tāzlār, 100
Yanisarı b. Ḥāfiz, 24
Yaqūpova, Salīma, 232
Yāshen, 149
Yaushev and Sons, 150

Yaushevs (Kulja), 150–51
Yaushevs (Troitsk), 154
Yenikeyev, Ḥalilullāh, 1, 2
Young Turk Revolution, 212
Youth, 197, 198, 199, 200–3, 211
Yūldız, 162, 223
Yūnus b. Iwānāy b. Usay, 24, 25, 26, 156
Yūnusov, Ibrāhīm, 123
Yūsuf kitābi. See *The Tale of Joseph*

zakat, 82, 152, 196
Zungars, 27, 40, 70

Danielle Ross is assistant professor of Asian history at Utah State University.

www.ingramcontent.com/pod-product-compliance
Lightning Source LLC
Chambersburg PA
CBHW030530230426
43665CB00010B/826
* 9 7 8 0 2 5 3 0 4 5 7 1 3 *